"[A] truly creepy true-crime story. . . . This portrait of an evil prince needs no embellishment." —*People*

"In her selection and treatment of the Fahey murder, [Rule] might have created her masterpiece."
—*The Plain Dealer* (Cleveland)

"Even crime buffs who followed the case closely are bound to gain new insights. . . . The courtroom scenes of Capano are especially compelling."
—*The Orlando Sentinel* (FL)

"[Rule] tell[s] the sad story with authority, flair, and pace."
—*The Washington Post*

"[A] compassionate portrayal of the victim and a chilling portrayal of her killer. . . . This is a true page-turner."
—*Booklist*

BITTER HARVEST

"A must-read story of the '90s American dream turned, tragically, to self-absorbed ashes." —*People*

"Impossible to put down. . . . A tour de force from America's best true-crime writer." —*Kirkus Reviews*

"[A] tension-filled, page-turning chronology and analysis of a psychopath in action. . . . It is Rule's expert attention to detail that makes this Medea-incarnate story so compelling. . . . [A] gripping saga of sin and murder most foul."
—*Publishers Weekly* (starred review)

Books by Ann Rule

Every Breath You Take
. . . And Never Let Her Go
Bitter Harvest
Dead by Sunset
Everything She Ever Wanted
If You Really Loved Me
The Stranger Beside Me
Possession
Small Sacrifices

Ann Rule's Crime Files:
Vol. 8: Last Dance, Last Chance and Other True Cases
Vol. 7: Empty Promises and Other True Cases
Vol. 6: A Rage to Kill and Other True Cases
Vol. 5: The End of the Dream and Other True Cases
Vol. 4: In the Name of Love and Other True Cases
Vol. 3: A Fever in the Heart and Other True Cases
Vol. 2: You Belong to Me and Other True Cases
Vol. 1: A Rose for Her Grave and Other True Cases

The I-5 Killer
The Want-Ad Killer
Lust Killer

ANN RULE

LAST DANCE, LAST CHANCE

AND OTHER TRUE CASES

ANN RULE'S CRIME FILES: Vol. 8

POCKET BOOKS

NEW YORK   LONDON   TORONTO   SYDNEY   SINGAPORE

The names of some individuals in this book have been changed. Such
names are indicated by an asterisk (*) the first time each appears in the
narrative.

An *Original* Publication of POCKET BOOKS

POCKET BOOKS, a division of Simon & Schuster, Inc.
1230 Avenue of the Americas, New York, NY 10020

ISBN: 0-671-02535-X

First Pocket Books printing January 2003

10 9 8 7 6 5 4 3 2 1

POCKET and colophon are registered trademarks of
Simon & Schuster, Inc.

For information regarding special discounts for bulk purchases,
please contact Simon & Schuster Special Sales at 1-800-456-6798
or business@simonandschuster.com

Cover design by James Wang

Printed in the U.S.A.

For my grandchildren: Rebecca, Matthew,
Olivia, Tyra, and Cooper

Acknowledgments

Acknowledgments

Many thanks to the people who lived *Last Dance, Last Chance* and were kind enough to revisit some tragic years in western New York with me: Debbie, Ralph and Lauren Pignataro, Caroline Rago, Denis Scinta, Shelly Palombaro, and Rose Gardner; Sarah Smith's family: Dan Smith, Sandy Smith, Barb Grafton, and Russell Grafton; Erie County, N.Y., District Attorney Frank Clark and his staff: Frank A. Sedita III, Carol Giarizzo Bridge, Charles Craven, and Sharon McVeigh-Simon.

To the dozen detectives who solved the other cases in this Volume Eight of my Crime Files. Many of them have retired, but I remember the following investigators and salute them for their brilliant and dogged work: Lt. Austin Seth; Sergeant Ivan Beeson; Benny De Palmo; Ted Fonis; Wayne Dorman, Seattle Police Department Homicide Unit; Sheriff Harold Sumpter; Grays Harbor County Detective Ted Forester, King County Police Department; George Ishii, Western Washington Crime Lab, and Dr. Donald Reay, King County Medical Examiner. Special thanks to K. Casey and Pat Jacque.

It takes a lot more than one woman working at a computer to nurture a book from the selection of interesting cases and carry the idea into bookstores. I am ever grateful for my friendly and talented team at Pocket Books:

Acknowledgments

My publisher, Louise Burke; my editor, Mitchell Ivers, and his assistant, Joanna Goddard; Art Director Paolo Pepe; Managing Editor Donna O'Neill; Production Supervisor Stephen Llano; my publicist, Louise Braverman; and my "Legal Eagle," Felice Javit.

And I have my own "staff" of friends and family in Seattle who help me with every book. "First Reader" Gerry Brittingham Hay, and Mike Rule, Leslie Rule Wagner, and Andy Rule, who help with everything from my newsletter to getting a manuscript to the airport.

Three decades later, my original—and only—literary agents, Joan and Joe Foley, are still with me and I appreciate them more every year. My theatrical agent, Ron Bernstein, is responsible for getting most of my books on television and actually bringing *me* to the bright lights of Hollywood now and then!

More than a year has passed since the Snohomish County Critical Incident Response Team raced to New York City from Washington State to assist New York police officers as they dealt with Post Traumatic Stress after September 11. My admiration for that team—Dave Coleman, Phil Nichols, Joe Beard, and Chuck Wright—knows no bounds.

Contents

Contents

A Note on Liars

In a sense, all my stories are about liars. Some of the killers I write about have lied all their lives, and some have lied only to throw their victims off balance so that they became vulnerable. Once a lie is successful in giving the murderer what he or she wants, it grows and multiplies, burnished and perfected until it works every time. It's a sad irony that the more honest a potential victim is, the more innocent, the more likely such a person is to become prey. Honest people don't expect to be lied to, because they wouldn't lie to someone else. That doesn't matter at all to dedicated liars. They only smile.

"Last Dance, Last Chance" is about a world-class liar, if there is such a thing. "The Accountant," "The Killer Who Begged to Die," "The Beach," and "The Desperate Hours" are all about repeat offenders whose ability to twist the truth made them as believable as preachers in the pulpit—and as evil as the dark forces any minister decries.

All their crimes were examples of conscienceless cruelty. Perhaps more shocking is the fact that they were so often forgiven and were offered so many chances to start over. In the end, each reverted to type; they were as dangerous as a rabid lion in the street.

Last Dance, Last Chance

Prologue

As I begin my twenty-first book and look back over three decades of writing about true-crime cases, I have come to a place where I am no longer surprised by the unusual requests I receive in phone calls, letters, and e-mails. Hundreds of people send me suggestions about cases for book topics, and a third of them actually offer me stories from their own lives. Predictably, most of them are victims' survivors. Very rarely does a convicted killer's family look for an author to write a book. Many long-time readers can spot the characteristics I look for in a criminal case, and I appreciate that, but I can choose only a small percentage of the suggestions presented to me. Try as I might, I can write only two books a year. Back when I was the Northwest correspondent for *True Detective* magazine, her four sister magazines, and the Justice Stories in the *New York Daily News,* I could report on many more cases. My accounts were much shorter, naturally, but I was able to write two crime stories every week.

Fortunately, I saved copies of all of them, and some stand out sharply in my memory. In the true-crime files that follow, I came to know many of the people involved very well. Sometimes I knew them before the path to crime escalated to violence, and sometimes it was long after. The victims' parents or siblings often became my friends through my membership in our Washington State support group: Families and Friends of Victims of Violent Crimes and Missing Persons. For twenty years I was a familiar visitor in various homicide units from Seattle, Washington, north to Bellingham, and south to Eugene, Oregon. The detectives I met shared their investigative techniques and their gut feelings about murder with me.

This book is different from all the others. To my great surprise, in the long title case—*Last Dance, Last Chance*— I heard from both the would-be killer and the victim, albeit two years apart. I probably wouldn't have remembered the first call from the convicted man if an alert reader hadn't sent me an e-mail. She wanted to tell me about a story in her city that she thought would make an interesting book. It sounded interesting—even more interesting when she gave me the name of the accused, which sounded vaguely familiar. I dug deep into a box of newspaper clippings, letters, and my own notes scribbled on fading yellow legal pads and found something that matched my recall. I finally located what I sought—notes on a phone call from a physician in Buffalo, New York. He had called to persuade me to write a book that would unveil the shabby treatment he felt he had received from the New York State Department of Health. They had taken away his license to practice medicine for reasons, he said, that were entirely prejudicial.

I remember that he was very well-spoken, with a deep authoritative voice, and that I felt some sympathy for him as he told me his life was in ashes. I explained to him that I wasn't an investigative reporter and didn't write the kind of book he wanted. I suggested that he contact a reporter in Buffalo who might be interested in exposing the roots of a medical scandal.

He seemed to understand, and he even introduced me to his wife, who was listening on an extension. Although he knew I couldn't write his book for him, he insisted on sending me the biography his wife had written about his tragedy. A few days later, I mailed him the eight-page handout I have put together for aspiring writers. He sent me the manuscript of his biography, which was more than a hundred pages long, single-spaced, and full of details about his life, especially about his career in medicine and its disastrous ending. Titled *M.D.: Mass Destruction* and written from the point of view of the doctor's wife, the manuscript was ponderous, although the spelling and grammar were correct. His wife obviously idolized the doctor, and she went on for chapter after chapter about how wonderful and kind he was, how brilliant and dedicated. The story wasn't for me, and I have to admit that I didn't read it all: it was overwritten, overwrought, and very one-sided.

It wasn't a true crime case at all. At most, it dealt with civil matters and possible medical malpractice, and I had a book deadline to meet. I was so involved with writing *The End of the Dream* that I promptly forgot all about the New York doctor.

If someone had asked me six months later the name of the Buffalo physician who called me, I probably wouldn't have remembered it. But when someone told me the name—Anthony Pignataro—it certainly had a familiar ring. Curious, I reread the manuscript he had sent me and realized that it had to be the same heartsick doctor who had lost his license to practice medicine in 1998. By 2000, he appeared to have even more problems in his life.

When I heard about the charges against Dr. Pignataro, I contacted the District Attorney's office in Erie County, New York. The Pignataro case was being handled by the chief assistant D.A. in charge of the Special Investigation Unit: Frank Sedita. I told Sedita about my short correspondence with Dr. Pignataro. Because I knew that Pignataro had read my books, I sent Sedita two volumes that I thought might have significant ties to his current investigation: *Everything She Ever Wanted* and *Bitter Harvest.*

Frank Sedita eventually passed them on to Deborah Pignataro, Dr. Pignataro's estranged wife.

And one day, she called me. She told me of an all-too-true scenario that seemed almost unbelievable.

This story began quite routinely as a civil matter, but it became an incredibly tangled spiderweb of pretense, deception, deadly plots, and tragedy. Once again, just as I had been when I researched *And Never Let Her Go,* I was drawn back to a place where I had lived long ago. This time it was western New York State, where I spent two years when my then husband was assigned to an antiaircraft battery in the middle of the Tuscarora Indian Reservation. We lived in a small trailer a few miles from the tiny village of Youngstown, New York, in the farthest northwestern corner of New York State.

My first child was born in Niagara Falls at Mt. St. Mary's Hospital. Army pay for second lieutenants was $300 a month, so we rarely had money enough to go to Buffalo, the closest big city in the area. I remember seeing *Guys and Dolls* and *High Society* in a luxurious Buffalo theater, and then driving home across Grand Island, hungry because we couldn't even afford to buy hamburgers and Cokes after the movies.

Erie and Niagara Counties were wonderful in the summer and fall when the fruit trees of western New York were laden with apples and peaches, and bitterly cold in the winter when the wind roared inland from Lake Erie and Lake Ontario. At 28 degrees below zero, the waves near the shoreline froze into giant icy "doughnuts." Before living there, I hadn't realized that moving water could freeze. But Buffalo gets so cold that Lake Erie turns to ice even as it crashes against the shoreline.

Just as I never thought of Dr. Anthony Pignataro after our brief phone meeting in 1998, I never expected to return to Buffalo or Niagara Falls or the thin eastern belt of Ontario where the land barely separates Lake Ontario from Lake Erie. But the twists and turns of our lives are nothing if not unpredictable.

In 2002, I went back to the place where I had lived as a very young wife. Fittingly, it was winter. The bitter cold was still a shock, although Buffalo natives barely acknowledged it. They did acknowledge the blizzard that brought ten feet of snow and virtually paralyzed the city at the end of 2001. When I arrived two weeks later, the billowing drifts had diminished, but they were still there.

Going back to my own early days was the only way I could explore the labyrinth of lies that defined the story of Anthony and Deborah Pignataro. Their falling in love and getting married once seemed like the happy ending to a dream romance. Sadly, it wasn't.

Part One

Debbie

Part One

1

It was so hot, *and the air was heavy and muggy with humidity. Even rain didn't cleanse the air; it only became thicker and harder to breathe. The woman who lay on the couch had been sick for so long that she couldn't remember feeling well. Sometime earlier—last week or maybe last month—she had been able to walk. But now her feet and legs had become leaden stumps, unwilling to accept any messages from her brain.*

Her brain wasn't working very well, either. She knew she was still living in her old familiar neighborhood, but it all looked as if it were underwater or as if someone had painted it a different color. She remembered that when she could still navigate, the street signs were wavy and jarring, and she got lost. She remembered vaguely that she had walked into a neighbor's kitchen, a neighbor she barely knew. She didn't know why she was there, and the woman who lived there certainly didn't either. It was embarrassing to be led home.

When she looked into a mirror, her own face looked alien to her. It was all bloated and puffy, with black circles carved beneath her dark eyes. She looked a hundred years old, but she couldn't remember growing old. She couldn't remember when she got sick.

Sometimes people came and went, and her friends'

faces seemed to float above her, their expressions worried and concerned.

How do you feel? they asked, but she couldn't answer them. She couldn't describe how she felt. Sick. Sick. *Sick.* And so tired that she could not imagine cooking a meal or making a bed or walking to the mailbox ever again. When she could fix her mind on her children, she wept inside for them. They no longer had a mother, only a useless, swollen blob who sat propped up in a recliner chair while the world went on without her.

The doctors didn't seem to know what to do about her. The one man she trusted most assured everyone that she was doing just fine, and that he would take care of her. Sometimes he said that all she needed was to have her gall bladder removed. He didn't think there was anything really wrong with her. And he, of all people, would surely know.

But nothing changed. She sat in her chair for what seemed like months. He lay on the couch nearby, rarely leaving her alone. Sometimes it seemed to her that he was watching over her with concern, and sometimes he didn't seem to notice her any more than if she were a piece of furniture. The ice clinked in his drink as he watched television, clicking the channel changer often. His voice slurred, and he dozed off, but he never did anything, despite the questions people kept asking him.

Why don't you take her to the hospital? they asked him.

They have a skeleton staff on the weekends, he told them. *She's much better off here with me . . .*

And so, day after day, the sun came up with pale washed skies, grew bright and hot at noon, and faded until the room was again in shadow. And Debbie Pignataro was still there.

At length, with what rational thought she could manage, she began to believe that she would die there, surrounded by people who loved her—people whom she loved—and yet somehow beyond all hope of rescue.

2

Deborah Rago was born in Erie County, New York, on July 22, 1957. Her mother, Caroline, was a housewife, and her dad, Frank, supported the family with hard physical labor. She had an older brother, and she was the little girl her parents had hoped for. They were both children of the fifties, that rather innocent time in America sandwiched between World War II and the Vietnam War, the calm between storms.

In 1957, the year Deborah was born, the first reports suggesting that smoking might contribute to lung cancer appeared, but smokers weren't really alarmed. Actor Humphrey Bogart, a heavy smoker, died of throat cancer that year. But a huge segment of the population still smoked, sure that it wouldn't happen to them.

Father Knows Best and *The Roy Rogers Show* were popular on television, and *Leave It to Beaver* was in its first season. Elvis Presley's performances on the small screen were deliciously shocking and were only allowed to be filmed from the waist up on *The Ed Sullivan Show*. John F. Kennedy was a senator, and Billy Graham was a young evangelist. Americans were somewhat worried about Russia and Cuba, but most people felt safe. Young families had four or more children without a thought to the dangers of population explosion. "Young Love" was top-ranked on *Your Hit Parade* during most of 1957. Pat Boone was a rosy-cheeked twenty-two, and he still wore white bucks. So did a lot of people.

There was crime and murder and scandal in the fifties—there always is—but it wasn't omnipresent, because the vast majority of American citizens only read about it in the newspapers or listened to coverage on the radio. Tabloid television was yet to be heard of.

Debbie Rago grew up cosseted by her extremely close and loving family. Her father worked in construction. He was considered an artist at building forms for concrete and in the timing of its pouring and hardening. Caroline worked part time in Krasner's, a ladies' dress shop, and Debbie's brother, Carmine*, five years older than she was, was a typically protective big brother. They all lived in a nice little house in Williamsville, out Kensington Avenue northeast of Buffalo. "We lived there from the time I was one," Debbie recalled.

Frank Rago belonged to the laborers' union, Local 210, an all-Italian union, and it provided backup and friends. Like many other East Coast cities, Buffalo was—and still is—part Italian, part Irish, and part Polish, part African American with strong ethnic neighborhoods.

Debbie and Carmine went to Maple West Elementary School, Mill Middle School, and Williamsville South High School, as did all their friends. At Christmas, their extended family got together—all the aunts and uncles and cousins—and Caroline Rago roasted a turkey and made two hundred raviolis.

Their lifestyle changed dramatically when Frank Rago had a massive heart attack when he was only thirty-eight.

*See note on copyright page.

Everyone was afraid he wasn't going to make it, but he survived. However, he never came all the way back to the strong man he had once been. Debbie's father was disabled and couldn't return to the rigors of construction.

Frank became a house-husband long before the concept was generally accepted. Carmine was grown and out of the house, and Frank stayed home to look after Debbie while Caroline worked full time at the mall. Their roles changed, but their family stayed as solid as the concrete that Frank had once poured. Debbie grew closer to her father because he was home taking care of her, unlike her friends' fathers, who were at work all day. She accepted that there were luxuries she couldn't have and that she wouldn't have an easy ride to college. Instead, she had to work for spending money and bought her own clothes and helped her parents as soon as she was old enough.

"I went to work when I was 16," Debbie said. "I sold clothes at the mall, too—and then I got a job in a pharmacy. I was a pharmacy technician, and I stayed with Georgetown-Leader from 1975 to 1982."

Carmine grew up to be a very tall, husky man and went to work for the Niagara Falls Transit Authority (NFTA) as a bus driver. He was still protective of Debbie, even though she had a feisty personality and insisted she could take care of herself. Caroline and Frank Rago had done a good job raising their children despite Frank's illness. They didn't have a big house and financial security, but that didn't matter. Their church and their extended family meant a lot to them, and to Carmine and Debbie, too.

Debbie Rago was very pretty, with dark hair, huge eyes, and a great smile. She was five feet four and weighed only a little over a hundred pounds. Like all teenagers, she perceived flaws when she looked in the mirror, and she hated her nose, sure that it was too big, and unable to see how attractive she really was. Debbie dated only casually through her teens, and she had never fallen in love.

After high school graduation, Debbie lived at home and paid her share. She was skilled at counting out pills, checking them to be sure they matched prescriptions, and dealing with customers. The Ragos were such a solid family unit that she had no particular desire to find an apartment of her own. There would be time for that later.

Debbie was 20 before she met the man who seemed to embody everything she had ever hoped for—and more. On Friday and Saturday nights, her crowd of friends stopped in one bar or another, not really to drink but to socialize and dance and, hopefully, to meet someone special. It was a summer when young people were consumed with disco dancing, inspired by movies like *Grease* and *Saturday Night Fever.* Many years later, it was easy for Debbie to remember every detail of the night she met Anthony Pignataro. Their meeting followed the scenario she had carried in her head for years. It was like a scene from a movie.

It was in early July, 1978. Debbie knew right away that Anthony was perfect for her. "I met him first in the parking lot of The Lone Star," she recalled. "I was with a girl-friend and I was driving and I cut the wheel too hard and hit a wall—just grazed it a little bit. Anthony was watching, and he kidded me about my driving. He said I hit the wall because I was too busy looking at him."

In a way that was true. Anthony was "very good looking," almost six feet tall, and Debbie was instantly attracted to him. He had a full head of hair and classic, balanced features, and she thought he could have been a movie star—he was that great looking.

But he was dating one of her acquaintances, so technically he was off limits. Debbie stood at the edge of the crowd and watched Anthony a little wistfully as he danced with Karen.

In the days to come, she saw Anthony often at the night spots where they all went on weekends. And then, on the Fourth of July weekend, he asked her to dance. Just as Debbie had pictured it, she fit into his arms perfectly. She had never felt like that with a man before.

Although she could be strong-willed, Debbie had never been assertive with a man; she was much too shy. That night, she surprised herself. "We were dancing, and the record changed from slow to fast. I remember that it was Donna Summers singing 'Last Dance.' I guess the song title got to me; if I didn't speak up, he would be out of my life. So I looked up at Anthony and I said, 'I wish I'd met you before Karen did . . .' "

He smiled down at her and seemed pleased. She sensed that he apparently felt the same way she did.

Anthony broke up with Karen that night. He asked Debbie to go out with him on July 8. Would she like to see the movie *Grease?* She accepted happily.

It was a golden summer for them. Anthony and Debbie went out several times a week and talked on the phone every single day. With the winters in Buffalo so bitterly cold, summers were packed with events scheduled to take advantage of the balmy weather. They went dancing, of course, and to movies, picnics, concerts, and the beach.

When they talked about birthdays, Anthony said his was on May 12—her mother's birthday! Such a coincidence had to mean something. Debbie was surprised to learn that Anthony was actually ten months younger than she was, although he seemed far more sophisticated. He was going to college at Lehigh University in Bethlehem,

Pennsylvania. He was a junior, majoring in mathematics, although he didn't seem very interested in math. He belonged to one of the top fraternities there: Phi Gamma Delta—whose members were known as Fijis. She dreaded the fall when he would be going back to college, worried that he would drift away from her. Sometimes she was afraid that she was only a summertime girlfriend.

Anthony's world was so different from Debbie's. He had never known anything but wealth and privilege. His father, Ralph Pignataro, was a prominent surgeon in the Buffalo area, and Anthony had grown up in a lovely home in West Seneca. He'd attended the Nichols School, a private school where the tuition was $11,000 to $15,000 a year. Anthony had an older sister, Antoinette, and younger brothers, Ralph Jr. and Steven. None of them had ever known what it was like to wish for something their parents couldn't afford. Dr. Ralph Pignataro wanted his family to have the best. Anthony told Debbie that his father was wonderful and that he could always count on him for advice. He idolized the older man, and Dr. Ralph was beloved throughout Buffalo.

Her first months with Anthony were a wonderfully exciting time for Debbie. She was so much in love that her parents worried sometimes that she might end up with a broken heart. When Anthony left in late September, it was as if somebody had turned the sunshine off in her world. Debbie continued to work in the drugstore, but she lived for the weekends and vacations when Anthony came home from Lehigh.

Debbie and Anthony wrote to each other at least three times a week, and talked on the phone when they could. Anthony came home for Thanksgiving, Christmas, and then Easter. He seemed to be just as interested in Debbie as he had been during their first summer. And she certainly never looked at another man.

In June 1979, they were together again and jubilant that their romance had survived the long school year. During their second summer together, Debbie and Anthony were with each other constantly. Both sets of parents felt left out sometimes because the couple seemed joined at the hip and spent little time with their families, but they knew it was the natural progression of life. It was only natural that Anthony and Debbie could see only each other.

Frank Rago was an old-fashioned Italian patriarch and very protective of Debbie. In the beginning, it was fine with Frank for Debbie to date Anthony, but she was afraid her father would hit the roof when she asked to visit Anthony at Lehigh for a weekend. He gave his permission only after she explained that a girlfriend was going with her and that the two girls would share a hotel room off campus.

By that time, Anthony was in his senior year. They weren't kids, and they could be responsible for their private relationship. Anthony wanted Debbie to be there when he performed in one of his avocations: boxing. He boxed at Lehigh and was a champion in his weight class. He'd won the Eastern Regional NCAA middleweight tournament in his junior year, and he'd lost only one fight in thirty.

In 1980, he was so sure he would win his final college boxing match that he insisted Debbie be there at ringside, bragging to her that he'd seen the other finalist and had no doubt he was going to win. He promised Debbie he would give her the championship trophy over dinner afterward.

Instead, Anthony received the worst beating of his life. His eyes were blackened and swollen, and he could barely see out of the slits between his eyelids. Debbie had rarely seen him lose at anything. His obvious discomfort and humiliation only made her love him more.

Anthony graduated from Lehigh University in May

1980. Debbie attended the graduation ceremony with his parents, Dr. Ralph and Lena Pignataro. Henry Kissinger was the commencement speaker. It was a glorious, sunny day, and Debbie was very proud of Anthony.

Despite their intense attraction, Debbie and Anthony were to have a very long courtship. He explained that he didn't want to marry her until he knew what he was going to do with his life, and he was having difficulty settling on a career. Debbie accepted that. She found Anthony so intelligent and realized that he could do any number of things well; he just wanted to be sure that he chose a profession suited to him. They spent a lot of time discussing Anthony's future. He knew that his father wanted him to go into medicine. His sister, Antoinette, was already in her first year in med school. Dr. Ralph was happy about that, but what he really longed for was to have his son follow him into medicine.

Anthony told Debbie that he didn't want to let his father down, but he explained that he didn't want to let himself down either. He believed that he had been blessed with special gifts and had intellectual capacities far beyond most men. He saw the tremendous future there would be in computer science, an embryonic industry in the late seventies. Most people had no idea how important computers were going to be, he told Debbie—and he knew he would be a natural. But he was also fascinated by the prospect of becoming a doctor. He admired his father tremendously, and Anthony liked the idea of two physicians—father and son—working side by side.

Anthony believed he could do anything. He was supremely self-confident. Debbie admired that in him, but she also saw that some people they knew were turned off by Anthony's ego. He could be full of such braggadocio. In the first years of their being together, she chose to see his confidence as strength rather than an overblown ego.

In the end, Anthony decided to apply for medical school. His father was very pleased. Neither of his brothers had showed an iota of interest in becoming doctors, but once he had decided, Anthony glowed with enthusiasm about his chosen career. He filled out applications to several top medical schools, wondering which one he would choose when the acceptances came in.

Dr. Ralph had always been very kind to Debbie. Anthony's mother, however, was another matter. They had dated for weeks before he took her home to meet his parents, and Debbie would never forget the first time she went to the Pignataro home in West Seneca. She was impressed with how beautiful it was, with the landscaping and the swimming pool, and she wondered whether she would ever fit in. As she stood somewhat hesitantly in the foyer, she heard shouting from upstairs. It was Anthony's mother, Lena. She was shouting at her husband: "What do you think I am? Stupid? I saw you with her!"

Debbie and Anthony had come at a bad time. Anthony's parents were having a fight. Debbie was so embarrassed that she wished she could sink into the floor.

"But his father was very warm," Debbie remembered, and she recalled what he said about Lena. "He told me that she had no manners—but that's just the way she was."

Anthony had some of Lena's bluntness as well as her lack of tact. As Debbie began to feel more secure with him, she also saw him with clearer eyes. She was humiliated sometimes when he made loud remarks that hurt people's feelings. He never seemed to understand that he had done anything wrong. But they had been together for so long. She loved him and considered his occasional rudeness as one small part of his confident personality. She told herself that most people found Anthony completely charming.

Sometimes, Debbie wondered if Anthony's mother would ever accept her. Surprisingly, Lena came to be very fond of Debbie and often took her side when she and Anthony had a disagreement. As time passed, Debbie and Lena Pignataro became good friends, and Debbie understood why Lena was sometimes snappish with people. Her own background had been hardscrabble and miserable.

"Lena was a change-of-life baby," Debbie explained. "She was born into a very, very poor family in Port Colborne, Ontario. Her parents died when she was young, and she was never close to her brothers and sisters."

But Lena Wakunic, christened Sabena, was beautiful. She was Ukrainian and had pale blond hair, ice-blue eyes, and a lovely figure. As a young man Ralph Pignataro met Lena at Crystal Beach, a resort a few miles east of Port Colborne. She was alone in the world, and he fell in love with her and vowed to make up for all the things she had never had. He even put her through high school. When she was angry or "uppity" with people who had less than she did, Ralph knew it was because of the dark times she had lived through. He always tried to smooth the way for her and to make excuses for her.

By the time Debbie met her, Lena Pignataro was a very attractive middle-aged woman with the body of a girl in her twenties, as fair as Dr. Ralph was dark. Her blond hair had turned white and looked platinum rather than gray. She wore expensive but modest clothing with high necks and long sleeves, although she usually wore high heels and a delicate gold ankle bracelet.

Dr. Ralph himself looked like Vic Damone, a popular singer of the era. All of Ralph and Lena's children were good looking, with Antoinette and Ralph resembling Dr. Ralph and Steven and Anthony looking more like their mother.

In time, Lena came to accept Debbie as Anthony's girlfriend. Still, Debbie realized that Lena might not make the most nurturing mother-in-law if she and Anthony should ever marry. Lena adored Anthony and was partial to all of her children. She had great difficulty refusing any of them anything, but Steven was clearly her favorite.

Debbie knew she wasn't a debutante or anything close to it and that Anthony could have had any girl he wanted. Sometimes she still marveled that he had chosen her. She was glad that she had had the courage to tell him how she felt about him.

She never minded that their relationship was all about him. Anthony had such great dreams for the future that she was happy to be part of them. When he told her he was going to follow in his father's footsteps and one day become a surgeon, Debbie knew that medical school and internship would take many years, but she was willing to wait. She promised Anthony that she would work and help him through med school if that's what it took. They would be together forever and have the children she longed for—the children she believed he wanted, too.

Remarkably, Debbie Rago and Anthony Pignataro ended up dating for seven years before their marriage—mostly a long-distance courtship. It would have been nice if they could have become engaged sooner than they did, but he explained to her that they would have to wait until he finished medical school. He needed to concentrate totally on his studies, he said, but he assured Debbie that being apart was as difficult for him as it was for her because he loved her completely.

It turned out to be a *very* long-distance romance. To

his shock, Anthony wasn't accepted by any medical school on the mainland of the United States. The top universities accepted only about five percent of those who applied, looking for applicants who had the best grades and the most well-rounded personalities. Given the option of choosing a straight-A student with no other interests or extracurricular activities, and one with less than perfect grades but a broad base of friends and community service, the second possibility usually got the nod.

Anthony Pignataro didn't make the cut, probably because he had done little to prepare for the test, counting on his intelligence alone. He didn't even come close. The MCAT scores for those chosen by Harvard's med school averaged over 11, and Anthony's were far below that.

The only med school willing to take him was the nonaccredited San Juan Bautista School of Medicine in Hato Rey, Puerto Rico. One drawback to attending a Puerto Rican med school was that the courses there were all taught in Spanish. Anthony was quite willing to learn the language, and he mastered it quickly. From 1983 to 1985, he attended the Universidad Central del Caribe in Bayamon, Puerto Rico. There, students could enter with an MCAT score of 6.7. The tuition was almost as steep as it was at Harvard, but del Caribe accepted over fifteen percent of those who applied. Anthony didn't have to worry about the tuition; Dr. Ralph Pignataro was willing to pay it. Even though it was taking so long, the realization of his dream of having his son practicing with him meant so much to him.

Dr. Ralph Pignataro gladly paid $24,000 a year tuition and all of Anthony's living expenses in Puerto Rico. Whether his medical training was as thorough or as current with medical care advances as taught by medical schools in the continental United States was a question.

Top-ranked American medical schools had 3.8 instructors for every student; del Caribe had only 0.4 instructors for each student.

Still, Anthony Pignataro was very intelligent, more so than his undergraduate grades indicated. When he set out to do something, his brain fairly sizzled. He often said that he viewed himself as a modern-day Galileo, and he prided himself on the way he visualized original concepts. His first goal was an M.D. degree—but that, he assured Debbie, was only a jumping-off place for what he would later accomplish.

He first planned to become a specialist in obstetrics and gynecology. "I found genuine pleasure in obstetrics . . . assisting in the giving of life," Anthony commented. "It was the gynecology addendum to the OB/GYN that did not thrill me."

"Female problems" didn't interest Anthony, and treating such ailments had none of the drama and joy that came with presenting a new baby to its parents. Beyond that, Anthony cited family loyalty. His father was a surgeon, and he leaned toward a surgical specialty of some kind that would complement his father's practice. He searched for a residency program where he could learn more.

With Anthony undergoing intensive training in Puerto Rico, he and Debbie were even farther apart than when he was at Lehigh. But she waited for him faithfully, happy in the knowledge that they would be together forever after four or five years. Debbie kept working and saving her money for that day. She "practically commuted" to Puerto Rico, and she and Anthony seriously discussed having her move there to live with him.

"But we couldn't do that," she recalled. "With our religious beliefs and our families, living together just wasn't something we felt comfortable with."

Sometimes it seemed that their wedding would never happen; Anthony was spending their early and middle twenties in college and med school. Finally, they set June 15, 1985, as their wedding date, almost exactly eight years since Debbie had first run her car into a wall, staring at Anthony.

She could hardly wait to start their life together.

Part Two

The Doctor

3

Anthony Pignataro and Debbie Rago were married in St. Bonaventure's Catholic Church before a gathering of more than three hundred and fifty guests. It was a joyous occasion and a beautiful wedding, the culmination of all their years of waiting.

Debbie had six attendants in mauve satin gowns. Her color theme was mauve and white. She was very slender and looked lovely in her white gown with its long train. A photographer took dozens of pictures of the bride and groom and the wedding party and family members.

Two handsome families blended that day, but the one member of the wedding party who photographed the best was Anthony. He was so photogenic that it was hard to get a bad picture of him. He had his mother's fair complexion, and his hair was much lighter than his father's. The moustache he'd grown after achieving his status as an M.D. only made him look handsomer.

Debbie and her parents had wanted the reception to be held at Samuel's Grand Manor, a very nice facility chosen by many newly married couples. It would hold all their guests comfortably. Anthony agreed—at first. But Ralph and Lena Pignataro argued that it would be preferable to have the reception at their country club. Anyone could book a reception at Samuel's Grand Manor, but only a small number of newlyweds could have their reception at the Wanakah Country Club. Anthony told Debbie that that made sense, just as he always agreed with his parents' wishes. After much discussion, he convinced her to honor Ralph and Lena's request that they move the reception to their exclusive country club.

Still, Debbie had her doubts. The posh club was lovely, but she was afraid that it wasn't nearly large enough. When the day came for their reception, she saw she was right. It was a very warm night, and their guests were hot and crowded. In a way, it became Ralph's and Lena's day rather than the bride's and groom's.

Always anxious to please his father, Anthony made a glowing toast to Dr. Ralph, but his toast to Frank Rago, perhaps meant to be humorous, came off as demeaning and insulting. Debbie was so happy to be Mrs. Anthony Pignataro that she forced herself to keep smiling, but inside she was crushed to see her father trying to mask his hurt. She worried about her dad. Frank Rago's health was failing, and it was all he could do to walk her down the aisle and dance with her at the boisterous Italian wedding reception. Frank and Caroline Rago wanted Debbie to be happy, and they were happy, too, to see her a bride at last.

Debbie was 28 years old. She had waited all those years for Anthony, and now she was married to her young doctor. Thanks to his father's connections, he was scheduled to begin his first year of surgical residency on July 1 at St. Agnes Hospital in Baltimore, Maryland. St. Agnes was a satellite of the Johns Hopkins system, yet Anthony always referred to his first internship as being *at* Johns Hopkins, a prestigious name in the world of medicine.

Right after their wedding reception, Debbie and Anthony flew to Los Angeles, where they boarded a cruise ship that would take them to exotic ports of call on what Anthony called the Mexican Riviera: Puerto Vallarta, Mazatlan, and Cabo San Lucas. Their two-week honeymoon should have been idyllic, but there were jarring moments.

Debbie had long accepted that Anthony had no particular talent with people. She didn't know why, but he just wasn't a people person.

"Sometimes he seemed conceited," she recalled, "so arrogant." He had never had many friends, but she didn't mind that at first; they had so little time to spend together that she had been glad that his free hours belonged to her.

All through school—high school and college—Anthony had only one close male friend. He had gone to the private and expensive Nichols School, and he rarely mingled with anyone from public schools. Graduates of Lehigh University later remembered him as "very conceited. He always had such a high opinion of himself."

Debbie knew Anthony turned people off, but never his loyal buddy from school. She assumed that he would change once he wasn't so laden down with studies. It was just that he was always in a hurry, she told herself, trying to cram too much into too short a time.

So she was a little shocked on their luxury cruise when Anthony's blunt and artless conversation annoyed people and isolated them from the other travelers.

"He embarrassed himself one night," Debbie said. "There was a Jewish couple at our table, and he made awful remarks and jokes about Jews. They asked to be moved to another table."

Debbie was mortified. She had always tried to be kind to people and think of their feelings. It bothered her that her new husband had been so rude and that he seemed completely oblivious to what he had said. He shrugged his shoulders when she told him why the couple had moved to another table.

But when Debbie later looked at their wedding and cruise pictures, she saw again how perfect they were together. She had never really felt pretty, but she felt beautiful on their honeymoon. She was very much in love.

Debbie was a typical Italian-American wife of the seventies. Despite the strides being made in the women's movement, she sublimated her needs and desires to her husband's wishes, content to stand in his shadow and know that she was helping him reach his goals.

They moved to Baltimore, and Anthony was immediately plunged into the life of the fledgling doctor at St. Agnes Hospital. He began a two-year program in general surgery, his intern years, and he was on call every third night. Sleep was elusive, as it was for all young doctors.

Debbie and Anthony found an apartment they could afford. It was quite pleasant, but it was in a section of the city that had a relatively high crime rate. When Anthony was at the hospital all night, Debbie was afraid, hearing sounds that woke her often. She had a job during the daytime in a plastic surgeon's office, and that time raced by, but she dreaded the nighttime when she was home alone.

Sometimes Debbie socialized with the other interns' wives, but mostly she lived a solitary life in Baltimore. Anthony was studying when he was home—or sleeping. She had expected this—it was what they had both worked for; he was going to be a doctor, a surgeon, and all their sacrifices would be worth it. They lived on one salary and banked the other, saving for the future when Anthony would build his own practice.

The early spring of 1986 brought both joy and sadness. Debbie was thrilled when she became pregnant, but she miscarried before the third month. "Anthony felt bad, too," she recalled. "He was very comforting to me, and told me we would try again and it would be all right."

And it was. By July, she was pregnant again. Anthony teased her because they were both so busy he wondered how they'd ever had time for conception to happen, but they were both elated. This time, Debbie felt wonderful, and she continued to work while carrying the baby.

Anthony had completed his first year of internship in general surgery and begun the second. He was sure that two years at St. Agnes would set him up nicely in his career as a surgeon. So was Debbie, although she wasn't really aware of what was going on at St. Agnes. Living with a man as mercurial as Anthony was, and as brilliant, she had long since learned to make the adjustments necessary to keep him happy. She listened when he told her of his life at the hospital, but she didn't question him when he didn't want to talk.

By March 1987, Debbie was more than eight months pregnant and a little nervous about being alone. One night when Anthony was at the hospital, Debbie awoke to a sound that wasn't the usual creaking of their building. Her heart beating wildly, she crept to where she could peek into the living room. Someone was moving outside the sliding glass doors of their apartment. The doors had never fastened correctly, and suddenly one slid open. There stood a tall naked man inside her apartment, raving incoherently.

She was terrified, but she remembered the gun Anthony had purchased. "I found the gun where Anthony put it in the dresser, and I held it on that man. That seemed to snap him out of his delusions, and suddenly he wasn't talking crazy any longer."

She managed to call the police as she held him at gunpoint, and they came and took him away. "It took three officers to get him in the car," she remembered with a shiver. "I was really scared, but thank God, I didn't go into premature labor."

A few weeks later, Debbie gave birth to her baby by cesarean section. On April 4, 1987, she had a son—just what Anthony wanted. They named him Raphael Frank after Anthony's and Debbie's fathers. He was a beautiful baby, and they were both enthralled with their dark-eyed child.

Everything was moving along on schedule for them. Anthony was only a few months away from the end of his first two-year program, and he had decided to continue on at St. Agnes for another year. But he was stunned and then outraged when his contract was not renewed.

"They only renewed one of the residents," Debbie said, "and it wasn't Anthony. He talked to an attorney to see if he could sue them, but he didn't go ahead with it."

During this, the third year of their marriage, a tiny network of fissures appeared for the first time. Debbie noticed a number of hang-up phone calls coming into their apartment. One time, a female voice actually gave her a message to give to Anthony. "Just tell him 'hello,' she said."

Debbie was puzzled but not overly alarmed. Anthony was a very handsome man, and she knew women often got crushes on doctors. It was probably some woman who had come into the hospital. Still, she had a wife's insecurity. She realized that she never really knew where Anthony was at any given time; that was just part of the nature of his career. She had always trusted him.

Debbie had almost forgotten about the odd phone call, but then she answered another call from a woman. It was their last night in Baltimore, and Debbie was happy that they were getting ready to go home. This time, the woman's message was for her. "Go look in the back seat of your car," she said with a hard edge to her voice.

Making her way out to the car, Debbie opened the door, hoping that it was just a hoax. Instead, she found a cassette recording, a letter, and a Christmas card. Her hands were numb as she opened the letter and the card, reading what seemed unfathomable to her. She played the tape, and there was no question that it was Anthony's voice on the tape, obviously talking to another woman. There was no other way to view the items in the back seat beyond accepting that her husband had been having an affair.

Debbie Pignataro might have been a loyal and patient girlfriend, and then a wife willing to work and postpone having a nice house to help Anthony through his years of residency and postgraduate training. She was a faithful wife, her marriage blessed in the Catholic church and sacred to her. But she was no doormat. Whatever else might be wrong with their relationship, she had believed in Anthony's fidelity. Now, she had proof that he had been cheating on their marriage—and she erupted, as angry and hurt as she had ever been in her life.

"Get home right now!" she shouted, when she got him on the phone.

"He came home," she said, "and I screamed at him and cried, and I hit him—not hard, but I hit him. I was so angry that he betrayed me like that."

Anthony was stunned, and shocked when he realized that Debbie actually intended to leave him. He didn't call his father for advice this time; he called Debbie's father and said, "Debbie wants to leave me, and take the baby." Then he handed the phone to her.

"What's goin' on?" Frank Rago asked her.

"I don't know, Dad," she said, worried that this wasn't at all good for her father's health. Her dad had been going downhill since her wedding three years before. But he kept asking her what was wrong, and he was a very strong man, despite his illness. Finally, she told him that Anthony had been unfaithful to her.

"Debbie," her father said sternly after a long pause. "Listen to me. You forgive *once*. Now hang up and go make your marriage work."

Anthony certainly appeared to be truly repentant. He insisted that he loved her and the baby, and he could not bear the thought of losing her. The other woman didn't matter at all—she was just some crazy girl. He would never see her again, and he begged Debbie to stay with him and go ahead with their plans until he got another residency. They had too much invested in their marriage—all those years together—to throw it away now.

Her father's words played over and over in her head: *You forgive once.*

So Debbie did. She had loved Anthony for ten years; she still loved him—and she was pregnant again. She would stay in the marriage. And it wasn't long before she believed that things were going to be all right again. She wanted so much to believe that.

They had already decided to leave Baltimore after Anthony had lost his residency at St. Agnes, and it was too late to get into another residency program for the 1987–1988 year. They agreed to move back to Buffalo until Anthony found a better venue for his third year of residency. Debbie was relieved that they were going to be far away from the woman who had called her.

Together, they packed everything they owned into their car and a rental truck and headed home to New York State. They could stay with the elder Pignataros until they found a place of their own.

Anthony took a job at a walk-in emergency clinic, the Mercy Ambulatory Care Center, in Orchard Park, New York. In essence, he was a "Doc-in-a-Box," but he was at least practicing medicine, and he certainly saw any number of injuries, maladies, and illnesses. It was a comedown for him, though; he was in the trenches instead of in the much more rarefied air of a Johns Hopkins' satellite.

Anthony began to keep a journal, documenting his reaction to the events of his life and putting forth his philosophies. It would one day become his book, *M.D.: Mass Destruction*—a paean to himself. This was the manuscript he later sent to me, telling me that his wife, Debbie, was the author. He must have thought it would be better received if someone other than himself wrote it.

Two years later, he would have more than a hundred pages. The first page began with his accomplishments. Anthony seemed confident that his talent as an author was as brilliant as his skill as a physician. His style was a throwback to novels from the nineteenth century. It was clear that he wrote with a thesaurus close by—he chose the longest words possible in his almost archaic narrative. He sometimes referred to himself in the third person. The vast majority of his book was about his brilliance as a physician; only occasionally did he mention his family life.

There were some situations that he didn't mention at all. He included nothing that might cast a negative light on his prowess as a physician, although he was quick to blame the bad judgment of others.

Anthony was less than three years out of medical school, and the young doctor didn't have the experience that older physicians had. All doctors make mistakes once in a while; they are only human, but most of their slips or misdiagnoses are not life-threatening. However, Anthony made a really bad call. He allegedly failed to diagnose a patient who had a severe inflammation of the lining of the heart: bacterial endocarditis. Such an ailment can be mistaken for pleurisy or pneumonia, but it can also be fatal if not treated. This patient died, and a wrongful death suit was filed. Eventually the suit was dropped, but it was a scary thing for both Debbie and Anthony.

Nevertheless, being back in Buffalo gave the young Pignataros a time of calm in their lives. Everyone fussed over baby Ralph, and it was good to be home again after years away. Even though it tore at Debbie's heart to see her father so ill—any effort at all made him gasp for breath—he still had the strength of character that endeared him to everyone in his family. To his siblings and cousins, nieces and nephew, Frank Rago was "Uncle Junior," a vital and integral part of a wide, extended family. His advice was always solid. Everyone called Uncle Junior for counsel or for comfort.

Debbie followed his directive to forgive her husband *once,* but it was to be the last advice her father would ever give her. On November 16, 1987, Frank Rago slipped into severe congestive heart failure and was taken to the hospital to undergo diuresis in an effort to remove the fluid that was drowning his lungs. Caroline and Carmine were at the hospital with him, and Debbie was home with her infant son, waiting for word. But Anthony had gone deer hunting with his father at dawn. He assured Debbie he would carry his pager with him in case she needed him. Hunting was very important to Anthony—both hunting for deer in New York and later for big game in faraway countries.

Debbie needed him that day, and needed him badly. Oddly, Anthony chose to immortalize that last day of Frank Rago's life in his book by prefacing it with a description of his successful shot into the heart of a whitetail deer.

"I was confident he was dead," Anthony wrote of the buck he shot. "As I descended from my stand I knew that no animal could withstand such a violent penetrating chest wound. As I followed the trail, my pager began to beep. I canceled the signal and caught up with my trophy. Knowing my passion for this sport, neither my answering service, nor my wife, would risk the wrath of my response to the disturbance of a loud audible beeper in the silence of the forest. I had the deer gutted and field dressed as soon as possible, and began the half-mile drag back to our vehicle with the innate fear that the page was real . . ."

Even so, when Anthony learned that his father-in-law's condition had worsened, he stopped to shower and change. "But I neglected to shave," he added. "Stepping off the elevator, we presented to the ICU, Carmine, my brother-in-law, greeted us with the most crestfallen expression of bereavement as he simply shook his head, 'No.'

"Deborah erupted with the most gut-wrenching expression of pain that I ever remember. Her best buddy was gone. I knew that nothing has hurt her as much as this . . ."

Debbie Pignataro withstood several emotional losses that year. Her father was gone. Her husband had been unfaithful, and more and more he was often missing when she needed him. Still, she was made of steel as well as velvet, and she kept going. The Pignataros made Debbie welcome. The news of Anthony's dalliance with another woman was apparently common knowledge in the family, because Lena took Debbie's side, confiding to her that she understood how Debbie felt. "It happened to me, too—twice," Lena said.

That shocked Debbie, but it reassured her, too; Dr. Ralph and Lena certainly had a strong marriage now.

"In many ways," Debbie remembered, "we had a wonderful year. I was pregnant again. Anthony was always sending me flowers and cards saying he loved me. I didn't worry about him cheating on me, and we were both looking forward to summer when our new baby would be born."

The prospect of a new baby proved to her that life went on after all, even though she still grieved for her father. After her second cesarean—this one an emergency procedure—Debbie's baby emerged on June 5. It was a girl, just as the ultrasound had shown. But the atmosphere in the delivery room was strangely stilted, and the newborn was whisked away for what they told her was "testing and stabilization."

Her name was Christina Marie—just as they had planned—but there was no joy in her birth. Her head was enlarged and misshapen. "She had a brain tumor that had been growing for months before she was born," Debbie said sadly.

Christina had no significant brain function, and neonatologists agreed that she couldn't survive without being on a life-support system that would breathe for her. Even then, barring a miracle, the baby girl would never move beyond a vegetative state.

Debbie and Anthony made the heartbreaking decision to give their permission to take Christina off the life support system. They arranged for a simple burial service.

"I was still in the hospital," Debbie said. "Anthony, Lena, and my mother went to the cemetery to bury my baby. There was no funeral. I didn't even get to go to her burial."

Before Debbie could recover from the surgical birth and the grief over the baby she never saw, Anthony left Buffalo. He had been accepted into another residency program, this time at Georgetown University Medical School in Washington, D.C. He told Debbie that she and Ralph should stay behind with his parents until he found suitable housing for them.

It was necessary for him to go—he couldn't be board-certified in any specialty until he completed a residency program. Both Debbie and Anthony had struggled for too many years to give up on Anthony's dreams now. But it was such a lonely time for Debbie, and she grieved for her father and her lost baby girl on her own.

Anthony's third year of residency began on July 1, 1988. He found a town house to rent in Alexandria, Virginia, and Debbie and Ralph joined him in late July.

"The neighborhood wasn't what I'd expected," Debbie said. "It was nice, but everyone was older, and no one had kids. We moved later to Wheaton, Maryland, and that was better."

Anthony became critical of Debbie's appearance. She was never thin enough or pretty enough for him. She recalled, "He would ask me, 'Have you looked at yourself in the mirror? Do you think I want to be with someone who looks like that?' "

So Debbie began to diet and tried harder to please him, but her self-confidence drained away every time Anthony let her know that she wasn't quite good enough for him. In truth, she was still a very attractive young woman, but she saw herself through Anthony's critical eyes.

Anthony had switched his speciality to otolaryngology, which dealt with diseases of the ear, nose, and throat. It would take two more years of training for him to be certified. Anthony wrote in his continuing journal that he was doing rotations in plastic cosmetic surgery and had become fascinated with facial reconstructive surgery.

"These were the areas that interested me the most," Anthony wrote. "I always believed this was the logical extension of my prior engineering school, and the many summers I spent working on construction. It was the perfect match of intellect and artistry."

If Anthony could help people with this combination of

specialties, Debbie would be proud. She prayed that this program would be smooth. In two years, they could move home to Buffalo for good, and Anthony could open a practice that would provide them a good living but, more important, would be beneficial to his patients, giving them hope and a new life.

But Anthony ran into more problems. Later, he blamed his troubles at Georgetown University on the fact that he lost his mentor, the one senior physician he felt understood his potential. Dr. Louis Gilbrath* was as important an influence on him, he said, as his own father was. But Dr. Gilbrath had coronary artery disease, which required bypass surgery. The surgery was only partially successful, and Anthony's idol and teacher was forced to retire early.

Despite this explanation, it was more than losing Dr. Gilbrath that marred Anthony's years at Georgetown. Even with his intelligence and goal-oriented lifestyle, Anthony still had no skill in dealing with people, especially his own peers.

"As is often the case with the changing of the guard, turmoil ensued," he wrote. "Subversion and discord pervaded both the staff and the resident team . . ."

It was true he wasn't popular with the staff and his fellow residents. He was boastful and, as some of his fellow students thought, conceited. In a residency program where no one ever had enough sleep or free time, the team had to pull together, and many of his peers felt that Anthony was only out for himself.

Beyond Anthony's arrogance, there were other reasons why he wasn't doing well at Georgetown: He broke rules that should never be broken. At Christmastime in 1988, Debbie took Ralph, who was twenty months old, home to spend the holidays with his grandparents. Anthony couldn't go; he was scheduled to be on call. But on New

Year's Eve, he walked out of the ER. He went to a bar and got drunk. This total lack of regard for the residency program at Georgetown did not go unnoticed. He was chastised severely. When Debbie heard about it, she was horrified. She held her breath, hoping that Anthony wouldn't be dismissed from the program. In the months that followed, she relaxed a little. He remained at Georgetown.

Debbie became pregnant again in February 1989, eight months after they had lost their first baby girl. Her obstetrician hastened to assure her that Christina's tumor had been a very rare thing, and no more likely to happen again to her than to anyone else.

It was a good pregnancy. Debbie carried her baby to term, listening throughout her last months of gestation to Anthony's growing dissatisfaction with the otolaryngology department at Georgetown. He was gloomy and disgruntled because, once again, he was not being treated with the respect he felt he deserved.

In Wheaton, Maryland, on October 2, 1989, Debbie had a third cesarean and gave birth to a perfect little girl. They named her Lauren. Now they had one of each, and Debbie was fulfilled. Any further pregnancies would be risky for her after so many surgical deliveries. She lived through her children and her husband, content to stand behind them.

Anthony called the situation at Georgetown a "maelstrom" and said he didn't think that he could finish out the two-year residency. No one appreciated his knowledge or listened to his theories. If Dr. Gilbrath were still in charge, things would have been different, Anthony said. Gilbrath understood what he was capable of. With this new regime, no one recognized his talents.

Perhaps Anthony could see the writing on the wall. He

would say later that he got out just in time. "I adroitly avoided this maelstrom by placing into a final PGY-V [senior year] at Thomas Jefferson University Medical Center in Philadelphia."

Anthony had not completed the two-year program, and he had virtually slipped back to where he had been two years earlier. Of course, it meant another move. In June 1990, the Pignataros packed up again and relocated to Marlton, New Jersey, a suburb of Philadelphia, on the other side of the Delaware River.

Anthony was still seeking his credentials in otolaryngology. Although he described himself as "gregarious and personable [and a man] who worked well with people," that clearly wasn't true. He was no more popular at Thomas Jefferson than he had been at Georgetown. This time, he blamed it on the jealousy of the other residents. He was entering at the senior level, and he felt the others resented that. "As hard as I tried to break the ice," he remarked, "I was never truly accepted as part of the new team. There was an almost tangible air of envy because I had come from such a reputable program. The others had paid their dues together, and hadn't seen the sort of road I already had."

It was true that he had just spent two years studying the human ear, nose, and throat, and he was repeating much of what he'd done in Washington D.C., but he was not particularly adept. Worse, he clashed with almost everyone he worked with. Ironically, Anthony's patients adored him. He had a charismatic bedside manner, and they preferred him to some of the other residents.

Debbie had begun to dread spending time with the other residents and their wives. In social situations, Anthony could be counted on to say something offensive. Debbie, of all people, knew that he could insult people and never know it—or care. She loved him still, but she could see why he wasn't successful in human relationships. He had so many grandiose dreams and such confidence in himself that he seemed to forget that other people had their own issues. "I was embarrassed," she said, "and I usually tried to talk about it with him afterwards. He just said 'I was only kidding' or told me I had no sense of humor. He didn't seem to understand that he was constantly hurting people's feelings or making them mad with his 'jokes.' "

He hurt Debbie's feelings, too. He continued to complain that she was "too dumb" or "too fat" or incapable of keeping up with him socially in his climb to the top. Anthony had always found time to keep himself in top physical shape, and he expected perfection in his wife, too. Debbie had gained a little weight in her four pregnancies, but she wasn't fat—not to anyone's eyes but Anthony's.

Debbie got a part-time job in another plastic surgeon's office, leaving her babies at a day care center. She hated leaving Lauren and Ralph, but she had no choice; they needed her income. One of her features that Debbie had always disliked was her nose, and her employer gave her a greatly reduced rate to make it smaller. She was thrilled with the difference in her appearance, and Anthony was so impressed that he decided he would get *his* nose fixed, too. He fretted about his appearance a lot, and he was devastated because his hair was thinning rapidly.

Debbie made lots of friends among her neighbors in Marlton, and she liked her job, but the evenings were not pleasant; she had to listen to Anthony complain about his rejection at work. It was a monotonously familiar theme.

Anthony was not only a resident physician, he was also an inventor. He was always tinkering with better ways to do things, and he talked about getting patents for some of the ideas he'd come up with. On weekends, he went fishing with his son and his father—an activity that he said helped him survive what was going on at Thomas Jefferson.

"It made the countless hours of abject isolation in the workplace seem meaningless. I simply looked forward to the opportunity to begin my private practice. Soon we would be headed home again to take root and pursue this goal."

Debbie looked forward to a bright spot in the onerous year: a trip to Maui for a medical conference, where they joined the rest of the residents' class. Lena stayed with Ralph and Lauren, and Debbie hoped the excursion would be like a second honeymoon. But it turned out to be a disaster. They had one of the worst arguments of their marriage, which ended with Anthony storming off and leaving her, once again, alone.

Anthony actually thought the trip went well. He presented a paper on a bizarre patient he had treated, a man he said had tried to commit "suicide by scissors." The patient had driven the scissors' blade tips into both his eyes. Anthony had worked on him for more than nine hours and had saved not only the patient but his eyesight. Anthony's paper on the procedure was well received, and he was elated.

But in June 1991, Anthony's evaluation at Thomas Jefferson was so negative that once again he failed to be invited back for the second year of a residency program. That made him ineligible to sit for the American Board of Otolaryngology examinations. Once again, he had failed to complete a program. He was an M.D., but it was unlikely he would get hospital privileges—a kiss of death for a physician.

Residents are expected to achieve at least a grade of 4 on a 1 to 5 scale evaluating their skill in otolaryngology. The records of his evaluation by teaching doctors gave him scores of 1 to 2.5. They commented on his performance in brutally frank terms. One termed him a "medico sociopath," while another wrote "major questions regarding integrity raised by a large number of resident peers." Many of the physicians who worked with Anthony found that he had a severe deficit in basic knowledge of the speciality of otolaryngology.

For all of his boasting about his own brilliance and skill, when Anthony took the preparation test for the Board Certification test, he scored abysmally low. His raw score was in the 20th percentile, and was only in the 7th percentile for a resident in his year of standing, and in the 3rd percentile of his "year group." Ninety-seven percent of his fellow residents in their senior year of otolaryngology scored higher than he did.

But his peers were his harshest judges. Anthony was dead-on when he complained that nobody liked him or listened to him. "Simply put," one resident wrote, "he is unreliable, poorly informed, dishonest and dangerous . . . do not rehire . . . the responsibility is too great, the risks innumerable . . . I fear that lives are truly at stake . . ."

Other evaluations were just as damning: "I found many errors in patient care . . . His response was that 'It could happen to anybody' . . . A major problem with Tony is that he will not change his behavior, even if he is directly confronted with a problem . . . I feel that he has no detectable positive attributes as a physician."

"I find him to be dishonest, manipulative and conniving. He has demonstrated a lack of fundamental medical knowledge . . . his dishonesty and lack of medical knowledge combined with his arrogance make him dangerous."

Anthony Pignataro was finished with residencies. He vowed that he would never go through another two-year program.

"He believed in his mind that he had completed the process," Debbie said. "We moved back to Buffalo, and he prepared to hang his shingle as an expert in otolaryngology in West Seneca."

Despite her doubts, and without full knowledge of why her husband had not been asked to return to the Thomas Jefferson program, Debbie Pignataro tried very hard to believe that their future had begun. Even though life hadn't happened quite the way she pictured it, she had long since grown accustomed to accepting life the way it was.

Part Three

Private Practice

4

It **was wonderful** to be back in Buffalo. It was home, where everyone was wrapped up in ice hockey with the Buffalo Sabres, baseball with the Buffalo Bisons, and football with the National Football League's multichampion Buffalo Bills, where O.J. Simpson was once a revered hero. Debbie and Anthony watched the thousands of tiny white lights illuminate the Peace Bridge to Fort Erie, Ontario, and they ate the best pizza in the world, Buffalo wings, and "beef-on-a-wick," the thinly sliced roast beef on a Kimmelwick roll that was Buffalo cuisine. The air smelled of honeysuckle and the salty spray of Lake Erie.

Debbie felt as if she had finally come out of a long dark tunnel. She didn't have to pack up the kids and move any longer, and she could be close to her mother and brother. Anthony assured her again and again that he didn't need any more of the controlling, prejudiced, two-year residencies. After all, he'd spent almost five years trying to fit into their stupid, confining little boxes, and he knew more than the lot of them. He was ready to treat patients in his own practice. Debbie wanted to believe him; the stress of his repeated failures in his two-year programs was almost too much to bear—for either of them.

Anthony didn't want to join a group practice or a

health maintenance organization (HMO)—if, indeed, he was eligible. And there was his own research.

"I needed to pursue my own ideas," he recalled. I needed the freedom to go to the lab at my own discretion. I could not be held down by the demands of a group, where the youngest physician members obtain the least amount of personal time."

Once again, Debbie and Anthony were living with his parents—but that was all right; they would soon have their own home. Ralph Pignataro had always helped and mentored his son, and he was still there for him. If he was disappointed by Anthony's scholastic and residency-program failures, he didn't speak of it.

After a few weeks, the younger Pignataros moved into a small two-bedroom apartment of their own. They planned to build a starter house to live in while they paid off some of their debts and saved up enough to open their own clinic.

Anthony's father and his best friend owned several acres of land in West Seneca, not far from Dr. Ralph's home. It was zoned for residential building, and the older men envisioned streets lined with new home construction as Buffalo's burgeoning population spread to the western suburbs.

Anthony and his brother Steve were given one lot along the otherwise empty street. They borrowed money to start construction on a duplex. Steven would live on one side of the three-story duplex, and Anthony and his family on the other. Although they would contract most of the actual labor out, they would oversee the building. Anthony and his brothers had worked summers in construction when they were teenagers, and they understood the principles of building.

It wasn't a good summer. Buffalo is usually hot and sunny all summer, but in 1991, rain came down in torrents, making the project take longer and longer as the brothers slogged through a sea of mud. They finally set their moving-in date for February 1992.

It wasn't a good omen when Debbie and Anthony stopped to check their new house three days before their moving date and found that someone—probably teenagers—had broken in through a basement window. Since their place was the only home on the long street, it was a natural target for someone looking for a spot to have a beer bust. Empty bottles littered the interior. Their unwelcome visitors had vandalized the house, smearing linoleum glue on the walls, cabinets, and carpets. Debbie sobbed. They had been so close to having a home of their own, and she knew that their insurance wouldn't cover their losses. They would have to tear up the brand-new carpet and replace it.

Anthony was enraged, and rightly so. He slept on a cot in the empty house every night to be sure that no one broke in again.

Finally, in March, after living for nine months in a cramped apartment, and for years without a real home of their own, they moved in. It was lonely for Debbie at first. There were no neighbors to have coffee with, and no grocery stores close by. But they were close to her in-laws, and she and Lena were by now good friends. Caroline Rago wasn't far away, either, although Anthony wasn't enthusiastic about Debbie spending much time with her family. Caroline had to work, and her visits were limited to weekends.

They settled in. Anthony was now completely free to work on his plans to be granted hospital privileges, where he would meet future patients. He applied to several hospitals in western New York, telling them that he was eligible to sit for the otolaryngology boards. But it was simple enough for the hospitals to verify this—and most of them did check and found it wasn't true. Anthony had never been notified that he had achieved this eligibility, and he was bluffing.

Anthony found a way in, at least temporarily. An elderly physician in Warsaw, New York, was recovering from a coronary bypass and also had diabetes and hardening of the arteries. He needed help with his small country practice. The older doctor, a native of India, offered Anthony a job assisting him for two or three days a week. It meant an income to add to Debbie's, and that was important. Anthony applied for loans to remodel an office he leased in West Seneca for his primary practice.

Largely because he was helping a well-known local doctor, Anthony was given conditional privileges at the Wyoming County Community Hospital in Warsaw, almost forty miles east of Buffalo.

Debbie set up Anthony's office books and did all the paperwork for his fledgling practice. There were considerable expenses in setting up a solo practice. Beyond the office and examining room furniture and equipment, there was malpractice insurance, and leasing fees for the equipment Anthony could not afford to buy outright. In time, he would need to hire office personnel and medical assistants. Debbie was doing everything she could to help him get started. For the moment, they were on a shoestring budget.

Anthony planned an operating room in the basement of his building. That might take a while longer, but he wanted to get to a place where he was autonomous and would never again have to depend on anyone but himself. If he had his own operating room, it wouldn't matter if hospitals didn't accept him. Of course, he didn't include his father as someone he didn't want to depend on. His father's approval and support were vital to him.

Even in the beginning, Anthony designated Wednesdays as special days set aside for his "current research endeavor." His ultimate goal had always been plastic surgery. As he had said, it was "the perfect match of his intellect and his artistry."

For now, he treated patients with ear, nose, and throat problems, and most of the time, he seemed to be competent. At last, the Pignataros were enjoying a comfortable, if not luxuriant, lifestyle.

Ralph was 5 and in kindergarten. Without discussing it with Debbie, Anthony bought a German shepherd puppy, which he named Polo. Ralph had been named for his grandfather, and Debbie had chosen the name Lauren because she liked it. Polo's name was Anthony's little joke because of the "Ralph-Lauren" combination: a dog named for a men's cologne. The dog grew to be huge—too big for Debbie to handle—but Anthony pointed out that Polo was a good protector for their household.

"Anthony always had a dog when he was a kid," Debbie said. "But he was so mean to Polo. He didn't train him, and when Polo did something to irritate him, Anthony would hit him or kick him."

Polo remained loyal to Anthony, and Ralph loved the big dog.

Anthony was determined to be board-certified, if only for economic reasons. Patients with any savvy knew enough about specialists to ask that vital question. Reference services were more likely to recommend board-certified physicians. He attended a few seminars, and he read medical journals with articles about plastic surgery. He usually traveled to seminars on his own because Debbie was so busy with Ralph and Lauren. He was piling up hours of study, although some of the conferences he attended were too experimental to qualify as continuing medical education (CME) courses.

Part of Anthony's Wednesday research was grotesque.

He worked on female cadavers as he experimented with underwires beneath the skin to maintain breast implants. He even thought he might be able to bypass implants entirely. He wanted to come up with techniques he could use when he was doing breast plastic surgery—something that would make him appeal to the mass of prospective patients who were looking for plastic surgeons.

But perhaps more than anything, Dr. Anthony Pignataro wanted to be famous, renowned for his brilliance and innovative thinking. He still thought of himself as a "modern-day Galileo," a man of such vision that he saw far beyond the ordinary man's imagination.

Most of his research didn't concern life-threatening illnesses. Rather, he was almost entirely focused on ways to improve the physical appearance of his future patients. The way he looked mattered so much to Anthony that he assumed everyone was as self-focused.

In the meantime, Anthony's practice was growing, but his conditional privileges at the Wyoming County Community Hospital ran out in September 1994. The official reason was that he was still not eligible to take the otolaryngology board exams. However, there may have been another reason.

One of the most delicate procedures in otolaryngology is surgery in the frontal sinus area. Only a paper-thin layer of bone separates the sinus area at the top of the nose from the brain itself, and any surgeon operating there must have a steady and educated hand.

On August 3, 1994, Anthony operated on a deviated septum (the center cartilage in the nose) in a 30-year-old man. He clumsily entered the outer layer of the brain, a critical mishap that greatly increased the patient's susceptibility for brain abscess, meningitis, and nerve damage. In this case, the patient's brain fluid actually leaked into the nasal passages, but Anthony told no one and sent the patient home from day surgery.

A senior otolaryngologist who studied the case reported that there were serious questions, of both "omission" and "commission," about Anthony's surgical technique. The specialist questioned whether Anthony had the credentials to continue doing endoscopic sinus surgery.

The following day, Anthony's hospital privileges were canceled. He was fortunate that the young man with the deviated septum didn't develop deadly meningitis.

In 1992, Anthony had fortuitously added a second hospital that gave him temporary operating privileges, Our Lady of Victory Hospital. But in February 1993, Anthony operated on a seventy-one-year-old patient who agreed to elective surgery to remove a laryngeal tumor for biopsy. It was, in some aspects, a routine procedure, but any time a patient is operated on deep in the throat, his main route to get oxygen to the lungs can be compromised. Sensitive tissue can swell or hemorrhage.

Anthony's patient died.

A hospital board reviewed the operation and immediately restricted his privileges. After that, he was not allowed to do elective procedures involving the airway after 1:00 P.M., and before that hour, he had to be monitored. The chief of surgery and chief of otolaryngology met with Anthony to explain that it was extremely important not to disturb laryngeal tumors any more than necessary, and that he should have been prepared for swelling and excessive bleeding at the site of surgery.

Anthony was indignant that they should lecture him as if he were a mere intern.

Anthony's privileges at Our Lady of Victory expired in September 1993, and the hospital did not renew them.

Anthony no longer had *any* hospital where he was

welcome to operate or treat patients. He applied for privileges in otolaryngology and plastic surgery in Irving, New York, and at Buffalo Mercy Hospital. He wasn't accepted because he had no proof to back up his statement that he was board-certified in those specialties.

Anthony suspected that one of the department chairmen at Thomas Jefferson Hospital in Philadelphia might be blocking him by failing to endorse him as a doctor of good moral character worthy of taking the board exams. He fought back by suing his last training hospital and the chairman.

Thomas Jefferson submitted the names of seven ear, nose, and throat specialists to serve as arbitrators. Any one of them was competent to evaluate Anthony's level of skill in this speciality.

Characteristically, Anthony balked. He came back with his own list of three otolaryngologists. That was no problem for Thomas Jefferson Hospital; they agreed to let the matter be decided by the very first doctor on Anthony's list.

Although Anthony was intelligent enough, he was ultimately self-defeating. In his rage at *anyone* who had the temerity to block him from doing what he wanted, he often failed to reason things out carefully. He apparently expected the past to disappear into a kind of mist where no one remembered details.

"Dr. H.," the physician whom Anthony himself had chosen, set about gathering statements that were either for or against the subject. He interviewed specialists who had worked with Anthony Pignataro. Usually physicians tend to close ranks and protect each other. So many things can go wrong in diagnosis, treatment, and surgery that they are hesitant to point fingers at other doctors, knowing that they too could make mistakes. Not this time.

In the end, Dr. H.'s report was scathing. The doctors who had worked with Anthony in Philadelphia recalled that he was lazy and slipshod when he came into the residency, and that he never improved while he was there. "He would routinely show up late for rounds, claiming he had done work he had not done, say he had seen intensive care unit (ICU) patients that he had not seen, fabricate laboratory data, fabricate physical examination data, fabricate information about postoperative patients that he had not seen. This was routine . . ."

Anthony scoffed at his evaluation. "If I had been such a bad doctor . . . practicing for four years . . . If I were as bad as I'm made out to appear, I'm sure that something would have happened by now."

As indeed it had. More than one "something" had happened. He had simply forgotten the dead biopsy patient and the young man whose brain had been pierced by an errant blade.

Dr. H. said that no one at Thomas Jefferson should be compelled to recommend that Anthony take the otolaryngology board exam. He concurred that Pignataro was in no way qualified for either skill or good moral character. Stung, Anthony challenged the findings of the arbitrator he himself had chosen, and he requested a review in federal court.

In May 1995, Anthony withdrew his lawsuit, and it was dismissed.

Actually, he cared very little about the practice of otolaryngology. It was only a stepping-stone for him on his way to plastic surgery. He had had minimal formal training in that delicate art, although he still attended every conference he could afford where plastic surgeons gathered. He leaned toward techniques that were more experimental than accredited. Aware that there was a lot of competition in plastic surgery, Anthony focused on procedures that were new and dramatic, something that would attract patients to him.

And he continued to work on his permanent subcutaneous underwire to lift sagging breasts.

5

Dr. Ralph Pignataro could see no wrong in his doctor son, nor could his wife. Anthony considered his father his greatest mentor. He had always spent hours on the phone with his father, discussing the cases he saw in medical school and residency. Anthony said he idolized his father, and that was probably true.

Both Dr. Ralph and Dr. Anthony were bald. There was a strong balding gene in the Pignataro family, and Anthony had started to lose his hair when he was only 23. He continued to be vain about how he looked. He tried comb-overs held in place by hairspray, and then toupees held down with glues, clips, and tie-downs. He even resorted to intricate weaves that combined human hair from someone else with the rapidly retreating rim of hair that still remained.

He concluded that women wanted large, perky breasts and men wanted hair. Anthony figured—correctly—that there would be an unlimited market for an expensive real hairpiece that would never blow off or even slip sideways. As an intern, he had once seen a technique called implantology in which surgeons used snaps to anchor artificial eyes, noses, and even ears. Further, Anthony recalled that dental surgeons had successfully implanted teeth in a procedure known as osseointegration, in which the replacement tooth was threaded into the softer bone tissue of the jaw. After about four months' healing time, the teeth had literally grown into the bone.

What if a man—or a woman, for that matter—could have snaps implanted into their skulls? Anthony thought it could be possible to have the receptacle part of the snap sewn into a hairpiece. Actually, the more he thought about it, the more it seemed to him that putting snaps into a skull would pose less danger of infection than putting a tooth into a bacteria-laden mouth.

"I recall that at the time, it seemed like a crazy idea," Anthony said. "I initially exercised caution with whom I would discuss the details of the project."

Other doctors, including his own father, found his research bizarre, but Anthony kept on. He knew that bolts were routinely inserted into human skulls to give patients with unstable spines traction until they healed. Why not move up the side of the head and somehow insert the male part of a snap into the bone?

He felt he was on to something big. But who would test it? There had to be a guinea pig willing to be a modern-day Frankenstein with semipermanent metal "bolts" protruding from his head. Men were not likely to stand in line for that operation, even if the metal would never show beneath the attached hairpiece.

Anthony thought of Sy Sperling, president of the Hair Club for Men, a successful entrepreneur whose familiar television commercial featured him saying, "I'm not only the president; I'm a client!"

It dawned on Anthony that *he* should be his own first patient. If he truly believed that his invention was sound, he should be willing to undergo the necessary surgery. "Would it not be a tremendous advertising advantage to proclaim that I'm not only the doctor, I'm the patient?" he mused. "Who would perform the first surgery? Who did I trust? Who had the skill and confidentiality to be trusted with my technique . . . which, if successful, I hoped could be patented. The answer was patently obvious: my own father. He certainly had the necessary skills and could be trusted."

It took some convincing for Anthony to persuade his father to operate on him. Finally, Dr. Ralph Pignataro agreed, and Anthony noted that a distinguished dentist, experienced in prosthetic surgery, assisted.

Afterward, Anthony proclaimed the procedure no more painful than having a cavity filled. His father had drilled four holes in his bald head. After three and a half months of healing, an implant was integrated into the surrounding bone, and then the center screw was removed and a protruding bolt with a socket remained just above the skin. "The female or ball portion of the attachment was fastened to a custom skullcap cover with synthetic hair— which was then easily snapped into the socket of the bolt."

Anthony was elated. His invention worked, and he would be the main model. His "hair" stayed on beautifully. It was, he believed, the first of many triumphs—but this one meant the most to him because he saw new respect in his father's eyes. He began to research how he could best sell his new process and get the most publicity out of it.

Debbie was happy for Anthony and enthusiastic because *he* was so overjoyed about having hair again—but then, she had always thought her husband was handsome. Their family life was going well—as well as it could when she lived with a man of such energy and mercurial temperament. They did things as a family, going for ice cream or to the wonderful Buffalo Zoo. Ralph still went fishing with his father and grandfather, and Anthony promised him he could go hunting with them as soon as he was old enough.

Hunting was important to Anthony, although it seemed a little strange that a doctor enjoyed killing things. He shot a cheetah on a safari and proudly had it stuffed and mounted, and then placed it in the great room of their duplex. It gave Debbie a start whenever she looked at it, but Ralph thought it was sensational. He was a little boy who thought his father was perfect.

Sometimes Anthony and Debbie took vacations in Florida, where Anthony's brothers lived. Steve and Ralph Jr. were in the ice cream business there. His sister Antoinette was a physician. Vacations there were fun, with trips on family boats, although Debbie sometimes felt a stinging sadness that she was so removed from the celebrations on her side of the family. She talked to her mother on the phone, but that didn't seem enough. She wanted her to be more a part of her life. Even during the years when Frank and Caroline Rago were struggling to meet their budget, they had wonderful parties with their extended families. Now, it seemed to Debbie that there were so many things to do for Anthony that there never seemed to be time to be with *her* family.

Anthony considered himself to be from a higher class than the Ragos. After all, his father was a distinguished surgeon much beloved by the community, and their home was definitely upscale. Country clubs and private schools had never been part of the Ragos' world.

Anthony continued to be critical of Debbie. It was almost as if he deliberately set out to tear down her self-confidence. She could never be thin enough for his tastes, and he reminded her of that repeatedly while still wanting her to cook whatever he fancied. Anthony worked out at

Gold's Gym almost compulsively, and with his new fail-proof toupee he looked better than ever.

He wasn't home a lot. He had the long commute to Warsaw to take over his elderly benefactor's patients, and at the same time he was struggling to get his own clinic going.

And his Wednesdays were sacrosanct. Nothing interfered with his research.

6

By 1994, Dr. Anthony Pignataro was moving rapidly toward the specialty he aspired to—that of a plastic surgeon. But for every success he had, there were red flags and censure raised. He chose to ignore them for the most part. He always had a smoothly crafted explanation for any negative event in his life.

In 1994, he was sued by a patient for an allegedly negligent face-lift and blepharoplasty (eyelid lift) that caused the seventy-one-year-old patient to seek further surgery to correct Anthony's mistakes. Anthony blamed the problem on the patient, insisting that she had failed to follow his postoperative instructions. He also said she had gotten a second opinion from a competitor who spitefully encouraged her to sue. The lawsuit was eventually settled by a $75,000 payment from his malpractice insurance to the patient.

Also in 1994, Anthony was investigated for the first time by the New York State Department of Health/Office of Professional Medical Conduct. He advertised for clients enthusiastically, something physicians rarely did then. Not only that, despite the fact that it was not true, his ads said he was "Board-Certified in Otolaryngology."

He claimed that he was affiliated with "Cosmetic Plastic Surgeons International." Debbie said later that Anthony had formed some sort of alliance with a plastic surgeon in Canada and then had used that man's name to become "international." Anthony referred eye-lift and skin care patients to the Canadian doctor, whose face-lift patients were referred back to Anthony.

His operating room in the basement of his office was finished to his satisfaction, and Anthony advertised that his facility provided "state-of-the-art care in outpatient surgery." He sent coupons to hair salons in his area, offering them $100 for every patient they sent to him for a hair transplant. He was not yet using his snap-on-snap-off technique; instead, he was taking hair grafts from the back of the patient's head and transplanting them to the balding area.

"This was a long and laborious technique," he recalled. "The state of the art had advanced. Minigrafts and micrografts had become the standard. Minigrafts are four to eight hair grafts, and micrografts are one- to three-haired grafts."

It took about a thousand of these per session, and Anthony and his transplant team, mostly office help and licensed practical nurses, would take five or six hours to manage this. Now, he invented what he called the Micrograft Implanter. He was pleased with it because it worked "even in untrained hands," and it cut down on the time needed, allowing him to operate on even more patients.

He felt so relaxed doing hair transplants that he sometimes sent out for pizza to eat during the surgery. One patient, as easygoing as Anthony, joined him in eating the slices of pizza.

But Anthony's advertising brought an investigator from the State of New York, a physician who questioned him about the plastic surgery he was performing in his office. He was cagey when he answered her questions, saying he didn't *really* do plastic surgery in his office. He did admit that he was doing occasional tummy tucks, but everyone knew those were "easy."

Asked about what he used as anesthesia, Anthony shook his head and said he used only "sedation" and never considered general anesthesia. He used narcotics for the sedation. When the visiting doctor pressed him to specify which narcotic, he answered, "Versed." Versed is a powerful drug given intravenously.

It was apparent to the investigating physician that Anthony Pignataro did not have the training to become legitimately board-certified by the American Board of Medical Specialities in Plastic Surgery. The investigator wasn't reassured at all by his glib responses and his unctuous, confident manner. She stared Anthony Pignataro in the eye and said, "You had better stop these [plastic surgery] procedures in the office before you kill somebody."

He stared back at her, neither angry nor insulted. He was hardly impressed. In his own mind, he was confident that he was far more skilled than any board-certified, hospital-approved physician. Far beyond the mundane doctor, he had imagination and the ability to see beyond the staid old methods. It was only that other doctors were envious of his skill.

Later, Anthony would write about that interview, and it was as if the doctor's warning was a hollow shout into the wind. Anthony's own version of the meeting demonstrated his talent for twisting the truth to suit himself: "With the surgical suite fully operational, the cosmetic practice improved as more patients were able to afford the procedures," he wrote confidently. "In this state, physicians are overseen by the Department of Health . . . The Department of Health has always maintained a justifiable vigil on physicians doing more and more procedures in the office. Nonetheless, this was the trend in the 1990s. A cadre of health department officials had already reviewed the practice and done an on-site review of the facility. Having not a single violation was a comforting, positive sign."

He had forgotten the investigator's warning that he might kill someone with his office surgery; he saw only a "comforting, positive sign . . ."

In 1995, Anthony Pignataro became partially "certified" by the American Board of Cosmetic Surgery and Facial Cosmetic Surgery. But to do this, he had had to prove he was board-certified in otolaryngology, which, of course, he was not. Instead, he faxed the Facial Cosmetic board a forged diploma dated October 31, 1991, guaranteeing his good standing in otolaryngology.

He took only the first part of the test, deciding to get more "practice" in the coming year before he took the part that encompassed cosmetic surgery on the entire body. "Having passed the standard written portion, I would only have had to face the eight hours of grueling oral examiners again—a bone-chilling prospect at best."

He hated probing questions, but now Anthony was very optimistic. "In April, 1995, I took and passed the written as well as the oral exam for facial cosmetic surgery. Recognizing the sacrifices my family and office staff had made so that I could steal away for hours of study, I treated the entire family and staff to a five-star meal at a nearby restaurant . . . This was the true validation of my long-enduring academic history. I had definitely paid my dues. The day the notice came in the mail, I opened the envelope at about 11:00 A.M. No one of the staff was aware . . . It was 4:00 P.M. before anyone was made aware of my success. I needed those five hours to savor the moment just for myself . . ."

It apparently didn't matter at all to him that he had used a forged diploma to qualify to take this exam. If Anthony Pignataro was anything, he was expedient. Whatever it took to accomplish his goals, he did without a backward thought. He had so much to offer the world that he couldn't allow "small thinkers" to impede him.

Anthony continued to claim that he had current hospital privileges. One lie begat another, and Anthony's lies continued to pile up. In 1995, he was terminated by the Individual Practice Association of Western New York, Inc. In November, he applied to an HMO to be part of its staff. But once again, he lied, claiming that he had never been the target of malpractice claims or illegal actions and had not been denied hospital privileges in the previous ten years. He lied and said there were no proceedings currently against him, that judgments had never been brought against him, and that he had never been the object of peer-review proceedings. Indeed, he had been beleaguered by every one of these questions. Everywhere he turned, it seemed that someone was investigating him or suing him.

Debbie Pignataro had no idea how many lies Anthony was telling. As far as she could see, his practice was going well. He was very popular with his patients, and she believed him when he said he knew everything there was to know about ear, nose, and throat ailments. She no longer spent much time in his office; he was doing so well, he assured her, that he had hired a full staff so that she could spend most of her time with their children.

Anthony seemed happy and fulfilled at last. He was working hard to hone his skills in plastic surgery, traveling often to attend teaching conferences in this medical art. He wanted to be able to offer his patients a full range of cosmetic surgery, including breast reduction or augmentation.

It also never occurred to Debbie that Anthony might be unfaithful to her again. That early affair had happened so long ago, and they had worked through it and stayed together. Anthony had been so sweet for the whole year after she found the tapes and cards in the back seat of their car. He had literally begged her to forgive him, and he had promised that he would never cheat on her again if only she would take him back. Her father had warned her not only to forgive but to forget, and to give her marriage another try. They had survived the death of their baby and all of the disappointments Anthony had in his residency programs. They had been together all the way. Debbie felt that any couple who had been through so much had forged a bond that could never be broken.

Debbie loved her home, her husband, and her children. Their duplex in West Seneca was very nice, with a big kitchen, dining room, and living room. Upstairs, there was a master bedroom, and Ralph and Lauren each had their own room. They had a rec room in the basement, where the windows were now protected by bars to ward off any other vandals who might try to get in.

But that was less of a danger now; building was going on around them, and families were moving in all up and down the street. She had friends and neighbors close by.

Debbie told herself there were no perfect marriages, and she accepted hers for what it was—the good and the bad. Anthony was still critical of her, and he seldom helped around the house or suggested that she take some time for herself. He was drinking more than he should, and that worried her. But the good times offset the bad, and although Anthony could make her cry when he complained about her appearance, Debbie never thought about leaving him now. They were both close to forty, and they were settled down. At least, Debbie was settled down. She never looked at another man; she hadn't since the moment she first saw Anthony.

Despite what Anthony had told the investigator, he was doing a lot more than tummy tucks. He needed to make as much money as he could from plastic surgery to offset jobs he had lost. The part-time practice in Warsaw ended when the elderly doctor returned to his office after his recovery from open heart surgery. Anthony felt he had been dropped because the doctor was East Indian and that he was jealous of how popular Anthony was with his patients.

"I had done an outstanding job of keeping the practice going for him," Anthony said. "So I was shocked and disappointed that his first order of business was to remove me from his office. He didn't like the rural populous [*sic*] of the area preferring a white American doctor without a heavy foreign accent."

So once again, Anthony felt that jealousy had made another doctor turn against him. He said he was just as happy to be able to devote full time to his own practice.

And he was about to become a national celebrity. The Associated Press carried the syndicated story of the doctor who had the answer to the prayers of bald men all over the country.

"Anthony Pignataro reached under his hair," reporter Stephen Sobek wrote, "and—pop! pop! pop! pop!—in a matter of seconds, held most of his thick brown locks in the palm of his hand . . ."

Anthony agreed with Sobek that his invention might sound "too science fiction" to the layman, but it was commonplace for him. He described the surgery in which his father had implanted the four titanium bolts into the top of his skull. The snaps would never need maintenance, and the hairpiece should last about four years. The initial investment was $4,000, and Dr. Pignataro said he had already done about a hundred of the procedures for men from all across America who had flown into his West Seneca clinic.

The AP story that appeared in most papers around the world caught the interest of all forms of media. Anthony and his invention were mentioned on *CBS Nightly News* and by Tom Brokaw. *GQ* and *Esquire* had short articles on the lifetime hairpiece system. He appeared on the *Maury Povich Show* and on *Hard Copy*. Anthony Pignataro was finally enjoying the public attention and the accolades he had wanted for so long. The only place he felt he didn't get enough press was Buffalo. His contribution to bald men—and women—was widely accepted.

Money rolled in.

Anthony had another favorite project, which he had been working on since 1994. He envisioned a kind of bra that would fit under the skin of the breasts. Not all the women who came to see him needed breast implants; some were suffering only from the pull of gravity. Mastopexy (a breast-lift) worked, but Anthony wasn't happy with the scarring that often resulted.

His answer was his invisible bra, a concept that he tested on female corpses in a medical school anatomy lab. His test subjects could not complain if the under-skin brassieres should prove to be uncomfortable.

"Several materials were tested," he wrote in his book. "Ultra-thin silicone sheeting seemed to have all the right qualities. Though not originally patented this way, a thin, lightweight underwire of implantable titanium forms the framework for implantation below the breast. Multiple devices, such as screws, metal sutures, and anchor were already approved and in use."

Again, he referred to himself in the third person but quickly slipped back into using "I":

"Anthony would never see those clinical trials [of the inner brassiere]. I would be remiss if I did not recognize the personnel of the local anatomy laboratory, who provided invaluable assistance to my research. Innumerable hours were spent working with different materials, methods, and cadavers, with surgery going into the late-night hours. They were always accommodating. Without such perdurable assistance, the entire endeavor may never have been possible. This research had consumed him [me]."

But this was one invention he could not test on himself, and it didn't sound all that comfortable. He put off testing it on a human being. He had, however, progressed to doing breast implants and lifts in his basement surgery. Business was good: men flew into West Seneca to have bolts implanted in their skulls, and women arrived to have breast augmentation.

Anthony believed in advertising and marketing. His was a service like any other business. Why should doctors be so hesitant to compete for business?

Anthony saw everyone he met as a potential patient, and he wasn't shy about approaching them. He gained several patients at the sports club he frequented. He took before-and-after pictures of his breast enhancement patients and showed them naked on the Internet. He advertised his hair replacement system in the sports section of local papers, figuring all men would see them there.

Probably his most unusual and innovative approach was to convince a Buffalo radio station to award a free breast enlargement to the winner of a contest. Anthony offered free consultations to the finalists: the contestants went on the air to tell why they needed their breasts enlarged, and Anthony explained what would transpire in the consultations and offered his easy-pay financial plan for those who didn't win.

As fate would have it, the woman who won never had the surgery, and it may have been a fortunate thing that she hesitated for so long.

One of Anthony's many out-of-state patients was a woman from Virginia. Her name was Moira* and she was an "exotic dancer" in polite terms but a "stripper" in reality. Her chosen career demanded full and nondrooping breasts. She came to Anthony for her surgery. He found her stunning as she was, and irresistible after he inserted saline implants that increased her bust by two cup sizes. In a way, he felt like her Pygmalion.

Moira was an attractive if bizarre-looking woman. She had a tattoo on her back from the nape of her neck to below her waist. Anthony had always favored anything that smacked of the upper class—private schools, country clubs, exclusive restaurants, and fine cars—but he quickly became besotted with Moira. She was different from any woman he had ever known.

Moira was delighted with her surgery and appreciated Anthony as her doctor, but she wasn't initially attracted to this married man with the strange—if well-fitting—toupee.

Anthony pursued Moira for a year, only tantalized by her coyness. He bought a new car, a red Lamborghini, and he lavished gifts on Moira.

Debbie had no idea that Moira existed.

7

By 1996, Anthony was not only a faithless husband but an oblivious father. Debbie knew that he had never learned how to be a father; Dr. Ralph had always been working when Anthony was growing up. Anything Anthony learned about playing ball or sports he learned from the elder Pignataros' neighbors. The family pattern was repeating itself. Anthony had no time for Ralph or Lauren.

"He wasn't what I'd call a 'hands-on father.' He grew so cold," Debbie recalled. "There was no love or affection for me—or for the kids."

But Anthony had never been known for his warmth. Debbie thought his removed attitude was due to his involvement in his practice. Ralph was almost 10, and Lauren was 7. They were very nice, smart kids. They didn't lack for things that money could buy. They were attending the Nichols School, the exclusive private school Anthony had gone to when he was a boy. Debbie drove them to all their extracurricular activities. Lauren studied gymnastics, and Ralph was active in sports—ice hockey in the winter and football in the autumn. He was a natural. Aside from bragging about his children's victories, Anthony didn't seem to care about their daily lives. His eyes clouded over with disinterest when Debbie tried to share their experiences with him.

He continued to express his temper when he didn't get

his way. On June 15, 1996, he was driving his Jeep in Depew, New York, when he cut off a Pontiac Firebird driven by a woman from Cheektowaga, New York, forcing her to the shoulder of the road. When both cars stopped for a red light on Transit and Broadway, a male passenger from the Firebird got out and confronted Anthony, who claimed later that the man had hit him in the face several times.

Anthony grabbed the .380 caliber handgun that he always carried with him, walked over to the car, and fired one shot at the Firebird. Fortunately, neither occupant was hit. Still outraged, Anthony called the police from the nearby home of a patient. He was arrested on charges of reckless endangerment and discharging a firearm.

"Maybe I was right—maybe I was wrong—for shooting at him," Anthony said. "But when you get punched in the face . . . I was only protecting myself. I didn't shoot at him. I could have easily got him, but I just shot to scare him off."

The reckless endangerment charge was dropped, but Anthony lost his pistol permit for a year: harsh punishment for a man who loved guns and hunting.

It was one more humiliation for Debbie, but she swept it under her conscious mind, where she had swept so many other disturbing incidents.

By now, Debbie didn't resent being virtually a single parent; she loved being with her children. But she began to have health problems that made it difficult for her to be responsible for everything around the house. During one of their trips to Florida to spend time with Anthony's brothers, she was injured in a boating accident. Antoinette's then husband, Allan Steinberg, was driving the boat while Debbie held Lauren and Anthony held Ralph. When Allan had to swerve suddenly, Debbie pitched toward the deck. "I could have broken my fall if I'd let go of Lauren, but she would have been hurt, so I held on to her and hit so hard that I broke my ribs," she said. "But there was more damage to my neck. In the three years between 1996 and 1999, I had to have five surgeries on herniated cervical disks to stabilize my neck."

Anthony ignored her pain. "We were hardly speaking to each other," Debbie remembered. "He was just never there. Not for me and not for the kids."

Debbie's neck injuries were extremely painful, and her orthopedist prescribed painkillers. When she needed them, however, she noticed that there were far fewer in the container than there should have been. There was only one explanation: Anthony was taking them.

At that point, a more sophisticated wife than Debbie Pignataro might have recognized the classic signs that her husband was having an affair. His new red sports car was one, and the frequency of trips away from home was another. His obsession with his own appearance increased. He'd already had his nose reshaped with plastic surgery, but now he got cheek implants. He had eye surgery to correct his vision, and he bought the most expensive toupees. All were indications that Anthony was trying to impress someone—but not Debbie.

"After winning several collegiate boxing tournaments," Anthony wrote in his book in his odd third-person voice, "the doctor was very principled in the virtues of exercise and diet. His medical school education served to reinforce his commitment to personal training. He often referred to exercise as a form of mental therapy. Medical science has proposed the 'endorphin theory.' To Dr. Pignataro, this was not [just] a theory . . . He struggled to find the time to work out. He would skip his lunch break to make it to the gym four or five times a week."

In truth, not all of Anthony's habits were healthy. He drank pitchers of tequila margaritas, and he sometimes seemed so out of touch that Debbie wondered if he might be on drugs—more drugs than the pills missing from her own prescription vials. Certainly, he was working very hard, and he had a lot on his mind—far more than she realized. He had to do some fancy time-planning to keep enlarging his practice, to preserve his sacred Wednesdays for research and invention, and to allow ample time to court the elusive Moira. Often, he came home only to sit in his recliner and drink until he fell asleep.

Debbie, who had weighed 110 pounds when they were married, had gradually put on about 40 pounds. It didn't seem to matter whether she dieted or not; Anthony would always find something to ridicule about the way she looked.

When Debbie was recovering after one of her neck surgeries, she was given steroids that made her face puffy. Anthony stared at her and said, "Look at you. Who would want *you?*"

Little by little, he wore down her belief in herself. Even so, she kept trying harder to please him and make his life more comfortable.

Things got worse in the spring of 1996. They could both see that Anthony's father wasn't well. As Anthony himself wrote—back in his third-person voice: "The doctor's world began to crumble."

Dr. Ralph Pignataro had always been brilliant and sharp, Anthony's example and hero, the one person whom Anthony continually tried to impress. He was the man who had never had time for his son until Anthony, too, was a physician. In a sense, he defined Anthony's world. While Anthony's mother had pampered him, his father was the god he never quite lived up to. But given enough time, he was sure that his father would be astounded by what he could do. His father was the audience Anthony played to, and it was Dr.

Ralph's ultimate approval that would assure Anthony that he was finally a man and a doctor of great excellence.

That was not to be. Gradually, the family had to acknowledge that Dr. Ralph was often confused, fumbling for words, and forgetting things that had become second nature to him. He had always possessed a mind fully capable of handling myriad details. Now, they realized that he was trying to hide his symptoms, which had become so profound that they could no longer be concealed. An MRI scan showed what Anthony had feared: his father had a large tumor in the frontal lobe of his brain. Always a very heavy smoker, Dr. Ralph also had many tumors in his lungs and liver. Buffalo area specialists gave him six months to live.

Anthony researched all the advanced treatments for the type of cancer from which his father suffered. He took charge and strongly recommended that his father travel at once to Houston for treatment. Dr. Ralph refused. He knew that he had only months to live, and he wanted to spend them in Buffalo with his family, doing the things he loved best.

In Anthony's view of an idyllic world, he had always planned to return to Buffalo as a physician and to work side by side with his father for decades. Now, he blamed a cruel fate that would rob him of his father only four years after his homecoming. He hadn't let the imminent death of Debbie's father disturb his first day of hunting season, but now he beat his breast and cried, "Why *me?*"

And it *was* "Why *me?*" and not "Why my *father?*" In Anthony's narcissistic world, every event was important only as it affected *him.* For Anthony saw himself as the center of the world, with other people spinning around him, ready to answer his needs. Any human consumed with such raging self-love is difficult to deal with; a physician who thinks only of himself is a disaster on the way to happen.

A month after his father was diagnosed, Anthony inserted breast implants into a patient and told her she would need Demerol for postoperative pain. He wrote a prescription for a hundred 50-milligram tablets and sent her husband to a drugstore to get it filled. The worried husband rushed to get the painkiller and gave it to Anthony. But the patient never got any of the Demerol. Anthony kept it, apparently for his own use.

Dr. Ralph Pignataro died on November 23, 1996. There was no Thanksgiving for the Pignataros that year. Dr. Ralph was only 62. He left behind his family and the patients he had served well over the preceding thirty-five years. Anthony announced that a piece of himself had died along with his father. But he added that his father had taught him to be strong and accept the reality of life, often advising him, "The dead are best left in the past. One can never forget, but one must move on."

Anthony moved on.

After conducting a year-long campaign to convince Moira to go away with him, Anthony finally persuaded her to join him on a trip to Puerto Rico. He planned to set up a hair clinic there. The wealthy and the bald could get bolts and snaps in their heads or hair transplants in an exotic setting, combining recovery with a vacation. Labor would be cheaper for Anthony, too.

The Friday night before he left, Anthony was an uncharacteristically attentive father. He took Debbie, Ralph, and Lauren to the Erie County Fair. They all had a good time. It was the kind of family occasion that Debbie had always longed for. They had so much fun that she wondered whether things *could* work out for them.

The next morning, she drove Anthony to the airport and kissed him goodbye as he headed to New York City to catch his plane to Puerto Rico. He gave her the number of the hotel where he would be staying as he worked out the details on the new hair clinic.

But Anthony wasn't alone as he boarded the Puerto Rico flight. He and Moira flew south together.

Debbie stayed home, unaware that her husband's trip was anything more than a business venture.

Debbie was faithful and supportive. She wasn't particularly assertive, and she was long-suffering, living with a man who could be totally charming to his patients and potential patients and mean and critical at home. Now, he often compared her unfavorably with other women they saw.

Long-suffering, yes, but Debbie was not saintly, and she certainly wasn't stupid. She placed a call to the hotel in Puerto Rico where Anthony was staying to ask about his flight. She was startled when a woman's voice came on the line.

"Who *is* this?" Debbie asked.

"Moira."

At first, Debbie thought she might have the wrong room, but she asked for Anthony anyway, and the woman didn't think very fast.

"He's not here right now—"

"Who are you and what are you doing in my husband's room?" Debbie pressed.

"I'm . . . er . . . a model. Dr. Pignataro did my breasts."

But Anthony wasn't in Puerto Rico for a breast clinic; he was supposed to be there for a hair clinic. A familiar sick feeling rolled over Debbie. She remembered the woman who had left evidence in their car in Maryland. She reacted like a mother tiger whose young are threatened, shocking herself with her vehemence.

Debbie's voice had an edge of steel. "Well, tell him his wife called," she began. "And I don't know who you are, but if you ever come near him or my family, I'll fucking kill you! Now get out of my husband's room!"

A long time later, Debbie recalled that Moira packed her suitcase and literally ran from the Puerto Rican hotel.

"I went to Anthony's office in West Seneca, and I asked his secretary if she knew anything about some woman named Moira," Debbie said. "She knew, all right. She knew all about her."

Panicked when he heard that Debbie knew about Moira, Anthony tried to get Debbie on the phone all day. When he finally succeeded, he begged her to fly down to Puerto Rico. "Please come down, Deb," he pleaded, "so we can try to save our marriage."

Debbie booked a flight to Puerto Rico. Once again, Anthony was chastened and frightened by her anger. He rushed out and bought her an expensive pair of diamond earrings, thinking that he could smooth over his infidelity with money.

But this time, Frank Rago was gone and so was Dr. Ralph. Debbie had taken her father's advice the first time, and she had forgiven Anthony once, but that was all her father made her promise to do. This time, it wouldn't be easy to forgive—or forget.

Debbie didn't leave Anthony. She would honestly admit that she still loved him, even though she would never again really trust him. They'd been together for almost twenty years, and she had two children who deserved a good life with two parents.

But now she thought she knew whom she was dealing with. She wouldn't forget this time, and when Anthony was away she never again trusted that he was where he said he would be.

8

In the year after his father's death, Anthony seemed to be back in control. As far as Debbie knew, he was no longer seeing Moira, whom she now knew was an exotic dancer. That had baffled her. If he'd gone off with a snobbish society woman, she might have expected that. But a woman who danced in a sleazy club? That didn't seem like Anthony, who always insisted on the very best of everything.

Debbie took some satisfaction in remembering the way she had frightened Moira with her threats. She never knew she had that much guts or that such strong language would come out of her mouth. Now she knew she was tougher than she had thought. Their marriage was different from how it had been before. Anthony didn't pick on her quite so much. He wasn't as nice to her as he had been after his first affair came to light, but he was better than usual. Once in a while, he even cooked supper.

"Steak and lobster," Debbie said. "Nothing but the best."

Anthony was pleased with his basement surgery suite. It was convenient, and it was economically advantageous. He was frugal about spending extra money on staff that he felt were unnecessary. He employed a secretary and a licensed practical nurse from a local trade school, and he used Debbie when he needed a trained medical assistant. Although she had worked for many years in a pharmacy, and had also been employed in doctors' offices while help-ing to put Anthony through his five years of residencies, Debbie wasn't a trained nurse or even an L.P.N. Anthony told her that didn't matter—that his skill, and his ability to train her for the specific kind of surgery he practiced, were far more important than any nursing school curriculum.

Whatever trust Debbie might have lost in Anthony as a person, she still believed he was a good doctor, even if he wasn't a good husband. But Debbie was aware of only a fraction of the disasters that had happened in Anthony's surgeries. He hadn't told her about most of them.

The worst thing Debbie remembered was the time he left her alone to do a chemical peel on a patient without enough instruction. The woman suffered burns and sued both her and Anthony.

But now, Anthony seemed to know everything there was to know about plastic surgery. And he had refined his practice so that breast and hair surgeries made up 70 per-cent of his scheduled operations. All he needed Debbie for was to monitor body functions.

Anthony certainly didn't believe he needed to have an anesthesiologist present during operations in his office. Their fees were outrageous, he thought, and there wasn't anything they did that he and Debbie couldn't do. He had worked out his own combination of pills to relax his pa-tients before surgery. Later he combined the pills with in-travenous drugs to lull the patients into forgetful sleep while he practiced what he considered his art.

Anthony felt it was important for students at Nichols School who wanted to go to medical school to have some practical experience. He often hired teenaged boys at minimum wage to do various chores in his clinic.

He was still traveling to continuing medical education courses and other seminars, learning more about plastic surgery—or at least he told Debbie that's where he was going on weekends. One day soon, he would unveil his subcutaneous bra. He believed that would make more headlines than bolts for toupees.

In the first part of July 1997, Connie Vinetti* went to Anthony's office in West Seneca for a consultation. She wanted to ask him whether liposuction on her abdomen would be effective in making her stomach flatter. She also wanted to be sure that Dr. Pignataro was board-certified. Having done some research, she knew that was important. The sight of a framed certificate on the wall of his office reassured her. It said "American Board of Cosmetic Surgeons," and his name was there, all right, in flowing script.

After she asked him the questions she had written down, Pignataro checked her stomach and told her flatly, "Your abdominal muscles are shot."

Connie was embarrassed; she hadn't realized that she was in such poor condition. The doctor recommended that she consider a procedure called an abdominoplasty. It would take only about an hour to an hour and a half and would leave a discreet 4-inch scar. He assured her that she would be back to work in a week with taut muscles.

"I would throw all those pieces of fat in the garbage," Dr. Pignataro said crudely, "and you will have a V-like waistline."

The surgery would be a bit more expensive than liposuction, which cost between $1,500 and $3,000. Abdominoplasty would be $4,000, but he told her that she would be much happier with the result. Pignataro urged Connie to reconsider, stressing that she was "the ideal candidate" for the operation he suggested.

She could expect to pay $2,000 up front and another $2,000 on the day of the surgery.

But Connie Vinetti had another concern. She was going to have a hysterectomy (the removal of her womb and ovaries) at Buffalo General Hospital in two weeks. She asked if he could coordinate the abdominoplasty with that surgery and said she would rather have it all done at once than undergoing two surgeries.

"I'll try to do that," he said, "but you will have to talk to my office manager about it."

Connie came back to see Pignataro on July 13, but when she asked again about doing the abdominoplasty at the same time as her hysterectomy at Buffalo General Hospital, he told her that he couldn't do that because his "schedule was full."

What he didn't tell her was that he didn't have privileges at Buffalo General. He had no privileges at *any* hospital.

Connie Vinetti asked if her insurance would cover the plastic surgery on her abdominal muscles, and Dr. Pignataro told her he'd found that 90 percent of the time a hernia was involved when stomach muscles were as badly out of shape as hers were. The presence of an actual medical reason for an abdominoplasty would then fit within insurance guidelines. Pignataro smiled as he said that he could really "stretch it" on the forms for her insurance company.

By now, Connie was convinced that she needed to have the abdominoplasty. They agreed that she would come to Dr. Pignataro's office at 8:30 A.M. on August 5.

Connie arrived with her husband at the appointed time, but was told the doctor was still waiting for the results of some of her blood tests. An hour later, he was ready to operate and suggested that her husband leave and come back for her about 1 P.M.

The next several hours would be blurred for Connie Vinetti. She remembered being taken to an examination room, where she changed into a gown. At that point, Pignataro had given her seven or eight pills. She would remember that one was red and the others were white. She noticed that the doctor was watching her closely to be sure she swallowed them all.

Then a nurse whose name was Betty led Connie through the waiting room, and she was embarrassed that she had to walk past other patients in bare feet, wearing only a gown.

In the operating room, Connie was washed down with betadine to fight infection. Another woman was there, wearing scrubs, who said her name was Jean.

Connie recalled hazily that Jean had trouble getting a needle into her vein and that Dr. Pignataro had to do it. She was left alone for a while and then taken to the "surgical center" downstairs, where she was asked to lie facedown on the operating table.

She was feeling a little woozy, but she remembered seeing a young boy in the room who looked to be in his teens. He wore scrubs, too. So did a young female nurse.

She felt another needle in her vein, and then only a soft blackness. Connie remembered nothing more until she finally woke up at 4:30 in the afternoon.

Her husband was waiting to drive her home, and he helped her to their car. But on the way Connie realized that she was bleeding so heavily that the blood was oozing scarlet splotches through her clothes. She couldn't walk, so her husband carried her into the house. She couldn't even sit upright on a chair.

Connie Vinetti kept hemorrhaging, so much so that the carpet beneath her turned bright red. Her husband was very worried, and he called Dr. Pignataro before six that evening.

The doctor didn't seem at all concerned. He explained that he got "these calls all the time. I know it looks like blood, but it's really just drainage," he said soothingly. "Connie has a lot of fluid in her."

What, the worried husband asked, were they supposed to do to stop the bleeding? Pignataro suggested that he purchase some sanitary napkins to absorb the leakage from the incision. They would be more absorbent than a regular bandage.

They tried that, and Connie pressed the super-size sanitary pad against the gash in her abdomen. It wasn't a sterile bandage, but she didn't think of that. The bleeding continued, leaking through the layers of the pad. Soon, she was in excruciating pain as whatever Dr. Pignataro had given her wore off.

"I tried to tough it out over the next two days," Connie recalled.

By Thursday, August 7, she could no longer bear the pain. She went back to see Dr. Pignataro early in the morning and waited for twenty minutes until he hurried in, not apologizing for being late. By that time, the *upper* part of her belly was severely swollen.

Pignataro examined Connie and told her he had found the problem; the girdle he'd placed around the incision after surgery should have been located higher. "That's why you have this swelling," he said easily. But as he pushed against the swollen spot, she began to bleed again.

He suggested that she come back early Saturday morning. He was going out of town later in the day, but he would see her at 6:30 A.M.

And then Connie Vinetti watched in shock as Pignataro summoned Sue, his young nurse. "Sue will take care of you next week," he said.

"Sue, do you know how to suture using staples?" he asked.

"No," she said, shaking her head nervously.

He brought out what appeared to be a surgical stapler

and touched it to Connie's bloody incision. She wondered if it was sterile. She thought probably it wasn't when he put it back on the shelf without even wiping it with alcohol.

How was Sue going to take care of her when she obviously didn't know anything about patching a wound back together?

"Your drainage tubes are pointing up," Dr. Pignataro muttered.

"What . . . ?"

"They're supposed to be pointing in the other direction," he said, as if someone other than himself had put them in.

At that point, Connie Vinetti lost all confidence in this doctor, who had seemed so professional when she first visited him. She was in terrible pain, she probably had some kind of infection, and he was simply going to go out of town and leave her in the care of a girl who clearly had next to no experience.

Connie got up from the examining table and said she'd be back, but she left, determined never to see him again.

Connie got even sicker as Thursday wore on, and her husband called the ER at Buffalo Mercy Hospital. He said his wife was very sick and in pain, and was told to bring her in.

Dr. K., the physician who examined Connie in the ER, saw that her abdomen was grossly distended and her temperature was soaring. Removing the elastic bandage commonly used after liposuction, he saw that her incision was badly infected with bacteria. Pockets of pus had formed. Some of the flesh around the incision was necrotic (dead). The swelling was so profound that he suspected she might have an ileus, a temporary paralysis of the bowel that sometimes follows surgery in which the walls of the abdomen have been perforated.

The ER doctor admitted Connie Vinetti at once to Buffalo Mercy Hospital. He went a step further and took Polaroid pictures of the incision. The wound had been stapled so clumsily that it looked like a crazy quilt, with all the edges of the incision mismatched.

One of the nurses on duty recalled Connie's condition with a shudder. "It was terrible," she said. "It looked as if someone had opened her abdomen with one of those old-fashioned can openers; it was all jagged and infected. I'll never forget it."

On Friday, August 8, Dr. Anthony Pignataro visited Connie in the hospital. He appeared to be his usual blithely confident self. But he looked at her with surprise and asked, "What *happened?*" as if he couldn't understand why she'd gone to the hospital.

Before she could protest, he examined the incision.

"There's nothing medically wrong with you," he said firmly. He picked up her chart and wrote that she should be discharged.

Nurses watched him and summoned doctors who did have privileges at Buffalo Mercy. They asked Pignataro to leave.

But he was back again on Saturday morning at 6:30, asking Connie, "What are you still doing here?"

She stared back at him as if he were crazy. You didn't have to be a doctor to see she was sick. He picked up her chart again and studied it, telling her that she had no fever and her blood work was perfectly O.K.

Once more, Anthony Pignataro was asked to leave the hospital. His visit had not been sought by the patient, and he had no authorization whatsoever to be in her room, to be reading her chart, or even to be in the hospital.

* * *

Later, Dr. K., the physician who was treating Connie Vinetti, placed a phone call to Dr. Anthony Pignataro. Eventually, the call was returned.

"I hear you're seeing one of my patients," Pignataro began smoothly. "What seems to be the problem?"

Dr. K. explained the problems he had noted in the acutely ill patient.

"That's nothing," Pignataro scoffed. "There's nothing wrong with her. I've seen worse."

Dr. K. was stunned. "This is bad, Doctor," he said. "You shouldn't be doing these procedures in your office."

"It isn't an *office*. It's a surgery center," Pignataro countered huffily.

Dr. K. tried once more to convey how very ill Connie Vinetti was and to describe the extent of her infection. He suggested that Pignataro was hurting people with his heedless approach. He was blunt.

"Well," Anthony Pignataro said, "I'm sorry you feel that way. Maybe we could have lunch and talk this over, before things get out of hand."

It was akin to a conversation out of *Alice in Wonderland*. How could any medical doctor be so oblivious to the dangers of septic infection in a terrible stomach wound? Dr. K. hung up, shaking his head.

Connie Vinetti spent another five or six days in the hospital, taking strong antibiotics to fight her raging infection. She survived, but she would never again want to wear a bikini.

Anthony Pignataro had another black mark against him, but it really didn't matter to him. He still believed that he was a superior surgeon and that other people had simply overreacted to the occasional medical mishaps that could happen to any doctor.

He was in denial. Some might say he was having a

breakdown, that he was overwhelmed with grief at the loss of his father nine months earlier. Those less charitable would lay it squarely upon his narcissism, a personality disorder, enhanced by drug use and alcohol.

There were four people in the world, however, who genuinely cared about the future of Anthony Pignataro, despite the times he had disappointed and betrayed them: his mother, Lena; his children, Ralph and Lauren; and his wife, Debbie. They all loved him.

But that wasn't enough. Anthony plunged into more office surgeries. He had learned nothing from the disastrous operation on Connie Vinetti.

To reassure himself, perhaps, Anthony's writing alias, "Debbie," added more validation of his skills to his manuscript:

"For better or for worse, how many of us have spoken these vows with the sincere belief that it will, for the most part, always be for the better?" "Debbie" wrote. "For me, there was no reason to believe that it would be anything but glorious. As a third-generation Italian American, of humble but virtuous means, all I ever desired was to marry a decent man who loved me and provided me with the emotional support I needed. If good fortune were to bestow on me any more than middle-class fare, this would not matter.

"Anthony S. Pignataro, M.D., my husband, found genuine success and fulfillment in his career as a Cosmetic Surgeon. It was his sixth year in private practice and we had just begun to see the light at the end of the long and arduous academic tunnel . . . We began to talk about a real house for our children. The winds of fate, however, would not blow in that direction . . .

"The practice had grown steadily over six years. Anthony enjoyed his work. Hair transplants, liposuctions, and breast implants were a mainstay of the practice. Having been published in the medical literature several times, the doctor frequently gave conferences and was active in the cosmetic academy as well as many other medical societies. Always eager to learn the latest new technique, he would travel to continuing medical education conferences. Ironically, it would be one of these new techniques that Anthony would use the day our world fell apart."

But it wasn't Anthony's or even Debbie's world that truly fell apart. It was the world of a young wife and mother named Sarah Smith.

Part Four

Sarah

9

Connie Vinetti recovered, and Anthony moved on, unconcerned that the New York State health authorities were still watching him. He was intrigued by a revolutionary new procedure in breast augmentation that he had learned about at one of the conferences for cosmetic surgeons. He had never been pleased by the scars that often remained under the patient's arms or beneath her breasts after breast implants were inserted. This new technique was known as TUBA (transumbilical breast augmentation), and it involved "tunneling" from the navel (belly button) to the axillary (armpit) area next to the breast.

An endoscope formed a tubular space through the fatty tissue just beneath the skin, an "expander" widened the area, and then a tightly folded sac was pushed through the groove into place, where it could be filled with saline solution. Any scars would be around the navel, but those would virtually disappear.

If gallbladders could be removed through the navel, why not use that route to insert breast implants? Board-certified plastic surgeons were having success with the navel approach. Anthony visited one physician in the Southwest and observed a few of the navel-to-breast procedures. He returned to Buffalo, convinced that he was fully prepared to add this new technique to his practice.

And, in this case, "practice" seemed to be the correct word. An article by one of the pioneers in this new surgery discussed both its positive and its negative aspects. He maintained that, using TUBA, most of the common dangers in any plastic surgery—bleeding, infection, and poor healing—were less likely to occur than in implants placed through larger incisions. However, he warned, "What is the greatest danger from (any) breast implant surgery? *Having it done by someone who is not qualified to do it.* Many doctors not certified by the American Board of Plastic Surgery are taking quick weekend courses about breast augmentation, including the through-the-navel method, and then just doing it. It is possible for a patient to die from any type of anesthesia and any kind of surgery. Every person should check out the qualifications of the surgeon and the anesthesiologist."

The physician who authored the article recommended that even a very proficient surgeon who wanted to learn TUBA had to be prepared to take an intense and comprehensive training course that lasted a full week. It wasn't something that could be done in a weekend of observation. Surgeons who used TUBA also had to be very skilled at using an endoscope, an internal instrument whose workings could be observed only through a magnified video image. The surgeon had to be able to do this without looking at his hands. "This is an ability that not all surgeons happen to have—even some skillful ones."

But Anthony Pignataro didn't want to take a whole week away from his office; he couldn't afford to close it down that long. He counted on doing at least three surgeries every week. And he continued to maintain an almost miserly budget in his office surgeries, still believing that anesthesiologists were unnecessarily expensive. After giving sedatives in the form of pills before surgery, Pignataro used his own concoction of intravenous anesthesia: sodium pentothal (known to many people as "truth serum," and Versed, a narcotic similar in action to Valium.

He could start the solution flowing into his patient's vein himself, and then have a member of his staff inject more into the line when he felt it was needed.

He used only the most basic machines to monitor his patients during surgery. A pulse-oximeter device to show the percentage of oxygen in the blood would be clipped over the end of a finger. If the pulse-ox reading dropped too low, an alarm would sound. A blood pressure cuff would indicate if the pressure fell dangerously low. Both of these were routinely used in hospital operating rooms. However, anesthesiologists also keep track of the heart rhythm and stability with an EKG (electrocardiogram) and maintain an airway in the throat so that the anesthesiologist can breathe for the patient if that should become necessary.

There is no way to know how many TUBA operations Anthony performed in the late summer of 1997. Apparently, they took place without incident. His operating room staff was sparse at best. Janie Krauss* was twenty-two years old, a recent graduate of a vocational training school. She was not a registered nurse. She was a licensed practical nurse with very little experience. Tom Watkins* was seventeen, a high school junior at Nichols School, who was interested in becoming a doctor someday. Anthony allowed him to dress in scrubs and a mask and observe operations, paying the teenager the minimum wage—around $5 an hour.

Debbie Pignataro sometimes served as Anthony's third assistant. She was not a nurse, a nursing assistant, a licensed practical nurse, or an anesthesiologist, but Anthony told her she was fully capable of the tasks he assigned to her. He was a medical doctor, after all. He felt supremely confident in his own ability to teach his pieced-together staff what they needed to know to help him.

Usually, Anthony didn't know his patients all that well. The women came to him with their worries about being too fat or too flat-chested. The men came because their scalps were shining through their thinning hair. He didn't know about their spouses, their families, their jobs—and he didn't care. He was providing a service. He might see his patients once in a preoperative appointment, again as they lay stuporous on the table below him, and once more for a postoperative visit.

Sarah Smith was prettier than most of his patients: a very slender woman with porcelain skin, clear blue eyes, and blond hair. She came to see Dr. Pignataro because her husband's younger sister had a roommate who recommended him highly. He had performed plastic surgery on her, and she was completely satisfied with her new and fuller breasts. That roommate was Janie Krauss, now Anthony's L.P.N.

Seven months earlier, in January 1997, Sarah had undergone some plastic surgery on her nose to fix a deviated septum and her surgeon had also removed a small bump on the bridge of her nose. That operation was completely successful, and she felt generally confident about having more surgery done.

To anyone else, Sarah looked flawless. At 26, she was a lovely and vibrantly happy young woman. Her husband, Daniel, couldn't imagine that anything might make her more appealing to him. He had loved her since she was 14 years old.

Sarah was born Sarah Grafton on May 14, 1971, in Springville, New York. Sarah Grafton and Daniel Smith had grown up in Springville, a town of four thousand people on the Cattaraugus River between Buffalo and Jamestown. Her mother, Barbara, came from a family that had lived there for several generations. Her father, Russell Grafton, remembered her as "Sarah—just Sarah," but his eyes filled with tears as he recalled a "bouncy" little girl full of energy and curiosity.

Most parents will agree that each baby has its own little personality, recognizable even at birth. Sarah was a sunny, happy baby, who slept through the night from the beginning. It was fortunate that she was so easy to care for, because her parents were about to face crushing news. When Sarah was six weeks old, they took her brother David, who was four, to Children's Hospital in Buffalo for testing. The news confirmed what they had feared. David had a progressive disease: muscular dystrophy.

Because David needed so much care and attention from her mother, Sarah sometimes resented him—but she loved him, too. David couldn't do chores, so Sarah had to do them all. "She never complained about this role thrust upon her," Russell Grafton said. "She became David's friend, confidante, and protector."

Her parents divorced in 1979 when Sarah was eight. Shortly after the divorce, Russell Grafton lost his job in the Buffalo area and was forced to move to Iowa for another position. Her mother had to work, and Sarah pitched in to help. Her father managed to visit Sarah and David every month or two for the next few years until the children became accustomed to his being gone. They always kept in close touch by phone.

Sarah did well in school, although her report cards sometimes noted that she was more interested in her social life than in studying. In the fifth grade, she took violin lessons, and she practiced faithfully all through high school, playing in the school orchestra at Springville-Griffith Institute. She had lots of friends, but she always had time for her brother, David, who was now in a wheelchair.

During her senior year at Springville-Griffith, Sarah was thrilled to be selected as a cheerleader for the basketball team. There were a lot of boys who would have loved to date Sarah, but she never really looked at any of them after she started dating Dan. He was a junior and she was a freshman when they began to go steady. Sometimes high school romances do last, and Sarah and Dan's relationship was like that. Although they had occasional short arguments, they went to every prom and every football game together. They were as welcome in each other's homes as they were in their own. They took Sarah's brother to the movies with them, and the three of them often sat around talking about music. David was a special part of their lives. Sarah wouldn't have fallen in love with anyone who wouldn't feel compassion and responsibility for her brother.

"It was harder for Sarah growing up because her brother was sick," Barb Grafton said, "but it made her a more compassionate and responsible adult."

Dan was one of Tim and Sandy Smith's four children—Laura, Dan, Paula, and Matthew. When the Smiths moved away from Springville, it meant a 45-minute drive for Dan to see Sarah.

"People were always predicting that we wouldn't last," Dan recalled. "They said when we lived that far apart, we'd break up pretty soon. But we kept dating. When I went off to college, they said we'd drift apart, but we kept dating. They didn't understand that nothing was going to break us up. We kept beating the odds. I called her my 'All American Country Girl,'" Dan said, "because

Springville was mostly dairy farms, and Sarah just looked like a pretty, kind of old-fashioned girl."

Sarah's brother David went to Edinboro University in Pennsylvania, but he didn't live to see his graduation. His health failed, and he died on February 12, 1990.

It was a sad spring, but Dan and Sarah were married on June 12. They got a little apartment in Lancaster, New York, halfway between Barb Grafton and Tim and Sandy Smith. When their first baby, a boy they named Nathan, was born, they started talking about the day when they could buy their own house.

Nathan bonded strongly with his mother. "He bonded to me, too," Dan remembered. "But there was something special between him and Sarah."

Every year that they were together, Dan and Sarah celebrated that fact. "We still felt as though we were beating the odds when we saw how many couples we knew were breaking up. We toasted each other every year. We were soul mates, and we knew it."

Sarah was the optimist of the pair, and Dan admitted that he tended to look at the negative side of things. "She gradually taught me to look on the bright side—she was always positive."

Dan was very tall, broad-shouldered and handsome, and strangers might have found Sarah a little docile at first because she was quiet. "But she was feisty," her mother-in-law, Sandy, recalled, "and she was very strong emotionally. They decided what they wanted out of life together."

Dan worked as a drafter/designer, and Sarah began work as a courier for a law firm. She had always been fascinated by the law and hoped to be a paralegal one day. Both Sarah and Dan worked full time, and he had his own business that he'd started in college: custom crating for companies that wanted to be sure their products, mostly heavy machinery, arrived in good shape.

"We called it 'DSS' for Dan and Sarah Smith," Dan said.

By August 1995 they had saved enough for a down payment on their first home. Sarah did most of the legwork on the legal documents they needed, and it saved them some money. It was a "starter" house in Depew, New York, another hamlet near Buffalo, close to Williamsville, where Debbie Pignataro grew up, and near the Buffalo-Niagara International Airport. It had three small bedrooms and a bath-and-a-half, and even though it looked like millions of other houses where young couples start out, Dan and Sarah were thrilled because it was theirs.

Dan built a shed in the back, and Sarah discovered that she loved gardening. It wasn't a very expensive landscaping project, but it looked great, and Sarah took great satisfaction in it.

"Our home was our hobby," Dan said. "We fixed it up outside, and Sarah planted flowers. There was a whole section in the backyard where she planted packets of wildflower seeds. We called it our potluck garden because we never knew what was going to come up. Daisies were her favorite flowers."

Three years after Nathan's birth, Amanda was born. "Nathan was like his mother," Sandy Smith said. "Thoughtful and strong, too. He was his mother's son, and he thought she was the most special mother in the world. When Sarah had Amanda, she was a miniature version of her mother. But Amanda's emotions were more on the surface."

Dan and Sarah's time off work was spent with their children, their parents, and good friends. "Friday nights were special to us," Dan said. "We rented kids' movies and made popcorn, and we all bundled up in blankets on the living room couch. We usually fell asleep there. Sometimes, in the summer, we went for drives on Friday nights."

Nothing interrupted those family nights. They also loved to go over to swim in the elder Smiths' pool and share a barbecue. They spent Christmas Eves with Sarah's mom, Barb, and then went to Dan's parents on Christmas Day. Dan loved his mother-in-law. Although Sarah's father had married again and lived in Iowa, Sarah remained close to him. Russell Grafton called her every second Sunday, and they visited back and forth.

Dan was proud when they entertained several of his friends, and the men commented on what a wonderful wife he had. "They told me I was so lucky because she was such a great person, and I knew I was lucky," he said. "She was young, funny, vibrant, and outgoing. She just put a smile on your face."

They argued sometimes. Dan and Sarah didn't have a perfect marriage, but they came close. "We just believed that you should work things out," Dan said. "We always figured that marriage was what you put into it."

Chillingly, they had a few somber conversations that might have surprised people who knew them. "We'd only been married a year or two," Dan said, "and we started talking about 'What if? What if one of us would die; how could the other one go on? I remember that we asked each other what we would want for the one that was left."

Sarah told Dan that her biggest fear was that he would be miserable without her. And how would he take care of Nathan and Amanda? "Don't stop living," she told him. "If I wasn't here, remember that I would want you to go on and be happy. I'd want you to find somebody to love."

And then she laughed. "And if you found the wrong one, I'd let you know before you married her. I'd drop a drink in your lap or something to get your attention!"

* * *

Dan's parents, Sandy and Tim Smith, used to feel blessed, too, by their good health and their four kids, who had turned out well. Then, in the spring of 1997, Tim suddenly became very ill. For three weeks, doctors couldn't diagnose what was wrong with him. His kidneys weren't functioning as they should. Finally, they honed in on Wagner's disease and were able to get him stabilized.

It made them all realize how vulnerable they were to the vagaries of fate—that there were no guarantees for them, or for anybody. They cherished their family all the more. They all felt as if they had dodged a bullet.

Dan and Sarah had a big project the summer of 1997: they worked together to remodel their bedroom. "We steamed off the old wallpaper," Dan said, "and sanded everything down, put up new wallpaper, and painted. Sarah used stencils to paint designs, and we got some bedside tables. We didn't spend that much. It was mostly our own work we put into it."

The elder Smiths had always welcomed foreign exchange students into their home. "We had them from France, Spain, Peru, Ecuador, Germany, and Russia," Sandy laughed, "all through the years after our own kids were grown."

The 1996–1997 students were from France, and they were due to go home in the third week of August. As usual, Sandy and Tim Smith threw a big farewell party for them out by the pool, with the requisite barbecue.

"It was on August 16," Sandy remembered. "Sarah was on the pool deck in her bathing suit, and she looked beautiful. But she always wanted boobs. For six years, she'd been talking about having breast implants. She used to ask me, 'How can I have two kids and no boobs?' And I'd tell her she had a beautiful figure, but she never believed me. It didn't matter to Dan. In fact, he didn't want her to ever have surgery because he worried about her."

No one looking at Sarah Smith could have imagined

that she felt unhappy about her appearance, but perfection had become a goal of many young women in the nineties, bombarded as they were by images of movie stars and top recording artists. Most of them didn't realize that most of the exquisite models' and stars' photographs were air-brushed to remove the slightest flaw and that expert makeup artists worked over them for hours. Sarah stared at her modest bustline and felt inadequate.

There had been a medical reason for her nose surgery. There was no reason at all for her to have breast implants—nothing at all beyond Sarah's own perception that she really wasn't very attractive.

When she got a job promotion six months earlier, her salary was enough so she could save for the operation. She wouldn't have taken money meant for her family, but now she had enough to pay for it.

When Sarah had her first appointment with Dr. Anthony Pignataro, she was impressed. He told her she was a good candidate for the new surgery he had perfected. Since everything had gone so smoothly with her nose surgery in January, Dan wasn't worried about Sarah's operation, although he still didn't see any need for it. She explained to him that Dr. Pignataro had told her about a brand-new procedure that he was using. "He said it worked so well that he would be charging more for it soon—but he would give her a special price," Dan said. "He talked to her the way a salesman talks."

Dr. Pignataro noted on Sarah Smith's chart that he had given her a complete physical examination, although he did not do any X-rays or give her an EKG, explaining that it wasn't necessary because she was under forty. He did take all the requisite blood tests, and he advised her hurriedly of the possible dangers in surgery. She signed releases, and her surgery was scheduled for 9:30 on the morning of August 25, 1997.

Few people knew that Sarah had made an appointment to have her breasts enlarged. "She told me and her mother, of course," Sandy said. "And her sisters-in-law, but she wasn't the type to tell people she wasn't really close to."

As Sarah enjoyed the barbecue party for the French exchange students that Saturday night, Sandy noticed that she was "super happy. She came over to me and whispered, 'Take a good look because this is the last time I'll look like this in a bathing suit!' "

Sandy forgot about that conversation soon after the party when Tim Smith suddenly became very ill. He was taken to the hospital and they were all afraid that his earlier illness had returned, but it was only his gallbladder. He was home by Tuesday, August 19.

On Friday, August 22, Dan and Sarah had their movie-popcorn family night camp-out in the living room with Nathan and Amanda. It was almost Labor Day. School would be starting for Nathan soon, and Amanda would go to preschool.

Dan Smith drove Sarah to Anthony Pignataro's office on Monday morning, taking a book with him to read in the waiting room while she was in surgery. He sat down with her to wait, and then she was taken to the back room, where she said the doctor would give her some "relaxing" pills. Dan was surprised when she came back out to the waiting room. He could tell the pills were affecting her; she was beginning to feel woozy.

Evidently Janie Krauss was late and they had to wait for her to arrive. When she came rushing in, Sarah was taken back through the closed door to have her surgery. Dan prepared to wait, but Dr. Pignataro came out several times and urged him to "go do some errands or something, and you can come back later."

"I didn't want to go," Dan said. "But finally he said he

was going to lock the door. He didn't exactly throw me out, but it was clear he wanted me to leave."

In his book, Anthony, writing as "Debbie," would recall that August 25 was the day *his* "world fell apart." For Sarah Smith, it was far worse than that.

Debbie Pignataro had been called on to assist her husband that morning. Wearing hospital scrubs, she had to keep a sharp eye on the pulse-ox device on the patient's finger and to check that her blood pressure was stable. Janie Krauss was in charge of adding meds to the tube going into Sarah Smith's arm, and seventeen-year-old Tom Watkins stood at the head of the operating table, mostly observing, but ready to run an errand if Anthony requested it. There was no anesthesiologist, no nurse-anesthetist, not even a registered nurse present.

The TUBA procedure began. But within less than an hour, sirens screamed as emergency medical units arrived at Dr. Anthony Pignataro's office. The scene in the surgical area in the basement was one of horror and chaos. No one who was there would ever forget it.

10

Dan Smith came back to Pignataro's office between two and two-thirty. As he walked into the waiting room area he heard someone whispering. "They were saying, 'The husband's here,' and a woman who said she was Debbie Pignataro asked me to go with her into a back office."

Debbie had taken a deep breath, trying to find a way to begin. Finally she said, "We've had a little problem . . ."

Dan looked at her quizzically. He wasn't worried yet.

"Your wife was not breathing—but she's breathing now," Debbie hurried to reassure him. "She's on the way to the hospital. I'll drive you."

Why would she want to drive him to the hospital? Dan started to explain that he was perfectly capable of driving himself, but there was a funny pinched look on the doctor's wife's face, and he followed her to her car.

It wasn't until he got to the hospital and a priest and nun came to talk with him that Dan Smith realized his world had tilted off center and something was terribly wrong. Someone led him to the intensive care unit, and he saw Sarah lying there with several tubes coming out of her body.

"It was just like somebody grabbed my ankles," he remembered. "I fell on my knees with shock. I realized then."

Sandy Smith, still on the job at the school where she worked, could hardly recognize her son's voice on the phone. Usually it was soft and calm. Now he was screaming something over and over that she could not understand.

And then she did. Dan was shouting, "She's flat-lined! She's flat-lined!"

At first, she couldn't figure out who he was talking about. Her husband, Tim, had been really sick, but he had recovered rapidly from the gallbladder attack. Sarah was supposed to have her surgery on this Monday, but her daughter-in-law had laughed at Sandy's concern, "It's not even a real operation," Sarah had said. "I won't even be put under anesthesia. He's just going to give me a local and something to relax me."

No, Dan couldn't be talking about Sarah. Sandy had worked as a medical assistant herself, and she knew what "flat-lined" meant. No brain activity, no heartbeat or breathing unless a machine did that for the person. Sarah was only 26 years old, and she was healthy.

But Dan *was* talking about Sarah. His voice quivered with shock as he said he was with her at Buffalo Mercy Hospital, and he wanted his family to come. Sandy called her daughter, Paula, and they raced to the hospital as fast as they could get there. Barb Grafton, Sarah's mother, was already there with Dan. Both of them were crying.

All Sandy could think of was that Barb had lost her son, and now she might lose her daughter.

Sarah was in a little cubicle, surrounded by curtains, in the hall of the intensive care unit. When Sandy Smith was allowed to look in, she gasped, "Oh, God!"

Sarah lay pale and still, a respirator hooked up and breathing for her. It didn't seem possible to Sandy that her spunky little daughter-in-law could be so still and unresponsive.

A nurse looked up at Sandy, and when their eyes met, Sandy knew the outcome was going to be as bad as it could get.

"Get a lawyer," the nurse said softly. "Get a good one—this guy has put five people in the hospital in the last few weeks."

"Will she get better?" Sandy asked, a hopeless tone in her voice.

"Not unless she comes back very soon," the nurse said, but her face said more. Sarah's chest rose and fell in the odd, mechanical way a patient on a respirator breathes. Sandy kept seeing the image in her mind of Sarah only nine days earlier as she grinned and said, "This is the last time I'm ever going to look like this in a bathing suit . . ."

Sandy and Paula went to the waiting room to join Dan and Barb, and saw that Dr. Pignataro and his wife, Debbie, were waiting there, too. Debbie Pignataro appeared to be in shock, but the doctor seemed calm.

"He kept talking about how everything was going to be all right. I asked him what had happened, but he didn't give me any specific answers," Sandy Smith remembered.

Pignataro turned to Dan. "I don't know what happened," he said plaintively. "Was she taking anything?"

"No—no!" Dan said. "What happened?"

"I don't know what happened," the doctor kept repeating, as if he had nothing to do with what was wrong with Sarah.

Sandy thought that Debbie was trying to shelter her husband from the bleak outcome of Sarah's condition. She appeared to be a gentle woman, and her skin was pale with concern as she scanned his face. Of the two of them, Debbie Pignataro was the one who seemed upset and aware of the tragedy that was taking place. The doctor only tried to make excuses for himself. Whatever had happened, he wanted everyone in the room to know that he was in no way responsible.

Debbie told Sandy that she had been in the operating room during Sarah's surgery. "She said she'd worked as a medical assistant in doctors' offices—but I'd done that, too, and I knew she wasn't certified to assist in operations because *I* wasn't."

She knew that Sarah had been very impressed with Dr. Pignataro, but now Sandy found him too glib and calm, given the circumstances. "Maybe it's because I'm older and I've got more experience, and it's harder to fool me," she said. "Sarah was only twenty-six, and she totally trusted him."

They all waited, forming a mostly silent tableau: Sarah's family and the Pignataros. The waiting room was hushed as the clock ticked and there was no change at all in Sarah Smith's condition.

The days wore on, and Sarah didn't wake up. As he had with Connie Vinetti, Anthony Pignataro came into Buffalo Mercy Hospital to check on Sarah Smith. The nurses there recognized him, and they moved to block his access to Sarah. Dan called the law firm where Sarah worked, and they quickly arranged to ban Pignataro from the hospital premises.

Dan Smith could not bear to go back to the little house where they had been so happy. He and Nathan and Amanda moved in with Sandy and Tim Smith while they waited to see what would happen, but Dan spent all his time at the hospital, coming home only to shower and change clothes. Dan refused to even think that Sarah might be in a permanent coma.

Sandy took care of the children while Dan and Barb, and later Sarah's father, Russell, who had flown in from Iowa, waited at Buffalo Mercy. Nathan was 7, and he knew something was wrong when the family decided it would be best not to take him to see his mother. "My mom's really sick," he murmured, half as a statement of fact and half as a hopeful question.

But they all thought he would be more frightened if he saw the silent bloated shell that Sarah had become. "It's not a good idea for you to visit her right now," they told him, and he answered sadly, "My mom's not going to come home." He knew it, but he didn't want to talk about it.

Amanda was too young to understand. She was getting a lot of attention from friends and family who had gathered to wait and pray, and she seemed to feel safe, hopping happily onto the laps of women who tried to comfort her.

The doctors told Dan that there was no chance that Sarah was coming back to him. If she lived, she would "be a vegetable." He couldn't accept that. It simply wasn't possible that she could have been healthy and happy and not even apprehensive the last time he saw her, and now have no brain waves or any sign at all that she was aware of him or their children.

The doctors were cautiously advising him to let her go, but he couldn't do that. Not yet.

Gradually, gradually, Dan began to think that maybe he could let Sarah go free of the body that trapped her, but he still went back and forth in an agonizing inner dialogue. He had heard of people in comas who were oblivious to anything around them for months—years even—who suddenly woke up. What if that could happen to Sarah? If that should be true, it would be terrible for him to turn off her ventilator. But if she was suffering needlessly, if she had already gone on without him—that part of her who thought and felt and loved—it wasn't fair to keep her alive.

Dan talked to Sarah's parents, because they had to be part of the decision, too. There could be no more agonizing decision for any of them.

The press hovered, wanting to know how Sarah Smith was doing.

Anthony Pignataro returned to work as usual. He had other surgeries scheduled, and he saw no reason not to carry on. When his staff asked him if he was doing all right, he shrugged off their concern.

"That could happen to anyone," he said. "We just have to go on."

In fact, he did a few more TUBA procedures for breast augmentation. He knew that the New York Department of Health's Medical Board was watching him and that they might try to shut him down. He said as much. "They're probably going to take my license," he commented mat-

ter-of-factly. "I need to do as many operations as I can—
get some money put away."

Debbie was heartsick. Anthony had left it up to her to
tell Dan Smith that his wife had been rushed to the hospital. She had wondered how in the world she could tell
him. She agonized over the impossible task Anthony had
delegated to her. Once again, Debbie had been left to
clean up after one of Anthony's disasters. She had no idea
what had gone wrong, and she had listened as her husband cried that he didn't understand it either. Debbie
hadn't known what to think as she sat in the suddenly
silent office with the surgical suite still in complete disarray. Anthony was a good doctor. She knew he was. He
had to be after all those years of medical school, all those
years of residency programs.

Hadn't she warned him in time that Sarah was in trouble? She wondered if the disaster might be her fault. No,
she had watched the blood pressure monitor and the pulse-
ox so carefully, and Anthony had been annoyed with her
when she tried to tell him that something was wrong.

She tried to tell herself that Anthony felt terrible about
what had happened, just as she did. But she had come to
know what was going on in Anthony's mind, and she
wasn't sure. Maybe he just didn't feel things the way
other people did. He'd put up a kind of a steel wall around
himself when his father died, and he kept moving forward, doing whatever he wanted to do.

He spent more time doing body-building exercises at
his sports club, and he drank a little more tequila in the
evening, but he didn't seem worried or remorseful.

Debbie herself was so concerned about other people
that she could not comprehend someone who didn't care
at all. She had been making excuses for Anthony for
decades—not only to others but to herself. And he had

been keeping secrets from her for just as long. There were so many things in his life and in his career as a doctor that she didn't know.

It was Labor Day, 1997, when Dan Smith made the most anguished decision any man has ever had to make. He told the doctors that he would sign the permission form to take his wife off the respirator. Sarah Smith legally died on September 1.

For the first time, Dan went back to their little house in Depew to spend a few hours alone and try to get his head straightened out. He had to find a way to tell his children that their mother was gone forever.

"But it was already on the news," Sandy Smith recalled. "And we all knew Nathan and Amanda needed to hear it from Dan first, so he hurried to our house. Nathan was stoic. He didn't cry—he just wanted to go upstairs and be alone with his cousins. Our oldest girl, Laura, has a son, Michael, who is a year older than Nathan, and those little boys kind of sat together quietly. Amanda cried.

"I heard her tell one of her little playmates that moms die when they get to be 26—that her mother was probably going to die, too, when she got that old."

They had a wake for Sarah, and crowds of mourners attended her funeral in the Hoy Funeral Home in West Seneca. It was forty miles from the site of her funeral to the cemetery where she was to be buried next to her brother. The church where she and Dan were married was just across the street. The procession of mourners' cars stretched out for more than a mile.

The television cameras followed them.

* * *

Sandy Smith became a substitute mother for two little children, decades after she'd raised her own.

"And all those flowers that Sarah planted," she said, "kept coming up long after she was gone. She worked so hard on her garden; it would have made her happy to see them, but it made us cry. Dan never lived there again, but his sister, Paula, did—until he could sell it."

"Everyone kept telling me to sue," Dan recalled. "But it wasn't going to bring Sarah back. My goal was only to be sure that people knew there were doctors like Pignataro out there. I didn't even push to have him go to prison for the maximum time because I knew he had two kids at home. I didn't want to take him away from his family. I thought if he just lost his license and couldn't practice, we'd have one really bad doctor out of the system."

For a time, at least, that wouldn't be a concern. On August 29, 1997, Anthony Pignataro's license to practice medicine was suspended by the New York State Department of Health. He had been correct in assuming he wouldn't be able to continue operating on patients when he rushed to increase his income before that happened.

His malpractice insurance made a settlement with Dan Smith, and Dan put it in a fund for his and Sarah's children.

Part Five

Last Dance

11

What *had* **happened** to Sarah Smith to cause her brain to die? The answers weren't easy, and it would take the combined efforts of medical investigators, skilled detectives, and clever prosecutors to find them. They could not bring Sarah back, but they wanted to know whether she had died because of some undetected prior medical condition or through an outrageous instance of medical malpractice.

The first of the investigators were the local police. Captain Florian Jablonski and Detective Robert Fiscus of the West Seneca Police Department visited Anthony Pignataro in his office at 531 Center Road in their town on August 29, 1997, two days before Sarah was declared dead. At ten that Friday morning, they were ushered into the doctor's office. He told them that his attorney had advised him not to talk to anyone about Sarah Smith. But then he smiled and said that since Jablonski and Fiscus were detectives, he would be glad to talk with them.

Asked who was present during Sarah's surgery, he said that Janie Krauss, the LPN who worked for him, was there and that his wife, Deborah, had acted as a gofer to get the instruments as he needed them. He explained Sarah's operation to the two detectives, saying that he had given her a local anesthetic and then something that allowed her to drift in and out of consciousness.

119

Pignataro gave them a description of the TUBA procedure. But somehow, he said, something had gone wrong, and he detailed how carefully he had given emergency aid to Sarah Smith when she went into cardiac arrest.

Doing breast surgery through the belly button sounded very peculiar to the two detectives from West Seneca, but Anthony Pignataro assured them that it was common in California and that it would soon be "very popular" in New York State.

When his patient had suddenly stopped breathing, he had administered immediate resuscitation efforts, of course, and instructed his office personnel to call for help. During this interview, four days after Sarah Smith went into a coma, Anthony assured the investigators that his prime concern had been for his patient and her recovery. But now, he said, he had to apologize to them because he had patients to see, and he could give them no more of his time.

Two days later, Sarah Smith was dead.

Frank Clark, the district attorney of Erie County, New York, oversaw an office with numerous assistant district attorneys to handle the different divisions. Like any city, Buffalo had its felonies and misdemeanors, domestic abuse, sexual assaults, arson, robberies, drug violations, and, of course, homicides.

Although there were ongoing investigations into the medical skill—or lack of it—of Anthony Pignataro, M.D., before September 1, those had been under the aegis of the New York State Department of Health. With the death of Sarah Smith, the Erie County D.A.'s office was drawn into the case of a doctor who had a disturbing history of patient care. While the Department of Health works with local law enforcement departments, the Buffalo-based D.A.'s office has sixteen of its own special investigators, most of them seasoned detectives with years of experience in other agencies. Jonathan Coughlan, Chief of the Special Investigations/Prosecution Bureau at the time, called two of the D.A.'s prime investigators and asked them to look into Sarah Smith's death.

Pat Finnerty and Chuck Craven were the "odd couple" of the D.A.'s office, but they worked so well together that they fit like a pair of gloves. Their only shared traits were that they were both Irish and had grown up in the same South Buffalo neighborhood.

Buffalo is rife with nicknames, and Chuck Craven was called Chickie because the old-timers remembered that was his dad's nickname when he was a sergeant in Homicide in the Buffalo Police Department. Chickie Senior cast a long shadow. He was a great detective and an athlete who played his last hockey game when he was sixty-nine.

Craven had an Irish mug, but then so did Finnerty, who liked to say that he was a "potato-faced Irishman." Craven's hair was brown with a red cast, and Finnerty's was gray with a reddish glow—or red with some gray, depending on how the light hit it. Craven's easygoing grin belied the fact that he was a relentless and clever detective. Finnerty was taller and burlier, and he looked grumpy even when he wasn't. He was also a merciless practical joker, enlisting Craven in his plots to catch the gullible unaware.

"Pat liked to walk down the hall," Craven said, "and pretend to walk into a doorjamb and bang his head. Then, if somebody laughed because he was clumsy, I had to whisper that he was blind in one eye because of an injury he suffered when he was in the Secret Service, and he couldn't help it. Then, naturally, they were embarrassed—and he had them. But he's probably the best investigator I've ever worked with. I've learned more from Pat than any detective I ever knew."

Pat Finnerty was once the Special Agent in Charge for the U.S. Secret Service office in Buffalo. Although one of its divisions guards the President of the United States, the Secret Service's primary function is to protect the financial integrity of the country. Finnerty knew everything there was to know about the way money changes hands—for both legal and illegal uses. He could follow a paper trail like a bloodhound. He knew the many facets of white-collar crime; there was never a scam invented that fooled Pat Finnerty. He was a complete professional, and he distrusted anyone who was remotely connected to the media.

But still, he could send victim's advocate Sharon Simon and Chuck Craven into muffled laughter with the tricks he played on young prosecutors or detectives. Finnerty kept a fake "Wanted" poster of David Janssen as the Dr. Richard Kimball character on *The Fugitive* tacked to his office wall, convincing them that Kimball was still out there and needed to be caught.

"They believed him," Craven remembered, "and when he got on a crowded elevator and pretended he was having a panic attack because he forgot his 'big pill' that day, people who didn't know him were squeezing against the wall. Pat is a very big guy."

Humor is vital in police departments and prosecutors' offices. Without it, there is no relief from the tragedies that come through their doors day and night.

Chuck Craven was born and raised in Buffalo, the only son in a flock of five sisters. He joined the U.S. Air Force and was sent to Clovis, New Mexico, where he met his future wife, Laurie. Six months later, he was ordered to Vietnam, where he fueled airplanes. After a stint in Thailand, he came back to New Mexico and reenlisted for three more years. He and Laurie moved to Peterson Air Force Base in Colorado Springs, where their daughter,

Christine, was born. And then, probably genetically driven, Craven transferred into the Security Police.

But Chuck Craven's goal was to work in a civilian police department, and he joined the Clovis Police Department. At the same time, he finished college with an A.A. in Criminal Justice and a B.A. in Liberal Studies. The Cravens moved West, and Chuck joined the Scottsdale, Arizona, Police Department. He worked narcotics, one of the more dangerous units in any police department. He was usually unshaven and dressed like the people he hunted.

He shrugs it off, but Craven was nearly killed when he was shot during a drug raid. Hit in the neck, he was very lucky that the bullet narrowly missed his carotid artery. Still, it would take a long time for him to recover—and his department told him he would never be cleared for full duty. He didn't want a desk job; he wanted to be out in a squad car and, eventually, to be a detective.

Instead, Craven was given a full retirement when he was only 36. He was not about to give up police work, although it would take more than a year of physical therapy to bring back the use of his arm. His physical therapists didn't think he could do it, and they were amazed.

"We realized that the only grandparents our children had were in Buffalo, so we came home," Craven recalled. "I got to play softball with my father. It was a good move."

Craven was hired by the Erie County D.A.'s office in 1989. Until then, he had investigated accidents and narcotics, but now he would be tracking every kind of criminal there was. Craven also became a certified fingerprint examiner and an expert at drawing crime scenes to scale.

Between them, Craven and Finnerty would handle everything from bunco to murder for hire. Each case they were assigned to had a different spin, but one or the other of them had the experience to winnow out the truth. Together, they were formidable. Now, they were about to learn a great deal about the practice of medicine.

On September 3, 1997, Pat Finnerty and Chuck Craven knew only that Sarah Smith had died during what was allegedly a routine procedure in Dr. Anthony Pignataro's office. They needed to interview all the office staff who had been present, as well as the paramedics and EMTs who had responded to the 911 call the morning of August 25.

They found Janie Krauss first. A very pretty young woman, she was the very epitome of what blond jokes portray. She hadn't mastered the correct terminology for techniques or medical instruments, and the two detectives exchanged dumbfounded looks while Janie struggled to explain what had happened.

Janie said she had arrived late on that Monday morning, and that Sarah Smith was already in the basement surgery, conscious but drowsy from preoperative pills. She said that Sarah had been given 20 milligrams of Valium before her surgery. Janie's assignment was to inject the anesthesia into a port in the tube to the patient's arm. She had given sodium pentothal 6 cubic centimeters, and then Versed, 3 cubic centimeters. Janie wasn't sure what those were for. She thought it was to control pain. Dr. Pignataro had then asked her to inject a second syringe of sodium pentothal, 7 cubic centimeters, into the port.

Janie said she had been present for a dozen other operations like this one, although she couldn't remember the name of this procedure. "He started with that sharp thing—I forget what it's called . . ." Janie began.

"A *scalpel?*" Finnerty asked.

She nodded. "That's it—and then he put this thing in and he was tunneling under her skin. It's like a hockey stick . . ."

"A *hockey stick?*" Finnerty echoed, amazed.

They realized later that the expander Anthony had used to burrow under the patient's skin *was* shaped like a hockey stick.

Sarah Smith had said "Ouch" several times, and the doctor had told Janie to give her a third dose of sodium pentothal—7 cubic centimeters.

The two D.A.'s investigators didn't know much about anesthetic substances, and they nodded, unaware that this third injection was an excessive amount.

Janie explained that Debbie Pignataro had been in the operating room, and that a boy from the Nichols School named Tom had been there, too. She didn't know his last name.

Within a few moments after the third injection, the pulse-ox on Sarah's forefinger began to sound the way it did if the oxygen level fell too low, below 85. Janie said the blood pressure monitor went off, too. She had tried to read the blood pressure and gotten nothing, and then tried to get a manual blood pressure reading, but she couldn't do that either.

"What does it mean when the pulse-ox hits 85?" Craven asked.

"I don't know," Janie said in a puzzled voice. "I just know that when it hits 85, it isn't a good sign."

She remembered that they had all worked over the woman on the table, trying to get her to breathe again, but she didn't know for how long.

Now Janie Krauss told them that the doctor had asked that the patient be hooked up to the electrocardiogram. "There was just a flat line. And he didn't have a 'Bamboo Bag.' "

"What's that?" Finnerty asked.

"You know—that little masky thing you put over someone's face when you want them to breathe?"

"Like an oxygen mask?"

"That's it!" As Janie tried to explain it, the two detectives realized that she meant an Ambu-Bag, necessary to intubate the patient in an effort to give her oxygen. If it hadn't been so tragic, her description might have been humorous. But it was all too clear that Anthony Pignataro not only hadn't hired an anesthesiologist or a nurse-anesthetist, he was operating with an L.P.N. who had never had the proper training or experience to do the job he expected of her.

The only other people in that surgical suite were a 17-year-old boy and Debbie Pignataro. Until now, the investigators hadn't realized they were there.

Janie said that Dr. Pignataro had sent Tom scurrying to find an Ambu-Bag, but all he could find was one for a child. Then the doctor had tried to use a flat piece of metal to open an airway, and finally had screamed for a coat hanger.

The detectives winced. They weren't medically oriented, but they could see that Pignataro hadn't been at all prepared for an emergency. They wondered if indeed he had *caused* the emergency.

Finally, Janie said, he had given up and told Tom to call for help. Once Tom called 911, Janie thought that the rescue workers had arrived in about five minutes.

Finnerty and Craven thought it would be a good idea for Janie Krauss to talk directly to the assistant district attorneys on the case, and she went with them willingly. On the way, she became animated as she told them about her exciting weekend.

"She told us that she went to a concert and she got to go backstage and meet Mick Jagger," Chuck Craven said. "There's a young mother with two little kids dead, and she's excited about Mick Jagger . . ."

Debbie Pignataro was considerably more affected by Sarah Smith's death. She looked at Lauren and Ralph and thought how she would feel if anything happened to her and they were left without a mother. She went over the operation again and again in her mind.

Her only assignment had been to keep an eye on the pulse-ox device and the blood pressure cuff, but she always watched the patient, too, whenever Anthony asked her to help him during operations. She wasn't familiar with the dosage of anesthetics. She had worked in the pharmacy so many years ago, and there they filled prescriptions—not doses of anesthesia.

"But I was watching her face," Debbie would say a long time later. "And I could see that her skin was getting gray. I tried to tell Anthony, but he was too busy with what he was doing. When the pulse-ox started to sound, he told me to take her fingernail polish off, so I could see the nail bed better. And he said to jiggle the pulse-ox because it was probably just some loose wires."

Debbie had become more and more concerned, but Anthony ignored her until the other alarm went off—the blood pressure alarm. Only then did he look up at his patient. And, at that point, he realized that she was comatose. But Debbie realized to her horror that he had made no preparation whatsoever to have the instruments needed present in his "surgical suite."

On September 9, Chuck Craven and Pat Finnerty met with representatives of the New York State Department of Health, the Vigilant Fire Company in West Seneca, and attorneys from the Erie County District Attorney's Office. Other than Pignataro's staff and his wife, the fire department's rescue squad personnel were the only people in Anthony Pignataro's office on the day Sarah Smith stopped breathing. They were able to reconstruct the scene of panic they encountered when they answered the 911 call.

Dave Koehler, the first assistant chief, had been the

first to respond. He drove to the fire station to pick up the Life-Pak that would trace the heart's rhythm and send it to a doctor in the ER, and could also be used to shock a heart into beating. When Koehler arrived at the Center Street office, he was met by a young man, who pointed toward the basement steps.

Koehler told them that he knew the doctor socially and recognized him. He knew Debbie Pignataro, too. She was wearing surgical scrubs but was standing off to one side as Pignataro tried to open an airway and a young woman was doing closed chest compressions.

"She just went out," Pignataro had gasped. "She had no history of medical trouble." He asked Koehler if he had a stylet for an intubation tube. He seemed to be having a great deal of trouble getting a breathing tube down the patient's throat.

At the time Koehler arrived, he saw three leads hooked up to an electrocardiogram in the room, but the screen was blank. He himself attached two pads from the Life-Pak to try to obtain any sign of heart activity. The only response he got was a slight reaction to the closed chest compressions. He heard Pignataro shouting for a clothes hanger.

Koehler recalled that Pignataro was begging to no one in particular, "We can't lose this one!"

Firefighters Lou Gimbrone, Rich Cramer, and Paul Bernardi rushed in, followed by David Willman, the second assistant fire chief. When the Rural/Metro Team arrived a few minutes later, Koehler heard the doctor ask them for their intubation equipment. Koehler looked to see if there was a crash cart in the surgery and saw none. What he saw was Pignataro and Janie trying to work the yellow wire clothes hanger into the victim's throat so he could get an oxygen tube into her lungs.

Jim Cavanaugh had been the last paramedic to arrive. The emergency medical personnel were attempting to get oxygen into the silent woman on the operating table. Like the rest of them, Cavanaugh was shocked to see that she was so young. They had expected an older person.

Pignataro was frantic, and he was getting in their way more than helping them. However, he left the room once "to get a cup of coffee," and then returned and pointed at his EKG machine. "Look at my EKG," he shouted. "Mine's better. Can't you guys shock her? We've got to save this one!"

Anthony Pignataro had then grabbed the Rural/Metro team's defibrillator and moved toward his patient as if he were going to use it, but the paramedics stopped him. Whatever his reason, he hadn't used his own defibrillator. They didn't know if it even worked.

Paul Bernardi wished mightily that someone would get Pignataro out of the operating room. He was so out of control that he wasn't helping the patient. He was hindering the rescue workers, attempting to remove some tube from the woman's chest area, fighting clumsily to intubate her airway. Bernardi and the other emergency medics carried Sarah Smith on a gurney to the rescue rig, where they were able to get oxygen going and shock her heart into beating. As they prepared to race to Buffalo Mercy Hospital, Pignataro attempted to jump into the back of the rig.

He was too agitated for them to deal with, and Dave Koehler volunteered to drive Pignataro in his vehicle and follow the ambulance.

It had been nineteen or twenty minutes since Sarah Smith received any oxygen—far too long for a human brain to survive without profound damage.

Debbie was left behind. It would be up to her to explain to Dan Smith why he couldn't pick his wife up and take her home for the few days of rest that Anthony had assured Sarah was all she would need to recover from his miraculous surgical procedure.

And, of course, there had been no easy way to tell Dan Smith that his beloved wife was in such critical condition. His loss was something that would come to him in a series of searing revelations over the next seven days—and indeed for the rest of his life.

A postmortem examination of Sarah Smith's body was performed at 9:45 on September 7, 1997, by Dr. Fazlollah Loghmanee, associate chief of the Erie County Medical Examiner's Office. If, as Anthony claimed, Sarah had a preexisting medical condition that had killed her, Dr. Loghmanee would find that out.

The term "autopsy," roughly translated, means "to see for one's self."

Dr. Loghmanee dictated into a tape recorder at the beginning of the postmortem examination. Sarah was five feet, five and a half inches tall and weighed 124 pounds. She had very little fatty tissue on her body. Her breasts were small.

The forensic pathologist could see the beginning of an operation: the semicircular incision around her navel and an odd "tunnel" above her muscles but through the soft tissue from her navel to her right breast. A bag containing less than 20 cubic centimeters of blood-tinged fluid rested within the breast. The left breast was normal; her surgery had stopped before the second half had begun.

All the signs in the organs of her body were normal. She had a sound heart, lungs, kidneys, arteries, liver; all were normal save for changes that had occurred after she was deprived of oxygen for twenty minutes. The only trauma had come from the breast augmentation surgery.

Dr. Loghmanee's final notation read: *Cause of*

Death: Asphyxia due to Inadequate Ventilation Under Anesthesia.

As always, it would take several weeks before the results of a toxicology screen were available. When the results came in, Sarah Smith's blood and urine had tested positive for lidocaine, codeine, diazepam, midazolam, and thiopental—all drugs administered by Anthony Pignataro.

Chuck Craven and Pat Finnerty began learning everything they could about anesthesia. The advent of the Internet had made it possible to find out anything about anything, and they punched in their questions and rapidly got up to speed. As soon as they learned the basics, the two investigators began to interview doctors who specialized in anesthesia.

When they compared what they learned to the sedatives and painkillers that had been given to Sarah Smith, they were stunned.

"We knew he wasn't meeting standards in the proper care of a patient," Craven said. "So now we had something to hang our hat on."

They moved ahead, gathering evidence to present the case of Sarah Smith's death to a grand jury. At the same time, the New York State Board of Health continued its meticulous investigation to see whether Anthony's medical license in that state should be suspended permanently.

For the moment, Anthony had continued seeing patients. His opinion was that Sarah Smith had been taking some over-the-counter herbal additives she hadn't told him about. In Anthony's opinion, that was the only way *his* anesthesia could possibly have harmed her. As always, Anthony Pignataro believed that he never made mistakes. Any problem had to be the patient's fault.

12

Frank A. Sedita III, now head of the Homicide Investigation Unit of the Erie County D.A.'s office, would be designated as the assistant district attorney working on the case of Sarah Grafton Smith. Like most of those involved in this medical tragedy, Sedita's family went back many generations in Buffalo. His grandfather, Frank A. Sedita, had been the sixty-third mayor of Buffalo, and he had been an awesome hero to his son and his grandsons.

The first Frank Albert Sedita was born in New Orleans in 1907, one of eight children of Italian immigrant parents. When the Seditas moved to Buffalo, Frank was 4, and by the age of 10, he was selling newspapers on downtown street corners to help support his family. As his son and grandson would do later, he attended Canisius College, but he had to work his way through as a busboy and a salesman.

It was 1931 and the height of the Great Depression when Frank Sedita earned his law degree; the next year he was admitted to the bar. He had many jobs over the next several decades: deputy sheriff, secretary of the Division of Water, city clerk, and city court judge. As a judge, he saw the plight of the homeless and the alcoholic, and he worked to help them. As the city's mayor for three terms, he quelled incipient race riots in Buffalo and appointed blacks for the first time to high city positions. The African-American population had come to Buffalo in large numbers in the 1860s as they escaped from the South through the Underground Railway. With Canada just across the water, Buffalo was a prime passageway, but many running from slavery chose to stay. Mayor Sedita gave them respect, just as he fought for urban renewal.

He was a man ahead of his time, dealing with issues that most of America would ignore until much later. "FAS," the first, was a staunch Democrat and the first mayor of a large city to endorse John F. Kennedy in 1960.

Ill health forced Mayor Frank Sedita to resign in 1973, and he died at 68 on May 2, 1975. His mammoth desk now sits in the foyer of Frank Sedita III's home in the city's historical section, North Buffalo. It is the young prosecutor's proudest possession.

Frank A. Sedita, Jr., is a New York Supreme Court judge, and Frank III's cousin Joe is an attorney. "He's the smartest of all of us," Sedita comments. Perhaps. The fact is that they are *all* smart.

As in so many other East Coast cities, Buffalo's 305,000 residents belie its small-town atmosphere. Families who settle there don't leave, and connections are forged through decades. Buffalo has seen its struggles, first with the history-changing excavation of the Erie Canal and then with both the wealthy and the criminal elements, who flocked to the crowded harbor to make their fortunes.

But by the 1990s, Buffalo was designated an All-American City. Today, it is a city rich in tradition and culture. The legal community is tight, and friendly—at least *outside* the courtroom.

In the 1930s and 1940s, all the Italian Buffalonians lived on the west side. Three generations ago, the first

Frank Sedita and Anthony Pignataro's grandfather—for whom Anthony was named—were contemporaries. Anthony's grandfather owned a restaurant/bar, Scottie's, where the menu featured clams and pasta. It was a very popular hangout for the "guys," where they could smoke and drink undisturbed, and the first Frank A. Sedita and the first Anthony Pignataro knew each other well. A similar establishment, across the street, was where organized crime gang members met, and neither the mayor nor Anthony's grandfather patronized that spot.

Of course, Anthony's father, Dr. Ralph, had a fine reputation in the community and was welcome at any hospital. The Pignataros were well thought of. Though perhaps not quite as solid as the Seditas, they were an integral part of Buffalo history.

At first, Anthony thought that the old-time family connections were a good omen for him and that the prosecutor Frank Sedita would look upon him more kindly because of that. It was a flawed assumption.

"I never met him," Sedita recalled. "I had a vague memory of reading his ads in the Buffalo Sunday newspaper. I kind of chuckled at the hair implant and breast implant ads."

Although he looks as Italian as his name, with dark hair and eyes, the "third FAS" explains that he is half Italian and half Scots—which he is. His dog is a West Highland Terrier, and his son is named Mac. His thick brush of a moustache and his suspenders sometimes give him the appearance of a Buffalonian of a much earlier generation.

Frank Sedita met his wife, Leslie, at a party, where they explored their mutual Scottish roots. His ability as a chef, however, comes from a cousin on his Italian side with whom Sedita lived while he was going to law school. Sedita's biggest triumph in the kitchen is probably his chicken marsala. Frank Sedita knows the words and the orchestration of every song Frank Sinatra ever sang; they are both "Frank Albert" (although Sinatra's given name is Francis). Sedita has a deadpan sense of humor that can be off-putting until you get to know him and realize that he's teasing.

In the courtroom, Frank Sedita, III, is a tenacious opponent. Leslie Sedita attributes that to his intense preparation and the fact that he approaches his cases backward.

"He starts where he knows he wants to end up, and then works back to what he wants in a jury." Like most attorneys involved in major trials, Sedita is consumed with preparations for the weeks in court and during the time the case is being heard. So, at home, there's the "trial Frank" and the "regular Frank," according to his wife.

Leslie's career may not be as high profile as her husband's, but it is just as vital to the citizens of Buffalo; she runs the Buffalo Sewer Authority's Industrial Waste section.

Together, the Seditas are restoring their century-old house, bringing it back to the way it was in its glory days. Some of the original wood is magnificent, even though it was referred to as "scrap wood" left over from the Pan-American Exposition of 1901.

All up and down their block and the blocks around them, homeowners are doing the same. These were the streets where Frank Lloyd Wright chose to build the Martin House Complex when he was only thirty-six years old, a very avant-garde weaving of brick and beam structures with square clean angles commissioned by Darwin and Isabelle Martin. Most people connect the country's most famous architect with the Southwest, but the young Wright chose Buffalo to build this outstanding example of his Prairie House era in the early years of the twentieth century.

By 2003 standards, the North End streets are narrow, but they are ablaze with Christmas lights in December, and they bloom with flowers when the frigid Buffalo winters finally give way to spring and summer.

Almost everything about Anthony Pignataro's bizarre saga is interwoven with the Seditas. The threads of lives are braided together so that the characters almost seem to change sides as a new "game" begins. Initially, Debbie Pignataro would view Frank Sedita as her enemy and a threat to the family she had struggled for two decades to keep intact. She could never imagine that a time might come when she would welcome Frank Sedita into her home.

As for Anthony, as the nineties moved toward the millennium, Frank Sedita III, became the most dogged enemy he had ever faced. He despised Sedita just as he hated anyone who criticized his superiority.

"The first time I ever really thought about Pignataro," Sedita recalled, "was when the D.A. called me in and said, 'This is a *very* unusual case. I want you to think about it.' I was on my way to a death penalty conference, and we agreed we'd talk about it when I came back."

It would turn out to be not one case, but three—and they were the most memorable of Sedita's career to date.

Pat Finnerty and Chuck Craven had located everyone who was in the basement operating room when Sarah Smith stopped breathing except for Tom Watkins, the high school junior from Nichols School. The private school attended by the scions of Buffalo's richest families was very protective of Tom and reluctant to let detectives talk to one of their students. It was November 1997 when Finnerty and Craven finally met with Tom, his attorney, Terry Cotters, and Frank Sedita.

Sedita explained to Tom that they weren't trying to incriminate him in any way. He said, "Listen, I don't know what the attorneys have told you, but we're not interested in prosecuting you. We just want to find out what happened that day."

As soon as Tom and his mother understood that they simply wanted to know the teenager's recall of the operation, "The dam opened up," Sedita said.

The investigators quickly understood that Tom had been in the operating room as a gofer. Sedita asked if Tom had ever assisted with the intravenous sedatives.

Tom shook his head, obviously relieved. He was clearly very intelligent and quite willing to talk to them. He said that Dr. Pignataro had come to Nichols in late spring looking for someone who would be an "intern" at his office over the summer vacation. Tom was interested and visited Pignataro's office, where he observed him doing a hair transplant. Where most people might be nauseated, Tom was fascinated. He wanted to be a doctor himself one day. He began his "internship" in late June, 1997, and earned $5 an hour for working three to six hours a day for four or five days a week. He said Dr. Pignataro paid him periodically by check.

Tom said that some of his duties were to sterilize the surgical gowns and instruments and help the nurses set up the surgical trays. He was allowed to watch many operations, including breast augmentations. He agreed with the other witnesses that the breast patients were usually given pills and water upstairs, and then walked to the operating room in the basement. The doctor, Tom said, kept all medications in a safe, sending him or one of the nurses to get them. On occasion, he—or a nurse—had mixed them, but always with precise instructions from Dr. Pignataro.

As for machines to monitor the patients' condition, the

only machines Tom ever saw the doctor use during the operations were the pulse oximeter and the blood pressure cuff.

He recalled that during July Dr. Pignataro had gone to California to learn the new technique of inserting breast implants through the navel, and Tom said the doctor was very excited about it. He had bought some new equipment to tunnel under the skin. Pignataro never measured or marked the skin of a patient before he started cutting.

Sedita asked Tom about the pulse-ox machine. Tom said that he had been present two or three times when a patient's oxygen level had dipped below a 70 percent reading during surgery. When that occurred, the doctor had rapped the patient on the head or on the sternum and then had the patient given oxygen by a mask. But they always came back. He said the doctor was never worried if the reading was in the 80s. The men questioning him knew now that readings below 85 percent were dangerous.

For Sarah Smith's surgery, Tom recalled that it was Mrs. Pignataro who had become concerned about the patient's lack of oxygen, but that the doctor kept right on with his operation, not even glancing up. Debbie Pignataro had quickly put an oxygen mask over the patient and had tried to get her husband to check on Sarah. She sent Tom to get nail polish remover so they could see the color in Sarah Smith's nail beds more accurately. He brought it to her and then they could see that the patient's nail beds weren't pink, and her oxygen reading didn't go up.

Finally, the doctor had "broken scrub," gone to the patient's ear, and shouted at her to breathe. Mrs. Pignataro had frantically tapped her on the chest, but there was no response.

Tom felt that it had taken about ten to fifteen minutes while he was sent to look for things, and then the doctor had sent him up to find the Ambu-Bag. He had mistakenly grabbed one that was too small and was sent back for an adult size. By this time, he thought that either the doctor or Mrs. Pignataro was doing closed chest massage and the doctor was telling Janie to get the "shockers" ready.

But even with a bigger Ambu-Bag, Tom said the patient's lips were pale blue. She wasn't getting any oxygen. Tom said he tried to follow the doctor's directions to hold her jaw while the surgeon used a piece of metal that broke, and finally a coat hanger, to open an airway. And all this time, Janie was saying she didn't know how to use the "shockers."

"Did you see the heart monitor?" Sedita asked.

The boy shook his head. He had never seen any sign that either the EKG machine or the "shocking machine" were turned on.

Dr. Pignataro had shouted at his wife to call 911, but when she stood frozen, Tom said he took the initiative and made the call. When the paramedics arrived, they had taken over and put the patient in the ambulance.

The boy said that the doctor had located him later that day and warned him about what to say. Tom was to stress that he was only observing the operation. Anthony wanted him to say that he was employed by the clinic to answer phones. A few days later, Dr. Pignataro had called Tom and asked him, "Isn't the media coverage wild?"

Tom had no idea what to say to that.

Only a teenager, Tom Watkins had given them the most comprehensive report of anyone who had been there in that chaotic scene in the operating room.

This was definitely a different version than Anthony himself had written in his report, which was only three quarters of a page long. Whatever he lacked in technique in surgery, he made up for in his very professional-sounding report. He had always been good at making excuses and explaining away mistakes. In his report, his actions sounded entirely proper.

But as brilliant as the report sounded, it was very difficult to explain away a dead patient. Perhaps only a man who viewed the world as Anthony Pignataro did would have chosen to blame the patient. He covered it in his "biography."

"What could have gone wrong? What information that, if available preoperatively, could have prevented this tragedy? Sure, an overdose of herbals taken in an attempt to 'purge' one's system, leading to an extremely low potassium [count] could explain the events, yet one got the distinct sense that there was an unknown—an unknown that the husband may have well known."

Anthony even pondered that lawyers for Dan Smith were keeping everyone who knew the secret from talking.

"Several days later," Anthony wrote, still in Debbie's voice, "it was revealed that illicit drugs may have played a role in the patient's response to the sedation used during the surgery. The office manager reported an anonymous phone caller who stated that he/she felt that it was not fair the way the media was crucifying the doctor and that he [the doctor] should know that the patient had been partying with her boyfriend and doing cocaine the night before the surgery to celebrate her new breasts . . . I do not want to believe this. A brilliant mind and career [Anthony's] may have been sacrificed for this error in judgment. Yet, too many subsequent coincidences occurred to call it paranoia."

The Debbie voice in the unpublished memoir was vehement that *Anthony* had brought Sarah Smith back and started her heart beating again. He actually blamed the hospital and Dan Smith for pulling the plug on her respirator, and laid out a plot whereby a conspiracy connected to the Erie County D.A.'s office had begun a spurious investigation into his actions, whereas he, the surgeon, had tried so heroically to save Sarah.

"What had taken thirty-nine years to build," Anthony wrote, still using his wife's voice, "was destroyed in one week. Anthony was so bereaved that he could scarcely get out of bed in the morning."

Anthony quoted everyone from Kenneth Starr to the Bible to make his argument. He insisted that Sarah Smith had come to him with a defective heart and liver dysfunction, and that her own actions and those of her husband, the hospital where she died, and the District Attorney had brought him to the end of his career.

Reading Pignataro's manuscript isn't easy, because he continually changes narrators, usually writing as his wife but occasionally forgetting and slipping into his own voice. Anyone who talked with Debbie Pignataro could see that it was obvious, however, that Anthony had written every word. She didn't have his vocabulary, his knowledge of medical terms, or his hubris.

Anthony added yet another conspirator. His attorney had sent an unsolicited package of information on the case to the famed Dr. Michael Baden, former Chief Medical Examiner of New York City, an expert in forensic science, enclosing a check. The attorney didn't know that Baden was out of the country for an extended period. When Dr. Baden returned, he read only as far as Anthony's attorney's cover letter and knew this was not a case that he could confer on. Baden worked directly with the New York State Police, and any consultation on Pignataro's case would be a conflict of interest.

Baden returned the material unopened and sent a for check the full amount to Pignataro's attorney. (Baden's secretary had deposited all checks that came in to his bank account while he was out of the country.)

Nevertheless, Anthony created several scenes in his book in which Debbie had conversations with Baden. Debbie—using perfect medical terminology that never was and never would be part of her vocabulary—"wrote" of her many conferences with Michael Baden.

Anthony's mind, now approaching frank paranoia, believed that Dr. Baden had conspired with the Erie County D.A.'s office to bring about an indictment. Anthony wrote: "Did the doctor [Baden] believe that there was more career potential on the prosecutorial side of the fence?"

It was a laughable accusation. Dr. Michael Baden had already reached the pinnacle of his career as a forensic pathologist and had far more work to do than he could ever accept.

Although grand jury hearings are closed to the public, and testimony given there is not available to the press or the public, there were two main areas where the Erie County District Attorney's office felt Dr. Anthony Pignataro's care of Sarah Smith had been so far below accepted medical standards that they merited criminal charges. The administration of anesthesia had put the patient at an unacceptable risk, and the resuscitation efforts—or lack of them—were gross deviations from acceptable conduct.

And, of course, Anthony was outraged that anyone should ever come to those conclusions about him. He wrote of his shock that his story had received bigger headlines than Princess Diana's death, but he was secretly pleased. The media coverage was "wild," and he had always reveled in seeing his name in print and his face on television.

Still, as autumn came to western New York State and the orchard trees became heavy with fruit to be harvested,

Anthony had to be aware that both the Department of Health and the Erie County D.A.'s office were closing in on him. His office revenues were falling like stones from a cliff, and he knew he needed to keep paying his malpractice insurance. If he was forced to stop practicing, a patient could bring a retroactive malpractice suit against him for two and a half years after he closed down.

Including a suit filed by Dan Smith, fifteen other patients were now suing Dr. Anthony Pignataro. Others were charging back on their credit cards, refusing to pay him.

Although the Pignataros still lived in the duplex in West Seneca, Anthony was a big spender. He had his Lamborghini, he loved to travel, and he had taken yet another mistress. Tami Maxell* was in her early forties, an attractive woman with blond-streaked hair, and she regularly worked out at Gold's Gym, where Anthony did. She was a widow and a grandmother, but you couldn't tell that by looking at her. Tami owned a cleaning business, and she found Anthony exciting and attractive.

Debbie had undergone two surgeries on her injured neck already. She was coping with that, raising Ralph and Lauren, and trying to support Anthony as he bemoaned the disaster that had befallen him. Although she knew all too well of his past liaisons with other women, she didn't know about Tami. With her neck, Debbie couldn't exercise at the gym, and she naively assumed that Anthony had so many problems that he was far too busy to cheat on her again. Not now. Not when she was his staunchest ally.

That might not be exactly true. Anthony's mother, Lena, might qualify for that position. As far as Lena was concerned, Anthony could do no wrong. She implored Debbie to stick by him, no matter what. And Debbie promised that she would. Somehow, they would get through this—for their children's sake. Somehow, they would make a life again, even if Anthony couldn't be a doctor any more.

Anthony's mother invested money in a business Anthony thought might help restore their finances. He and Debbie would sell workout clothes through the mail. That venture never really got off the ground.

It seemed to Debbie that nothing else could go wrong. What had taken them so many years to build had collapsed in such a short time. All they had left was each other and their children. She counted on Anthony's strength to save them all.

13

For Frank Sedita, the turning point in the case against Anthony Pignataro in the death of Sarah Smith came when he met Dan Smith. "We were very hesitant about this case at first," he recalled. "We thought that maybe it was just a malpractice suit. When a doctor kills a patient, it's usually a civil suit that follows. But when we got into the investigation, we found out that his conduct was so incredibly egregious that it became a criminal case."

Hearing Dan Smith's story solidified Sedita's feelings. That the young husband had literally been shooed out of Pignataro's office by the doctor himself, believing that his wife was in good hands, only to return to find that she was comatose, was far more than a civil matter. Clearly, both Dan and Sarah Smith had been deluded and deceived, and they had been ultimately trusting. Now, their life together was gone.

Anthony had started with a malpractice attorney, Carmen Tarantino, representing him, but Tarantino soon saw that the case was far more than that and brought in another lawyer to help. Terry Cotters was a high-powered criminal defense attorney and had also advised Tom Watkins, the Nichols student.

The grand jury hearings continued. Sedita admitted later that he "raked Debbie Pignataro over the coals" as he sought to find out what her part, if any, had been in Anthony's operational procedures.

A long time later, Debbie said, "I'll tell you this. I'd much rather have Frank Sedita for me than have Frank Sedita against me!" She frowned as she remembered the assistant D.A.'s relentless questioning.

But grand jury hearings are secret. Buffalonians interested in the outcome would have to wait to see whether the infamous plastic surgeon would be indicted.

It was reported that a woman named Connie Vinetti was seen entering the grand jury room, but few knew that she, too, had suffered grievous injuries from a bungled tummy tuck and that Anthony had attempted to release her from Buffalo Mercy Hospital against medical advice when she was critically ill.

The outcome of the grand jury hearings was that Anthony Pignataro was indicted on six counts on January 27, 1998:

- Manslaughter in the second degree (for recklessly causing the death of a patient by asphyxia).
- Assault in the second degree (for recklessly causing serious physical injury by means of a dangerous "instrument"—drugs).
- Criminally negligent homicide.
- Falsifying business records in the first degree (for falsifying his report on Sarah Smith's operation).

- Reckless endangerment in the second degree (for attempting to discharge Connie Vinetti from the hospital).
- Criminal possession of a forged instrument in the third degree (for displaying a forged American Board of Otolaryngology diploma).

Anthony was baffled and outraged. Still writing in Debbie's persona, he used whole chapters of what was essentially his autobiography to rant about the blindness of justice and the venality and conspiracy practiced by the Erie County District Attorney's Office.

"One can never imagine the enormous emotional pain and pressure events such as these can put on a family," he wrote. "Anthony became ever more distant and retracted. He would lie awake at night trying to make sense of it."

So did Dan Smith, alone with two little children who had lost their mother, just as he had lost his wife.

There was no question that Anthony's family was suffering, although he scarcely took that into account except when he scribbled over his tortured chapters about his own innocence. Not only was he narcissistic, he was also bizarrely untalented as an author, with a forced and artificial writing style and little or no grasp of proper sentence structure. The kindest critique would say that he could at least spell.

Anthony's mother, his wife, and his children continued to support him emotionally during the long spring of 1998. He bemoaned the fact that the entire medical profession had not rallied around him, although he presented his attorneys with numerous letters from physicians who praised him while denouncing the State Board of Health and the District Attorney's office for hounding him.

* * *

There were, however, many doctors who either kept quiet or offered to testify against Anthony. Anesthesiologists in particular were outraged that Sarah Smith had died needlessly.

At one point, Anthony even became suspicious of his attorneys. They were urging him to consider a plea bargain. They tried to impress upon him that if he insisted on going ahead to trial, he could serve far more prison time than he might get if he pleaded guilty. Dan Smith was a most sympathetic accuser, despite his terrible loss. He had said he didn't want Anthony to be away from his family for years and years.

Sharon Simon was a victims' advocate who worked in the Erie County District Attorney's office. A warm-hearted smoky blond with startling green eyes, Sharon spent most of her days—and nights—helping victims and their families deal with the shock of loss. She virtually held their hands as she led them through the tortuous maze of the justice system, even though her heart ached for them and her dreams were haunted by the tragedies of strangers.

On the other hand, she had an infectious giggle when something struck her funny—which it often did, despite her job. Her best qualification for her career was that she was empathetic and human and had never become jaded by the horrors she saw every day.

She tried to prepare Dan Smith and Sarah's family for the ordeal of a trial. The Pignataro hearings and the trial that was surely imminent was a cause celebre for the media in Buffalo, and television cameras followed the participants on both sides as they entered and exited the courtroom. The Smiths and the Graftons were still reeling from Sarah's death; she had been gone only a short time.

Debbie Pignataro was not a victim—not in the eyes of the law. Anthony's family and his lawyers reminded her continually that it was essential for her to stand by her man. If she had her moments of doubt about his lack of concern for the young woman who died on his operating table, she didn't allow herself to dwell on it. Her mother-in-law, who had been her friend and supporter for many years, was always at her side, steering her to the court-room's front-row seats, which Lena had claimed as their own. Anthony beamed at her and clasped her hand; he was far more attentive than he had been in years. Sitting in the front row, bolstered by other people who still believed wholeheartedly in Anthony's innocence, Debbie felt a surge of hope.

Dan Smith and his father always sat in the last row of the courtroom. To Dan, it seemed that both Anthony Pignataro's mother and his wife glared at him during the legal proceedings. He tried to understand that they were afraid and that they must love their son and husband. Dan was a very kind young man, and he put himself in Anthony's place, unaware that empathy for other people was an emotion completely alien to the doctor who had killed his wife.

As the courtroom emptied after each session, Sharon Simon put her hand gently on Dan's arm, signaling to him and his father to wait. Predictably, the reporters and cameras followed Anthony and Debbie. Anthony handled their questions deftly, but Debbie was overwhelmed. Lena Pignataro reminded her to hold her head up, to stand loyally beside her husband.

The time for trial approached rapidly. At the last minute, Anthony listened to reason. He could not visualize himself spending years in prison—something that could very well happen if he were convicted in a trial. Even though he found it outrageous that a physician should be accused criminally just because he had the "bad luck" to lose a patient, his lawyers hammered at him. They couldn't be responsible for what might happen if his accusers propelled him to trial, or if he should take the stand—something they were convinced he would do.

As much as he longed to seize the witness chair and use it as a soap box to denounce those whose small minds couldn't grasp his talent and potential, Anthony agreed to do as his attorneys advised.

On June 8, 1998, he pleaded guilty to criminally negligent homicide before Judge Ronald H. Tills. He also agreed to withdraw all his pretrial motions, waived any right to appeal his sentence, and agreed to surrender all his licenses to practice medicine. Sentencing was set for August 4.

Still, he couldn't step back without making a statement, and his passionate words before he was sentenced would return to haunt him. He spoke, as always, of *his* pain: "The loss of one's patient will forever haunt any moral doctor. Whatever determination you may decree cannot be worse than this pain. This pain alone, I assure you, would be sufficient to deter any physician from making the same mistake in the future.

"But my pain is even greater than that. If you could see the look of disappointment in the eyes of my son . . . the look of fear in my daughter's eyes . . . If you could see the pain in my wife and my mother's heart . . . the disgrace in failing your [my] father's memory and reputation, you would know the pain I feel every moment."

And having learned that the judge was a Shriner, Anthony shamelessly threw in a quote from that organization to cinch his plea for a light sentence—or, preferably, no sentence at all.

He was shocked to hear himself sentenced to what Frank Sedita had requested: six months in jail, plus five years probation, 250 hours of community service, and a fine of $2,500.

The final ignominy came as he was handcuffed and led off like a common criminal. Debbie fainted. The television cameras caught it all. Anthony Pignataro was the first medical doctor in the region's long history to be convicted on a charge of criminally negligent homicide.

Debbie vowed to wait for Anthony so that they could try to rebuild their marriage. "I was an old-fashioned Italian wife," she recalled later. "I was there for Anthony, supporting him all the way. He made the decisions, and I went along with them."

What Debbie still didn't know was that another woman was also waiting for Anthony Pignataro.

14

Jail in the Erie County Correctional Facility in Alden, New York, was a profound shock for Anthony Pignataro. He was used to the best, and he considered himself to be among the upper echelon of society in intelligence and breeding. Now he was forced to mingle with the kind of people he had never associated with—except, perhaps, in his early residency years when he worked in the ER. But those people had been patients, not his peers in any sense. This prison world of walls and bars was totally alien to him, and he was afraid, although he also believed that he was savvy enough to get by on his charm.

"The prospects of going to prison," he wrote, "are

without a doubt the most fearful dilemmas one could imagine . . . Given the high profile nature of my case and the incredibly intense media coverage, it was anticipated that I would be a target for other inmates."

He didn't know the half of it. Con-wise prisoners salivate at the prospect of meeting a wealthy and infamous prisoner. Celebrity prisoners often have money to share, and they are ultimately naive about dealing with the inside of "the joint." A man like Anthony Pignataro was a pigeon to be plucked, even though he bragged that the guards were all on his side and were looking out for him. One guard, he said, even brought another prisoner to his cell with instructions to "show Tony the ropes."

Whether that was the way they met doesn't really matter, but Anthony soon looked upon fellow prisoner Arnie Letovich* as his friend and protector—a special angel to look over him. He never questioned why Arnie seemed to be looking out for him.

Some of the other prisoners, especially the African Americans, viewed Pignataro with genuine amazement. He wasn't allowed to wear his toupee inside, but he still had the metal screws protruding from his bald head. One of them became infected and had to be removed, so his head looked a little lopsided after that. The African-American cons dubbed him "Frankenstein" and figured he had to be just plain crazy.

Anthony bragged about how rapidly he fit in in jail. He felt he was popular and well liked, but he was careful not to cross invisible lines drawn by different groups. He had been assured that with time off for good behavior, he would have to serve only four months. It seemed a minuscule sentence for the life of a 26-year-old woman, but it was all the law could decree. Even so, four months seemed like four years to Anthony.

Like the other prisoners, he lived in an 8-by-12 foot cell that had a cot, a desk, a sink-and-toilet combination with a mirror made of shiny steel, all of it bolted to either the floor or the walls to prevent suicide attempts.

Anthony used his superior education to keep from "screwing up" and losing out on his two months of "good time."

"I was able to read, write, work out, and practice my faith," he wrote. "I made it my goal to adjust and befriend everyone."

From his own description of his activities in jail, he was the model prisoner. He studied in the law library an hour a day, and he finished twenty-two books during the time behind bars—a book a week. However, Anthony wasn't quite the paragon of perfection that he said he was. He needed items that weren't provided in prison—items that were, in fact, frowned upon.

Debbie had realized for a long time that her husband was "borrowing" the painkillers and tranquilizers her doctors had prescribed for her neck pain. And Anthony had held back most of the painkillers he prescribed for his surgery patients. Now, all his usual sources of drugs had dried up—and the jail mess hall didn't serve tequila.

He was pleasantly surprised to learn that Arnie Letovich could hook into an illicit chain that could bring heroin inside the walls. Heroin took the sharp edges off his worries and made doing time a lot easier. Heroin more than replaced the painkillers and tranquilizers he took before his imprisonment.

Ironically, he was also working on keeping in top physical shape. He jogged three miles around and around the yard each morning and spent his afternoons exercising. "I left that facility, at forty years old," he recalled, "in the best shape of my life."

For the record, he added pages to his journal about the "unbelievably dirty business" of drugs in prison, and mentioned that he was in the "wrong place at the wrong time" and was forced to observe some drug transactions in the yard. He wrote that he had tried to look away from all of this because it was none of his business. He was "afraid" of the tough guys who dealt drugs.

Anthony never lost touch with Debbie and his children, with his mother—or with his girlfriend. Like any prisoner, he could phone out as long as his collect calls were accepted. And they always were. His family visited him as often as they were allowed to, twice a week.

Ironically, this was the first time in a long time that Debbie knew where he was and whom he was with. But her earlier disillusionment with her marriage had begun to vanish, anyway. During his court hearings, and now locked up, Anthony was as loving and sweet as he had been almost twenty-five years earlier when they first started dating. She began to hope that they *could* start over. Anthony couldn't be a doctor any longer, but they would find something else. He had such a creative and inventive mind, she knew he would work his way to the top again. All he needed was some encouragement and the love of his family.

Tentatively, his children, Ralph and Lauren, started to write to him. He had never been the kind of father who had much time for his children beyond the occasional trip to the zoo, a boat ride in Florida, or a drive to buy ice cream. Now, they wrote to him almost every day, and he answered their letters. They began to look forward to the time when he would come home to them.

Anthony wrote that he knew that the national media were fighting to interview him, but he had wisely turned them away. Comparing himself to Amy Fisher, the "Long Island Lolita," in terms of public interest, he was afraid that the tabloids would "devour" him, too. "Sure she was guilty," he wrote of Amy. "But she was also a victim."

And he certainly considered himself a victim. The more law books he read in the prison library, the more convinced he became that the attorneys who had represented him had led him down the garden path. Even in his embryonic study of the law, he had found any number of legal loopholes they might have used in defending him.

All through Anthony Pignataro's journal, when he became too overwhelmed by his terrible luck and the unfairness of the justice system and the New York State Board of Health, he added a little wry comment that seemed to make sense to him, although its meaning was vague. He blamed his bad luck on timing:

"Well, this is the Nineties!!!"

Whatever illegal activities Anthony Pignataro might have engaged in in prison, he was not discovered. He won his two months' good time, and he was released on Friday, December 7, 1998, in time to spend Christmas with his family. Debbie was waiting, and his children were thrilled.

That first day, Anthony spent the whole afternoon watching videos of the junior high school football games Ralph had starred in while he was gone. Ralph was thrilled to see his father so interested. His team had an undefeated record, and Ralph was the quarterback. Although he was still thin and lanky, Ralph had broad shoulders, and he was an excellent athlete as well as a top student.

Lauren, a petite girl, was a budding gymnast, and her dad was enthusiastic about that, too. Debbie watched them all with tears in her eyes.

They went out to have a steak dinner with Lena, Antoinette, Ralph, and Lauren at Anthony's favorite restaurant, E.B. Green's. Debbie and Anthony decided to spend the weekend just getting to know each other again. Their new life would be different, Debbie agreed, but it didn't have to be worse.

When they talked of bad times in the past, Anthony and Debbie decided they would have a truly fresh start to their marriage. They would renew their wedding vows at St. Bonaventure, the same church where they had been married. They wanted to prove to each other that they really were starting over with a fresh slate.

Anthony wasn't drinking, and his time with his family was different now. He was really with them. He had 250 hours of community service to perform as part of his sentence, and he chose to volunteer at a therapeutic riding center for underprivileged and handicapped young people. He did such a good job that the director of the center wrote a glowing letter to the probation department, extolling his "responsibility, kindness, and tremendous work ethic."

Debbie paid off Anthony's $2,500 fine.

"Mom," Ralph said to Debbie during that first week of Anthony's freedom, "do you think we have a real dad now? He's not anything like he was before."

She wanted to believe that, too, probably more than her children did. But Anthony had been home only a week when Debbie got a letter that was so shocking she almost felt it burn in her hands. She read it over twice, disbelieving, and yet finding it all too familiar. All those years ago, when Ralph was only a baby, she had received the phone call from the girl who told her to look in the back seat of their car. And she had found the cards and the audiotapes that proved absolutely that her husband was having an affair. And there had been the "Moira incident" in Puerto Rico.

Debbie had forgiven Anthony twice. She had walked through fire for Anthony, and she believed now that they had come to a new place in their marriage.

But Debbie didn't know that Anthony had been having an affair with Tami Maxell even before he went to jail, and that he still was. Once more, she never knew exactly where he was, and it had always been easy for him to deceive her. Tami was older than Debbie and in good shape because she worked out regularly at Gold's Gym, Anthony's sports club.

This time, the letter in Debbie's hands wasn't from Anthony's mistress. It was from Tami's ex-boyfriend, who was obsessed with her and violently jealous of her affair with Anthony. She recognized the signature on the letter. Several strange phone calls had come to their house, but someone just hung up. Debbie had punched *69 after a few of them, and the name Sam Picone* and his phone number had come up. The name meant nothing to her. She had just assumed he was some kind of nut.

Picone was an attorney, and he evidently believed that misery loved company—or perhaps he wanted to make Anthony suffer the way he was suffering without Tami. He decided that the best way to get back at both of them was to tell Pignataro's wife.

It was a mean and sneaky thing to do, and it almost broke Debbie Pignataro's heart. Picone enclosed a letter that Anthony had written to Tami from prison.

Far more than most women, Debbie had clung to her marriage. But the letter in her hands proved that Anthony hadn't changed. She knew he never would change. All of her children's hopes that they finally had a "real dad" were going to be shattered. She had stood beside Anthony while he was accused and convicted, and she had visited him every chance she could. She had suffered such terrible humiliation and stress, answered all the hard questions in grand jury, and seen herself on the front pages of the Buffalo paper and on television news.

And it had all been because she still loved and trusted a man who was a liar and a cheat and an adulterer. This time, she couldn't go back.

But this time Debbie didn't explode in a rage or accuse Anthony of being unfaithful. She told him about the letter from Picone, but she let him believe that she was still the deluded, stupid wife. She was buying time, trying to figure out what was the best thing for her children. If she left Anthony, she didn't know whether she could support them. If she stayed, Ralph and Lauren could probably stay in Nichols School with their friends, and they could have their own home and their own rooms and a chance to go to college.

And as ashamed that she was to admit it, Debbie still loved Anthony—or perhaps she still clung to the way she wanted to love him.

The "honeymoon" period of their "new" marriage had lasted such a short time. Because she had pinned her hopes on a fresh start, it was harder for Debbie to accept that it was all a facade. Little shards of the shiny surface began to crack and fall away—just a few at first, and then they began to tumble until Debbie saw too much behind Anthony's mask as the reformed adulterer.

The pain in her heart hurt far more than the pain in her neck. She had endured four surgeries after the Florida boat accident, and none of them had completely taken away the pain. Now, she needed yet another operation on the discs in her neck.

Debbie was biding her time to protect her children's future, but Anthony proved to her almost at once that she couldn't count on him to work out their desperate financial problems. The Lamborghini was long gone, of course. But Anthony went out and bought her a new Cadillac to celebrate their remarriage.

"We couldn't afford a new car," she said, "much less a Cadillac. We had a van, and that was fine for us."

And, as it turned out, Anthony was the one who drove the Cadillac; Debbie still drove the SUV. He'd always believed that expensive and showy cars were necessary to make a man look successful.

But he wasn't successful in the least. Anthony had been unable to find a job in the months he had been home, and he wasn't trying very hard. They were rapidly running out of money. His mother helped him. Debbie never knew how much Lena gave Anthony, but she did note the regular withdrawals from their bank account almost every day, usually in the amount of a hundred dollars.

Anthony was on something—something more than tequila. She and the children all noticed it. He drank, yes, but the way he kind of zoned out and fell asleep in his chair made Debbie worry that he was on something much stronger than alcohol. When she added his odd behavior to the frequent bank withdrawals, she suspected drugs of some sort.

Debbie didn't know anything about heroin. Not then.

Anthony apparently didn't realize how utterly betrayed Debbie felt now that she knew about Tami. Arnie Letovich was out of jail, too, and the two had reconnected. Anthony spent his days working out in the gym, writing down his thoughts in his "book," spending time with Tami, or visiting Arnie. Tami often accompanied him to Arnie's place.

On February 26, 1999, Debbie passed the house where Tami lived and saw a Cadillac parked there—a Cadillac that looked exactly like Anthony's gift to her. She pulled in closer so she could read the license number, and saw that it was her Cadillac.

"I knew he was with her," Debbie recalled. "I was so mad that I parked the van and used my key to drive the Cadillac home. I was picturing the look on Anthony's face when he came out and saw the van there. I wanted him to know that he wasn't fooling me—that I knew where he was and who he was with."

She would have liked to have seen that look on Anthony's face when he came out and realized what had happened. But he was apparently too afraid to face her. He picked Ralph up at his ski club and dropped him off at home, but he didn't come in.

He called her later with the oldest excuse known to wandering husbands. "Debbie," he said fervently, "it isn't what it looks like . . ."

The perfect, passive Italian wife had finally come to a place where she could hang up on him. Anthony didn't come back. She told herself that she didn't care where he went or who he was with. But she still did care. She confronted Tami Maxell and asked her bluntly, "Are you sleeping with my husband?"

Tami fled without answering.

Debbie had the locks changed so Anthony couldn't come sneaking back in with more vows of love and commitment. She also cleared out their joint checking account, leaving him $5,000. She didn't talk to him when he called every day, but Ralph and Lauren did. She knew Anthony was back to his familiar pleading mode, telling them that he wanted to come home to be with his family.

But Debbie didn't relent. The locks stayed locked.

Anthony used the money he had left to get his own apartment in West Seneca. Although he called every day, he wouldn't give Debbie or their children his phone number. Debbie was sure that he was spending much of his time with Tami.

After her outrage subsided, Debbie Pignataro sank into a depression that was far worse than any she had ever known. She had been through a great deal in the first forty years of her life, but she had always managed to come back from grief and despair. Now, she wondered if she could do it again, knowing that there was no hope any longer for her marriage. It was as if all her losses were stacked one atop another in a tower of misery that had no stability, wavering in the slightest breeze. Just one more stress would surely make the whole structure collapse and fall down—and take Debbie with it.

Debbie was in recurring physical pain from her neck injury—pain that held her neck in a vise and shot down her arms to her hands. A solid night's sleep became impossible for her, and she was always tired. She put on the best possible face for Ralph and Lauren's sake, but it wasn't easy.

Debbie had been seeing a psychiatrist for a year—since a month after Anthony's indictment for Sarah Smith's death. And the therapist had told her what she already knew: she was suffering from anxiety and depression. She dreaded leaving her home and suffered from a mild case of agoraphobia, meaning "fear of the marketplace." And why wouldn't she, with cameras pointed at her and her husband's faces, with their names in the headlines day after day? Staying at home with the curtains pulled seemed so much safer than venturing out.

While Anthony was in prison, Debbie was alone during the darkness of night while the winter winds off Lake Erie screamed around the house. They had Polo to protect them, but she longed to have Anthony beside her. He had come home, and she had felt safe for only a week. Now she could never be sure where he was or who he was with.

Debbie's psychiatrist prescribed Xanax to quiet her anxiety and ease her depression. It took the edge off, but she still found it hard to sleep. Her exhaustion weighed on her.

Two days after Debbie discovered that Anthony was

seeing Tami, she took more Xanax than her prescription called for. Two pills didn't quiet her anxiety, and she took two more. Then, her mind dulled by a double dose but still racing, she unwittingly took more. It was not a suicide attempt; she was far too protective a mother and too devout a Catholic to even consider such a thing. She was just so tired . . .

The minute she swallowed the last tranquilizer, she realized she needed help. She called her mother and a friend.

Debbie was hospitalized very briefly on March 1, 1999, until the excess Xanax washed out of her system. She was relieved to be home again with her children, but the problems were still there—and growing worse. She could always count on her mother and her brother, although Anthony had managed to distance her from most of her extended family over the years.

And, somewhat surprisingly, Debbie could count on her mother-in-law. Lena Pignataro might be helping Anthony out financially, but she was furious with him for leaving his family. She had accepted Debbie as another daughter, and she doted on Ralph and Lauren. Lena thought it was disgraceful that her son was seeing some floozie, and she lectured him that he should go back to Debbie and the children.

In truth, Anthony was under far more pressure from his mother than he was from his wife. Lena was absolutely furious with him for leaving Debbie and Lena's beloved grandchildren. She sent him a scorching letter:

"I'm not playing games with you now or ever," she wrote. "You and your whore deserve each other. I hate you both.

"If you think you can do this to your family and get away with it, you are NUTS! . . . I will not let you hurt or scar my grandchildren. I will get even with you both before I die.

"Stop bothering daddy's friends. They don't need you and your whore. You don't deserve the Pignataro name."

Lena Pignataro told Anthony that she was writing him out of her will and that he was not to try to find out information about her buildings or even come to her funeral when she died. She planned to advise Debbie to sue him.

"I never thought I would say it but I'm glad daddy's gone," she wrote to her wayward son. "He can't see what you are doing to us."

Clearly, Lena's approach worked. Anthony came by to see Debbie and the children in March. She described their meetings as "distant." In April, he visited almost every day. To her surprise, they seemed to be getting along better. On April 21, she had a fifth surgery to relieve the pressure of a herniated disc in her neck. It eased her mind to know that Anthony was checking in on her and the kids.

Anthony confided to her that he had received a death threat letter. He said he'd kept it from her because he didn't want to upset her—but then he wanted her to know that they might all be in danger. Now Debbie wanted him to come back—she was so frightened.

It was a decidedly odd spring in West Seneca. As the months eased toward summer, vandals attacked the Pignataro house and property. Someone wrote "KILLER KILLER KILLER" on the sliding glass doors that led to the patio on the back of their house and "DIE FUCKER!" on the fence.

When Debbie told Anthony about the vandalism, he told her they had to take the threats seriously. It might just be stupid teenagers, or it might be someone with a more serious grudge against them. He said he had picked up the phone while he was there and heard someone who snarled "You will die!"

It was frightening to think that even though Polo was

there at the house, the vandals had managed to creep all the way to the patio door.

Debbie felt safer when Anthony visited.

Anthony applied for a job in Philadelphia. It was a position in a profession that Judge Tills had specifically ruled out in Anthony's sentence after Sarah Smith's death: the medical field.

But Anthony had always abided by his own rules and no others. With the family, he drove to Philadelphia and had what he considered a most encouraging interview. On April 28, 1999, he wrote to the vice-president of a surgical care product line located in a veterans' medical center.

"I want to thank you and your board for the courtesy you extended to me yesterday. I truly enjoyed the opportunity to present myself and my credentials.

"I also took the opportunity to take a short self-guided tour and talk with some of the staff. I was extremely impressed with the facility and its personnel. My family and I also enjoyed Philadelphia and the Zoo.

"I truly hope that we will be able to pursue this position in the future. I look forward to hearing from you soon.

"Respectfully,

"Anthony S. Pignataro, M.D."

"We never went to the zoo," Debbie remembered. "He was lying again."

He did not hear from the company about his application to become a manager. Although he intimated in his letter that he was new to Philadelphia, he had a rather unsavory history there from his days as a resident. He also added the M.D. to his name—a title he no longer was allowed to claim. In the era of computers, that would have been easy to check.

In May, Anthony asked Debbie if he could stay

overnight. Debbie felt protected when he was there, and she hadn't been sleeping well at all with the stealthy attacks on their property during the night. She asked him if he was still seeing Tami, and he assured her that that was completely over. Debbie and Anthony slept together in their own bedroom, and to her it seemed right.

Anthony reported the vandalism and threatening phone calls to the police. Although they failed to identify any suspects, they kept an open file on it.

Oddly, the suspect the West Seneca police kept coming back to made no sense. Polo barked at any stranger who approached the Pignataro house, but there was one person the big dog adored and trusted even when it was pitch-dark out, even if that someone came upon him unexpectedly.

And that was Anthony Pignataro himself.

15

On May 9, Debbie suffered such excruciating stomach pains that she had to go into the ER. The doctors felt that she was having an attack of acute pancreatitis. Her symptoms subsided, and she was allowed to return home.

It wasn't unusual for her to vomit and suffer from stomach pains; she had had bouts of nausea and pain since the first of the year, and she assumed that was just her way of responding to extreme stress.

But the stress and worry went on and on. Debbie's children were the most precious people in her world; she would walk over hot coals for them. Perhaps because she had lost two babies, she was understandably protective of Ralph and Lauren. She worried about their safety.

First there were the vandals and the phone threats, and then the most terrifying thing of all occurred. A disturbed student at Ralph's school had apparently harbored deep hatred for several of his fellow students. A note, allegedly written by this boy, outlined his plan to smuggle a gun into school in his violin case. He wanted to eliminate his enemies and then kill himself. He had a list of the students he had targeted. Ralph's name was fourth on that list.

The note describing the planned attack had been intercepted in time, and the student was referred to counseling. But adding this aborted horror scene to the injustices he believed had been done to him and his family, Anthony blamed it all on the media and somehow on the justice system. He told everyone who would listen that he and his family were being harassed and threatened continually. He vowed to protect them.

In steady increments, Anthony had moved all the way back in with Debbie, Ralph, and Lauren. By July 1999, he had all of his clothes and belongings out of his apartment and into the duplex in West Seneca.

Debbie's expectations were nowhere near as high as they had been six months earlier when she and Anthony had their second wedding ceremony. "His mother made him move back, I think," she said. "If he hadn't come home, she was going to cut off his money, and he couldn't have that happen."

Anthony seemed to be trying to be nice to them, but it was hard to believe in him.

As for Anthony, he said he still felt edgy, believing that someone stalked them constantly—someone who watched their windows after the sun set. He blamed the planned student massacre, the event that was more than he could stand.

"This was the straw that broke the camel's back. We resolved that if there was any chance for reconciliation and healing that we needed to get out of the area."

All of Anthony's siblings now lived in Florida. His sister, Antoinette, was a physician there, and his brothers owned several Dairy Queen franchises. Anthony told Debbie that they would create a good job for him if only he could get the judge to grant him permission to leave the State of New York.

He was on felony probation, and if they were going to move to another state, his probation would have to be transferred. He hadn't bothered to consult Judge Tills about the job he sought in Pennsylvania; that was close enough to Buffalo that he might have been able to pull it off and still see his probation officer for his scheduled visits.

Now, he consulted an attorney who told him there should be no problem at all obtaining permission for him to move from New York State. But New York State said no. Judge Tills declined his request. The Department of Corrections and the District Attorney's office believed it would be too easy for Pignataro to disappear from the probation system if he moved so far away. Perhaps they all realized that Anthony was very familiar with Puerto Rico and that he might be planning to slip across the water from Florida. Indeed, if he got to Puerto Rico, he might even reestablish himself as a physician.

Debbie would have gone with him if Anthony had received a nod from the judge to move, but she dreaded the thought of leaving her mother and her brother's family behind. She was relieved when Anthony didn't get permission to go.

"What I didn't know then," Debbie would recall, "was that if we had moved to Florida, I would be dead now. There's no question in my mind that I wouldn't be here."

It is almost impossible for anyone who has not been the target of domestic violence—either physical or emotional—to understand just how many breakups and reconciliations have to take place in combative marriages before the battered party finally manages to separate for good. One support group for victims of domestic violence points out that it takes an average of *eleven* separations before a final split occurs. And it doesn't matter how intelligent or well-educated the victim is. Domestic abuse crosses all demographic boundaries. Friends and relatives often throw up their hands in frustration and disgust when they see one spouse, usually the wife, forgive and forgive and forgive. *Why can't she see what's right in front of her eyes? Why can't she show a little backbone? She's too good for him.*

But they haven't been there.

Tragically, some abused husbands or wives don't leave the relationship alive. Plans were already in place for Debbie Pignataro to become one of those casualties. But in the spring of 1999, no one could have convinced her of that. She had been systematically programmed over too many years to stay. As long as Anthony could persuade her—even a little bit—that he was sincere, it was still impossible for her to walk away from her marriage, even though it had become only a brittle shell of what she had once believed it was.

The comfortable living she and Anthony had finally achieved had long since been shattered. Debbie worked that spring as a receptionist in a pediatrician's office. It was the only income they had beyond help from Lena Pignataro, who seemed to have forgiven Anthony for his fall from grace with Tami. Like Debbie, she believed that her son was no longer seeing his mistress.

Anthony had failed to find a job. He complained that he could have worked for Dairy Queen if only Judge Tills had allowed him to go to Florida. He would be working with his brothers, and there was dignity in that. No one should expect him to apply for just any job. No one could ask a man who had trained to be a medical doctor to work in a bank or deliver pizzas.

By the time Anthony moved back home in July, their financial situation was desperate. Debbie couldn't work any longer. She was ill. It wasn't her neck; she had worked right through constant neck pain for years. At first she thought she had a really bad case of stomach flu, but her symptoms went on and on.

After her visit to the ER and her very tentative diagnosis of pancreatitis, she never felt really well. Throughout June, Debbie continued to feel sick to her stomach. She could no longer blame it on the flu; her illness had gone on too long. She didn't think it was psychosomatic, either, because on the surface, things were far better than they had been a few months earlier. Anthony hadn't left her after all. He had been virtually living with the family for weeks before moving back for good. No, she couldn't attribute her queasiness to sorrow over a broken marriage.

But she felt worse all the time. Debbie had severe pains in her abdomen, and it was bloated and distended. She vomited a lot. It became difficult for her to hold down any nourishment at all.

Over the years, Caroline Rago had usually come to visit her daughter and grandchildren on weekends. Debbie and Caroline had made it a habit to shop for groceries together at Tops or Wegmans supermarkets. Now, most of the time, Debbie was too sick to go. Caroline went alone, and Anthony would run to the store for a few things, although he didn't really like to shop for groceries.

He didn't like to cook much, either—unless it was something special that he could make into a big production. And they couldn't afford special foods any longer.

When Debbie was able to cook, she didn't prepare anything very exotic. At the time she first became ill, in May 1999—when she started having serious digestion problems—Debbie was the cook. "Then we had pasta, chicken, steak, hamburgers, salads." She cooked her own pasta sauce most of the time. Anthony didn't always like what Debbie served, and he often made an omelette for himself.

Debbie rarely drank alcohol. She occasionally had a wine cooler. Actually, she preferred Kool-Aid or juice. Anthony, however, was still a heavy drinker. "He drank tequila every day in May," she recalled.

In June, Debbie began to feel worse. Some days she lay in bed and could barely lift her head off the pillow. "I had good days and bad days," she said. But she couldn't come up with any common denominator that might explain why her sickness came and went. The fact was that she never felt really well any more.

On the days when she couldn't get up, Anthony cooked, or at least he made sandwiches for Ralph and Lauren and brought her Kool-Aid or some ice cream or sherbet. Debbie decided there had to be something the matter with her taste buds. Food just didn't taste right any more—sherbet in particular. She had always liked it, especially on hot days, but now it had a weird kind of metallic taste that stayed on her tongue as if she had licked a tarnished silver spoon.

Ralph and Lauren ate the sherbet, too, but they didn't find anything wrong with it. Debbie complained to Anthony that hers tasted like tin or iron or something like that, and she pushed it away half-eaten.

He stared at her oddly as if she might be losing her mind, but he didn't comment.

Some time in June, Debbie realized that she was having trouble remembering things. It was difficult for her to tell one day from another; they all blended into one endless blur of feeling sick. When she was able to get out of bed, she would walk into a room in her house and then forget what it was she wanted to do there.

One day, something happened that really frightened her. She left the house, walked half a block away, and entered the home of a neighbor she barely knew. The woman was in her kitchen and looked up to see Debbie standing there. She was startled, and Debbie was completely baffled. She had no idea at all why she was there, and she was embarrassed.

She didn't know what was the matter with her. She tried to figure out why she was forgetting so much and why she felt so sick all the time. Maybe that was what pancreatitis did to you. But if she really had an inflamed pancreas, surely Anthony would know. After all, he was still a doctor—at least in her eyes. If she had something really wrong with her, Anthony should be able to figure it out. But he didn't seem to have any answers either.

Anthony had moved the last of his belongings back to the Pignataro home in West Seneca as Buffalo baked in early summer. Debbie had marked the date—June 30—on her calendar. Then, she had expected everything to get better. But her condition had only deteriorated. She had worked just three or four days during the first week of July and then become far too sick to go in.

Although she was having trouble walking, Debbie sometimes managed to fix a light breakfast for Lauren and Ralph, but only dry cereal and orange juice. The thought of anything heavier made her nauseated. Most of the time, Debbie ate nothing for breakfast, but sometimes she tried to drink orange juice. It tasted like metal, too, and she spat it out.

She looked at the carton, and it wasn't outdated. It was the same orange juice she always bought at Tops or Wegmans. But it tasted so odd. Once again, Debbie complained to Anthony that *everything* tasted funny to her.

And once again, he stared back at her, saying nothing, as if she wasn't making sense. Maybe she wasn't.

When doctors or attorneys asked her later about what happened in July and August 1999, Debbie looked at them blankly. She simply could not access many of those memories. She didn't remember what happened. Again and again, her answer was "I don't know" or "I don't remember."

Fortunately, other records existed. Her physicians' files showed that on July 21, Debbie was back in the hospital. This time, the diagnosis of pancreatitis was firm. She had all the symptoms: nausea, severe stomach pain, and noticeable bloating of her abdomen. She was very, very ill.

But Debbie shook her head when doctors asked her what she had eaten. She couldn't remember. The month of July was one long gray mystery to her. She didn't know what she had eaten, or what Anthony, Lauren, and Ralph had eaten. Her mother came on weekends and cooked, and Anthony cooked every night.

When asked if she cooked supper, Debbie said no. She didn't know if the family had pasta or fish or meat, or if Anthony made the children sandwiches for lunch. She had no idea what she herself had eaten. "I was not at the dinner table . . . I was upstairs in bed."

Pressed, Debbie thought she might have eaten soup or perhaps crackers. She thought it might have been Lipton's chicken noodle soup, the dehydrated kind that came in a package to be added to boiling water. She liked that brand,

and it was easy to fix. How many times had she eaten it? "I don't know," she said wanly. "I don't remember."

Debbie did recall one day in July because Anthony was nicer to her than he had been in months. "I came downstairs to make myself some soup, and he said, 'No, no—I'll do it,' and I said, 'What?' He said, 'No, you go lie down. I'll do that for you.' I asked him, 'What's the change? Why are you doing this?' And he said, 'I can't be an asshole my whole life.'

"He must have brought most of the pan of soup to me in this huge bowl, and I told him I couldn't eat it, and he said, 'No, eat it. Eat it. It's good for you.' "

Debbie tried. She ate some of the chicken noodle soup that he made for her, but she couldn't keep it down long. Later, when Debbie came downstairs, she saw that Lauren was eating the soup that was left in the pan.

Anthony had gone to play baseball, so Debbie drove Lauren to gymnastic practice. She could still do that if she drove slowly and very carefully.

Debbie's biggest concern was for her children, and she did remember that Lauren had dished up a little bowl of the same soup for herself. That was the only kind of soup Lauren liked. A few hours later, when she was at the gymnastic meet, Lauren got sick, too, and threw up. She had to come home. Debbie managed to drive there and pick her up.

Later in July, there was no longer any question of Debbie looking after her family, driving, or visiting neighbors. She didn't know what her family was eating. Debbie was upstairs in bed most of the time, or on the couch. She no longer ate with her family, or ate much of anything. Sometimes she had a few spoonfuls of soup or just a few crackers. Everything tasted peculiar to her.

During Debbie's hospital visit on July 21, when her stomach pains were so bad that she could barely sit up, she didn't come home right away. She was admitted for tests and remained at South Buffalo Mercy Hospital until July 25. Her diagnosis of pancreatitis of "unknown etiology" meant that the doctors didn't know what had caused her pancreas to become inflamed. There could be numerous causes, and one of them was drinking too much alcohol. But Debbie hadn't touched liquor for months. If that was the cause, *Anthony* was the one who should have been in the hospital; he was drinking enough tequila to pass out most nights.

Debbie was home from July 25 until August 10, but she had no memory of that time. Her neighbors did. Her mother did. Caroline Rago was worried sick about her daughter, but she was not a confrontational woman—she never had been. If she asked Anthony too many questions, he might tell her she couldn't come into his home on the weekends, and she wanted to be there as often as she could to take care of Debbie and oversee the children.

Anthony had a way of dismissing questions from other people. After all, *he* was the doctor. If he thought Debbie needed medical attention, he would certainly see to it.

Debbie had a lot of friends along their street, although Anthony wasn't very convivial with the neighbors. His personality grated on a lot of them, particularly after a neighborhood meeting to discuss the construction of a Wilson Farms Store. The 24-hour convenience store would change the ambience of the area, and the neighbors gathered to discuss the pros and cons.

"Anthony got up and took over the meeting," one resident recalled. "Yes, his dad built our street, but he acted so superior, and he actually accused the people who didn't side with his views of being 'hired actors.' That didn't sit well with a lot of people."

Another neighbor was annoyed when he came into her

kitchen as she cooked dinner. "I was making souvlaki, and he reached into the pan with his bare fingers and started eating slices of beef. It was so rude, not to mention unsanitary."

One of Debbie's close friends was a woman who had lived a few houses down the block for eight years: Rose Gardner*. Rose invited her to attend a Tupperware party on Friday, August 6. Debbie had promised Rose she would be there, but she didn't show up. This was so unusual for Debbie that Rose came by to check on her the next day, concerned because Debbie had been sick for so long and seemed to be getting worse. She could see that her friend was very sick.

When Debbie was hospitalized on July 21, Rose had asked Anthony how she was. "He was very nonchalant," she recalled. "He said, 'Oh, she'll be all right—she just has a little virus.' I didn't question him because he was a doctor, but it seemed like he was always blaming Debbie's illness on one virus or another."

Rose was a petite woman whose slender figure belied the fact that she had borne six children. She took care of her home and flower garden and homeschooled her children, too, while managing to look as spic and span as her home. Rose was a devout Catholic and a very compassionate woman, but she wasn't afraid to speak up when something bothered her. There came what she called "a defining moment" when she had to say something.

It was Sunday, August 8, when Rose came to see Debbie again. She was horrified to see her friend propped up in a recliner chair in the corner of the living room. Anthony was lying on the living room couch with the TV remote in his hand.

"I looked at Debbie, and my heart just sunk. It was like looking at my mother-in-law, whom I had just lost," Rose said with a shudder. "It was the look of death—that's the only thing I can say to you. She was swollen, puffy."

As Rose moved closer to Debbie she saw that she was chalky pale, with huge purple circles beneath her dark eyes.

Debbie made no move to get up and offer her a cup of coffee or an iced tea—something she always had done. Rose realized that Debbie probably couldn't get up, but she insisted on giving Rose a check for her Tupperware order.

"She couldn't even hold a pen," Rose remembered. "It was just awful. She spoke to me, but her words were slurring, and I had trouble understanding her.

"I was so worried about her; she was so sick," Rose said. "I asked Anthony if she shouldn't be in the hospital, and he told me that she was better off at home, because hospitals weren't very well staffed over weekends. He said, 'I'm a doctor. Don't you think I would know what's best for her? She's much better off under my supervision.'"

Rose tried to argue with Anthony a little, but he dismissed her concern.

"When I went home, I cried," Rose recalled. "I told my husband that Debbie looked so bad that I was scared. I said, 'She looks like Ma did—just before . . . And I *was* scared. Debbie looked so bad, so bloated and funny, and she wasn't at all like herself."

Anthony's lack of concern was remarkably similar to his response to Connie Vinetti, the woman who developed a dangerous infection after he performed a tummy tuck on her, and not that different from his slow response when Sarah Smith stopped breathing. But this was his own wife. And still he lay on the couch watching television as Debbie sat so still in the recliner. To everyone else who saw her, she appeared to be dying, but he brushed their fears away. He was not concerned, and he refused to be rushed into taking her back to the hospital.

Debbie could barely walk. Her legs, feet, and hands were alternately numb and painful. Her stomach screamed with pain, and she was beyond nauseated.

Finally, finally, Anthony agreed to take her to see a doctor the next day. Caroline stayed with the children, anxious to hear from Debbie what the doctors had said. But Anthony came home alone. He told Caroline that Debbie was having tests at the hospital and he'd pick her up later. He did—but as Debbie tried to walk to her front door, she fell heavily. Caroline was frightened to see how she had failed over the space of a few days.

"I called her brother to tell him something was wrong," Caroline said. "Debbie was *crawling* because she couldn't walk. She was wobbling when she tried to stand up."

Caroline Rago was frantic, and so was Debbie's brother, Carmine. Anthony thought they were all overreacting. He greeted Carmine with his usual joking: "Hi, big guy!"

Anthony explained that Debbie probably had only the flu or something like it, and the tests would prove that. He didn't seem at all alarmed and thought everyone else was being somewhat hysterical.

Dr. Jahangir Koleini was Debbie's attending physician for the tests she had done that Monday in August 1999, with Dr. M. Reeza Samie consulting. Dr. Samie was called in because Debbie was having new symptoms: numbness and clumsiness in her right hand. After Dr. Samie examined her, she encouraged Debbie to return to the hospital.

But Anthony didn't want her to be admitted. He assured the examining physicians in the ER that all she needed was more pain medication. He would take her home and see that Debbie took her pills. He was sure she would be fine.

But she wasn't. Even Anthony's aversion to having Debbie hospitalized was overcome that night, and she was back in Buffalo Mercy the next morning.

What Anthony didn't know was that another doctor had been monitoring Debbie's condition for weeks. Dr. Michael Snyderman, a hematologist whose specialty was the blood and the blood-forming organs, had done a bone marrow test on her during one of her earlier hospitalizations. Snyderman found the results so bizarre that he wondered if Debbie might be suffering from some kind of poisoning. He spoke to Anthony on August 9 and asked that he bring Debbie in for more blood tests. But he didn't even hint at poisoning. He said only that he wanted to test for a condition known as porphyria.

When Dr. Snyderman told Anthony that he felt Debbie should really be in the hospital at once, Anthony said that he would have to consult with Drs. Samie and Koleini and see what they thought. That struck Snyderman as a patent lie; he had already consulted with them, and they had agreed with him that she needed to be in the hospital as soon as possible.

Finally, Anthony agreed to bring Debbie in to be admitted. Debbie's in-patient records began somewhat routinely, written, as all medical records are, without emotion.

"The patient is a 42-year-old white married female with history of recurrent episodes of major depression and pancreatitis two weeks ago. She was admitted to the hospital because of increasing ataxia on standing, distal sensory loss, and sluggishness of the ankle and knee reflexes. Two weeks ago, the patient had an episode of pancreatitis and about four days prior to admission the patient started to have the gradual onset of tingling, numbness and clumsiness of her hands and lower extremities. The patient was seen by Dr. Samie as an outpatient prior to admission and had an MRI of the brain done which was normal."

For the layperson, this meant that Debbie's history of crippling stomach pain now had new symptoms that didn't seem to tie into inflammation of the pancreas. The new symptoms had come on quite suddenly. She couldn't feel her hands and feet, and the tingling sensations had progressed to numbness and inability to pick up anything with her hands without dropping it or tipping it over. She did have the history of many surgeries to her neck, which could have caused numbness in her arms and hands, but her other symptoms couldn't be explained by cervical disk problems.

Once admitted to Buffalo Mercy, she could be given a whole array of tests to try to find out what was wrong with her.

What *was* wrong with Debbie Pignataro? Was it possible that Dr. Snyderman was right? Was it possible Debbie was being poisoned?

16

It was the hottest time of the year in Buffalo, and the towering snow drifts of winter seemed years away. Rose Gardner's flowers wilted and began to dry up as the neighbors watched the Pignataro house, saw Anthony come and go, and wondered aloud about how Debbie was doing. They had heard that she could not have visitors. Rose lit candles and said prayers for Debbie, even though she believed it would take a miracle for Debbie to survive. She was convinced that she would probably never see her again. There had been such a pallor of death about her the last time Rose saw her.

In the vineyards, the grapes hung heavy on their vines, and the apple and pear trees began to ripen. Wild berry pickers moved deep into the brush. Soon, the familiar roadside stands would be stocked with enough produce to make it worthwhile to leave downtown Buffalo and drive to outlying areas. Chuck Craven played golf, and the tourists flocked to both the American and the Canadian sides of Niagara Falls.

The best part of summer meant nothing to Debbie Pignataro as she lay on snowy white sheets in a darkened room. Her world was limited now to four hospital walls. Doctors struggled to diagnose her condition, ignoring Anthony, who assured them that there was really nothing wrong with his wife beyond a somewhat complicated case of gallstones.

They considered all possibilities. She had no history of diabetes; she had no history of alcohol abuse. Her temperature was 98.3, but her pulse raced at 120 beats a minute. Her blood pressure was 110/60 (ideal for an athlete in good condition).

As they listened to her heart and took her pulse, they asked questions, and she seemed alert. They didn't know that she would soon have no memory of what they had asked her. When she spoke, her words were clearly understandable. She had no head wounds; her ears, nose, and throat were fine. Her jugular vein didn't stick out, and the carotid arteries on either side of her neck had no ominous sounds when they placed their stethoscopes there. Her heart rhythm was normal; her lungs sounded normal.

They kept searching. The membranes in her eyes were a

little pale. She was anemic. She suffered from leukopenia—a very low white cell count, usually caused because new cells weren't being formed. Although her muscle tone was normal, she did have that lack of strength and the strange tingling and numbness in her hands and feet, more on the right side than the left. There were no deep tendon reflexes in her knees or ankles. The reflexes in her feet were normal enough to assure them that she hadn't suffered brain damage.

And yet, she staggered almost drunkenly when she tried to walk.

At this point, there were any number of diseases and conditions that had to be considered. In New York State, she could have been bitten by a deer tick and have developed Lyme disease, but she said she hadn't been out in the woods for months. She hadn't traveled to any other area where she might have contracted some disease. They had to rule out Guillain-Barré syndrome, a disease that can come on suddenly and completely paralyze a formerly healthy person—a malady that usually reverses itself in time.

The lab tests took longer than the questions and answers and the observation of skilled doctors. When the results came back, more possibilities were eliminated. A spinal tap produced crystal clear fluid. No meningitis.

There remained that one diagnosis that Dr. Snyderman didn't want to be right about: the diagnosis that most doctors don't turn to until all other options have been considered. They approached it gradually, asking Debbie if she was a gardener. When she said "Yes," they wondered if she had used toxic chemicals to kill weeds. She had, but she was stunned when they asked her if she had swallowed any. *Of course not.* And she hadn't ingested any rat poison, insect killers, or preservatives, either.

Had she ever worked where someone used heavy

metal poisons, or had she ever been exposed to them, to her knowledge? *No.*

But the blood tests and the urinalysis came back with a shocking result. Debbie Pignataro's 24-hour collection of urine showed that it contained arsenic at an almost unheard-of level: *29,580 micrograms per liter.*

To put that in context, it's necessary to know that we all have some percentage of arsenic in our systems, normally deposited through the environment. Soil has small amounts, and most seafoods—especially clams and oysters—have minute concentrations of the poison. Fuel oils and coal emit arsenic into the air when burned, and of course many weed killers and insecticides have arsenic as a component. Most humans have between 5 and 20 micrograms per liter of arsenic in their entire blood supply. It's nothing to worry about.

In 1998, according to the American Association of Poison Control Centers' (AAPCC) Toxic Exposure Surveillance System, there were 956 non–pesticide-related arsenic exposures with four fatalities, and 399 arsenic-containing pesticide exposures with *no* fatalities reported. Mystery writers often use arsenic as a way to kill characters; in real life, it is rare.

Blood arsenic concentrations should not exceed 50 micrograms per liter. In patients with arsenic poisoning, the blood arsenic concentrations usually range from several hundred to several thousand. But Debbie had 29,580 micrograms per liter of arsenic in her body, considerably more than even "several thousand." Indeed, that was far more than any of her doctors had ever seen—or heard of. She was alive, and she didn't seem to be in severe pain as long as she lay very, very quietly in her bed.

Every one of her symptoms made sense now. The numbness of her hands and feet was classic for chronic exposure to arsenic: it was glove or stocking paresthesia, in which the deadening of sensation perfectly fits the area where a person wears gloves or stockings. Her vomiting, diarrhea, and pain were signs of acute exposure. She apparently had swallowed both large and small doses of arsenic.

The rule of thumb for causes of arsenic exposure is almost always homicidal, occupational, or suicidal. Debbie had been horrified when her doctors asked her if she had taken poison deliberately. How could they even think she would do something like that? She would never, never leave her children. No, she was not suicidal. There was absolutely no occupational or avocational link between her and arsenic.

That left only the possibility that someone was trying to kill her. Nobody pointed that out to her. She was too sick and too upset for them to even think of bringing such a subject up.

Whatever the source of Debbie's massive poisoning, treatment had to begin at once. The preferred method of getting arsenic out of her system is chelation therapy. Debbie would be given capsules of Succimer (DMSA), an agent that would bind with the heavy metal of the arsenic in her bloodstream and render it weaker and weaker as it left her body, but she had so much arsenic in her body that they wondered if it wasn't too late. It would take nineteen days of chelation therapy to go through the whole course of Succimer treatment.

Somehow, Debbie had been poisoned with one of the most infamous poisons known to man—and yet, for the moment, she was alive. It would take a while to see how much permanent damage had been done to her liver, kidney, and heart functions.

Anthony doubted the diagnosis, and he didn't tell anyone about it. Instead, he demanded that Debbie have surgery to take out her gallbladder. That, he insisted, was her real problem. Until that happened, he was convinced that she wouldn't get well.

And her doctors looked at him, amazed. For her to undergo any kind of surgery in her condition would be akin to signing her death warrant. She probably wouldn't live long enough to waken from surgery. They stonewalled his demands.

With the diagnosis of arsenic poisoning by some unknown cause, it was mandatory for the Erie County District Attorney's office to be notified. Frank Sedita, Chuck Craven, and Pat Finnerty were not really surprised that they were hearing about Anthony Pignataro and a patient in critical condition only eight months after his release from prison. All kinds of possibilities came to mind. The wild card was that the patient was Pignataro's own wife— the same wife who had stood beside him with unflinching loyalty when he was investigated for Sarah Smith's death.

One of Sedita's strongest memories was a phone call from the Poison Control Center. "They asked me when the patient's funeral was," he recalled. "And I said, 'There is no funeral—she's alive.' They couldn't believe it. It was unheard of that anyone could have more than 29,000 micrograms per liter of arsenic in them and be alive. But Debbie Pignataro was."

Debbie had both disliked and feared Frank Sedita when he cross-examined her in the grand jury after Sarah Smith's death, but now he was on *her* side—although she didn't know that yet.

And so were Chuck Craven and Pat Finnerty. The two D.A.'s investigators had great expertise in any number of areas, but they had never worked on an arsenic poisoning case before.

"Both of us are interested in finding out new ways to

investigate," Craven recalled, "and we learn wherever we can. We're always watching shows like *Justice Files* and the Discovery channel documentaries on television. And we found a lot of information on the Internet. We played catch-up fast on arsenic."

There was a great deal of information on the Internet about poisons. Sedita, Craven, and Finnerty read everything they could find about arsenic poisoning. They learned that it is tasteless and odorless and that its crystals look like sugar. Absorption occurs primarily through the digestive tract, although some arsenic can be taken up through the skin. Once arsenic is in the body, it binds to hemoglobin, plasma proteins, and white blood cells and is then carried to the liver, kidneys, lungs, spleen, and intestines. After a few weeks, arsenic deposits can be found in the skin, hair, nails, bone, muscles, and even the nervous tissues. Ingestion of arsenic often leaves white marks on the fingernails, called "Mees' lines."

"We learned how to check for arsenic deposits by watching one of the *Justice Files* shows," Craven said. "You can find it by taking hair cuttings, fingernail cuttings, and urine samples. You can almost date the times the victim was given arsenic—particularly when they've been given large amounts."

Although they couldn't really question Debbie at the moment—she was fighting for her life—they would have heard answers that rang true for arsenic poisoning. Those with acute exposure suffer from nausea, vomiting, and diarrhea. They have low blood pressure and a rapid heart rate, and they may complain of a metallic taste in their mouths. Some have a garlic odor on the breath.

An armed guard was placed outside Debbie's room in Buffalo Mercy Hospital, and her visitors were carefully monitored. Anthony was her most faithful visitor, hovering next to his wife's bed.

Rose Gardner was surprised to find Anthony at her door the Thursday after Debbie was admitted to the hospital. He asked her if she had a Bible. Of course she had a Bible.

"Anthony said he needed to look up a certain passage of scripture. It was the part about 'An eye for an eye, a tooth for a tooth . . .' I knew it was in the Old Testament—probably in Exodus. I loaned him a Bible."

Anthony talked somewhat obscurely about people who might want to wreak revenge upon him because they blamed him for something he had done. Rose, of course, had read about Sarah Smith's death in Anthony's surgery. Anyone who read the papers or watched television in Buffalo knew about that. Later, when Rose thought about it, she sensed that Anthony was hinting that Sarah's husband or family might be plotting against him. But, for the moment, he didn't seem all that worried about Debbie's being in the hospital. He seemed more focused on his own fears.

"I asked him how Debbie was doing, and he said, 'Aww—she'll be all right.' That same lack of concern he always had."

Rose asked if she could see Debbie, and Anthony said he'd see what he could do.

"And he did. He called and said I could go and see her the next day—Friday. My husband came home early so I could go visit her."

In retrospect, Anthony's odd request of Rose Gardner may have been one of his initial steps to create a defense if suspicion should fall upon him. *He* knew what Debbie's diagnosis was; most people didn't—not yet. After that, without fail, his top suspect in Debbie's poisoning was Dan Smith. Wasn't it ironic, he would ask, that Debbie had gone to the hospital in August—the same month Sarah Smith died?

Rose prayed for Debbie, and she prayed for Anthony, too. But there was a niggling, stabbing doubt in her mind. "I did pray for him—I still do," she recalled. "But there was something . . . my gut feeling about him was that he was evil. I've never been aware of evil like that before. I've known people with psychiatric problems, but it wasn't that; it was almost that he was diabolical."

Rose went with Anthony on Friday, August 13, to see Debbie. He went ahead of her and pointed to the room in the intensive care unit where Debbie was. Rose was surprised to see the guard at the door. She wondered why. They had to wait, and she tried to make small talk with Anthony. She asked him how things were going.

"It was all 'woe is me,' " Rose said. "Nothing about Debbie, but his difficulties in finding a job and all the bad luck he was having. And then I went into the room after the guard cleared me, and I talked to Debbie, and she said, 'Rose, I've been poisoned.'"

"Poisoned?" Rose echoed, her voice full of shock. "Oh, Debbie . . . poisoned?"

All Rose could think was that Anthony had done it, but she couldn't say that to Debbie. It was clear that that possibility had never occurred to Debbie.

"It was very difficult for me," Rose said. "I knew Debbie, I knew the kids, and we were so connected. What do you say? It wasn't something I ever thought would happen to someone I knew so well."

Like several of their other neighbors, Rose noticed that Anthony seemed to be "on something." She didn't know if it was alcohol or some kind of drug, but he seemed so disconnected, and his affect was all wrong.

Caroline Rago was staying with Ralph and Lauren.

She would remember the moment her daughter called to tell her she'd been poisoned. "I was in the basement, and Anthony was doing something with his fax machine. Debbie told me what they found out—about her being poisoned, and I go *'What?'* and when I got off the phone, I said to Anthony, 'She's been poisoned. She's actually been poisoned,' and he says, 'Now, don't go telling everybody. Don't tell the family, because they're gonna be pointing the finger at me.'"

But Caroline told Carmine, her son. They had both been so frightened for Debbie.

"Anthony would take my hand," Debbie remembered, "and he kept telling me, 'You know *I* didn't do this, and I know *you* didn't do it, so we'll get through this—we just have to stick together. Remember that, Debbie, we have to stick together.' "

Anthony moved out of their duplex in West Seneca while Debbie was in the hospital, saying that he couldn't bear to be there without her. He and Polo went to live with his mother, leaving his children to be cared for by Caroline Rago or Carmine and his wife. Lena welcomed him with open arms and was once again completely supportive. Except for her fury over Tami, she had always given him whatever he wanted. Apparently, he had managed to explain that to her satisfaction, somehow managing to blame Debbie for all their marital problems.

Everyone in Debbie's neighborhood knew that she was very ill, but no one beyond her own family and, of course, Anthony's family knew about the poisoning diagnosis. Shelly Palombaro lived around the corner from the Pignataros' house. Although she and Debbie had never known each other very well, Shelly felt an urgent sense of needing to visit Debbie. Her son, D.J., had always been welcome in Debbie's house and was friendly with Ralph. Her daughter, Aly, was Lauren's age, and both girls were avid gymnasts.

"I kept calling and calling Anthony," Shelly said, "and asking him if I could go see Debbie, but he kept putting me off. I asked him what was wrong with her, and he told me this complicated medical thing and then said she had a rare virus infection of her nervous system."

For all Shelly knew about diagnoses, maybe Debbie did have that, but she was still determined to visit her. She left messages on Carmine Rago's phone and on Caroline's phone for Debbie. Finally, she went to the hospital, although Anthony obviously didn't want her there.

"I talked to the guard, and he let me in," Shelly said, "and I finally got to see Deb—and I couldn't believe how she looked."

Shelly was a hairdresser, and she had cut Anthony's hair before, but she didn't particularly like him—there was such an arrogance about him. Now, Debbie was telling her how good he'd been about coming to see her and standing by her, and it made Shelly's stomach go flip-flop. Like Rose, she had her suspicions.

One day Lena Pignataro came along with Anthony to visit Debbie. Caroline and Carmine Rago were there, too. They had planned to discuss what would be best for the children: who would take care of them until Debbie recovered.

It was the first time that Lena had come to visit Debbie since her hospitalization, and she swept into the room with an angry look on her face.

"What's wrong, Lena?" Debbie asked, puzzled.

"You know what's wrong," Lena said. "You did this to yourself, and you're trying to frame my son."

"If you believe that," Debbie said weakly, "get out of here."

Lena turned to Caroline and shouted, "You can have the kids!"

"Well, I'll gladly take the kids," Caroline said.

Lena left, with Anthony scampering along behind her. Caroline just stood there, stunned, but Carmine's hands gripped the arms of the chair he sat in. Carmine Rago was a huge man, a man that Chuck Craven described as "someone Pat and I *never* wanted to have mad at us . . . *never.*"

Carmine's hands alone would dwarf a football, but like many big men he was rarely angry at anybody. Now his face flushed dark red, and the veins stood out in his forehead.

Anthony had coaxed his mother to come back into the room and she stood with a pinched look around her mouth, staring at her paralyzed daughter-in-law with disapproval.

"My brother will take care of the kids," Debbie said quietly to Lena.

Whatever Anthony might have told Lena, she seemed completely brainwashed. "You know what you did—you liar," she spat at Debbie, who was completely confused by her attitude. "Liar!"

On this day, however, Lena Pignataro went too far. Carmine erupted before either Debbie or Caroline could respond. He picked up a table and threw it across the room as easily as if it were a pillow. His language was not polite as he ordered Lena to get out. It wasn't something that anyone ever expected Carmine to do, but he was worried sick about his sister.

"She left," Debbie said, "and Anthony just trailed after her. He had to stay on her good side."

A phalanx of nurses came running down the hall at the sound of the shouting and the clackety-clack of the table hitting the wall.

It was as if all their family relationships were turning inside out. It was unbelievable, and Debbie felt as though she were living inside a soap opera.

Lena didn't come back, but Anthony came back—again and again. He kept reminding Debbie that they were a team and that they must not let anyone on the outside try to split them up. *As long as we stick together* became his mantra to her.

Once Anthony had no choice but to accept Debbie's diagnosis as arsenic poisoning, he insisted on getting tests done on himself. He reported back to Debbie that he, too, had arsenic in his system. It wasn't true. He had no more poison in him than the average person. But it fit with Anthony's theory. He hinted that someone was trying to wreak revenge on him, and that would mean his family was a target, too.

Debbie was far more worried about her children than she was about Anthony. If someone had poisoned her, they might also try to hurt Ralph and Lauren. On August 12, as sick as she was, she insisted on having a nurse hold the phone for her so she could call their pediatrician and ask that they be tested to be sure they didn't have arsenic in their systems, too.

Debbie was not allowed to eat anything that wasn't prepared in the hospital. But Anthony brought her Snickers bars when he visited. They were still factory-wrapped, and she had no concern about eating them. But then, she had no concern about Anthony. Despite her family's and friends' worries that he had something to do with her poisoning, she never let such a thought approach her conscious mind. That would be too horrible even to contemplate.

She didn't tell anyone about the candy bars, however.

17

As the chelation therapy began to drain the arsenic from her system, Debbie's doctors started her on very gradual rehabilitation. By the time she left the ICU on August 27, the numbness in her arms and legs had become excruciating pain—a positive sign that her nerves weren't dead but represented an ordeal she would live through. "I couldn't stand up on my own or even with the help of three nurses."

Her physical therapists and doctors doubted that Debbie would walk again, so they concentrated on trying to bring back her arms and hands so that she might be able to feed herself, talk on the phone, and perhaps hold a pen again.

Debbie was gaining mobility by tiny increments when she suddenly had great trouble breathing and experienced pains in her chest. She was quickly transferred to the cardiac care unit. Tests showed that she had a small "whoosh" of blood into the pericardium, the tough, fibrous sac that surrounds the heart. Fortunately, it did no permanent damage.

Debbie longed to be home with her children, with her husband. Oddly, she asked no questions about the details of what had happened to her or why or even who was responsible. She was strangely passive and accepting of her condition.

In reality, she was fighting very hard *not* to ask herself any questions at all. She didn't dare focus on the huge, lurking possibility in her subconscious.

If Debbie was avoiding the obvious, D.A. Frank Sedita and his investigators Chuck Craven and Pat Finnerty were focusing intently on it, turning their suspicions like a many-sided puzzle and examining it, along with the forensic techniques they might use to prove what they suspected.

Less than three weeks after her massive dose of arsenic, Sedita, Craven, and Finnerty were all convinced they had found enough motives to convince a jury that Debbie Pignataro's husband had meant to kill her. But they were still a long way from arresting Anthony.

Not the least of their problems was the attitude of the victim. With Debbie Pignataro's complete denial that Anthony could have hurt her, they were at an impasse. At the moment, there was no chance she would testify against him. There was every chance that she, the loyal wife, would stick by him, just as she had in his previous court appearances. The three men knew they wouldn't be able to make a dent in Debbie's firewall of denial.

"We need Sharon," Craven said.

The other two men nodded their heads. If Debbie Pignataro was going to trust anyone from the District Attorney's Office, it would be Sharon Simon, their victim/witness advocate. Sharon had a fine, kind touch with people in crisis and too much empathy for her own good.

On August 26, Pat Finnerty and Chuck Craven visited Debbie in the hospital. They wanted two things: permission to search her home in West Seneca, and a lock of her hair. She gave them her O.K. to search, and she allowed them to snip hair from several spots on her head. She didn't ask why they wanted it. The dark brown hair would be sent to the National Medical Services Laboratory in Willow Grove, Pennsylvania, for hair segmentation analysis.

Debbie knew that she had been poisoned. She had known since two days after her admission to the hospital, but she was as baffled as anyone else about the source. They asked her again if she used any pesticides or gardening products, and all she could remember was Miracle-Gro fertilizer. "Last year, we had an ant problem," she said, "and Anthony sprayed the house."

"Have you eaten in any restaurants recently?" Finnerty asked.

"About three weeks before I went to the hospital," she said, "we stopped on Route 5, but I can't recall the name of the restaurant. But I was sick before that—I was so weak that I had to have help walking, and Anthony had to cut up my food for me. I'd started having the tingling in my arms and legs a few days before we ate there."

Debbie told them that she and her husband had been having marital problems earlier in the year, but she didn't elaborate beyond saying she had asked him to move out in February. She said she let him come back later in early summer, but she couldn't remember which month. Her memory was coming back in some areas, but she still had some difficulty putting events of the last few months in sequence.

Debbie was frank with them about taking too many Xanax in February, but she said that as soon as she took them, she called a friend for help. "I didn't want to hurt myself—I just was trying to relax and go to sleep. I was so tired."

She said they'd been having a difficult time financially. Her husband couldn't find a job he felt was suitable for him. "The only income we had was my salary from the pediatrician's office, so we were living on our savings, with help from Anthony's mother."

There were any number of things Debbie did not tell the two investigators, things they would find out later: She didn't mention the checks that Anthony wrote for "cash" almost every day—checks for $100. She hadn't known where that money was going, but she had an idea. Anthony seemed drowsy all the time. She wasn't ready to get into that whole discussion—not yet.

Debbie was pleasant enough to the two detectives from the Erie County D.A.'s office, but then they hadn't pressed her about whom she might suspect.

Later that day, Debbie called Chuck Craven and said she had told her husband that he and Finnerty had come to see her. "He wanted to know what I told you," she said, "and I told him only what I wanted you to know."

Craven wasn't sure what she meant by that. While Debbie had given them no information that would make her husband seem guilty of harming her, she might be unconsciously giving them a hint.

Anthony was loudly espousing his own suspect. The revenge theory became his cry. He wanted Dan Smith located and investigated. He was convinced, he said, that Dan had poisoned Debbie—and that he might even be behind all the vandalism around their house that spring. Somebody was clearly out to get his whole family.

Frank Sedita had kept track of Dan Smith, mostly because he admired his strength in adversity and wanted to be sure that Dan was doing all right. He learned that Dan had left the Buffalo area after Sarah died.

But shortly after Debbie became critically ill, Frank phoned Dan in the Midwest town where he currently lived. He wanted him to know that Tony Pignataro was a suspect in another medically connected crime. "This time it's *his* wife," Sedita said.

* * *

Chuck Craven learned that Debbie had asked to have her children tested to be sure they were safe. On August 27, he and Pat Finnerty found Anthony Pignataro at Children's Hospital. He explained that he was having his children admitted because the arsenic in their system was elevated.

He had come there with both grandmothers, Lena Pignataro and Caroline Rago, and was standing by to be sure his children were safe. He seemed anxious to get them home.

Later, Frank Sedita talked to the pediatric toxicologist working in the Poison Control Center. That doctor commented that Anthony *was* concerned when Ralph and Lauren had to stay in the hospital for further tests—but only because he wanted to be sure Ralph could play in a football game that Saturday.

Craven and Finnerty made an appointment to talk with Anthony the next day. He said he would meet with them at Buffalo Mercy Hospital.

The three men met in an office in the hospital, where Anthony was visiting Debbie. Asked about any chemicals that they might have in their home, Anthony said that they had the usual things for killing weeds and for pest control. All of those items were kept in a box in the garage.

"Do you know who might have brought arsenic into your home?" Craven asked.

Anthony looked baffled. "I have no idea."

"Who did the cooking?"

Anthony explained that Debbie did the majority of the cooking, although he occasionally cooked meat on the barbecue grill. The only thing he could recall fixing was some packaged soup for Debbie after she became ill. He said he didn't do the grocery shopping, and the only person who brought food into the house would be his mother-in-law, Caroline Rago.

When the two D.A.'s investigators asked him about

any troubles in his marriage, Anthony admitted to moving out in February. His wife had gotten very angry with him and changed the locks on him after she caught him with another woman. "But that's over now," he said earnestly. "Debbie and I have been working on our marriage."

Anthony told them he was very concerned because Child Protective Services in Erie County were apparently involved in the situation with his children. "Why would that be?"

Finnerty shrugged. "By law, the hospital had to notify them."

Anthony told them that he felt his family was being victimized. He wondered if the county water system had been tested. Perhaps some terrorist had poisoned the county water?

That was a long shot. No one else in their neighborhood had become ill. Indeed, there weren't any reports of mysterious viruses or unexplained gastrointestinal upsets anywhere in West Seneca. If the public water system were contaminated, surely many people would be affected.

The detectives asked Anthony if his wife could have taken the poison herself, and he shook his head. That wasn't possible, he insisted. "She's too close to her children to ever do that."

There was a long pause in the conversation, and then Chuck Craven asked the question that hung heavily in the air between them. The obvious question. "Did you poison your wife?" he asked, his eyes watching Pignataro's face.

The silence was even longer this time, and then Anthony answered in a calm voice without really answering at all: "I can see why people might think I would do that."

Oddly, Anthony wasn't at all upset or offended by Craven's question, while Debbie had been shocked and outraged when her mother-in-law asked her if she had deliberately taken poison.

Anthony was quite matter-of-fact, and his affect was very flat—as if he were giving the time of day. But, Craven and Finnerty noted he had answered neither "Yes" nor "No."

They asked him for permission to search his home, and he said that, personally, he would have no problem with that—but, of course, his wife would have to be the one to give permission. They already had that, although Debbie had stipulated that it be done when the children were not there. She didn't want them to see police going through their rooms and their possessions.

"How would someone obtain a poison like arsenic?" Pat Finnerty asked.

"I don't know," Anthony answered. "I'm a doctor, and I don't even know where you would get it." He mentioned an article he'd read in the newspaper about some man who had tried to kill his wife with cyanide. "He got it over the Internet. Maybe you could look on the Internet for arsenic."

He looked at them with a faint smile and clear eyes. He had answered their questions in a polite manner. He was now trying to help them do their jobs, offering them an idea of where they might find a source of arsenic. But it was only a guess on his part, he pointed out.

Finnerty and Craven had already been to the Internet and, not surprisingly, nobody was selling arsenic on eBay. They could sense that Pignataro viewed himself as vastly superior to them in intelligence and the ability to do research.

Craven and Finnerty looked back at Anthony Pignataro. He had no idea how serious they were about pinning him to the wall for what they believed he had done to the paralyzed woman who lay in bed down the hall from where they talked. And he clearly had no idea how good they were at their jobs. That was fine with them; let him see them as "dumb cops."

It seemed now that Debbie Pignataro was going to live. She had beaten unbelievable odds, but it would be weeks before she could leave the hospital. Craven and Finnerty had plenty of time.

18

On August 30, 1999, Ralph and Lauren were released from Children's Hospital after being tested for arsenic intoxication. Ralph showed no excess arsenic in his system at all, although Lauren had ingested a bit more than average at some time over the previous several weeks. There wasn't enough in her body to do her any harm. A few days later, Pat Finnerty and Chuck Craven talked to the children at their uncle Carmine's house.

Their search of the Pignataro home hadn't netted anything unusual or ominous. As Anthony had said, the box in the garage held nothing more than the usual garden products used to kill bugs and snails. A careful reading of the labels didn't reveal any arsenic in the ingredients.

One fascinating item, however, was a manuscript they found lying on the coffee table in the living room, almost as if someone had wanted them to read it. It was well over a hundred pages long, typed single-spaced: a book in progress titled *M.D.: Mass Destruction.* A cursory glance indicated that it had been written by Debbie Pignataro and that it was a kind of protest about the way her husband had been treated after the Sarah Smith case.

They had Debbie's permission to remove any item, and

they took it with them. Finally, Anthony had two readers who were very interested in the book he was sure would vindicate him. With Frank Sedita, he actually had three new readers.

In their uncle's home, the two detectives asked Ralph and Lauren about their family and what they recalled of the summer that was almost over. Any good cop hates to question children, always wishing that there were some other way to gather intelligence. But the Pignataro children were the only constant witnesses to the way things had been in their home.

Ralph was hesitant, protective of his mother, silent about his father, and very cautious about revealing family secrets. He was only 12, and he had been through so much in the past year: first his father's arrest and imprisonment, then a too brief period of happy reconciliation before his parents separated for a few months. His father had come back, but then his mother had grown so ill.

Ralph was obviously intelligent and responsible, mature beyond his years. But he really didn't want to say the wrong thing, and at his age he wasn't even sure what the wrong thing would be. He looked as if he had the weight of the world on his shoulders.

Lauren was more open, a pretty, bubbly little girl. She told them about how she got sick sometime in July. Her dad had made some soup for her mother. "I ate some of it," she said, "and I got sick and threw up at practice."

Lauren had a very small amount of arsenic in her system compared with the massive dose Debbie had ingested—but it *was* there. Anthony had said he didn't know where to get arsenic. Debbie said to Chuck Craven that they had had problems with carpenter ants. But arsenic isn't an ingredient in the kind of bug-killing spray effective against carpenter ants.

Lauren remembered that her daddy had put some little round tins out around the house to "kill ants." She had seen him placing them in various spots, and he had explained to her what they were for.

Prosecutor Frank Sedita was doing his own research on arsenic poisoning. In early September, he called Dr. Jahangir Koleini, the family practice physician who was the Pignataros' family doctor. Dr. Koleini had seen Debbie, of course, during July and August when she was admitted to the hospital, and said that Debbie was still complaining of pain when she left the hospital on July 25. That was not the typical post-pancreatitis pattern. She should have felt much better at that point because pancreatitis is an *acute* situation. Dr. Koleini had felt uneasy enough to try to convince the Pignataros to put Debbie back in the hospital for further tests, but Anthony didn't believe that was necessary.

Although he didn't share his thoughts with Pignataro, Dr. Koleini told the prosecutor that he was thinking that there might be "something toxic" involved. In his conversations with Anthony, Debbie's physician had found him "not too concerned" about her condition, whether it was her pancreatitis or even that she had been poisoned with arsenic.

Sedita spoke with Dr. Samie, too. Samie said she had agreed with Drs. Koleini and Snyderman that something "unusual" was going on. In fact, Dr. Samie had gone so far as to call the Pignataros on Saturday, August 7—three days before Debbie was hospitalized in crippled and critical condition. Anthony had told her only that his wife was "not herself." Samie said she had then suggested that an MRI (magnetic resonance imaging) test be done at once. Anthony had agreed to that willingly enough and the results were normal. Another MRI on Sunday showed nothing more than the residual effects of Debbie's neck surgeries.

Sedita asked if the MRI could have shown arsenic in her system, and Dr. Samie said it could not.

Frank Sedita was getting total validation of the written

medical records on Debbie Pignataro—directly now from the doctors involved. Dr. Samie explained that arsenic poisoning is often misdiagnosed initially as Guillain-Barré syndrome because the two conditions present very similar symptoms at the beginning.

Dr. Samie recalled the time when Pignataro was told that Debbie was suffering from arsenic poisoning. His first reaction had been to say, "Somebody must be doing this to *me*—because of what *I* went through before."

He was alluding to the investigation into Sarah Smith's death. And, as always, he saw events almost exclusively as how they affected *him*.

A few days later, Anthony had said to Dr. Samie, "You know that she has done this—tried to kill herself—before."

None of the doctors believed that Debbie Pignataro had deliberately poisoned herself. Now, when Sedita asked Dr. Samie about the expected progression of arsenic poisoning, the doctor was not optimistic. She explained that first the gastrointestinal system is affected, and then arsenic affects the nerves, where it can cause terrible damage. In Dr. Samie's opinion, Debbie's prognosis remained poor because she had suffered such severe damage to her nerves. She felt either that Debbie would lose the use of her hands forever, or that she faced a very long period of recovery before she could hope to regain normal use of them.

Dr. George Jackson, division head for the Criminalistics Department of National Medical Services, helped Sedita interpret the lab results from tests on Debbie's hair. Dr. Jackson, who has a Ph.D. in toxicology, explained that the hair samples, clipped carefully by Chuck Craven and Pat Finnerty on August 26, had been divided into three segments. As hair grows, the markings left by heavy metal will stay, and if more poison is ingested, other marks will be left closer to the hair root.

Segment 1 of the samplings was considered to be hair growing from the root between August 10 and August 26, measuring 0.4 centimeter. Segment 2 would have grown between June 30 and August 10: 0.4 centimeter to 2.3 centimeters, and Segment 3 was hair grown from May 31 to June 30. It was 2.3 centimeters to 6.4 centimeters long.

The rule of thumb for normal hair growth is about 1 centimeter a month. Jackson pointed out that the most dramatic increase in the arsenic level in Debbie's hair was in the segment that had grown between August 10 and August 26. This corresponded to the dramatic worsening of Debbie Pignataro's symptoms and to the fact that her urine had tested positive for arsenic on August 11, showing the highest level ever recorded by the New York State Health Department.

The date of Debbie's most significant poisoning had been narrowed down to a two-week period—probably less than that. It had taken a while for the chelation therapy to "catch" the arsenic in her system and gradually remove it.

Meanwhile, Debbie's agony was terrible to watch. She was prescribed as much painkilling medication as possible, but it wasn't enough. Even the sheets of her hospital bed hurt her feet. Her hands and feet got worse instead of better, and she began to accept the awful possibility that she might never walk again or be able to feed herself, hold a pencil, or comb her own hair. The nurses who cared for her felt helpless; there was so little they could do for her.

Frank Sedita, Pat Finnerty, and Chuck Craven met to go over the progress of their case. It was building steadily. They had made headway in both circumstantial and physical evidence. They knew now that if human beings are given arsenic in boluses big enough to produce acute symptoms, their hair will develop a crude "calendar" that gives macabre information.

After two series of tests on Debbie's hair—both without marks and with hair that showed the presence of arsenic—the Medical Services lab had been able to measure the exact amount of arsenic there. Debbie's hair before June 1999 showed that her baseline (normal) level of arsenic was 4 micrograms per liter. In June, when Anthony began to sleep over often in the family home and eat with them, it increased to 6.4 micrograms per liter. However, in July, when Anthony moved in completely and took over as the cook, it jumped to 18.9 micrograms per liter.

From all they had learned in their intense research into arsenic, they could deduce that Debbie had initially been suffering from chronic arsenic poisoning, ingesting small doses at a time since sometime in June. Certainly she was nauseated all the time, but she hadn't lost feeling in her extremities or developed the staggering walk until early August.

Just before August 10—when she was hospitalized in critical condition—damage to her hair showed arsenic present at *81.5 micrograms per liter!* As Sedita pointed out, this was sixteen times her original baseline figure. Human blood didn't leap from 4 to 81.5 micrograms per liter of arsenic without a good reason. There was only one conclusion: Debbie had been poisoned both chronically *and* acutely.

There was something diabolical and coldly plotted in that picture. They looked at their records of Tony Pignataro's probation to see what was happening with him in July. They knew that he'd asked permission to go to Florida to work with his brothers in the fast food business in the early summer—and been denied. They also knew that Debbie had gone into the hospital on July 21, stayed for four days, shown significant improvement, and gone home on July 25—home to her husband's cooking.

When acutely ill patients go to the hospital, improve fairly rapidly, and *then* have a relapse when they return home, an analytical mind sees the correlation. Something in Debbie's home was making her sick.

While talking to the various physicians who had treated Debbie, Frank Sedita learned that Anthony had not simply ignored his wife's condition. Although he certainly had no bedside manner with her and he hadn't talked with her about the funny taste in her mouth and her constant vomiting, he *had* sought a surgical remedy for her condition.

On August 2, Anthony had called Dr. Michael Rade and said that *his* analysis of Debbie's biliary scan (a CAT scan to find the source of her digestive problems) proved to him that Debbie had a nonfunctioning gallbladder. Anthony then practically demanded that Dr. Rade operate on her immediately. Rade didn't agree with Anthony's diagnosis and refused to operate.

"If she'd had that surgery in the weakened condition she was in," Sedita suggested, "she probably wouldn't have survived. And even on autopsy, it's not likely that they would have found any arsenic in her system—it's not a usual test they do. But that plan didn't work—if it *was* a plan on Pignataro's part."

Sedita, Finnerty, and Craven had known for a long time that they were dealing with a very calculating mind. All of their scenarios came full circle—back to Anthony Pignataro. Because Debbie's poisoning was both chronic and acute, Sedita would have ammunition to rebut what he fully expected Anthony's defense would be—that Debbie herself had taken arsenic in a long, slow suicide plan.

It didn't make sense that she would have taken lots of little doses, then taken some big gulps, and then gone back to the small amounts. They had all learned how painful arsenic poisoning was. Who would ever choose to die that way—with agonizing symptoms—over a period of months?

Anthony's other prime suspect was Dan Smith, but any defense attorney would have a very difficult time if he tried to accuse the gentle young widower of poisoning Pignataro's wife so he could get revenge on the man who had killed *his* wife. Even if Dan was that kind of man, he had been living many states away from western New York.

No, they were dealing with someone who was perfectly willing to plan ahead and wait and watch while his (or her) target withered away and died. Who—other than her husband—might have a reason to want Debbie Pignataro dead? She was a sweet woman obviously devoted to her home and her family, and she didn't have any enemies—not unless one of Anthony's girlfriends wanted him enough to kill his wife to get him.

Frank Sedita went over the motivation that Anthony might have. Again, any wish to have Debbie dead all seemed to come back to him. Debbie had a $100,000 life insurance policy, and her husband was the beneficiary. It wasn't a huge amount of money for an insurance policy, but a check of Anthony's bank records had showed them that his checking account was tapped out. For months he had been trying to get out of New York State and move to Florida. They assumed he would then cross the Caribbean to some out-of-the-way spot where he could set up practice as a doctor again. A wife with ties to the States would only get in his way. And he had at least one woman waiting in the wings for him: Tami Maxell.

"But he can't divorce Debbie," Sedita said. "If he did, his mother would cut him off from his dad's estate—which is considerable."

As awful as it was to contemplate, poisoning Debbie might have seemed the only way Tony Pignataro could be free of the constraints of his marriage and still inherit his share of Dr. Ralph's estate from Lena.

19

Debbie Pignataro was probably the one who could give the investigators the best read on her husband, but she seemed oddly loyal to the man who had put her through so much. She appeared to be more confused than angered that someone had poisoned her. It may have been that she couldn't bear to look at it head-on.

In September, Frank Sedita and Sharon Simon, the victims' advocate, went to Mercy Hospital, but Frank stayed in the lobby while Sharon went up to visit with Debbie.

Sharon empathized with women in a way no man could ever hope to. She hadn't grown tough during her years of dealing with victims, and she considered Debbie a victim—perhaps someone who had been a victim for a very long time.

"I know they call me Ms. Morgue, Dr. Death, or Morticia," Sharon recalled with a laugh. "I'm 'the one who talks to dead people.' I'm the one whose beeper sounds at the most impossible times, calling me out to a murder crime scene."

Like most professionals who work with the saddest events of life, Sharon had become used to the black humor they need to keep from crying. Her job required that she had to spend a lot of time at homicide scenes, morgues, and funeral parlors as she comforted the survivors of murder victims.

"When Frank Sedita called me, he had such a serious

tone in his voice that I wondered what was wrong," she said. "I went down to meet with him and our District Attorney, Frank Clark. I'd heard about the Pignataro case, and now they wanted me to work on it with them."

Sharon Simon hasn't had an easy life herself, which may have a lot to do with how she identifies with victims. She had been married for twenty-three years—happily, she believed—when she was served with divorce papers in 1992. She was grateful that her two sons, Yuri and Damien, were grown when her marriage crumbled. They stood by her, but she lost the home she had lovingly restored with countless hours of hands-on work. Sharon knows how to communicate with women where they live, but she empathizes with men, too. It was Sharon who had sat with Dan Smith throughout the painful hearings about Sarah's death. She had seen Debbie then, but had never spoken to her.

Now Sharon would be on the other side, helping Debbie—if Debbie would let her. She wondered if Debbie would recognize her from their earlier courtroom time together. And if she did, would Debbie even give her the time of day?

Like most women, Sharon had been through the wars of love herself, and she had also been a crime victim. "I grew up in Union City, New Jersey, and I'm a fighter. My response when I'm in danger is always immediate—and it's to fight back."

Once Sharon was walking home from a visit at a girlfriend's house when two men began to follow her. One of them jumped out and tried to push her into their car. "I scratched this guy's face and drew blood. I saw the look on his face, and I thought, Now I've done it. He punched me and fractured my jaw, and I lost a tooth besides. My own instinctive response isn't very healthy. Sometimes you shouldn't fight back. You can only do that in certain places. If you're in an elevator, you're not gonna be fighting back. Every guy's different. Fighting back might buy you some time—or fighting back might get you killed. So I tell women if you hit someone, be prepared that they're going to hit you back."

Sharon McVeigh Simon got to know law enforcement well in New Jersey. Two of her uncles and a grandfather were Jersey City detectives. "It was an Irish Catholic family," she said. "My father was one of eleven children. I was one of three girls."

After going to Catholic school, Sharon attended the University of Kentucky on two scholarships. "Moving to Lexington was like going to a foreign country for me. I had my bags packed every weekend to go home, but I stayed. I majored in English because that's what my scholarships dictated."

Her then husband was working toward his master's degree, and Sharon worked as a cocktail waitress in a country club in Louisville. "That was an experience because I was a Yankee—the only one who ever worked in that country club. On Sundays, they had a dance floor in the front, and they'd open up a beer garden in the back for people over 21 who didn't belong to the country club. My job was to sit on a bar stool and pat people down for weapons!"

Coming to Buffalo with her husband, who wouldn't consider moving to New Jersey, Sharon graduated from the University of Buffalo with a degree in philosophy and criminal justice. "I always called my curriculum 'head in the sky—feet on the ground.' "

It took her a long time to finish by going to school at night. Along the way, Sharon gave birth to her two sons.

The courses she took at the University of Buffalo were the perfect combination for the job Sharon would have in the nineties. "I didn't know it then, though," she said. "I also think that good cops use life experience—bad things that happen to them that they turn into knowledge. I had my share of those."

Initially, Sharon had wanted to go to law school. She took her first LSATs to prepare for that, "and I did terribly," she laughed.

She waited to take the law school aptitude test again, and volunteered at the rape crisis center in the interim. "I went through training there and did a year of volunteering, and then the coordinator's job for the Erie County Advocate Program for Sexual Assault Victims opened up in 1979."

It was only part time to begin with, a fledgling program, but Sharon was hired. She realized that she was doing exactly what she was meant to do. She was a natural.

Before long, the experimental program became a full-time job—more than full time, really. Sharon was always on call as an advocate for victims of sexual assault, and of course her hours were never nine to five. She wore a beeper and was summoned at all hours of the day and night.

Seeing how many agencies become involved in sexual assault cases, Sharon wrote a protocol so that when a victim came into a hospital in Erie County, her office was automatically notified so the victim wouldn't have to go through the procedures alone.

"I lost half my volunteers the first year because I told them we *had* to respond. The hospitals had been disillusioned because they hadn't always been able to count on advocates. I went to the hospitals and *guaranteed* that someone would show up—which meant *I* had to go to half the calls myself. When I started, we had two hospitals who called us; when I left, we had eleven. We had a program with credibility, and we had lots of volunteers we could count on."

When Sharon stopped to think about it, she realized

the job was making up for a marriage that wasn't working. She and her husband divorced.

Sharon Simon wrote grants and gradually was able to hire other advocates for her one-woman office. "It was only me to begin with," Sharon recalled. "When I left fourteen years later, there were six staff members, and we'd expanded to helping victims in court cases, opened a speakers' bureau, and taught prevention programs. I was trained by the best; I traded off teaching with the FBI so I could go to their classes, and I never thought about taking the LSATs again.

"But there came a point where I was teaching in the police academy, teaching police officers, teaching the doctors—but I realized *I* wasn't learning anything, any more."

Sharon had handled at least 8,000 sexual assault cases when she was hired by the Erie County District Attorney's office on November 1, 1993. Although she once said she wanted nothing to do with murder, she would be going to homicide scenes, too. She had seen the stress in sexual assault cases, and she sensed that the stress had to be so much more in homicide cases. It was.

Sharon soon wrote another proposal on what might be done to help victims, their families, hospitals, the detectives, the medical examiners, and even the funeral homes who were called in to murder crime scenes.

For the first two months, she learned about every facet of her new job as Assistant Coordinator of Victim/Witness Assistance. Even though she was a woman and from the D.A.'s office—not the most welcome visitor in mostly male homicide units—Sharon knew the chief and a lieutenant in homicide in the Buffalo Police Department. She introduced herself there and then visited smaller departments around Erie County.

"Then I went to the morgue. I told them I didn't need to see an autopsy, but they showed me around the whole place. And then they walked me out the back, and into an autopsy. It was on a baby. I didn't lose it. That was 'the test,' and I managed to pass."

At first, Sharon went only to the hospitals and the morgue to talk with relatives of homicide victims. Later, she went into the field with homicide detectives, starting with bombings in three Erie County cities. "I was watching TV and I saw a lieutenant I knew in Cheektowaga, and he was talking about the five victims. Then my phone rang. They were asking me, 'How long will it take you to get out here?' I wanted to say, 'I don't do bombings,' but I didn't. I was there in ten minutes. I had to walk a path as they were escorting me to the basement of the police department where all the agencies involved were meeting. I passed by agents who had plastic evidence bags with charred hands and fingers in them. That was literally my initiation by fire."

Everyone was in shock—from the deliveryman who delivered the exploding packages to the relatives to the detectives to the neighbors. Her new job had begun in earnest.

Once again, Sharon had no staff, although she worked in the same offices with Chuck Craven and Pat Finnerty. At any given time, she was responsible for seventy-five homicide cases—not in solving them, but in serving as a hand-holder, comforter, court companion, adviser, explainer, shoulder to cry on, friend to those caught in the tragic circumstances of violent crime. Some people called her once a year, and some called once a week. Homicide cases never close until they are solved, but there are often long periods when detectives have no new information. It's difficult for family members to understand that, and Sharon tried to explain to them that the victim they loved has not been forgotten.

In 2001, the homicide rate in Buffalo went up 69 percent, and some months Sharon spent more time in the homicide unit than she did in her own home. Still, no case affected her as deeply as Debbie Pignataro's.

The Pignataro case was different from anything Sharon had handled before. She had a living victim—so far—but one who really didn't want to know the truth.

Sharon would never forget what Debbie looked like when she first saw her, even though weeks had passed since she was admitted to the hospital in critical condition.

"She was totally paralyzed," Sharon said. "At one point, I answered the phone for her because she couldn't reach for it. I stuck it under her chin for her.

"I was nervous," she admitted. "I tried to explain to her why I was there, and that I could understand why it would be quite natural for her not to talk to someone from my office, but that my purpose was a little bit different. I wouldn't be asking the same kind of questions that they did."

To Sharon's relief, Debbie Pignataro was willing to talk to her. In fact, the two women quickly established a bond, cautious as it was. Listening to what Debbie had been through, and knowing what probably lay ahead for her, Sharon felt so sorry her. That touched Debbie, and for the first time, she allowed herself to talk about who might have given her poison. Carefully, she began to edge out of the safe place she had put herself in.

It was going to take a lot of time.

The two women were very different. Sharon had seen more of the ugly side of the world than most and had learned to deal with the cruelties of human against human. She had learned to look at a murdered body without flinching, and she was fiercely independent because she had to be. Debbie's life had been as sheltered as it could be, considering that she was married to a serial adulterer.

She had clung so tightly to her home, her marriage, and her belief that somehow she could make it right.

Both women loved their children more than anything else in the world.

When Sharon visited Debbie, she realized that "everything was always about Tony." She had seen Debbie at her husband's hearings after Sarah Smith's death, and it was clear then that her world revolved around her husband. So, apparently, did the world of her mother-in-law, and Tony himself certainly saw himself as the central person in the universe.

The D.A.'s personnel always referred to Dr. Anthony Pignataro as *Mr.* Tony Pignataro, ignoring his pretentious "Anthony" and refusing to call him Dr., fully aware that he had long since lost his medical license.

Sharon's assignment in the investigation was to help Debbie build some confidence and at the same time try to find information for the state about the crimes against Debbie. "And, personally," Sharon recalled, "I wanted to help her walk through this."

Sharon knew that it was going to be a long ordeal, although even she could not have known how long. Initially, her most challenging goal was to help Debbie Pignataro focus on herself instead of on her husband. She had seen herself as an extension of Anthony for two decades and had always put herself second.

" 'I just want to hear about Debbie Pignataro,' " I said. "And she couldn't seem to grasp that."

"Tell me about *Debbie,*" Sharon would say, and Debbie would look at her, confused. Somewhere along the way, the real Debbie had gotten lost. It was almost impossible for her to verbalize who she was, what her hopes and dreams were, what *she* liked to do. She was "the doctor's wife," or "Ralph and Lauren's mom," and she knew how to be those people, but she had forgotten how to ask for anything for herself.

"She couldn't even see her life without Tony, although she always called him Anthony," Sharon recalled. "That's how she defined herself. She'd always start with 'and then Anthony . . . Everything was described through his eyes. She started in the middle of her life, and I asked her to go back to the beginning of her life."

After Debbie had been told for twenty years that she was too fat, too dumb, too clumsy, and too unimportant to deserve a man like Anthony Pignataro, it wasn't easy for her to find any self-confidence. It was harder when she was well nigh paralyzed. But Debbie began to look forward to Sharon's visits.

"It was a process," Sharon said. "I've been trying to think if I can recall a specific time when Debbie realized that Tony was trying to kill her, but I come up with nothing. I think that's because the first time I spoke with her in the hospital, I sensed that she knew it was him but didn't—or wouldn't—believe it."

Sharon kept asking Debbie to recall her life from birth to the present without talking about her husband. And that almost made Debbie tongue-tied. She had a very difficult time visualizing her life except in its connection to Anthony. Slowly, Debbie was able to tell about how *she* felt and what had happened to *her.* Sometimes, Sharon would interrupt and comment on how difficult and heartbreaking some events of her life must have been. The deaths of her baby girl and of her father had been tremendous losses. Both women ended up in tears.

"That's just too much," Sharon said later, as she evaluated how tragic Debbie's life had been. "You've gone through all this with your husband—which had to be major denial, even while you're sitting in the courtroom and watching him being sentenced. And you said, 'Yeah, the world's trying to screw Anthony and us'—and it was genuine. It wasn't the way most people blame the system. And then you went through the girlfriend—and the letter. Bad enough something like this happens . . ."

She broke off. She hadn't been able to say it aloud to Debbie. She was nowhere near ready to face it.

Sharon voiced her own feelings about how steadfastly loyal Debbie had been to her husband and her family, always the supportive partner in the marriage. Debbie needed to hear that. Even though she was a woman in pain, her limbs frozen by paralysis, she still felt guilty, as if she had failed or somehow hadn't done enough for her family.

As they moved through the years to the present—late summer, 1999—Sharon asked Debbie to help her with a timeline on when she began to be sick and how her illness had progressed. Again, she focused on how this affected *Debbie*—that it was her story. It was easier for Debbie to look at it that way, rather than to talk about what was essentially a criminal act—a criminal act that her own husband had almost certainly committed.

"I could tell that all this woman wanted was to be a wife and mother and enjoy and share the love that this 'should' bring," Sharon remembered. "I also knew that she was trying to hold on to something that didn't exist—at least in that marriage."

Almost any woman who's ever been married can identify with Debbie's struggle to believe in her husband. Once she said out loud that he was probably the person who had given her deadly poison, she would have to let go of all of her dreams.

Sharon rejoined Frank Sedita in the lobby, and she remembered telling him that she felt Debbie knew it was Tony who had given her the arsenic, but that too much had happened to her for her to take it all in. "She can't accept it right now," Sharon said. "Not yet. You can't ask her to."

For her part, Sharon Simon was horrified to learn that Tony Pignataro hadn't been totally reviled by the medical community. Some Buffalo area doctors had even sent him letters of support, adhering to the "good old boy" system whereby doctors stick together, no matter what. Sharon's own physician complained to her: "Doctors shouldn't be investigated by the D.A's office. That's wrong."

Sharon changed doctors.

Anthony was still a regular hospital visitor, and he appeared to be as doting and supportive as ever. He searched Debbie's face to be certain that they were still clinging tightly together, still strong in their trust in each other. She didn't know yet that he was telling other people that she was suicidal and had probably taken the poison herself.

Debbie remained in the hospital in September as school started, her children's world so separate from her own. She had always been the kind of mother who made sure they had a good breakfast and clean clothes to wear to school. She'd waved goodbye to them in the morning and was waiting at the door for them when they came home. She'd made sure they had helmets on if they rode bikes, and worried if they had even a slight fever. She rarely left them overnight, preferring to take them along on vacations. Now all she could do was pray that they were safe.

Anthony wasn't looking after their children. He told Debbie he was too overwhelmed with emotion over what had happened to them all to take care of them. Ralph and Lauren were better off, he said, with Carmine and his wife.

But he assured Debbie that he was going to Ralph's football games. Ralph was still something of a football phenomenon. Anthony went out of his way to show everyone that he was a complete "football father," proud of his son and right there to cheer for him.

"He would run up and down the sidelines with Lauren on his shoulders," their neighbor Shelly Palombaro remembered. "He made such a spectacle of himself that it didn't ring true. He'd be shouting, 'Look at Ralph, Lauren! We've got to call Mom and tell Mom!'

"It was like watching some actor in a play. Several people commented about the way he seemed to know that every eye was on him, and he was showing them what a great husband and father he was."

As he had done before when Anthony went to Ralph's games, he ignored the parking area for visitors. Then he drove his Lamborghini right up to where the coaches parked, despite signs that said he couldn't park there. Every time he was told he couldn't park where it said "Coaches Only," he waved his hand and walked away, ignoring the rules. Now he parked his Cadillac there.

"The rules never applied to *him*," one of the other fathers said.

Anthony didn't live at home or oversee his children's day-by-day activities. He lived with Lena in her big house a few miles away from his own duplex. Debbie had no more visits from Lena, and her mother-in-law's complete reversal in attitude toward her disturbed her. Ordinarily, if Debbie was ill, she could depend on her mother-in-law for backup. Over the years, Lena had never had to work, as Caroline Rago had.

Debbie had always been able to count on Lena Pignataro. Sometimes Lena was angry with Anthony, but her grandchildren or Debbie could call her for anything. "She used to say to me, 'Debbie, I'm always here if you need me. It takes me seven minutes from my house to get there,' and she was always there when I needed her—always in seven minutes.

"Even when I found out about Tami, Lena was right there on my side. She was absolutely furious with Anthony."

Debbie's mother, Caroline, agreed, but with just a little sniff at Lena's failings as a cook—something Caroline excelled at. "Lena was a terrific grandmother," Caroline said. "Before the poisoning, she was on Debbie's side. But she couldn't cook. The kids always came home to eat because Lena only cooked things like hot dogs and macaroni and cheese. Dr. Ralph used to cook, and he was good. He would cook veal cutlets. They were his speciality."

Ralph and Lauren loved their grandmother Lena. But now she was out of their lives, too. Apparently, she had dropped them for her own reasons. She was standing by Anthony. Her maternal support was fiercely protective of him, and that was odd because no one had even accused Anthony out loud. There was no reason at this point for her to make any decision about whose side she was on. Anthony and Debbie saw each other every day, and Debbie had yet to say an accusatory word about him.

"I don't know what Anthony told her about me," Debbie said later. "It must have been something terrible for her to just walk out of my life like that. And for her to drop her grandchildren that she had always adored—that was hard to take."

20

If Anthony thought the Erie County District Attorney's office had forgotten about him, he was mistaken. Arsenic poisoning is an unusual crime, and the investigators needed direct physical evidence and even more circumstantial evidence to be sure that they had a case so defense-attorney–proof that nothing or no one could disassemble it. Frank Sedita knew where Anthony was, and he was still on probation, so he couldn't leave the area without being arrested. They monitored his movements, although he didn't know it, and they kept building their case.

One remarkable piece of good luck came into Sedita's office on August 30: a possible witness who, if he was telling the truth, would be worth pure gold. However, he was a jailhouse witness, and such people have been known to snitch and even make up stories to work out a plea bargain. Snitches are not preferred witnesses for either the prosecution or the defense, but Frank Sedita was willing to listen to what he had to say.

The man, Arnie Letovich, had contacted Captain Florian Jablonski and Detective Edward Tyszka of the West Seneca Police Department when he read about the poisoning of Debbie Pignataro in the Sunday *Buffalo News*. While most readers of the *Buffalo News* were shocked by the story, Letovich said it hadn't been very surprising to him. He knew Tony Pignataro, and now he wanted to talk about him.

At 2 P.M. that Monday afternoon, Frank Sedita, Chuck Craven, and Pat Finnerty, along with the two West Seneca officers, met with Letovich. Arnie Letovich was in custody, but only for two pending misdemeanors involving drugs. He wasn't looking at any hard time, and he might very well have the charges against him dismissed. He didn't have any particular reason to talk to the D.A.'s men except for his conscience.

Letovich was in his mid-forties, but he looked a little older. He seemed anxious to talk about Tony Pignataro, although Sedita informed him that no deals would be made in exchange for information. All Sedita could promise Arnie Letovich was that he would be given immunity for the information actually conveyed in this interview.

Letovich nodded that he understood. He began by explaining that he and Tony had been housed together in the Erie County Correctional Facility from some time in August 1998 until October of that year. One of the corrections officers had asked Letovich to keep an eye on Pignataro, because as a totally green prisoner he was in danger of being abused by other convicts.

Letovich said that while Tony was in jail, he had used both alcohol and heroin. That wasn't any shock to the D.A.'s men; there were always avenues for convicts to smuggle in both drugs and booze. Some with a bent toward chemistry even made their own alcoholic drink inside. Called Pruno, it was a noxious concoction of whatever could be gleaned from the kitchen: potato peelings or fruit or vegetables that were allowed to ferment. It tasted vile, but for serious drinkers, it was better than nothing.

As far as the investigators knew, Pignataro was a long-time drinker, and probably a user of prescription drugs, which he had been in a position to obtain quite easily, but they had never heard that he was a heroin addict. According to Letovich, that was a new habit Tony had picked up during his few months of incarceration.

Letovich said frankly that he had used heroin in the past and still did. He made no attempt to paint himself as any saintlier than he was. He had gotten along all right with Tony in jail, and Tony had told him he wanted to continue their friendship outside the walls. Tony had given Arnie his pager number.

Chuck Craven knew Pignataro's pager number: 555-3599. He asked Letovich what it was, and the convict gave it back to Craven instantly: "555-3599."

Letovich said he had been released from jail first, and he thought that Tony had been released on about December 2. He called Letovich soon after, and came over to his house, using the address he'd saved.

Tony Pignataro had had a woman with him. Her name was Tami, and Letovich said she was a rather attractive woman in her forties, with a very good figure. She looked as if she worked out a lot at a gym.

Tony's reason for visiting Letovich so soon after his release was immediately obvious. He wanted Letovich to "cop" some heroin for him, and Letovich had agreed to do that.

Craven nodded. He knew from his days in narcotics that there was a whole different language out there on the street. If he didn't know the right phrases, no "narc" could ever hope to fool the dealers, and might wind up a dead man. Craven had come close himself back in Arizona.

On Tony's first visit to Arnie's home, Letovich's girl-friend had been present. According to the witness, he, Tony, and both women had injected heroin in his house.

From the details he told Sedita and the D.A.'s investigators, it was clear that Letovich *did* know Tony Pignataro, and quite well. He knew that Tony had gone to medical school in Puerto Rico, that he was fluent in Spanish, and that he drove a black Cadillac Catera. Letovich said that Tony's father was a surgeon who had died.

From their initial meeting to inject heroin, Letovich said he had copped heroin for Tony over the next several months. Tony told him that he kept an apartment but that he had to move back in with his wife to make a good impression on Judge Tills so his probation rules would be modified. He wanted to leave New York State. His plans were to move to Florida and then eventually to Puerto Rico or the Caribbean, where he could start a medical practice.

What seemed to be eating at Arnie Letovich were two discussions he had had with Tony Pignataro beginning in May 1999. First, Tony confided in him that some guy was interested in Tami but was "screwing her legally." Tony apparently intended to get back at the man, but Letovich couldn't remember the other man's name. He thought Tony had mentioned that the guy had some connection with the D.A.'s office or law enforcement.

Letovich wasn't sure what Tami's other boyfriend's job was. But Tony wanted to get rid of someone. He was asking where he could get some poison. The only poisons Letovich had ever heard of were cyanide and arsenic, and he had no idea where to find something like that.

In June, Letovich said, Tony brought up the subject of poison again, but this time it was in a conversation about Debbie Pignataro. Tony complained about his wife. Evidently, she was always checking on him, and he told Letovich that it was driving him crazy because she paged him constantly.

Letovich looked down at his hands and sighed. He said he couldn't believe that Tony would actually harm his own wife. But he was insisting that she had to go. He planned to give her a "little bit" at a time, and Letovich assumed that he meant a little bit of poison.

Everyone in the room knew what the phrase "She has got to go" meant. Tony's statements about getting rid of his wife coincided with the time that Debbie Pignataro had first become ill. They knew now that in June, Debbie was suffering from chronic arsenic poisoning. That fit with Tony's statement about giving it to her a little bit at a time.

It looked as though Anthony had become impatient two months later and given Debbie a massive dose of poisoning.

Arnie Letovich had made some bad decisions in his life, and he was an admitted heroin addict. He was not, however, a killer. Now, he promised to do anything he could to stop Tony Pignataro from ever hurting anyone again. After that first meeting, he visited the District Attorney's office at least once a week.

Letovich said that when he was on the street, he and Tony had usually connected through Tony's pager. When Chuck Craven got a copy of phone records that listed calls made to Tony's pager, that information matched.

In order to assure themselves that Arnie Letovich wasn't exaggerating his position as a close companion of Tony Pignataro, Frank Sedita and the D.A.'s investigators pored through thousands of pages of financial records, telephone bills, and jail and hospital documents. It took a long time, but every detail of Letovich's story was verified.

Letovich said that he had gone to Mercy Hospital to meet with Pignataro sometime in the second week of July. He was sure that it was a Friday, and that would have been July 9. He said he'd paged Tony at the hospital and then gone over there, but Tony had already left. They had met up later—about 5 P.M.—when Tony copped more heroin.

Anthony Pignataro had apparently had an insatiable

appetite for heroin. Letovich said he copped heroin for him after they met at the Lafayette Hotel near the Buffalo Public Library. He had kept a running record of their exchanges. Letovich said he had provided heroin to Pignataro on July 21, July 24, July 28, and July 29. On the last day, he'd copped a ten-bag bundle for him.

Tony had told Letovich he was going out of town on a trip after that.

The only thing Letovich wanted in return for his cooperation in prosecuting Tony Pignataro was some help getting into a long-term drug rehab program. He no longer wanted to live the kind of life he had been living. The men observing him had heard that song and dance before from dozens of suspects and convicts, and they had reason to doubt. Only time would tell.

On September 1, 1999, Frank Sedita interviewed Tami Maxell and her attorney in his office while Chuck Craven and Pat Finnerty observed and listened. Tami's attorney asked for immunity for his client for any information she might divulge in this meeting.

Tami was a striking woman, although a little nervous as she recalled her relationship with Anthony Pignataro. She said they'd met sometime in March 1997 at Gold's Gym, where they both worked out. They got to know each other a little better when he showed her some rental space in a building near his Center Street office in West Seneca. By May, they had begun a physical affair.

Tami knew that Anthony was married, but that hadn't interfered with their mutual attraction, and they had dated until Anthony went to jail in August 1998. They hadn't really broken up, but while Anthony was locked up, Tami dated an attorney who worked in the probation department for three months, beginning the month Anthony went away. That relationship turned ugly, she said, and sometime in early December, Tami said she had filed a domestic violence report against Sam Picone, the attorney.

Interestingly, Tami's relationship with Picone ended a day or two after Anthony got out of jail. She saw Anthony again at Gold's Gym, where a group of people they all knew worked out together. Anthony gave her his pager number, although she understood that he was living with his wife.

But he wasn't working very hard on his marriage: Tami said that she and Anthony had resumed their affair in either February or March. Soon after, Anthony left his wife and moved into an apartment on Center Road.

Tami didn't appear to be much more faithful to romantic partners than Anthony was. On March 26, she had become engaged to yet another man. However, she continued to see Anthony three or four times a week.

Tami said that she had been confronted by an angry Debbie Pignataro in March. Debbie had a copy of a letter Anthony had written to Tami while he was in jail. Sam Picone had taken it without Tami's knowledge, and, of course, sent it to Debbie.

Debbie had begun to call Tami often, asking questions. Although Tami insisted that she wasn't having an affair with Debbie's husband, Debbie didn't believe her. Perhaps she wasn't sleeping with Anthony in *March;* it was difficult to chart when Tami and Anthony were together and when they weren't.

Tami said that Debbie had called her as recently as July, still suspicious that she and Anthony were seeing each other. Again, Tami had lied and said she was not involved with him.

Frank Sedita asked Tami about the last time she had been with Tony Pignataro. She guessed that it was in the first half of July. He had come to her house.

Tami said Anthony had confided in her that he was struggling with the court system, trying desperately to get his probation moved to Florida. He had it all planned out. His mother had a vacation house there where he could live, and his brothers owned several Dairy Queen franchises. Anthony had assured Tami that he would reestablish his medical practice in either Mexico or Puerto Rico.

Tami said they had talked about a future together, and in the beginning, Anthony had seemed quite untroubled about leaving his children with his wife after a divorce. But, gradually, Anthony had begun his familiar refrain about how unstable Debbie was. He said she was addicted to painkillers and that he was frightened for his children. How could he leave them with her?

He said Debbie was "unresponsive" to the children and that she was "bloating up" and going to several doctors. He told Tami of his wife's overdose but assured her that he had no further worries about her committing suicide. None of the doctors could diagnose what was wrong with Debbie, Anthony told her, but he felt it was pancreatitis, which she had inherited from her father.

Anthony himself, Tami said, was deeply committed to fitness and good nutrition and had dreams of opening an anti-aging clinic in Florida. Still, Tami said she hadn't been anxious to throw her lot in with Anthony. He had called her at either the end of July or the first part of August, leaving a message that he really needed to talk to find out what was going on in her life. He had been very resistant to ending their relationship.

Tami mentioned a sentimental card he sent her in mid-August, proclaiming his need for her and wondering why she wouldn't come back to him.

Tami left the interview with the investigators, but she was back in about ten minutes. She admitted that she

The Pignataro family in 1980. Left to right: Anthony, Lena, Dr. Ralph, Antoinette, Ralph Jr., and Steven.

Debbie and Anthony in the early 1980s, when they were dating steadily. She was so much in love with him from the very start.

Anthony's graduation from medical school in May 1985 in Puerto Rico. He stands between Dr. Ralph and Lena.

Debbie and Anthony pose with her family on June 15, 1985, their wedding day. Left to right: Her brother Carmine, his wife, Patti, Anthony, Debbie, Caroline Rago, Frank Rago. Carmine and Patti's children are in front.

Debbie with her daughter, Lauren, and her son, Ralph, at the elder Pignataros' annual pig roast in the summer of 1991.

The Pignataros pose for a family portrait in November 1996. Debbie and Anthony are smiling, but their world was beginning to fall apart.

Dan and Sarah Smith with their children, Nathan and Amanda, shortly before their lives changed forever. *(Dan Smith Collection)*

Shelly Palombaro, Debbie, Caroline Rago, and Lauren watch Ralph play football in November 1999. Debbie couldn't walk or use her

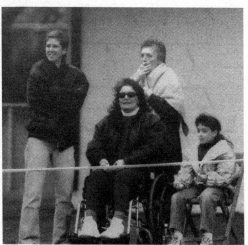

hands, but she was alive—and she was grateful. Shelly and her mother took care of her 24 hours a day.

Finally, Debbie's prayers were answered and her children returned home to her in the summer of 2000. She had conquered all medical odds to survive, for Lauren and Ralph's sake.

Chuck Craven, Special Investigator for the Erie County District Attorney's Office, worked on three cases involving Dr. Anthony Pignataro and discovered some startling information. *(Ann Rule)*

Frank Sedita III, Chief of the Special Investigations Unit of the Erie County D.A.'s Office. A daunting prosecutor to a defense witness and a strong advocate for victims, he found the Pignataro case his most unforgettable. *(Ann Rule)*

Denis Scinta, Debbie's cousin, fought for her in and out of the court-room. Even though it broke her heart, he told her the truth. *(Ann Rule)*

Carol Giarizzo Bridge and Frank Sedita, Erie County prosecutors who teamed up against Anthony Pignataro. They had a "conga line" of informants who proved invaluable to their case. *(Ann Rule)*

Sharon Simon, head of the victims' advocacy program in the Erie County D.A.'s Office. She helped Debbie face a tragedy too frightening to contemplate. *(Ann Rule)*

Shelly Palombaro and Debbie. Shelly's extraordinary friendship made it possible for Debbie to return home. *(Ann Rule)*

In Debbie's kitchen, five women celebrate a happy end to a horrific story. Left to right: Debbie, Shelly Palombaro, the author, Carol Giarizzo Bridge, and Sharon Simon, January 2002.

THE ACCOUNTANT

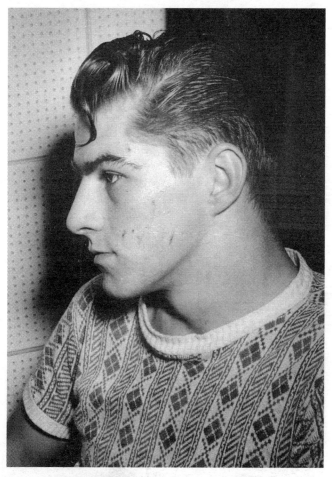

Jack Gasser in 1948 after his first arrest for homicide.
Note scratches the victim left on his face. *(Austin Seth
Collection)*

Jack Gasser, 20, shows King County Prosecutor Edmond Quigley how he disposed of Donna Woodcock's body. *(Police photo)*

Carhop Donna Woodcock, 22, was Gasser's first victim.

Austin Seth, 32, as a young detective in 1948, when he arrested Jack Gasser, and with the author fifty-four years later.

Sheriff Don Sprinkle. He and Seth were longtime partners as homicide detectives in the Seattle Police Department. Together they drew a shocking confession from Jack Gasser. Sprinkle died young, but Seth lived to see Gasser kill again. *(Austin Seth Collection)*

THE KILLER WHO BEGGED TO DIE

Using the Ninhydrin Process, Criminalist Ann Beaman of the Western Washington State Crime Lab lifted invisible fingerprints from the inside of a toilet paper roll. Later, these prints matched those of a killer captured in New Mexico. *(Ann Rule)*

Detective Benny DePalmo of the Seattle Police Department's Homicide Unit discovered a vital fingerprint clue that helped solve

Bertha Lush's murder. It was the last place anyone might look. This case was one of the most memorable of DePalmo's long career. *(Ann Rule)*

Photos from *True Detective* magazine. Top: Sergeant Jim Lehner. Right: James Elledge. *(Ann Rule)*

THE BEACH

Gaelisa Burton (left) and Tina Jacobsen. *(Police evidence photos)*

William Batten gave
two hitchhiking girls
a ride to the ocean.
He later went looking
for them. *(Police photo)*

Top: Two girls setting out on a beach vacation ate their last meal here at the Colonial West Restaurant. Sheriff's detectives finally found witnesses who saw them get into the killer's vehicle. *(Ann Rule)* Middle: The admitted killer lived in this trailer with his wife, only a short distance from the beach at Moclips. *(Ann Rule)*

This jumble of driftwood was a shelter someone had built next to the Pacific Ocean on the beach at Moclips. Beachcombers peeked inside and discovered a double tragedy. *(Ann Rule)*

Patricia Jacque opened her door to a killer on a dark December night. Kidnapped, she was forced to leave her children behind. *(Ann Rule)*

hadn't told them everything. Either her attorney or her conscience had become so insistent that she had to tell them the whole truth. She now recalled an incident that occurred after Anthony got out of prison. She had gone with him to a house on Washington to get some heroin. She gave Arnie's name and recalled that his girlfriend was there, too. She watched as Anthony injected himself with heroin there. She was under the impression that he was also using Darvocet, a painkiller.

Tami Maxell had just confirmed what Arnie Letovich had told them. It looked as though Tony Pignataro was so confident that he never thought anyone would betray him. Not his prison buddy/drug procurer or his mistress or his family—and certainly not his long-suffering wife. He seemed to think he was completely bulletproof.

He was wrong.

21

Debbie had been the complete wife, putting Anthony's wishes first, but she had always had friends on the long street where she lived, the neighborhood where her father-in-law and his lifelong friend had carved a small housing development out of a field. During the long summer just past, her friends had seen her health fail until many of them feared for her life. She had looked so pale and bloated as Anthony drove her away that most of them didn't expect her to come home from the hospital. As much as they hated to accept it, they thought she was dying.

At first, they had felt so helpless. Most of them were housewives, ill-equipped to confront Anthony with outright accusations. How do you say to your neighbor, "I think you must be killing your wife, and I want you to stop?"

Rose Gardner had come close to that, but in the end she walked away defeated. She sobbed in her husband's arms that Debbie was dying, and she didn't know how to save her.

Although she was deathly ill, Debbie didn't die. Debbie had recovered enough by the end of August to be moved to a rehab wing. She had been in the intensive care unit for almost four weeks when her doctors moved her to the rehabilitation floor. She needed a wheelchair, and she had braces on her legs. She had no balance at all and could do virtually nothing for herself. Her recovery wasn't a steady progression toward health. There were setbacks.

Although the move apparently wasn't responsible for the change in her condition, Debbie suddenly had trouble breathing. She was whisked to the cardiac care unit when her oxygen saturation point tested much too low. Her doctor told her that he would need to do a tracheotomy and insert a tube in her throat if her inability to draw in oxygen stayed so low.

"I immediately refused," Debbie recalled. "I didn't want to be kept alive by a machine. I fought so hard because my children needed me, and somehow I managed to breathe more deeply without any machine."

No one could tell Debbie whether she might ever walk again. She still couldn't feed herself, dress herself, bathe, curl her hair, put on makeup, or brush Lauren's hair. "I couldn't even turn over in bed. I couldn't move my legs or my arms or my hands."

Her brother Carmine came to visit often and urged, "Fight hard, Deb! Keep trying to move your fingers, your toes, your arms, and your legs!"

But days went by, and then weeks, and Debbie couldn't make her limbs work at all. She gritted her teeth and closed her eyes with the effort of trying to connect with nerves that wouldn't work. "It was so odd," she remembered. "Even though my arms and legs were numb, I always felt unbearable pain there. It was constant."

And then the worst thing of all happened. The Child Protective Service of Erie County served both Debbie and Anthony with a petition that said Ralph and Lauren were neglected children. "ADJUDGED that above named children are neglected children . . ."

Debbie was humiliated and horrified. Even though so many events in her life had made her feel like a failure, the one thing Debbie had always known was that she was a good mother. That anyone would consider her a neglectful mother was more than she could bear. She was terrified to read the words at the top of one of the documents from Family Court of the State of New York:

Notice: YOU ARE HEREBY NOTIFIED THAT IF ANY OF THE WITHIN-NAMED CHILDREN REMAIN IN FOSTER CARE FOR FIFTEEN OF THE MOST RECENT TWENTY-TWO MONTHS, THE AGENCY MAY BE REQUIRED BY LAW TO TERMINATE PARENTAL RIGHTS.

That meant that the state could take her children away from her and give them to someone else. Debbie knew that even if she never got over being paralyzed, her children would need her. And she needed them. She read the terrible notice with tears running down her face.

Fortunately for Debbie, her cousin Maria, who was Ralph's godmother, was married to Denis A. Scinta, a well-respected local attorney who specialized in family law. Denis promised Debbie that it would be all right— that no one who heard the whole story, not even a judge, would ever conclude that she wasn't a proper mother.

There was nothing she could do about it at the moment. On her own, she couldn't even move her little finger. And it would be a while before she could hope to return to rehab.

Anthony continued to visit her, although as the arsenic leached from her system and her mind cleared, she found herself questioning why he came and why he wasn't angrier that the state was trying to take their children away.

Why wasn't he raging and stomping his feet? *He* could move and shout, but he didn't seem worried about what would happen to their children. Sometimes she thought he only needed to be sure that she would never suspect him of poisoning her. And those were the times when Debbie remembered how often he had lied to her.

On September 14, 1999, Anthony sat beside her bed acting as he always did now—the perfect, concerned husband. Suddenly, Debbie's cousin Denis walked into the room. She was happy to have Denis and his wife, Maria, back in her life. If anything good had come out of her illness, it was that Debbie's extended family had returned to her life. Over the years, Anthony had discouraged her from seeing her relatives, preferring to celebrate holidays with his family.

Denis strode in, and he seemed very angry when he saw Anthony. His voice was steely as he said, "Anthony, leave. Get out of here and don't come back!"

Anthony turned pale, but he stood up and hurried out. Debbie turned to Denis with a question on her lips. Before she could ask why her cousin was so angry, her mother, her cousin Maria, and her brother Carmine and his wife walked in. They were all there to show their support when Debbie heard devastating news.

Denis, who was usually quite jovial, was deadly serious. "Deb, Tony sent his girlfriend a card while you were in the intensive care unit. While you were dying, he wrote to her, 'If you knew how much I missed you, you would be with me.' "

It may have seemed cruel, but Denis wanted desperately to convince Debbie that Anthony would destroy her if he could. "You have to choose. If you care about your kids, you've got to make up your mind. It's either Tony or the kids. And you can't trust Tony."

With tears in her eyes, Debbie looked at the serious faces of the people who loved her the most, and she knew Denis was right. There was no contest; Ralph and Lauren came before anything else.

"He won't be back, Denis," she said. "I don't want him here any more."

Then, something miraculous happened. "In the month of October, I'll never forget this," Debbie recalled, "I was lying in my hospital bed, and I moved one of my fingers. I lifted one of my legs. I was screaming out to the nurses, who then started screaming for the doctors that 'Deb is moving her fingers—she's moving her legs!' Everyone was ecstatic. Even the nurses were crying.

"I fought as hard as I could to regain my functions, but I knew I had a long way to go," Debbie remembered. "I was transferred to the rehab floor once again, where I worked so hard every day to try to walk again, to try to feed myself."

It was Debbie's women friends who rallied around her—not just Rose Gardner, but also Shelly Palombaro, who had become a close friend. Shelly would become the person who made the difference in Debbie's being allowed to live at home again, rather than languish in a nursing home designed for the elderly.

Shelly and Rose were very different, but they were both extremely loyal friends. Rose was very proper, wore her dark hair pulled tautly back from her un-madeup face, and had a very soft, precise voice. She was devoted to her religion, and she was stubborn. Shelly spoke loudly and firmly, wore her hair in sometimes outrageous styles in wild colors, with lipstick to match, but she was stubborn, too.

Like Sharon Simon, they understood that Debbie didn't need anyone judging her or giving her advice. Both Rose and Shelly could understand why Debbie still clung to a relationship with Anthony, even though it was probably a relationship that had never really existed beyond Debbie's hopes. Although *they* didn't like him, Debbie had loved him for such a long time.

"He was her *husband*," Rose said. "For all those years, she wanted to believe in him."

Debbie's survival *was* a miracle; nobody denied that. She should have died her first week in the hospital. That she survived was very impressive, even to toxicologists who usually based their conclusions on scientific theories. Nobody could have that much arsenic in their system and live. But Rose had been faithfully saying the Novena of the Little Flower of St. Therese, a special Catholic prayer. St. Therese has been elevated to a doctor of the Church, and Rose prayed to her for Debbie's recovery. Rose had also enrolled Debbie in a prayer chain so that she would be prayed for constantly by the Carmelite Sisters.

By the beginning of August, when her hold on life was the most fragile, Debbie had scores of people who didn't even know her praying for her. Rose considered her recovery a miracle, and no scientists spoke up to disagree with her.

Like Rose, Shelly insisted upon visiting Debbie in the hospital. "I only knew her from the boys' football games," Shelly recalled, "and I can't explain why I had such a strong need to go to her. She was just a customer in my shop, but when she came to my house a week before she went to the hospital I just knew something was wrong. I *had* to go see her in the hospital."

Actually, Shelly probably knew Anthony better than she did Debbie. Her terrific figure was partly Anthony's handiwork. "He gave me breast implants," Shelly said. Although she had an uneventful recovery, she had never cared much for Anthony. She cut his hair, but there was always something about him that grated on her. During that fall of 1999, while Debbie was still in the hospital, Shelly watched Anthony once during a football game played in a drizzling rain.

"There was something wrong with him," she said. "I didn't know if it was alcohol or what—but he was on something. I actually called the West Seneca Police because he was acting so strange, and I knew that part of his probation said that he couldn't drink or do drugs. They told me, 'Don't worry about it. We're watching him. Let him hang himself.' "

Shelly was a little surprised at their response, but then she realized she wasn't the only one keeping an eye on Anthony.

One of the coaches in the league where Ralph played football remembered a game night when it poured down rain; it might have been the same night that Shelly watched Anthony.

"I had mentioned loudly that the sidelines were so muddy that I needed some *boots,*" the coach said. "Anthony was on the sidelines within hearing distance, and he waved to me, and said, 'Here!' and tossed me his plastic water bottle. He must have thought that I said 'I need some *booze*' because as I took a sip from the water bottle, I realized I was drinking straight whiskey! He always had a plastic bottle with him on game day."

Both Rose and Shelly had happy marriages, but Shelly had survived a rough first marriage and she felt a lot of empathy for Debbie.

Rose and Shelly bolstered her spirits. They told her that her house was fine and they were looking after it. Shelly even packed up her hairdressing salon and took it to Debbie's hospital room.

"They weren't taking care of her the way she always did," Shelly said. "The nurses were wonderful to her, but they didn't have time to fix her up. Debbie was always very into her hair, and having her nails done nicely, and of course now she couldn't use her hands."

"She even came to the hospital and dyed my hair for me," Debbie remembered. "She did my nails and my makeup."

These attentions may not have been life saving, but they gave Debbie a boost when she had begun to feel like a useless lump lying in bed day after day with little hope. The sight of Shelly and Rose cheered her.

If they believed she was going to make it, she could believe that, too.

It wasn't until the last few weeks in October that her nurses, Teena Wise and Jackie Keller, could get Debbie into a wheelchair to maneuver her into the shower.

"I couldn't move or stand, so they'd have to grab me under the arms to get me on my feet," she recalled, "and the pain was so excruciating that I'd start screaming, 'I don't want to! I don't want to!' It just hurt everywhere, and it hurt to be touched. But somehow we'd make it to the shower down the hall, and then they'd have to drape me with towels so I'd be decent enough when they wheeled me past my guard."

One night on the 11-to-7 shift, the nurses on duty had given Debbie all the medication that they could, and nothing seemed to touch her pain. "They came in, and they started crying. They were telling me, 'Debbie, we don't know what to do. We don't have anything else to give you.' I knew I had to let it ride."

Debbie remembered when one of her physical therapists suggested that she use other ways to function. They could attach instruments to her wheelchair to help her feed herself, and a sliding board to help her from the chair to the bed. She didn't want to resort to that—it would be like admitting she would always be paralyzed.

"With the help of my wonderful physical and occupational therapists, my nurses and doctors, I overcame many obstacles," Debbie said. "Finally, I was able to walk with braces on my legs and a walker—just a few steps at a time. I was almost able to pick something up and put it in my mouth to eat. I was able to turn over in bed. You don't know how important those things are until you can't do them. With every little step, the staff was right there to cheer me on."

After two and a half months in the hospital, the time came for Debbie to leave. By the third week of October 1999, she had progressed as far as she could in the hospital rehabilitation center. She wanted desperately to go home to her own house. She was running out of health insurance. She had two choices: to go to a senior rehabilitation center (basically a nursing home) or go home with 24-hour care. She couldn't begin to afford full-time nurses, and she could not possibly live alone. She would need help in the most ordinary of tasks that other people take for granted, along with regular shots and injections, and her mother didn't think she could do that all by herself.

There was no question about Ralph and Lauren coming home. To add to Debbie's misery, the Children's Protective Services Agency of the Erie County Department of Social Services was moving ahead with their efforts to take away her custodial rights to Ralph and Lauren.

Debbie realized to her horror that perhaps *she* had inadvertently helped to bring their investigation into her capability as a parent down on herself. She had called her pediatrician and asked to have Ralph and Lauren tested for arsenic poisoning. Now, both she and Anthony were the objects of scrutiny. Her children were under a court order to stay in their uncle's home. Despite all the physical pain, the worst pain Debbie endured was emotional. She was being kept away from her children. They wouldn't be living with her when she went home, and the house would seem so empty without them, and without Anthony—or rather the hopes she had always had to have him be a real dad and a real husband.

It seemed such a ridiculous situation to anyone who knew Debbie Pignataro and her abiding love for her two children, but for now Ralph and Lauren were ordered to stay with Carmine and his wife. Still, in October 1999, Debbie believed that they would be allowed to come home to her if she could only recover enough to take care of them. Surely the CPS investigation would be over soon.

She could not have been more wrong.

But, for the moment in October, Debbie's biggest hurdle was trying to figure out a way she could go home and continue convalescing there. She had finally gathered the emotional strength to tell Anthony not to visit her any longer. He certainly wouldn't be there at home, and she knew in her heart that even if he was, he wouldn't take care of her. Beyond that, she had begun to accept that it was indeed Anthony who had fed her the poison that had almost killed her and had left her in the condition she was in. She didn't want to be around him any more.

So, just before Halloween 1999, Debbie was virtually helpless, and no one knew how far she would come back or whether she would ever improve beyond this point. After twenty-six years, Caroline asked to be laid off her job at Krasner's department store so she could move in and take care of Debbie. But they still needed one other person.

"I'll take care of you," Shelly Palombaro said firmly.

"You can't, Shelly," Debbie protested. "You've got a husband and a family, and you work all day. There's no way you could take care of me, too."

"Yes, I can. And I will."

Porches and windows were decorated with jack-o'-lanterns, and the air smelled of smoke rather than the flowers of summer, as Debbie was driven down her street for the first time in two and a half months.

"I arrived to an empty house," Debbie said, remembering how strange it seemed. The hospital bed took up most of the living room. Shelly and Caroline got Debbie settled in her wheelchair, combed her hair, and fixed her makeup. She hadn't told Ralph and Lauren that she was coming home for fear something might happen to delay her homecoming.

"They were at Carmine's house, and we wanted to surprise them, Debbie said. "Carmine and Patti made up this story about having to stop by our house to pick up some of Ralph's football equipment.

"When they arrived, I was sitting in the wheelchair, and they were so happy. *Mom was home!* No matter what condition I was in. They were just so happy that I was home."

Shelly had promised to take care of Debbie, and she did. For six months, Shelly arrived at Debbie's house every morning at 6 A.M. "She got me dressed, did my hair, put on makeup . . . She came back every four hours to help me," Debbie said.

"I brushed your teeth for a long time, too," Shelly reminded her, laughing. "You couldn't hold a toothbrush."

When Debbie first came home, her physical therapist had her crawl up the stairs on her hands and knees. She made it, but then she didn't know how to get down, and neither did the therapist. Shelly was irate, and she demanded that Debbie be assigned another therapist. She got someone whose approach was calmer and more in keeping with her physical capabilities.

But upstairs was out of the question. Debbie's whole world was the living room/dining room, the kitchen, and the little downstairs bathroom. Although Caroline Rago had given up her home and her job to move in with Debbie, there were still many things she was hesitant to do. Shelly helped Debbie with the most intimate chores—things that nurses do routinely. When Debbie was embarrassed, Shelly taught her how to laugh instead. Sometimes the two of them went into hysterical giggles.

Without Shelly, Debbie would have been lost. She wasn't exactly a quadriplegic, but neither her arms nor her legs worked very well. They were numb and unpredictable.

"One time, I thought I had Debbie safe, standing in front of her kitchen sink with her braces on, and I thought she could hold on," Shelly said. "I turned my back for a moment, and she fell right over backward. I felt terrible."

Shelly gave the intramuscular shots that Debbie needed. But once Shelly had to be away for four days, and Caroline had to do it. She didn't think she could. She was terrified—but she did it. "I was so afraid I'd hurt her," Caroline recalled.

Ralph and Lauren couldn't understand why they couldn't come back home full time, but the court order said they had to stay with Carmine and Patti. "I could only see them one hour per week," Debbie said. *One* hour . . .

Anthony never came to see Debbie after the day Denis Scinta threw him out of her hospital room. Oddly, he didn't fight his banishment. It was as if he was waiting for the ax to fall and didn't want to draw attention to himself.

"Anthony went to court and got visitation rights with

Ralph and Lauren," Debbie said. "Sometimes the kids were with me and he came to pick them up. If he stepped inside the door, he was in the same room with me because my hospital bed was right there. But we barely spoke— maybe we said a few words about the kids."

Debbie was shocked when she learned from the children that Anthony was working on them, trying to get them to believe wild stories and to believe his excuses for himself that were far beyond their ability to handle.

"He was telling them that the person who gave me arsenic was someone in Sarah Smith's family. And then he told them that his mistress's ex-boyfriend did this to me," Debbie recalled. "Finally, he even accused a neighbor from across the street!

"My kids were scared and confused—very upset. There wasn't anything I could say to help them. The things he told them weren't true, and they were totally inappropriate for a father to say to children who were only ten and twelve. Anthony was only interested in saving himself. He had never put the children's needs first, and he was still playing with their minds."

But Ralph and Lauren knew that their mother was the one who had always been there for them. The three of them had formed a bond that none of their father's wiles could weaken. Frustrated, Anthony gradually began to plead with Debbie. That had always worked before. Debbie had always taken him back, no matter what.

"I can't live with my mom," he said urgently. "She's driving me crazy. Deb, I want to come home."

For the first time in twenty years, Debbie didn't want him to come home. She never wanted to live with him again.

"He would still work on the kids, too," Debbie said. "He'd ask Ralph, 'Why don't we all go to the Buffalo Bills game?' As if somebody could load me into a wheelchair and take me up the stadium steps. I couldn't even get upstairs to the bathroom. Shelly's husband teased me and said, 'Sure, Deb, you go to the game. He can push you right up to the top row and send you over the edge,' and we all laughed. I was actually getting to the point where I could laugh about things that used to make me cry."

While Anthony Pignataro worked to get back into the good graces of his wife and made certain that he was observed being an excellent father, Debbie was learning that it was quite possible to live without him. The men who tracked him were jumping over all the hurdles they had to clear before they could hope to get an arrest warrant. They knew they had an essentially circumstantial case, but a solid circumstantial case can be as strong as, or stronger than, one based on physical evidence or even an eyewitness if it is constructed flawlessly.

Sharon Simon was still visiting Debbie or calling, Shelly and Rose and her mother were taking care of her, and Debbie was as happy as a paralyzed woman whose beloved children could not live with her could be. She tried not to think about what would happen if her paralysis was permanent. She focused on each day, thrilled when she continued to make tiny steps toward recovery. Debbie's doctors couldn't tell her what her prognosis was. They had never treated anyone with such profound arsenic poisoning before.

Anthony's mother never asked how Debbie was doing. One of Debbie's neighbors, an older woman they all called "Virginia, the Italian Kitchen Lady" because she was such a wonderful cook, was ill. Lena stopped by Rose Gardner's house to ask about Virginia, but she didn't even mention Debbie, who was only a few houses down the street, struggling to feed herself and to get up on her feet.

On one occasion, Lena picked Ralph and Lauren up

from Shelly's house. Shelly welcomed her with a smile and said, "Hi! Would you like to come in while they're getting their stuff?"

"Anthony's mother looked at me as if my house was filthy," Shelly said. "She stuck up her nose and wrapped her coat tightly around herself and took a perch on my porch. She said, 'I do *not* want to wait in *your* house!' "

22

Debbie was afraid to go out in public. She had come to dread the threat of camera strobe lights flashing and reporters confronting her with questions during Anthony's court appearances after Sarah Smith's death. She had seen her own startled image on the television news or in newspaper articles too often, her face a bleak study in stress. The Pignataros were big news in Buffalo, and sometimes it still felt to her as if she were a character in a continuing soap opera saga. She couldn't remember when she had last had peace in her life. She wondered if she ever would again.

But Shelly Palombaro wouldn't let Debbie hide in her house. As soon as Debbie could physically handle it, Shelly bundled her and her wheelchair up, loaded her into a van, and took her to Ralph's football games. With her arms and legs still as numb as if they were asleep, Debbie felt embarrassed—like an object of curiosity in her rolling chair. And yet, it was wonderful to be able to watch her son out on the field. Whenever Shelly thought Debbie was getting too housebound, she coaxed her into going for a drive and even to Kmart or the grocery store.

"People recognized me, I know," Debbie said, "but they were nice. A lot of strangers stopped to say they were pulling for me. It wasn't as bad as I thought it would be."

Shelly had such an outrageous sense of humor that she could usually get Debbie to laugh. She hadn't really laughed in years. When she fell down or dropped a forkful of food, they laughed instead of crying, and it felt good.

There were tears, too. Now that she was back in her own house, Debbie promised Lauren and Ralph that they would be home with her by the holidays. She was sure of it, because she was getting a little bit of feeling back every week. She knew she was too weak to spend a whole day and night at Carmine's house for Christmas with them. Having her children home for Thanksgiving and Christmas was her first goal, and Debbie truly believed that they would be able to come home as soon as she was stronger. She didn't know she wouldn't be able to keep that promise.

The state wouldn't let Ralph and Lauren live with Debbie, although they allowed agonizingly brief visits. The visits were over too soon. And then the kids would fight over who got to hug Debbie last.

"It was awful," Shelly Palombaro said. "We'd just have to peel the kids off Debbie, and they'd all be crying."

After they left their mother's house, the phone would ring in twenty minutes, and they'd talk and talk for two hours. Ralph and Lauren cried and wanted to come home, and Debbie tried to calm them down so they could sleep. They did little rituals, like "I love you, Mom." "I love you, too."

It made her heart hurt to know that their rooms upstairs were empty.

The holiday season was anything but festive for Debbie Pignataro. A year before, she had been full of hope. Anthony was home from jail, they had gone through a renewal of their wedding vows, and their future seemed bright. But it had all turned ugly so soon. Now, they would soon be divorced.

Anthony had cashed in his stocks and bonds to pay the legal expenses when he got in trouble over Sarah's surgery. His portfolio was depleted now, and he turned continually to his mother, who was ready to stand behind him. She hired one of Buffalo's most outstanding defense attorneys, Joel Daniels. Daniels was touched by the elderly woman who sat in his office and cried. He was a tenacious combatant, but he had a tender spot for white-haired mothers sobbing for their sons. Daniels agreed to defend Anthony in whatever legal travails lay ahead. Brian Welsh joined him as co-counsel.

The first fight for the Pignataros would be against the Children's Protective Service. But, oddly, Anthony didn't seem concerned about losing custody of his children, while Debbie was terrified of what the family court might do. Anthony bent CPS's charges to suit himself and get back at Debbie.

Both Debbie and Anthony were listed as defendants in the family court case. But Daniels and Welsh knew that far more serious charges were hovering over Anthony's head. They were convinced that Erie County District Attorney Frank J. Clark would attempt to indict their client in the poisoning of his now estranged wife.

And they were right. Joel Daniels sought an order that would compel the West Seneca Police Department to comply with Judge Marjorie Mix's subpoena instructing them to turn over all the information they had in the poisoning of Debbie Pignataro and—as rumor had it—her children. The West Seneca department balked at releasing their files, and the Erie County District Attorney stepped in to join the small police department. Their investigation was confidential, and they wanted it to stay that way.

The matter was left in abeyance, waiting for more evidence that either of the Pignataro children had had toxic levels of arsenic. Actually, tests on Lauren and Ralph hadn't shown alarming amounts of arsenic in their systems.

Anthony had visitation rights with his children on Tuesdays and Thursdays, but Carmine Rago told Frank Sedita that he had come to see Ralph and Lauren only once between August and November, 1999. Carmine suspected that Anthony had chosen to go to Ralph's football practices to speak to his son there—against family court Judge Marjorie Mix's orders.

When he could not get to Debbie directly, Anthony continued to work on their children. Ralph was a strained rope in an emotional tug-of-war. No matter how Debbie tried to protect him, Anthony always found ways to draw him in.

"Why is your mother doing this?" he asked his son, blaming Debbie for the divorce, for failing to let him come home, for all of their troubles. "We will have no more family. You know there will be no more vacations to Florida."

Carol Giarizzo Bridge, the D.A.'s assistant bureau chief for domestic violence cases, talked with Patti Rago, Carmine's wife, and learned that the children had permission from the Department of Social Services to go to the Buffalo Bills/Indianapolis Colts football game on January 2, 2000, with their father. But Ralph had come home with his mind full of Anthony's dire warnings of what would happen to their family if his mother didn't do as his father wanted.

"She [Debbie] cannot say I did this, because if she does, I will go away for twenty-five years," he had told Ralph. "If Daddy goes to jail, you will have to leave your house— but if Daddy stays out of jail, you can stay in the house."

It was clear that Ralph was supposed to persuade Debbie to stand by his father. If she didn't, Anthony had painted a world that would come tumbling down for Ralph and Lauren—a world with no home, no money to live on, and no family. Ralph was smart, probably far more intelligent than his father—but he was only thirteen. No responsible adult would ever have suspended him in the middle of this struggle.

The state wasn't ready to indict Anthony on attempted murder charges. Some questions hadn't yet been answered. There might be questions they could *never* answer. And all the time they were working on two fronts. While Frank Sedita was fighting to protect Debbie from the relentless pressure of unending hearings in family court, he was also striving to find enough evidence to arrest Anthony for attempted murder.

Chuck Craven was determined to find the source of the arsenic trioxide that had been used to poison Debbie. Even two decades earlier, it would have been easier. Most farmers then kept poison in their barns to kill rats and mice. There was even some horse medicine that contained arsenic: one to kill worms and another called Appitone that was given to them to stimulate their appetites. But the Environmental Protective Agency had long since ordered that the age-old preparations containing arsenic be taken off the market. One thing Craven learned was that there were virtually no cases on record of suicide by arsenic. It would have taken too long and hurt too much.

The only thing Craven really had to go on was the statement Lauren Pignataro had made about seeing her dad placing little round tins or cans around their house to kill ants. He searched hardware stores and the huge club stores for something that resembled that description, but it was winter, and the ant season in Buffalo was over.

Since Buffalo is so close to Canada, Craven wondered

whether Anthony might have gone out of the country to buy arsenic, but he didn't make any headway with that theory.

Craven heard about a product called Terro Ant Killer, but he found out that it had been removed from the market about a decade earlier. It had proved too toxic to sell to the general public. Several murderers, mostly female, had used Terro to get rid of spouses before the middle of the twentieth century, but it was long gone from store shelves in 2000.

The product had been manufactured by the Senoret Chemical Company in St. Louis, Missouri, and Chuck Craven called the company to talk to the staff there. It was true that Terro Ant Killer was a thing of the past after the EPA recall, but Stewart Clark of Senoret told Craven that there was a company in San Leandro, California, that sold an ant-killing product said to contain arsenic trioxide.

"It's called Grant's Labs."

Craven next talked to Lou Antonali, the chief operating officer at Grant's. Antonali confirmed that they did manufacture ant killer containing arsenic trioxide. It was made of a waxy substance that contained 0.35 to 0.46 percent arsenic trioxide with a sweetener. The sweet taste attracted ants.

"How much poison would that be?" Craven asked.

"Well, they come in what we call hand stacks," Antonali said. "Two hand stacks could conceivably give a 150-pound man a fatal toxicity level."

Craven held his breath. He then asked what a "hand stack" was—what it looked like.

" 'Grant's Kills Ants' is sold in small round tins—four tins per stack."

Exactly what Lauren had described to Craven: "little round tins." But all those little tins were gone when they had searched the Pignataros' house.

Craven found out that the arsenic trioxide used by

Grant's came from Kraft Chemical in Melrose Park, Illinois. He phoned that company and talked to an employee named Mattie Webb. When he asked her where they got the arsenic, she said it was imported from Mexico. However, most of their customers were in the Chicago area.

"Would you sell to Canada?"

The answer was no. It would be cost prohibitive and too much trouble to bother with customs. Mattie Webb knew of no sales at all to individuals. A single person attempting to buy arsenic would come under great suspicion. Kraft Chemical dealt only with major companies.

Frank Sedita talked to a company in Philadelphia to see if they had sold any arsenic trioxide. No. They hadn't had a single sale in 1999. They wouldn't sell it to an individual, either.

Frank Sedita tried another approach. He asked if the Pennsylvania company had any record of selling to Plastic Surgeons International, the Canadian corporation that Anthony was affiliated with. If not in 1999, then any previous year?

No.

As it turned out, finding an outlet for Grant's Kills Ants wasn't that difficult. It was right in front of them the whole time. Chuck Craven went to a Target Store in Cheektowaga, the Buffalo suburb. He headed toward the gardening and pest control section, and there it was on the shelf. There were several forms of Grant's Kills Ants. One was an ant trap to be placed on the floor; another was a metal spike that could be stuck in the ground around shrubs and bushes (particularly peonies, which attract ants).

The third form of ant killer containing arsenic trioxide was sold in the little round tins. Craven bought the products. He didn't look like a detective, and he certainly didn't tell the sales clerk why he wanted ant killer. He realized that was probably all Anthony had to do—just walk into a store and buy a product to kill annoying insects. They would never be able to trace his purchase now unless he'd used a credit card. Pat Finnerty was an expert on paper trails, but they didn't find any purchases of ant killer memorialized on either Debbie's or Anthony's credit cards.

Debbie Pignataro had told them that she usually drank Kool-Aid in the summer. It was sweet. She wouldn't have tasted a sweet and deadly additive. Later, of course, everything tasted strange to her—that silvery metallic taste. Even chicken noodle soup tasted off to her. She wouldn't have been able to recognize it if Anthony had put a massive dose of arsenic in her bowl of soup. She just got sicker, and she didn't connect Lauren's nausea to her own—not for a long time.

Sedita, Finnerty, and Craven felt that the soup poisoning was probably the one that took Debbie out of the chronic poisoning category and plunged her into acute poisoning.

It was time for them to move in. There was a very strong possibility that Anthony would bolt and run, perhaps even leave the country. He had confided his plans for an offshore clinic to reverse the ravages of aging to enough people to make them think he was serious. Anthony Pignataro might have an outlandish perception of himself as compared to the rest of society, but he was shrewd and intelligent. If he was free, and if he decided to leave Buffalo and West Seneca behind, he would figure out a plan—one probably financed by his mother, even if she had no idea that he was leaving.

On January 31, 2000, the net that hung over Anthony began to tighten, although he didn't know it. He was too focused on trying to convince Debbie to reconcile with him so he could improve his image.

Anthony's probation officer, Judith White, wrote out a

violation summary, attaching affidavits from Chuck Craven, Arnie Letovich, and Deborah Pignataro. When Judge Ronald Tills sentenced Anthony on August 7, 1998, two important probation conditions were imposed: (1) Anthony was to remain drug and alcohol free, and (2) he was forbidden to leave Erie County without permission of the Court and the probation department.

He had broken both of those provisos. Arnie Letovich's affidavit spoke of Anthony's heroin use and his plans to move far away and open a new medical practice. Debbie's detailed his alcohol consumption and the unauthorized trip Anthony took to Philadelphia. When he applied for the job at the Veterans' Hospital, he had taken her and their children with him as props, she realized, to support his "good family man" image. And he'd insisted that the hotel and car rental be charged to *her* Visa card so that he left no trail.

But he *had* left a trail. Chuck Craven had possession of four CDs from Anthony's computer; one contained Anthony's letter to the Veterans' Hospital where he had hoped to get a job. That letter substantiated that he had indeed left Erie County without permission from anyone. It was helpful that Tony Pignataro had dated it.

The arrest warrant, signed by Judge Tills, went out to "Any Police Officer, Sheriff's Deputy, or Peace Officer in this State.

"Whereas ANTHONY PIGNATARO . . . having violated the conditions of probation, you are commanded forthwith to arrest the above named ANTHONY PIGNATARO and bring this individual before this court for judgement."

Anthony was arrested on February 1, 2000, but Lena quickly posted $50,000 bail, so that he spent only one night in jail. When he left jail, however, he wore an electronic ankle bracelet that allowed authorities to monitor his every move.

On Valentine's Day, he was back in jail. Still positive that Debbie would never blow the whistle on him, he had called her on February 5, despite a no-contact order by the Court.

Debbie now had a restraining order to keep Anthony from phoning her. She had finally realized that she didn't have to see him or talk to him any longer. Anthony knew full well the danger of someone finding out that he'd broken most of the rules of his probation, but he never doubted that Debbie would save him. His calls to her were always choreographed to draw her over to his side, and he'd pulled out all the stops to persuade her that she had to take him back.

In his second arrest in two weeks, Anthony's bail was set so high that even Lena Pignataro decided against bailing him out.

Anthony was terrified of having to finish his five-year term for the death of Sarah Smith. If his probation was revoked, that was very likely to happen. Perhaps he wasn't really afraid yet of the far more serious charges that might await him.

Anthony was fairly certain that he could still pull Debbie back to him, but he was losing control. He had always been able to manipulate two women in his life: his mother and his wife. Now he felt his power slipping away, at least with his wife. He was aghast that she had actually reported him for calling her on the phone. The old Debbie would never have betrayed him like that.

"You hold the cards, Deb," Anthony had pleaded in his call. "You know I can't do five years. Can't I go for shock treatment instead? Can I go to a halfway house? At least, if I'm out of control, my mom will take care of you and the kids. I can't do it. I'll die in there if I have to go back to prison."

"You know what I thought?" Debbie asked, a long time later. "I thought, 'Well, I was supposed to be six feet under, so maybe his troubles weren't as bad as he thought. Maybe he had it coming.' "

The family court hearings continued in the early months of 2000, meeting for a few days here and a few days there. Each time, Debbie thought that Judge Mix would let Ralph and Lauren come home to live with her. She tried to follow every directive Judge Mix gave her and to answer every question. But the children were still living with Carmine and his family.

It was like a frustration nightmare where one escape door opens on another and another and another. Although Debbie was getting physically and mentally stronger all the time, she didn't have her children.

Anthony's attorney, Joel Daniels, had attempted to use the family court proceedings in Judge Marjorie Mix's courtroom to find out just what the D.A.'s office had uncovered about Anthony in the poisoning case. This was pushing "discovery" way beyond the point that Frank Sedita felt was either relevant or proper, and Judge Mix seemed to take forever to make a decision whether Anthony and his defense team could see all the files of their investigation.

Judge Mix's responsibility was to decide whether Ralph and Lauren Pignataro were neglected children. However, the judge would continually refer to Debbie's poisoning and say, "I have to get to the bottom of this." Solving the criminal case should not, Sedita felt, be a part of the matter of child neglect before Judge Mix. In a legal sense, it was apples and oranges.

The D.A.'s office had been granted intervenor status, and Sedita moved again to quash the subpoena that used the discovery option of the Family Court Act to obtain criminal investigative files from the West Seneca Police Department. If the subpoena wasn't stopped, Anthony and his attorneys would have access to all the information Sedita and the detectives had obtained in the poisoning investigation. That would grant them an "open sesame" to anything and everything the investigators knew about Pignataro.

Sedita pointed out in an order to show cause on February 4, 2000, that Anthony was currently on probation for a conviction on criminally negligent homicide charges, and that Debbie had almost died of sky-high levels of inorganic arsenic. "She survived the poisoning but has suffered serious and permanent physical injury."

Judge Mix seemed unmoved.

Further, Sedita said that a criminal investigation into that poisoning was being conducted by his office and the West Seneca Police Department. "The target of the investigation is Anthony Pignataro, respondent in the neglect proceeding."

Since the Pignataro children had no inorganic arsenic in their bodies, Sedita argued that there was really no need for the family court to continue on a "factually baseless petition's" information.

Sedita argued that Debbie should be named the legal guardian of her children and said that even the Department of Social Services agreed with that.

"Of all persons and bodies interested in the neglect proceedings, the only persons or bodies who object to its discontinuance are Anthony Pignataro and family court," Sedita argued, with a sense of frustration.

All through February, Judge Mix delayed ruling on releasing the investigators' records.

It should have been over sooner. For six months, beginning while she was still in the hospital, Debbie had felt like a target for the Child Protective Service. On February 23, 2000, even though she couldn't walk or even hold a little paper cup of water when her throat grew dry with nervousness, she was subjected to intense questioning on the witness stand.

It was all happening at once. Debbie took the stand in Judge Marjorie Mix's courtroom for two days of direct examination and cross-examination to explain why she was convinced her husband had poisoned her. She answered the questions put to her by Denis Scinta and then by Joel Daniels as well as she could.

Judge Mix was a mother and a grandmother, but she was also a jurist given to sudden explosions of temper, and Debbie was afraid of her wrath as she sat in the witness chair. Her cousin Denis tried to tell her during breaks that it would be all right. She sometimes wondered how that could possibly be. She was grateful to have Frank Sedita on her side, and Sharon Simon was always there for her in court.

Marlene Chemen, a senior child protection social worker who had seen the children in both Debbie's home and Carmine Rago's home, testified that she felt the children should be allowed to go home to be cared for by their mother and their maternal grandmother, Caroline. And then Chemen, too, was bombarded with questions by Joel Daniels about Debbie's "mental instability."

Ralph and Lauren's court-appointed guardian, Theresa Lorenzo, asked the judge to bring them to court so that they could tell her what *their* wishes were, but Judge Mix said she was already aware that they wanted to come home to live with their mother. "I have to strive legally to keep them from risk," she explained as she denied the request.

But it was Debbie who testified endlessly. She answered every question put to her to the best of her memory, telling the truth, because if she lost her children, she would have no reason to go on.

There was no disagreement that in February and March

1999, Debbie *had* been unstable—depressed, anxious, grieving, angry, and hopeless. The husband who had declared his undying love in December and remarried her the day he walked out of prison had left her after only a few months to be with another woman. For the purposes of these family court hearings, she had done the worst thing possible. After Anthony left her once more, to relieve her severe stress, she had taken ten to twelve Xanax capsules. Even though she had immediately realized that she'd done something foolish and dangerous and phoned for help, her "suicide attempt" kept coming back to haunt her again and again.

It didn't matter that a psychiatric examination she had submitted to found her reaction "transient and expectable" given the situation. That one act of desperation, quickly over, clung to her like moss on a tree in deep shade.

Now, as Debbie testified, the questions grew more and more daunting. Joel Daniels asked her a dozen ways who had poisoned her, while Denis Scinta and Frank Sedita objected to his attempts to slide over into the criminal case. Debbie could not prove who had poisoned her, but she answered, "I don't believe my children did this to me, and I don't believe my mother did this to me, and I did not do it to myself. The only other person was my husband."

So many attorneys were in the room that it made Debbie dizzy. Denis had told her that she didn't have to answer questions about things she didn't remember, and so much of the summer of 1999 was obscured by a fog of pain and disorientation.

The examination by Joel Daniels would have confused even a seasoned witness, and Debbie struggled to keep from giving the wrong answer to his rapid-fire questions. He wanted to know who had told her that her husband had poisoned her. He suggested that her cousin Denis Scinta had put the idea into her head.

Through discovery, Daniels had Debbie's medical records, and he went tediously—and accusingly—through all the pills and capsules she had taken over the past several years while she had five neck surgeries and was in severe pain. As the hours wore on, it was as if *she* were somehow guilty because she had been injured in the boat accident and then because she had been poisoned. She could not remember each incident of visits to a doctor, emergency room treatments, surgeries, hospitalizations. No one could have.

Denis Scinta reminded the judge that Debbie needed to change position because the blood would not circulate in her legs if she sat too long in one spot. Debbie's hand shook so much that when she needed water, her cousin had to hold the paper cup to her mouth.

Ironically, she had been called by Anthony's attorney, and it was her attorney, her cousin Denis, who cross-examined her. It was a relief when Daniels sat down and Denis walked toward her, smiling. Denis managed to move deftly as he questioned her so that he blocked her view of Anthony, who stared at her as if he could hypnotize her into retracting her statements. But even for Denis, Debbie could not recall much of the previous summer. She had been so sick. Her memory cleared somewhat as the questions moved on to the autumn.

"When you went home in October," Denis asked, "what were you able to do with your hands?"

"Basically nothing."

"And how about your feet? What were you able to do in terms of walking or using your legs?"

"They sent me home with a walker . . . it wasn't a regular walker."

"Would you try to describe for the Court what walker you were on at the beginning of your return home?"

"The walker was probably twelve inches higher than a

regular walker, and my hands had to be strapped into it. I couldn't grip."

"When you went home, were you able to feed yourself?"

"No, I was not."

Debbie explained that she had been having occupational and physical therapy four times a week. She had come to the point where she could use a regular walker and could now go upstairs once a day—to bed at night and down in the morning. She could use a knife and fork and drink out of a glass with a straw. She could take a shower if she had a shower chair.

"And could you tell the Court," Denis asked, "why is it that you have to sit?"

"Because I lose my balance."

He asked her the purpose of the braces on her feet.

"To help me walk."

"Are you able to walk at all on your own—any distance?"

"Yes, sir . . . I'd say ten to fifteen feet."

"All right. And while you're walking, are there people there to watch you in case you become unsteady?"

"Always."

"Mrs. Pignataro," Denis Scinta asked his cousin, "I know it's been asked and answered a number of times of you. I'm going to ask it again. Did you [deliberately] at any time during 1999 ingest any arsenic in your system?"

"No, sir."

"Did you at any time expose your children to any arsenic that may have been in and about your system or around your house?"

Debbie stared back at him with clear eyes. "No sir."

"I have no further questions."

There were so many lawyers. Edward McGuinness, attorney for the Erie County Department of Social Services, asked Debbie about her pain and seemed kind.

Frank Sedita rose to ask more questions. For a moment, Debbie's mind flashed back to Anthony's hearings over Sarah's death, and she remembered how intimidated she had been by Frank. But now, he was on her side. His dark eyes were serious. Try as she might, she admitted to herself that Frank still scared her a little. He was so smart and somber.

She wasn't sure what he was going to ask her, but she soon figured out that he was simply undoing the mass of accusations Anthony's attorneys had flung at her.

"Do you carry any diagnosis as a drug abuser, ma'am?"

"No, sir."

"Have you ever been institutionalized—such as like the Buffalo Psychiatric Center, any facilities like those?"

"No, sir."

"Have you ever had to go to any kind of outpatient psychiatric services? Just to give you some examples: Horizons, Lake Shore Behavioral Health Services, anything like that?"

"No, sir."

"Are you a convicted felon, Mrs. Pignataro?"

"No, sir."

Daniels and Welsh tensed at the defense table. They could see where Sedita was going. As long as he stayed within certain parameters, there wasn't a thing they could do to stop him.

"Have you ever been indicted for forgery?"

"No, sir."

"Have you ever been indicted for falsifying records?"

"No, sir."

"Have you ever been responsible for the death of another human being?"

"No, sir."

Sedita was walking a very careful line, never mentioning that Anthony Pignataro could have answered "Yes" to all of his questions.

He led Debbie through the spring and summer of the previous year, his questions seemingly innocuous as he asked who had cooked and cleaned and looked after the well-being of her children. "Myself . . . my mother."

And then she answered that after Anthony moved in, he had done some of the cooking. The time sequences were interesting, but Sedita didn't comment on them. They spoke for themselves.

"Have you ever done anything in your life to harm your children, Mrs. Pignataro?"

"No, sir."

"Have you ever done anything in your life to harm yourself, Mrs. Pignataro?"

"No, sir."

"Have you ever done anything in your life to harm your husband, Mrs. Pignataro?"

"No, sir."

"Who are the most important people in your life, Mrs. Pignataro?"

"My children."

Using simple questions that asked for short answers, Frank Sedita winnowed out the rhetoric of the defense and sliced it away. Since Debbie had come home, no one had gotten sick, and no one needed to be tested for arsenic poisoning. Debbie had had only a year in college; she had no four-year degree and no medical degree. She didn't even know what arsenic looked like, how to obtain it, or what doses were fatal.

"In the course of being familiar with that business [Anthony's Cosmetic Plastic Surgeon's International], did Mr. Pignataro at that time have a license to order drugs?"

"Yes, sir."

"Do you know exactly what kind of drugs he was ordering?"

"No, sir."

"Now, after your husband got out of the correctional facility, he began to author a manuscript. Is that correct?"

"Yes, sir."

"What's the title of that manuscript?"

"I believe it's *M.D.: Mass Destruction.*"

"From whose point of view is the book told?"

"Mine."

"Who actually wrote all the words—*all* the words in the manuscript?"

"My husband."

Judge Mix questioned Debbie directly about the time Ralph and Lauren were hospitalized to be tested for arsenic. Debbie said that their arsenic level was "slightly elevated," but that they hadn't needed to receive treatment.

"All right. You made reference to the process of clearing out the toxicity in your system during one of the painful parts of your hospitalization . . . Would it surprise you if I told you that the hospital records . . . reflect the fact that there was a consideration that your son— Was it your son or daughter who had the highest level?"

"My daughter."

"There was a possibility that your daughter might have to undergo the same process?"

"I did not know," Debbie said, her face worried.

The judge asked Debbie if she knew the children were ordered to eat only hospital food, and were not allowed off their floor, or to be released to anyone but her brother.

"I knew that, yes."

Denis Scinta called Anthony as a witness. And Joel Daniels leaped to his feet. "I will direct Dr. Pignataro not to take the stand, not to be sworn . . . The District Attorney intends to secure an indictment against Dr. Pignataro involving this case, and I will direct under no circumstances that he be sworn or answer any questions concerning the matter."

"Your honor," Denis Scinta responded. "Your Honor, I might just ask of the Court—that I think I've heard it several times in this court proceeding—maybe more often than I wanted to hear it, but that the sword cuts both ways ... The Court, when there was a discussion with Mr. Daniels, when he was directing the testimony of Mrs. Pignataro, you indicated that you would take into consideration her failure to answer any question posed to her at this hearing, and would weigh it as you saw fit?"

"Right," Judge Mix answered.

Frank Sedita argued that Anthony's refusal to even be sworn in seemed to be improper procedure. Under the Fifth Amendment, Anthony had the right to refuse to answer questions that might incriminate him, but that didn't mean he could simply refuse to take the stand and be sworn.

Joel Daniels would not even give his basis for argument. He said he simply refused to let Anthony be sworn in.

"Why?" Judge Mix pressed. "Can you explain that to me, Mr. Daniels?"

" 'Cause I just believe under the posture of this case and what's going on here and the District Attorney's office wanting so much to question him and wanting so much to even put questions to him—"

"I object to that!" Sedita said as tensions rose in the courtroom. "That's not true. I object to that."

Judge Mix noted his objection and allowed Daniels to continue.

"I would ask this Court to understand the situation we are in. We have been looking at an investigation for a long time. The District Attorney's office—they've followed him, they've surveilled him, they've talked to I don't know how many people in West Seneca. They have done anything they could to put this arsenic into his hands, and so far they can't do it and I'm not going to assist them in all of their investigation. We don't think they have a case . . . He's in jail now because of what Judge Tills did."

Edward J. McGuinness, the attorney for the Erie County Department of Social Services, agreed with Scinta and Sedita that Anthony Pignataro should at least agree to take the stand. How was the judge going to make a decision if she didn't hear what Pignataro had to say for himself? "I take the position he is in the default position."

Judge Mix attempted to placate the furious lawyers by saying she would take inference by Anthony's refusal to testify or answer questions, but she wouldn't force him to come up to the witness stand. She wanted to move the hearing along and to avoid "the charade of his nonresponse."

She refused to chastise Anthony or his attorneys.

Her stance only served to frustrate the attorneys for Child Protective Services, for Debbie, and from the District Attorney's office. Anthony Pignataro, through Joel Daniels, had just thumbed his nose at the judicial system, and the judge wanted no further discussion of it. She told the angry attorneys they could write their arguments or testify to them at a later date.

Anthony looked smug. He had never played by society's rules, and he was not about to start. He might be incarcerated at the moment, but nobody was going to make him testify.

It had been such a long, long day, and Debbie was exhausted, almost to the point of tears. She felt that Judge Mix didn't like her at all. Maybe all the strong attorneys in the world weren't going to make any difference.

* * *

Now, despite the common sense in Sedita's argument that the case against Debbie Pignataro be dismissed, Judge Mix declared that she wanted to continue the investigation of child neglect. And she denied the District Attorney's motion to quash the subpoena seeking their investigative files. Soon, Anthony's attorneys would be able to learn almost every bit of the intelligence they had carefully gathered against their client.

It was easy to understand why Anthony and his attorneys should want to keep a rich vein of information about the D.A.'s investigation open. What was baffling was why Judge Marjorie Mix was so adamant in continuing the case against Debbie.

None of them knew how long and agonizing Debbie's struggle to regain her children would be. Sharon Simon had feared it would be this way, but she hadn't told Debbie; that would have discouraged her before she began. Sometimes Debbie wondered if Ralph and Lauren would ever be allowed to come back to her. Maybe she would be an old woman and they would be grown up before the state would let them sleep in her house.

She accepted that Anthony had wanted her dead. And now, he was actually helping those who would take her children away from her. Anthony seemed to enjoy being on stage in family court. He made a big production about shuffling his legal papers and conferring with his attorneys.

An hour after he refused to take the witness stand, Anthony was found in contempt of court by Judge Mix and fined $1,000.

His mother would pay it for him. Lena Pignataro was always there, supporting her son. She walked with her head up, above the crowd. But she darted scathing looks at Caroline Rago and Debbie.

"She thought that money buys class," Caroline commented later in one of her rare criticisms of other people.

The old family court building in Buffalo was very cramped. All of its rooms and spaces were small and confining, all smelling of old radiators and the sweat and tears of thousands of people who had passed through over the years. Those who battled out old and new hurts there were forced together physically. The waiting rooms were always packed. If Caroline went in one room, she noticed that Lena made a big show of going into the other waiting room. But Lena and Caroline still had to pass by each other in the narrow hallways, almost touching. Lena never acknowledged Debbie's mother.

"We used to wonder what on earth Anthony could have told her about me," Debbie speculated. "She and I had been so close for so many years that it had to be something awful—that I was a drug addict, or cheating on him with another man, or something like that. I was the one in the wheelchair, but she acted as if I were the criminal."

Judge Mix seemed to think so, too. A few weeks after Debbie testified on February 23, she included her suspicions about just how limited Debbie's capabilities really were. "Illustrative of this claim was her repeated drinking of water from a cup held to her lips by her attorney," Judge Mix wrote. At other times in the hearing, however, "Ms. Pignataro absently put on and adjusted her glasses, held papers from which she read, and turned pages, creating a different impression."

And Debbie had come to a place where she could turn a page or push at her glasses despite the numbness in her fingers. But she could not manage a flimsy paper cup full of water without spilling it on herself.

Judge Mix postponed the hearings indefinitely.

Debbie had a supporter in Donn Esmonde, a columnist for the *Buffalo News,* who titled his commentary "Time to Drop Case Against Mrs. Pignataro."

"Anybody who thinks watching small boys pull the legs off a fly is entertaining would have enjoyed himself Wednesday in family court," Esmonde began his scorching criticism of the seemingly endless persecution of Debbie.

"How any of this makes Debbie Pignataro a bad parent is a mystery, unless ignoring your kids while fighting for your life is a crime . . .

"If this had been a boxing match, the referee would have stopped it. First arsenic, then a lengthy session with a hostile defense lawyer. . . . How much punishment can one woman take?

"Judge Mix says she wants to be sure the kids are safe. We hear that. But this system bends over backward—sometimes too far backward—to put kids back in homes with parents trying to beat crack addictions, with parents who say they're sorry for beating a toddler to a pulp. Yet now we've got a woman whose worst crime against her kids was getting poisoned, possibly by her husband, and the court case never ends."

What Donn Esmonde saw was obvious to almost everyone. No one had ever observed that Debbie was a bad mother. On the contrary, if she had a flaw, it was that she had often given up something she wanted so that her children would be safe and happy. She was worried that she would always be crippled, but her biggest fear was that Lauren and Ralph would be kept away from her forever.

On some days in Judge Mix's courtroom, it seemed that that was going to happen.

Part Six

Last Chance . . .

Last Chance

23

Debbie had once persuaded Anthony to go with her to a family counselor, hoping that a trained professional third party might be able to help them rebuild their marriage. The counselor perceived quickly that Anthony was a poster boy for Narcissistic Personality Disorder as it is outlined in the *Diagnostic Statistical Manual—IV,* the bible of psychologists and psychiatrists. His attitudes and reactions were certainly flamboyant, but he clearly was not insane. He might have been more responsive to counseling if he had been.

"Crazy" often gets better with drug therapy, shock treatments, and psychiatric help. But those with personality disorders embrace their approach to life and have no desire to change. Consumed by one of the half dozen widely accepted personality disorders, the narcissist sees himself as the center of the world, the most important person around, but he still seeks constant admiration, and he has almost no empathy with or sympathy for other people.

Narcissus, a Greek god, was a handsome young man who fell in love with his own image while looking into a clear pond. He was so enchanted by his own beauty that he slipped into the water and perished. The personality disorder named for Narcissus is easily seen in people who overestimate their own importance and accomplishments and boast of their achievements. They believe that they are special.

Anthony fell perfectly within the parameters of the disorder. Trying to fit him into a successful marriage counseling plan was akin to trying to teach a pig how to roller skate. He just didn't get it. He was constitutionally unwilling and unable to put himself into anyone else's shoes. He saw himself as a "co-therapist" and in no need of counseling. He consented to family counseling only to straighten out his wife's problems. When Debbie tried to say how *she* felt, he snickered. He simply could not see that his behavior might have any detrimental effect on her or his children.

And, of course, he had never accepted that he had any responsibility in the death of Sarah Smith.

When he looked into a mirror, his "pond," Anthony Pignataro saw only a handsome man with a full head of hair, a brilliant physician, a study in perfection. It was always other people who were getting in his way and stopping him from creating his world of accomplishment as a famed surgeon. And it was always other people he blamed when he encountered roadblocks.

Anthony was, if possible, even better looking in his forties than he had been in his twenties—at least when he wore his trademark toupee. And he was highly intelligent, but he was totally blind to his own faults. Indeed, he could see no faults.

Now, as the first crocuses poked through the snow in Erie County in 2000, Anthony languished in the ENE section of the Erie County Holding Center—but only because, in his mind, jealous and misguided people had thwarted him.

One of his prime enemies was Frank Sedita, who still titled his investigation "People v. Dr. Doe." Buffalo reporters knew that something big was going to happen with the Pignataro story, but nothing was official yet. As long as Anthony remained "Dr. Doe," the real investigation—the poisoning probe—would be harder to track. The District Attorney's office was in no hurry to expose the intricacies of their case until they were ready.

Sedita and his team continued to gather witnesses who recalled the seamy, shadowy life Anthony had lived after his release from jail on his first conviction. One informant was a woman named Doris Kline*. During the first months of 1999, Doris had lived with Arnie Letovich.

She said she had met Tony several times when he came over to her house about twice a week to get heroin.

"Did you ever see him with a woman?" Sedita asked.

She nodded, saying that he had brought a woman with him in the spring of 1999. Doris only knew her first name: Tami.

Asked to describe Tony Pignataro, Doris said he drove a late-model black Cadillac, and that he struck her as "nervous, paranoid, and arrogant." She described a night when he had unbolted his toupee from the top of his head to demonstrate his invention. That had to be Pignataro; there weren't a lot of men in Buffalo with bolts in their heads.

"Once," she said, "he actually asked if he could date my daughter. She's only twenty-three, and he has to be in his mid-forties. I didn't like that idea."

As for Arnie and Tony, she said they always seemed to get along well. Arnie copped the heroin, and Tony paid for it. She said she'd left Arnie in June 1999, but there was no big flaming breakup; their relationship had just kind of worn itself out. Arnie had never been physically abusive to her.

In March 2000, Anthony Pignataro was sentenced to sixteen months to four years in prison for violating his probation. That was a minor sentence compared to what might lie ahead. Buffalo residents were beginning to follow the Pignataro saga with great interest as significant events in the case were reported by the local media more and more frequently.

Because the grand jury was about to meet to consider the evidence in Debbie's poisoning case, Joel Daniels still refused to let Anthony take the witness stand in the marathon family court trial, which continued endlessly. He said he wouldn't even let his client take the stand and invoke his Fifth Amendment rights against self-incrimination because of the criminal investigation that everyone knew was going on.

Anthony, who looked as if he was eager to take the witness chair, listened to his attorneys and remained at the defense table. He had always considered himself to be extremely talented in persuasion, but for once he allowed someone else to hold the reins. Frank Sedita and Denis Scinta would have been delighted if he had overridden Daniels's advice. But he didn't.

Debbie hoped against hope that the neglect hearings were over, but they weren't. On March 10, Judge Marjorie Mix refused to dismiss the child neglect proceedings against the Pignataros in her court. A trial was scheduled for June 13, when both Debbie and Anthony would be defendants. Frank Sedita appealed Judge Mix's decision to the appellate division of the state supreme court in Rochester.

It was such a long spring.

In a hearing on April 4, Joel Daniels argued that "Deborah Pignataro has a long sordid history as a pill-popper" and said, "She very well may be lying" when she claimed that she had not tried to kill herself with arsenic after her 15-year-old marriage collapsed. That angered Frank Sedita. He protested that Daniels was trying to interfere with an upcoming grand jury probe into the causes of Debbie's poisoning.

It would have been a hard time for even the most confident of women. For Debbie, still in her wheelchair, it was totally humiliating. She *had* taken a lot of pain pills, muscle relaxants, and tranquilizers to deal with five surgeries on her neck, the disintegration of her marriage, and her way of life since the awful day when Sarah Smith suffered her fatal lack of oxygen in the operating room. But all those pills had been prescribed by Debbie's doctors, and many of them had disappeared down Anthony's throat.

Every secret corner of Debbie's life had been poked at, probed, and held up for the world to see. All of Anthony's mistresses, all of her perceived failures. If it hadn't been for Sharon Simon, Shelly, her mother, and her cousin Denis—who sometimes turned to wink at her in court when it got too painful—she wondered how she could bear to face Anthony, his attorneys, his mother, and the clamoring media.

On April 4, an Erie County grand jury began hearing evidence that might convince them to bring an indictment against Anthony Pignataro in the poisoning of his wife. All grand jury hearings are secret. Debbie had to testify once more, and now she had to do it alone. Even attorneys are not allowed behind the closed doors of a grand jury.

On April 27, 2000, Anthony was indicted on charges emanating from Debbie's poisoning: attempted murder in the second degree, assault in the first degree, and three counts of criminal possession of a controlled substance in the seventh degree. He had been transferred a week earlier to the Elmira Correctional Facility to begin his sentence for violating probation. He was being held in the reception area while prison officials decided where he should serve his time.

District Attorney Frank Clark refused to comment on the poisoning case. Defense Attorney Joel Daniels remarked that "There is no case, and we're going to fight the indictment and try to get it thrown out because we believe there isn't any real proof, only *imaginary* proof."

Contrary to popular belief, a prosecutor's case against a suspect does not have to have direct physical evidence or eyewitness testimony to make it viable. DNA, hair fibers, fingerprints, teeth impressions, tape recordings, and video are, indeed, wonderful tools for a prosecutor to hold. But circumstantial evidence can also be very powerful. If there are enough circumstances that point to a suspect who has a motive, a method, and a means to commit a murder, and if that suspect has behaved in such a way as to make him or her look like the only person with reason to want a victim dead, a gutsy prosecutor will take a chance. All that is needed for conviction is one pebble of circumstantial evidence following another that can be piled on top of still another until there is a wall of evidence—something that a reasonable juror can turn over in his mind until he comes up with the only possible killer.

Anthony Pignataro's patterned response when his back was to the wall had always been to draw his wife and family around him like a protective cloak. While he had neglected them in his hedonistic pursuits, he used them when he needed them.

On April 27, even as the charges against him were announced, Anthony wrote to his children:

"Hi,

"How,

"How are you guys. I haven't heard from either of you??[sic] Grandma said you wrote me, but I haven't got it yet?? I miss you both so much. Why don't you write to me?? I think about you all the time & I miss you both. Do you think you could at least write a short note & let me know how you are doing, how's school, sports etc. Did you guys get my letters and Easter cards?"

He gave them his new address: Elmira Correctional Facility, Box 500, Elmira, NY 14902—0500, although he expected to be moved one more time.

"How about sending me a picture or 2 of both of you?

"Try to see Polo. He doesn't get to see anyone & grandma can't handle him on the leash so he doesn't get out much. I know he'd love to see you both. Every day, I wait for the mail & hope for a letter from my children. Please don't let me down! Be good and look out and take care of your mother."

He knew what buttons to push. Polo, their German shepherd, had been their pet since Ralph was five, but Debbie certainly couldn't handle him. She felt lucky to be able to walk a few yards. Ralph ached for his dog, and Anthony knew it.

After he'd gotten out of his first jail sentence, Anthony had sat in his recliner chair drinking tequila or spent time with Tami Maxell. His only interest in Ralph had been when his boy was a football star, but now he heaped guilt and pleas for love upon his children.

Ralph wrote to his father that April 2000, and he asked him some hard questions.

"I have a lot of unanswered questions," he wrote. A topic I would like to start on is why you are telling everybody that Mom put you in jail for your probation violation. Do you know how hard it is for me to go with Grandma to help her buy a new car (You know I love cars!) and hear her say bad things about Mom? It hurts. And what is this about heroin? And heroin with Tami? Was Mom responsible for that? I can't believe you sometimes. I just want to ask *why?* Why did you have to be so stupid? Even I know not to do that sort of thing. You're a doctor; you should definitely know right from wrong. That was wrong!"

Ralph pleaded with his father to confess the truth to Lena Pignataro and admit his own flaws.

"Mom can't even afford the mortgage nowadays . . . we may have to move. How come Grandma can't help out? She always used to . . . She definitely doesn't care about Mom because that's what you're putting into her head, and I can tell by the way she talks about her.

"Well, write me back, but I don't want to hear just excuses." Ralph sounded more like the father than the son. "This letter is sincerely between you and me . . . I would absolutely love it if you stopped telling Grandma some things to make her feel otherwise and give me back the relationship I used to have with her. I feel like I lost all of that now. Please help out Dad; I know you want to in your heart! None of us ever wanted any of this to happen."

But all Ralph got from his father were excuses. He had no money. He couldn't help them.

"I will always love you, too & and don't you forget that," Anthony wrote to Ralph. "I'm sorry for what grandma says. It's not my fault. She is very stubborn. I never told her it was mom's fault for my probation violation. I also told her to stop saying anything about mom!!

"Your letter said, 'Please help out, Dad.' I do want to & I could as soon as this is over and I go back to work. Take care of mom. Hold onto the house till I get back to work. I'm sure you remember I told you I could help with the house as soon as I get out. I promise you."

Ralph had just turned 13. How was he going to pay the mortgage? But his father brushed that off. On May 10, 2000, Anthony wrote and reminded his children that his birthday was in two days and he would like a card.

"Please do not believe what you hear. A son and a daughter need their [*sic*] father. And I will be there for both of you. I'll never stop fighting till I prove my innocence . . .

"Grandma has to get rid of Polo. He's too much for her. I want to know if you both could take him for me till I get home. I don't want to lose him. Please help!!"

A week later, Pignataro wrote to Ralph with complicated instructions on how to start the hot tub, but then suggested he wait until he got home from jail, which would be soon.

Officially, Ralph and Lauren weren't even living at home yet, although caseworkers looked the other way as the family court hearings dragged on and on. Anyone who saw the children sob as they had to be pulled away from the mother they loved and forced to leave their own home would have understood their tears. It was an open secret that they were virtually living at home in West Seneca.

In late May, Anthony wrote to Ralph to explain who the real culprit was in the breakup of their family.

"Apparently, it is the District Attorney—D.A. Frank Sedita—who tore our family apart in September. The D.A.'s investigators talked to and scared Tami. She gave them the last card I had given her in late June or early July [1999]. The D.A. gave the card to Denis and told him I had given it to Tami while mom was in the hospital. Then Denis gave it to mom. I swear on both grandpas' graves that I never sent the card when they said I did & and I wasn't seeing Tami. All this will come out in the trial anyway because Tami will say so!! Besides she's married to someone else now."

It never occurred to Anthony, apparently, that bringing up his mistress wasn't the sort of thing most men would discuss with a thirteen-year-old son. He was too intent on putting the blame on Sedita. And, of course, he was still lying: Tami Maxell had admitted to Frank Sedita that Anthony had sent her the romantic card begging her to come back to him in August 1999—exactly when Debbie lay in the hospital fighting to live.

Anthony continued to insist that Sedita was the cause of all their troubles. "Then in February D.A. Frank Sedita got Judge Tills to sign an order preventing me from talking to mom without mom asking me to."

"After breaking up our family & putting me in jail, Sedita now seeks to put me away for 25 years. We won't let that happen!! I still love mom. I love you & I still love Lauren and I always will. I will never stop fighting for my family. I don't blame mom for what the D.A. did. She couldn't have known what they were up to . . . Please try to keep Polo for me. Take care of mom and Lauren.

"I love you so much,

"DAD"

Anthony wasn't far off when he characterized Frank Sedita as his enemy, but not for the reasons he gave his son. Sedita had seen the devastation of Dan and Sarah Smith's family, and the struggles of Debbie Pignataro, and he *did* want to prosecute the former doctor. Sedita and Carol Bridge were already prepared to go ahead with their case against Anthony Pignataro when they began to get a lot of help. Apparently, Anthony hadn't been any more popular in jail than he was in the straight world.

Carol Bridge laughed as she described the rush to snitch on Tony. "We never had so many informants. We had a conga line of them coming across Delaware Avenue to tell us about Tony Pignataro."

The first informant was not a jail inmate, although he was a man who "knew things." Mr. X had once been a patient of Tony's. Back in 1997, he had overheard the doctor complaining to his staff about patients who owed him money. Being an expert in collecting money, Mr. X let Dr. Tony know that he could probably help him get what was owed. But the doctor said that wasn't what he needed help with; what he was really looking for was someone to kill his wife.

"I took him seriously when he wanted to know if I could do it. I told him I'd get back to him on that."

However, when Mr. X came in to get the final check on his hair implants, Pignataro hadn't brought the subject up again. Mr. X was relieved, as he had no intention of hurting a woman. When he'd read in the paper about Debbie, he had recalled the conversation. But he didn't want to get involved. "I just wanted to tell someone," Mr. X told Chuck Craven.

This occurred months before Sarah Smith died.

They already had one witness who was willing to testify that Pignataro was thinking about killing his wife: Arnie Letovich. Arnie was prepared to get up on the witness stand, even though he knew that Tony would be furious.

However, the conga line continued. A woman named Trixie* talked to Frank Sedita, Craven, and Finnerty about her ex-husband, Paulie Cavalini*, who was in the Erie County Holding Center waiting disposition on a federal charge. Cavalini agreed to talk to the prosecutors. He described Tony Pignataro, beginning, as everyone did, with the bolts in his head. He remembered Tony as being weird and a "loner."

But Paulie and Tony had played a card game called International Spades to pass the time. The subject of Tony's prosecution on the poisoning case had come up, and the ex-doctor had bragged that "they can't put the arsenic in my hands." He said that the only one who might keep him from being found innocent was Arnie Letovich.

Of course, Tony added that he was innocent. Either his wife had done it to herself, or maybe her mother had done it, because she was over at his house at least five days a week.

Tony was very upset with Arnie, and he told Paulie Cavalini that he had found out that Arnie was going to court on May 23.

Cavalini said that Tony was looking for someone to either beat up Arnie or kill him before he could do harm to Tony's defense case. Paulie also recalled that Tony had said his girlfriend would never say anything about him to hurt him. Tami was in his pocket, and so was his mother. Paulie said Tony called his mother a lot from jail.

As always, Sedita told Cavalini that there was no deal, other than that anything he said during this interview would not be used against him. He also instructed him not to try to entice Pignataro into further conversation. It wouldn't matter what Tony said under those circumstances; it would be "fruit of the poisoned tree" and could not be used against him in any trial.

Cavalini said he didn't want anything from the D.A.'s office. He just didn't like Tony Pignataro.

On May 19, Pat Finnerty heard another version of Tony Pignataro's thirst for revenge from an inmate. Mohammed Kwamba* said he had been housed with Pignataro a couple of times. He described Tony as keeping things very close to his chest, but he had told Kwamba that he knew that a man and two women were going to be key witnesses against him in his trial, and that they were people he used to do heroin with.

Kwamba said that Tony was extremely frightened about what the man might say in his testimony. He had asked Kwamba to help him "scare the shit" out of Arnie Letovich so that Arnie wouldn't testify. He had asked Kwamba to find out through his Muslim friends in the holding center the exact pod and cell where Letovich was being held.

Kwamba had the impression that Tony was testing him. He had found out where Arnie was and reported that to Pignataro. Satisfied that he could count on Kwamba, Tony then asked him to spread the word among his friends to put pressure on Arnie so he would be too frightened to testify.

Tony had bragged to him that he was a doctor, Kwamba said, and he would never have gone after his wife and kids in any way he knew could be detected. But, when Kwamba asked him directly if he did do the poisoning, he only replied, "They will never find out."

Then Tony winked at Kwamba in a conspiratorial way. Pignataro had apparently believed that he could persuade Kwamba to assist him by offering to pay for a better attorney for him if he did what Tony wanted. What he didn't know was that Kwamba had already accepted a plea bargain and didn't need an attorney. Kwamba had only been toying with him, seeing how far he would go.

Feeling that he had Kwamba on his side, Pignataro asked him to get him some tobacco and other items that were contraband. Kwamba had assured him he would check with his circle of friends, but he'd never delivered anything to Tony.

Kwamba, too, was warned by the district attorney's office not to speak to or solicit information from Pignataro unless Tony himself started a conversation, and even then to limit himself to listening only. Kwamba said that Tony kept to himself most of the time and spoke only to a very few of the other inmates in the holding center.

Thanks to his mother, Anthony Pignataro had two of the most outstanding criminal defense attorneys in Buffalo representing him. But he was clearly not content to let Joel Daniels and Brian Welsh speak for him. He thought his plan was far superior and much more expedient. He was confident that he knew his way around the jail system. With his savvy and his mother's money, he could find insiders who would either frighten the witnesses against him or kill them to eliminate any chance that they could testify. Arnie Letovich, in particular, was the potential witness who worried Pignataro.

By July, he had found another likely hit man. And now it *was* a hit man he was looking for. After five months in jail, Anthony wanted to make sure that he didn't face another prison term at the end of the one he was already serving.

This time, the informant who contacted Frank Sedita was a native of Puerto Rico: Luis Perez*. Luis was thirty-five, and although he was housed in a different pod than Pignataro, they could see each other through their cell doors, and, like everyone else in the jail, Perez had noticed the man with bolts in his head. Later, they spoke often in the gym.

Tony was fluent in Spanish, and the two conversed in both English and Spanish. Tony explained that he was a surgeon and that he had gone to school in Puerto Rico, and they shared memories of Perez's home territory.

They had many conversations, the last on July 8, 2000. After they moved past casual comments, Perez said that most of their discussions had been about Tony's need to find someone to kill a witness against him: Arnie Letovich— whom Tony called "his problem on the West Side."

Tony explained that Letovich had copped heroin for him. He promised Perez that he would cop for him, too, although he warned him that Letovich would want to hold back a couple of bags for himself. Tony said that at the time of his own most recent arrest, he had quickly discovered where Letovich was being housed. He was in the Delta wing then, but Tony now believed Arnie had been moved to a rehab center over on Delaware Avenue. He was still seeking someone who could hurt Arnie enough to keep him from testifying.

Perez told Sedita that he had listened to what Pignataro had in mind. Tony was prepared to pay big money to have Letovich killed. He asked Perez if he or someone he knew might be willing to do that for money. He had worked out a plan that he thought would be foolproof. Through his sources, he knew that Arnie was due to be released from the rehab clinic within a few days, and he wouldn't be hard to find.

Whenever they met, Perez said, Tony had brought up the subject of killing Letovich. He thought it would be prudent if Perez spent some time convincing Arnie that he was his friend. The best way, Tony suggested, was for Luis to get him high, so that Arnie would trust him and expect that they would shoot up when they were together. It never occurred to Tony that Arnie Letovich might have kicked his habit while he was in rehab.

To be sure that Perez was carrying out Tony's plans, he wanted him to have someone take a picture of him and Letovich together. That way, he would know that Perez wasn't trying to pull anything on him, that he really had made contact with Arnie. He even promised Perez he would pay him $5,000 up front if he could produce a photograph of himself with Arnie Letovich. That would prove that Perez wasn't snitching to the cops.

Perez said he'd been curious about why Pignataro was willing to go as far as murder for hire, and Tony told him that Letovich was going to be a star witness against him in an attempted murder case. He asked him whom he had tried to kill.

"My wife," Tony had answered. "My wife. I'm gonna get that bitch." Tony had gone on to confide that his wife had tried to commit suicide when she found out he had a girlfriend, as if that were outrageous enough behavior on her part to warrant reprisal of some kind.

At this point, Perez decided that he should go to the

district attorney. He didn't need any more convincing that Tony was serious about having Letovich killed, and maybe he wouldn't stop with that. He seemed furious at his wife, too.

Now, Perez told the investigators that Tony had gone so far as to plot the best way to kill Arnie. Once they got used to shooting up together and Arnie trusted Perez, Tony suggested that Perez put poison in the syringe. Tony had specifically said that rat poison would probably be the best poison to use.

But Tony was starting to get anxious. His trial for attempted murder was getting closer, even though he thought Joel Daniels could get him some delays. Tony wanted to know when Luis Perez would be released from jail. Just as soon as Luis was out, Tony wanted him to write to him at a post office box address.

He gave Perez a precise description of Arnie Letovich, saying he was a skinny white male who looked like Jesus Christ. He had a lot of tattoos, the most outstanding of which was a Heroin King symbol. He described Arnie as looking like "a straight-up junkie."

With Perez's information, the D.A.'s investigators were convinced that eventually Tony Pignataro was going to find somebody behind bars who *was* willing to carry out a murder for the sake of the $10,000 he was offering. His only money source was his mother, although they doubted that she would give him the money if she knew what it was for. She had been an endless source of funds for attorneys and his living expenses, however.

One more informant was warned not to attempt to entice Tony Pignataro into a conversation. Frank Sedita told Perez that he would be violating Pignataro's constitutional rights if he started conversations about the attempted murder case. Anything Tony might tell him would probably be ruled inadmissible by the court.

Frank Sedita talked to the deputy superintendent of the holding center to see which, if any, of the conversations between Perez and Pignataro might have been caught on surveillance cameras. If they had been, they were gone; at the time, the tape in the gym camera was recorded over every two hours after corrections officers viewed them.

Oblivious to the fact that the prisoners he had approached were giving the D.A.'s office play-by-play descriptions of his attempts to set up a hit, Tony Pignataro continued his solicitation of murder. And Luis Perez made regular reports to law enforcement authorities about what Tony was planning. He spoke to Special Agent Richard Caito of the Career Criminal Task Force on August 7. He said that Tony had located Letovich's new address and even knew that he might be living with a woman named Sherry*. Perez repeated that Pignataro wanted Arnie Letovich's death to look like a drug overdose.

On August 8, 2000, Frank Sedita and Joel Daniels appeared before Judge Mario Rossetti to make motions about the date of Pignataro's trial on the attempted murder charges. Although Daniels argued vociferously for a delay, Rossetti made it clear that he intended to proceed with the trial on October 9.

A day later, Pignataro's defense team made a motion to have him released from the holding center while his violation of probation appeal was pending. Frank Sedita and Carol Bridge were puzzled over why they chose this relatively late date to protest. Way back in February, Judge Wolfgang had ordered no bail and told Pignataro's lawyers that he could reapply for lower bail, but they had waited five months to do so. Now, with the trial looming so near, Tony Pignataro suddenly was very anxious to get out of jail.

Knowing what they knew about Tony's animosity toward Arnie Letovich, Sedita and Bridge were uneasy. Either he was going to see to it himself that Arnie was silenced, or perhaps he was planning to run.

There was a third possibility. He needed a reason to get $10,000. Tony might have been planning to tell his mother it was bail money, knowing that she wouldn't even consider paying a hit man.

The next day, Sedita received a message from Pat Finnerty and Special Agent Rick Martinez of the Career Criminal Task Force. They had information that Pignataro might be making a phone call between one and two that afternoon: a call about Letovich. This call was not, however, a secret to law enforcement. Pignataro thought he knew the true identity of the person he was about to call, but he was mistaken. They had inside information about almost everything Tony was doing.

But the investigators didn't know yet whether he had already forwarded money to someone, or was about to send the money, to carry out his plan to have Arnie Letovich killed.

They moved quickly. Frank Sedita called the Erie County Holding Center and asked that the phone banks be visually monitored during the vital time period. If someone witnessed Tony at that time making a call, it would be additional backup for what was about to come down.

While Anthony believed he had finally contacted a hit man who would carry out his wishes to eliminate the most potent witness against him in his upcoming trial, he was strolling right into a trap. There was no way either the D.A.'s office or the task force was going to let Letovich get a hot shot of heroin or a dose of rat poison.

Luis Perez was with Tony when he made the call to the hit man that Luis had found for him. What Tony didn't know was that the man at the other end of the phone line wasn't a would-be killer hungry for $10,000. He was an Erie County deputy sheriff who spoke fluent Spanish.

Deputy Pedro Pabone listened as Tony Pignataro described Letovich. "He's skinny—looks like he has AIDS, lots of tattoos . . . one's a Heroin King tattoo."

Tony spoke excellent school-taught Spanish, but he was at a loss for slang phrases in that language. Pabone, who was fluent in both textbook Spanish and street slang, could tell that Pignataro was not speaking in his native tongue. When he stumbled in getting his thought across, Tony turned to someone with him—Perez—and asked him in English to translate the words in Spanish. He was trying to say "goatee" to describe Arnie's beard, but he didn't know how. Pedro Pabone could hear another male voice telling Tony what phrase to say. There were several instances when Pignataro spoke in English as he asked for help.

Perez had been transferred to the same pod—Echo Northeast—where Pignataro was.

Sedita and Finnerty went to the Career Criminal Task Forces offices to talk with Deputy Pabone and Special Agent Martinez. They handed over a copy of the taped conversation in which Pignataro spelled out what he wanted Pabone to do to Letovich.

"There may be a delivery to the 200 block of Massachusetts," Pabone said. If Tony did have someone who would arrange for the first $5,000 to be paid for the hit, that was where it was supposed to be delivered. Pat Finnerty contacted postal authorities and asked them to put a hold on mail sent to that address.

They halfway expected Lena Pignataro to drive up and

leave an envelope behind a bush or in the mailbox, and they put a surveillance team on the address to watch, but no one appeared.

Frank Sedita talked to Arnie Letovich and casually brought up the subject of tattoos, and Arnie mentioned that he had a Heroin King symbol, although Sedita hadn't mentioned the name. Looking at him, the D.A. saw that Arnie did have a Christ-like appearance—more so now that he was free of drugs. He had come from drug court that day, he said, and his public defender had told him that an investigator from Tony Pignataro's defense team had been fishing around in his court file. Arnie said his current address was in that file as well as the information about the location of the drug rehab facility he'd just left.

Letovich's public defender had moved quickly to have his file sealed.

Armed with the audiotape of Tony Pignataro talking to what he believed was a murderer for hire, Frank Sedita called for a meeting with Joel Daniels. After he told Daniels that he might want to rethink going to court because of what the Career Criminal Task Force and the D.A.'s office had found out, Tony's lawyer looked at him, surprised.

"What are you talking about?" Daniels asked.

"Your man's going to be charged with conspiracy to commit murder," Sedita answered.

"What?"

"I have it on tape."

The tape began to unwind, and two male voices filled the room. Daniels looked dubious while the conversation was in Spanish, but when Pignataro switched to English, his face sagged.

"There's no mistake whose voice that is," Sedita said quietly.

"Oh sh— . . ." Daniels couldn't deny that it was Tony Pignataro on the tape—Tony setting up a murder for hire. Even the best defense attorney in the State of New York would have a tough time explaining that away.

Pignataro had outfoxed himself, and he had lied to his own attorney. There would be no trial. After Joel Daniels spelled it out for him, Pignataro agreed to plead guilty to a lesser charge. He even promised he would tell the D.A.'s office where he obtained the poison used in the attempted murder of his wife.

When Debbie learned that Anthony had agreed to confess, it was literally an answer to her prayers. She had said a novena for nine days, praying that he would confess to save them all from another trial—and, perhaps, to lift a weight from his mortal soul.

In September 2000, one year after Ralph and Lauren had gone to live with their uncle Carmine and aunt Patti, Judge Marjorie Mix finally allowed them to return to live in their mother's home. She stipulated that Debbie's mother, Caroline Rago, must remain in the home, too. Debbie was just thankful to have them home at last; she would have followed any restrictions Judge Mix imposed. She and the children loved her mother and were delighted to have her live with them.

A month later, Debbie did something she never thought she could do. In October, she filed for divorce. Anthony was stunned. And worried. How many times had he reminded Debbie that nothing bad would happen as long as they stuck together? But even as Debbie started divorce proceedings, he was working hard to convince her that he still loved her, begging for her forgiveness and for a chance to rebuild their lives together.

She still had to see her almost–ex-husband in the crowded corridors of the courthouse. On Lauren's birthday, October 2, Anthony and Debbie passed in the hallway. He was in handcuffs, but he smiled and asked her to tell Lauren he would call her later with birthday wishes.

During one of the dozens of hearings connected with the multitudinous charges against Anthony, Debbie and Shelly met someone else in the hallway: Arnie Letovich.

"He came up to me and started to tell me that he was so sorry, that he'd done his best to protect me—" Debbie said.

"And we were scared," Shelly interrupted. "But not of him. We weren't supposed to talk to any witnesses, so we kind of mumbled and hurried away."

"But that was nice of him," Debbie said, of a man whose world was so alien to her own. "I do appreciate what he did. He may have saved my life."

Debbie had help from a lot of people she never expected to back her up. That fall of 2000, Debbie's former brother-in-law, Allan Steinberg, who was now divorced from Anthony's sister, Antoinette, organized a benefit to help her with house payments. Allan rented a fire hall, and donated food, a Chinese auction, and other enticements drew a crowd of people who showed their support of Debbie.

24

It was November 3, 2000, when Anthony Pignataro and Joel Daniels stood before Judge Mario Rossetti in the Supreme Court of the State of New York, County of Erie. District Attorney Frank Clark was there, too, and so were Frank Sedita and Carol Bridge. The assistant district attorneys were happy to know that Pignataro was about to be sentenced to prison, but it would have been more satisfying to see him go through the trial process. They had prepared for such a long time to prosecute Pignataro.

For those who prosecute crime, nothing is predictable. Preparing for trial is akin to going into training for a major sporting event; memorizing all the techniques, the plays, and the plans; and getting suited up for the big game—only to have it called because of inclement weather. Some trials go on for months or years, some end abruptly in days, and some never happen at all.

When it came down to it, Pignataro was a paper tiger, unwilling to have all the details of his crimes spelled out in a trial and on the front page of the *Buffalo News*. That incriminating tape would have been played on every radio and television station in Buffalo and Erie County, and Anthony didn't want that to happen.

Claudia Ewing from WGRZ TV, Channel 2, was in Judge Rossetti's courtroom with her film crew, hoping to videotape the proceedings. The defense didn't want her there, and Frank Sedita said simply, "The People have no position, Your Honor."

Judge Rossetti, bound by New York State law, denied Ewing's request.

Frank Sedita explained that it was his understanding that Anthony Pignataro was going to withdraw his not guilty plea to the original charges against him and plead guilty to attempted assault in the first degree, a lesser offense included in Count 2 of his indictment.

His guilty plea would be his admission that he had intended to cause serious physical injury to another person using a dangerous "instrument" (specifically, arsenic poison) and that person was his wife, Deborah Pignataro. The rest of the counts against him would be consolidated and dismissed.

But there were several conditions that Pignataro had to agree to: he had to withdraw all motions made to date, agree to waive his right to appeal, and admit that he was a second felony offender.

Frank Sedita had met with Debbie, and this plea bargain met with her approval. "Your Honor," Sedita said, "myself and Ms. Bridge urge the Court to accept the plea disposition."

The ex-Dr. Anthony Pignataro stood before the judge in handcuffs, no longer swaggering in the courtroom. He said, "Yes, sir" and "No, sir."

It must have been humiliating for him to have Judge Rossetti ask him if he had graduated from high school and if he could read and write English, but he answered only a meek "Yes," respectfully. He said he understood what it meant to plead guilty, and he understood his rights. He knew he had a right to a trial by a judge or a jury, and to confront witnesses against him. But he was afraid of what his sentence might be.

"Do you understand, therefore . . . that the Court is restricted to a determinate five years up to a determinate fifteen years . . . as a second felony felon?"

"Yes, Your Honor."

The judge explained that he had as yet made no commitment one way or the other.

"Did you," Judge Rossetti began, "on or before June 30 and August 10 of 1999 attempt with intent to cause physical injury by use of poison, that is, arsenic, attempt to cause the injury by preparing some food for your wife and having her consume that food?"

"Once, yes, Your Honor."

Anthony was again downplaying his crimes, admitting to less than the truth. Judge Rossetti didn't comment. Pignataro admitted that the poisoning had happened in Debbie's home in West Seneca.

"And you knew at that time, did you not, that the use of such poison, arsenic, could cause serious physical injury to your wife?" Rossetti continued.

"At that time, I did not know it was arsenic. I knew it was harmful."

"You knew it was harmful?"

"Yes."

"Did you attempt to use it with the intent to cause serious physical injury?"

"Yes, Your Honor."

"Nobody forcing you to say that—is that correct?"

"No, sir."

Judge Rossetti explained to Anthony that he would base his sentencing decision on documentation from Joel Daniels, a presentence memorandum, and any other documentation and letters he might receive. Any sentence would have to run consecutively with the sentence he was currently serving for probation violation.

Anthony pleaded guilty. His sentencing date was set for January 2001. There was no bail. He would spend Thanksgiving and Christmas behind bars.

Two days later, Erie County District Attorney Frank Clark broke the long silence of his office and spoke for his staff about the theory they had developed in Anthony's crimes against Debbie. Heretofore, Frank Sedita, Carol Bridge, Chuck Craven, and Pat Finnerty had agreed with Clark that the less information the public knew about Anthony Pignataro's game plan, the better.

Now the "Poisoned Plot" headline swept across the final edition of the *Buffalo News*.

Characterizing Pignataro's thinking as fiendishly clever, Frank Clark said his office had never felt that Debbie was poisoned for something as mundane as insurance money or even to set her husband free to be with another woman. It appeared that Anthony Pignataro had a far more complicated motive. He had hoped to show that *anyone's* wife could die in surgery—even his own.

Anthony had taken Debbie to the hospital in the third week in July and had agreed with her doctor's tentative diagnosis of pancreatitis. But tests didn't back that up. After she returned home, Pignataro had almost insisted that she undergo gallbladder surgery. A cholecystectomy is not a dangerous operation for most people, but, in Debbie's weakened condition, she probably would have died. Indeed, the D.A.'s team had lined up Debbie's doctors as witnesses who would testify that she would have been unlikely to survive.

"We now think," Clark said, "he was lobbying for that surgery with her physicians because he thought she wouldn't survive it. Then her arsenic poisoning would never have been discovered. And if she had died in surgery, we think he believed that would be vindication in the death during surgery of [Sarah Smith]."

Carol Bridge added, "Then he could say, 'Look, this could happen to anybody. I was a doctor practicing my trade, and it happened to *me.*' "

Pignataro's motives were many and interwoven, the prosecutors said, designed to take care of a number of his problems. First and foremost, he wanted his medical license back. Whoever had to be sacrificed to accomplish that didn't matter. As always, he wanted the very best out of life for himself.

Rumors and misinterpretation of lab tests had abounded, making the lay public believe that Ralph and Lauren Pignataro had been poisoned, too. But they never had, save perhaps for the small amount of chicken noodle soup that Lauren had eaten. The prosecutors stressed that the children had only the normal level of arsenic in their systems.

Many people had asked them why a medical doctor would try to kill his wife with arsenic and hope to get away with it.

Frank Sedita pointed out that tests for arsenic poisoning are not normally given in autopsies. "Historically, when defendants are prosecuted for arsenic poisoning, they usually have racked up a number of victims—not just one.

"This is the first arsenic case I know of," Sedita told reporters, "where there is only one victim; there are usually multiple victims before anyone gets suspicious."

And that is true. In fiction and in true crime, the prototype of an arsenic poisoner is the "Black Widow," a woman of a certain age who feeds arsenic to a series of husbands and boyfriends, or to the poor and helpless aged placed in her care. When the whole history becomes known and there are too many bodies, too many insurance payoffs, and too many instances of a weeping widow, then the poisoner falls under suspicion.

The Erie County prosecutor's staff had built a very solid circumstantial evidence case against Anthony Pignataro—one that almost any reasonable person might agree with—but they knew that Debbie Pignataro and her children didn't wish a vendetta on her husband and their father. They just wanted him to go away and let them live their lives.

25

But, of course, Anthony Pignataro didn't go away. As meek as he was in front of Judge Rossetti, he was already working to assure himself of a relatively light sentence. He had heard the judge say that letters and documents could make a difference in his sentence, and he figured that Debbie and their children would be the most impressive if they were to come forward and plead for him.

He was barely chastened when Family Court Judge Marjorie C. Mix finally made a ruling on the issue of the alleged neglect of Ralph and Lauren by Debbie and Anthony Pignataro. Judge Mix announced her decision only six days after Anthony pleaded guilty to poisoning Debbie. Although Debbie was found innocent of the charges, Mix convicted Anthony of child neglect.

"You are a miserable human being," she intoned, "who failed everybody. You have done something that is so wrong. You have destroyed your life and inflicted incredible physical and psychological pain on your wife."

Bleak revelations kept surfacing. After Anthony pleaded guilty, Debbie got a phone call from a neighbor who asked to come talk to her.

"She sat down and started to cry," Debbie said. "She

begged me for forgiveness. She said that Anthony had called her all the time and finally convinced her that I had deliberately poisoned myself. He wanted her to wear a wire and try to get something on me. She was so sorry, but all I could think of was how she had been brutal to me."

The woman said that Anthony was now asking her to find out how much time Debbie was going to ask the judge to give him.

Debbie was shocked to think that a neighbor she had liked and trusted had believed Anthony's lies about her, but she laughed when Shelly told her that he even had the temerity to call *her*. There wasn't a friend in the world who was more of a mother hen watching over Debbie than Shelly Palombaro.

Back at home with their mother, and in a new public school, Ralph and Lauren Pignataro blossomed. Sustained by their sure belief that their mother loved them, neither of them had ever buckled under the tragedy that tore through their lives. Their report cards in November spoke for their determination not to let their father's crimes rub off on them.

Ralph was in the eighth grade, and every one of his teachers noted that his effort was excellent and that he was "a pleasure to have in class." He received two 99s, two 98s, and a 96. In grade six, Lauren was rated just as high, with six A's and two A-pluses.

And still, Anthony continued to write his manipulative letters from prison. His sentencing was two months away, and he was afraid. He begged Debbie not to cut him off from his children: "You [once] said that jail is not the answer, that I should get therapy. *They* are my therapy, especially during the holidays. Please reconsider. I'm sorry. Love, Anthony."

To Ralph and Lauren (November 18, 2000): "Ralph and Lauren, Sometimes I just need to talk. Do not block the calls. I need you both, especially now at the holidays. Please!! Love, Dad."

". . . I know I made a mistake, and I'm so sorry. It hurts me every day. I need my children . . . Maybe you can visit me at the holidays . . . I'm so sorry I messed everything up.

"I feel so sorry for all the hurt I've caused. Please talk to me . . . I am so thankful you could forgive me, but please do not forget about me . . .

"Please forgive me. It was a very hard time for me back then & and I made a very bad mistake . . . Please try to talk to me . . . I'm so sorry."

As Christmas 2000 approached the litany in the letters Anthony scrawled to his children was repeated on and on and on. Sometimes Ralph accepted his phone calls. Sometimes he and Lauren sent a photograph or two. But they didn't really believe in him any more.

They hadn't been able to take Polo back into their home, despite their father's entreaties. But Debbie promised them they would find a dog. She had no money to buy a puppy, but she would find a way.

"We went to a football game at school, and some kids were giving away yellow Labrador retrievers," Debbie said. "There was only one left, but she was perfect for us—meant for us, I think. We call her Gabby."

In December 2000, Anthony sent a card to Debbie:

> *To My Wife, With Love at Christmas*
> *It's Love that makes Christmas so special . . .*
> *Merry Christmas with Love*

He added his own sentiment:

> *My heart aches so, Baby, and I don't know what*
> *to say to you right now. Except I'm sorry.*
> *Anthony . . . You know my heart.*

Indeed she did. Debbie opened the Christmas card with hands that could no longer feel, her nerves deadened as if they'd been injected with Novocain. She couldn't decorate their Christmas tree because she no longer had small muscle control. She couldn't kneel. She directed from her chair as Ralph and Lauren scrambled to hang the familiar ornaments. Ralph put up the Christmas lights.

Anthony's romantic card was shamelessly obvious. He meant to swing Debbie back over to his side. A supportive letter from the victim herself would surely have an impact on his sentence length.

Perhaps it didn't occur to him that because he had tried to plot murder for hire in jail, his mail was censored. Oblivious to this, he wrote to his mother, imploring her to intervene with Debbie:

12–6–00
Mom

>*Hi, it's snowing pretty good down here now.*

>*Please think about what I asked you. Even if it's all phoney & you don't truly mean it, you could do it for me.*

>*You will never have to see her again anyway.*

>*What she tells Judge Rossetti will determine how much time he gives me.*

>*Every Day that you save me is worth it.*

>*You wouldn't have to see her, you could just call on the phone and be nice.*

>*I know it would kill you but it will help me.*

>*If you have any doubts, ask Joel. I'm sure it didn't help for her to hear that you called Carmine fat again and that you told [a mutual friend] that you'll never get along with her again. Especially now in these critical days when she will speak to The Judge.*

I know she would accept your call & it will surely
help me (& the sooner the better.)
Please, Please, Please reconsider.

Thanks, Anthony

P.S., I know it will kill you. But please try.
That's all I want for Christmas.

It was too late. Whatever Anthony had told his mother about his wife to turn Lena totally against Debbie and to make her give up any relationship with her grandchildren, he had done a remarkably effective job. He wasn't able to undo his own handiwork. Even to save him years in prison, Lena could not lower herself to be nice to Debbie.

It is extremely doubtful that it would have made a difference. Debbie did write a letter to Judge Rossetti, but it wasn't what Anthony had in mind. It was seven pages long, typed single-space.

"For the last 20 years," Debbie began, "I have loved this man, Anthony Pignataro, unconditionally. No matter what has come our way, stood by him and supported him 100%."

Debbie didn't have to exaggerate as she simply recalled the events in her life and in her marriage since Anthony's release from his first prison term. Judge Rossetti already knew the details of her mysterious illness and her steady progression toward entering the Mercy Hospital ER.

"I am completely convinced my husband was waiting for me to die and I didn't. He probably couldn't understand why I was still living with the amount of arsenic I ingested. He knew exactly what he was doing. His only explanation to me so far as to why he did this is that he was terribly confused. He was in so much pain emotionally and he didn't know which way to turn.

"My response to him was then, 'Why didn't you take your *own* life?' His response was, 'I did [try]—but it didn't work.' "

Debbie's letter to the judge didn't leave one horrific incident out. In a sense, this was her first time to speak. She recalled Anthony's infidelities:

"He always told me how lucky I was to have him. He degraded me in front of people. He often said to me, 'Look at yourself, who would want you?' He made me cry all the time . . . I thought, as he got older and matured, he would come to his senses and realize how lucky he was to have a wife that adored him unconditionally and two beautiful children . . . How could he ever take a chance of losing that forever? He didn't care. He knew I would keep forgiving him. He would promise it would never happen again. Say how sorry he was, and buy me a piece of expensive jewelry and life would go on again until the next time."

For Debbie, the fact that her life had gone on was almost a miracle. She tried to put into her written statement the extent of her physical handicap.

"I have come a long way this past year, but my fight isn't over yet. I am now able to walk without braces on my legs or any other means of assistance. I can feed myself, bathe myself, and dress myself. Once again, taking care of my kids is a pleasure. I can also drive.

"My legs, from the knees down, are constantly numb and painful. I can only wear sneakers because I have severe foot drop as a result of the arsenic. I can no longer walk a mall with my children or do many things that we did.

"My hands are numb and painful. I have lost all the fine motor skill such as taking money out of my wallet . . . My hands still look like they are in a palsy state . . . But I am *here.* I am still alive. I can watch my beautiful children grow up into fine adults. I can enjoy their teen years with them . . . my job will never be done with them. Even when they are married with families of their own, they will always need their mother. Thank God, I am still here for them."

She told Judge Rossetti that she didn't want revenge; she wanted only to protect Ralph and Lauren. "When [Anthony] finally did the right thing and confessed this heinous crime, he said to our son, Ralph, 'I stood up like a man and told the truth—and look what they're doing to me now.'

"Once again, 'poor Anthony,'" Debbie wrote, "I don't think so. The kids and I are the victims here, not you."

Debbie had put a block on her phone because there were too many wheedling calls from Anthony, and then she removed it because Ralph thought he might want to speak to his father once in a while.

"I do not seek revenge. Someday he will have to answer to God why he did this unspeakable act . . . I ask you to determine, however, please let the punishment fit the crime. I do not feel safe with this man on the streets, nor will I ever trust him again with my children. Please help us to get on with our lives without him . . . I don't know how they will feel in the future regarding their dad, but the choice is theirs—he's still their father . . ."

There were dozens of letters to Judge Rossetti about the sentencing to come. Aside from Anthony's mother and some of his siblings, they all came from neighbors and friends who had no sympathy at all for his plight.

26

Anthony Pignataro's sentencing was delayed for three weeks, but on Friday, February 9, 2001, he finally faced Judge Mario Rossetti. As with so many convicted felons who have awaited sentencing in a jail cell for months, his skin was the greenish-white shade of jail pallor. He wore his own invention, his snap-on toupee, but it looked bizarre because his head was shaved beneath it, and it didn't blend smoothly with his own hair as it had been designed to do. Although he was still close to six feet in height, he seemed much diminished, a shadow of the super-confident persona he'd always affected.

He didn't look dangerous, but perhaps that was the image he wished to project on this cold morning in Buffalo. As Donn Esmonde of the *Buffalo News* observed, Pignataro had missed his calling. "[He] should have taken a few acting classes and headed for Hollywood. Instead of a felon, he could have been a star."

Frank Sedita and Carol Bridge were present to represent the People, and Joel Daniels sat beside Pignataro.

"There has been a presentence report," Frank Sedita said. "In my thirteen years as a prosecutor, it's probably the most comprehensive and detailed presentencing report I've ever seen."

And it was. It was all there: a written survey of a man's

life, a word picture eerily similar to the painting of Dorian Grey that festered and streaked and aged in a locked room while the human form of the character remained youthful and unlined. Anthony's sins against his patients, his fellow physicians, and his family had piled up year after year, and now most of them had been found out. All the plastic surgery and workouts that had been designed to keep him looking young for his age had been erased by alcohol, heroin, failure, and long confinement.

Frank Sedita said he had nothing further to add to what was already on the record. He did, however, wish to speak to a last-minute letter Anthony had given Judge Rossetti—a letter the prosecutor had just read.

"The defendant claims that he has had several 'heartfelt discussions with Mrs. Pignataro'—that's a quote—regarding her expressed desire for the leniency of this Court towards Mr. Pignataro. I showed her the letter, and she denied the claim by Mr. Pignataro."

Continuing his custom of whittling a fine edge off the truth, Anthony had tried a final foolish deception. He had written a letter in his own handwriting to Judge Rossetti to explain that he and Debbie had reconciled. That was not true, Debbie said firmly. There was not a wisp of truth in the letter. In the past year, Debbie had never discussed a reconciliation with Anthony, and she shook her head faintly as she realized he was trying to convince Judge Rossetti of that.

Indeed, Debbie was within a week of receiving her final divorce decree.

Even though she had been vindicated, this was a difficult day for Debbie. She had had such hope for Anthony—for them both. Now it had all turned to ashes, and she was sitting in yet another courtroom. At least she was walking under her own power, and everyone who had supported her was there with her: Denis Scinta, her mother, her brother, her cousins, Sharon Simon, Shelly Palombaro. They were all there beside her in the front row of the gallery as the man she had once loved waited to hear his sentence.

Sedita reminded the judge that Pignataro had promised in his plea bargain to admit to being a second felony offender at the time of sentencing. He added that Debbie had asked that there be a restraining order of protection against Anthony for three years *after* he served his maximum sentence. No one knew yet what that would be, but she feared that whenever Anthony got out of prison he would head for her door.

As for Anthony's two sentences, it was to be expected that Frank Sedita preferred that they run consecutively—one right after the other—while Joel Daniels wanted them to be concurrent. If Daniels got his way, Anthony would get two prison sentences for the price of one.

Debbie had asked to testify before Anthony was sentenced. She had always been fearful on the witness stand before, but this time she needed to speak. She didn't talk for very long, but her words were powerful as she described the few years just past.

"He has taken away part of me that I will never get back," she said softly, looking down at Anthony. "He put his own children and me through a living hell."

Anthony seemed stunned that Debbie could speak so well in front of a crowded courtroom, and that she would speak against him. She was his last and best hope for mercy.

Judge Rossetti explained that he had read the presentence report, the letters attached, the victim impact statement, a presentence memorandum that Joel Daniels had submitted, the letter from Anthony, and one from a minister writing on Anthony's behalf.

Joel Daniels spoke to what he had seen as prejudice against his client by the probation department. "First of all, he's paid a price for the Sarah Smith case—he went to jail for *four months* in the Erie County pen. He got out; his probation was revoked by Judge Tills. Judge Tills gave him another whack—he maxed him, gave him one-and-a-third to four . . . The point is, he's paid his price to society for whatever he owes on the Sarah Smith case."

Four months for the life of a young wife and mother. If Daniels's reasoning hadn't reverberated so tragically, it might have been laughable. Four months was a slap on the hand, and for Anthony it had been almost a vacation as he read books, took illegal drugs, and jogged around the exercise yard.

Daniels characterized Pignataro as being "victimized by word processors . . . regurgitating everything up about the Sarah Smith case from the old report." That was old news, Daniels implied, and had nothing to do with the current conviction.

Joel Daniels pulled out all the stops for his client, suggesting that the District Attorney's office was wrong when they insisted that Debbie had received more than one dose of arsenic. His was a scatter-shot technique, and he was a very good orator. He commiserated with the judge over how tough *his* job was.

"But look at the defendant, his family, everything about him . . . You know Anthony Pignataro—he has a wonderful family. His mother is here today. I didn't realize it, but she just had a birthday on February 1. She's seventy-one years old now. His two brothers are here from Florida; Ralph is here. Steven is here. His sister, Antoinette, I talked to her—but she couldn't get up here. As the Court knows, she's a doctor, and she's very, very busy."

Daniels began to wander, but Judge Rossetti let him talk. He spoke of how wonderful Dr. Ralph had been, of Anthony's schooldays, his boxing career, his years of training to be a physician, his children. "He was a devoted father to those children. Those children came first with him."

Now, incredibly, Daniels visualized a time in the future when Ralph might throw a 40-yard football pass, if he should get into St. Francis. "If he [throws that pass], I hope he pauses for a minute and says to himself, 'Thank you dad. Without your help, your confidence, I don't think I would have been able to do that.' "

Lena Pignataro's emotional pain had clearly gotten through to Joel Daniels. "She's a very, very nice lady. She's a fine human being . . . a good solid mother. She would come up to my office and she would cry . . . and say, 'Joel, when can I bring him home? . . . Joel, do you think he's going to be out before I die?' And I said, 'I hope so.' "

Daniels admitted that Anthony had just gone downhill, but he had no explanation for it.

Finally, the time had come for Anthony to speak, if he chose to. Most felons don't say a word at sentencing; some blurt out a paragraph or two. But Anthony held several sheets from a yellow legal tablet. His words weren't new to Debbie or to anyone who had seen the snowstorm of letters and cards that had come to her and her children since his guilty plea in November. But he turned them now into a dramatic soliloquy. His hands trembled, and his usually deep voice lost its timbre as he began to speak. Tears wet his face, and he choked as if he couldn't bear to go on.

Perhaps he *was* having trouble; he faced what, for him, was unthinkable. He certainly had the full attention of the courtroom onlookers, including reporters with their pens raised, waiting.

"What does one say?" Anthony began. "Where do I begin? How do I tell my family and this Court how very,

very sorry I am for what has happened? First and foremost, I want to apologize to my wife and my children. I want to apologize to the Rago family, and my family. I failed you all—not only my wife and children but my profession and my family legacy. Mostly, I failed myself. I was once so strong, both mentally and physically, and anybody can attest to that."

Within a paragraph, the prisoner was back to himself, lips quivering as he looked for someone to blame. He didn't blame his father, but marked his decline from his father's death.

"My professional career failed and I went to jail, after which an attempt in a private business venture with my wife failed, and in the process, consumed the majority of our remaining cash reserve.

"My pride was eating me up inside . . . The pressure of no income, being unemployable, the confusion, the pride, the frustration, consumed me. After years of dedicated study, I became a twenty-four-hour prisoner of my own demise."

Jail had been tough for him, he said. "I hit bottom."

He said he could not reach out to his wife because it would confirm his failure. "I lost sight of everything but bitterness."

He reached back to his dead baby girl, mentioned his children's athletic accomplishments, and asked only that the Court would allow him to help his family, to provide for their emotional and physical needs. "I truly am not a harmful man. I want to prove that. I am a good man . . . My soul aches with profound shame, sorrow, disgrace and loss . . . Please allow me a second chance."

Anthony claimed that his recent talks with his wife had elicited feelings of forgiveness from her, even though people with other agendas had influenced her.

"I want you to ask her if you question that at all. Our souls are still bonded, and I did the worst thing imaginable, but she has expressed her ability to forgive."

Anthony finished with tears streaking his face.

"Anything else?" Judge Rossetti asked.

"No, Your Honor."

Judge Rossetti had missed nothing in either Joel Daniels's or Anthony Pignataro's rhetoric. He observed that he knew the family history. He himself was Buffalo born and bred. He had been to Scotty's on Busti Avenue, and he had known Anthony's grandfather, if not Dr. Ralph. "There are a lot of Pignataros that I played ball with," he said.

But the judge was not about to be persuaded by an "old boys" plea, a plethora of local connections, or a river of tears. It was clear that he had paid far more attention to facts than to emotional oratory. He spoke with a wry solemnity.

"When you received your medical degree," Rossetti said to Anthony, "I believe you took the Hippocratic Oath . . . the oath embodying the code of medical ethics that doctors should perform during their practices.

"Whether the arsenic ingesting was acute or chronic is immaterial at this particular time . . . You had your wife consume [arsenic] which resulted in her going to the hospital—which resulted in her being close to death's door . . . All of the physicians were trying to find out what the basic problem was. They could not ascertain how to treat her because they couldn't find out immediately that she was poisoned with arsenic. It seems to me that [with] remorse, if anything, [you] should have said, 'I know what it is. I gave it to her. She has got arsenic poisoning—let's try to do something.'

"That is very, very troublesome to me.

"As a part of the marriage ceremony, there were vows to love, honor, cherish, obey, in sickness and in health. When you got out of jail, you renewed those vows. Certainly giving arsenic, in my humble opinion, is not living up to that vow."

Judge Rossetti blasted Anthony for reconciling with his wife and then returning to put arsenic in her food and watching as she consumed it. And then he had proceeded to blame other people for his own crime. "You pointed to the family of Sarah Smith; you pointed to the fact that she [Debbie] may have [almost] committed suicide.

"You have two children . . . This whole matter, as a result of your unprovoked conduct towards your wife, has led to an array of pain, of permanent damage to your wife—physically, emotionally—I remember arraigning you on the initial charge [Sarah Smith] . . . I remember your wife being here. I remember your mother being here . . . She's been here time and time again—and I'm not sentencing your mother. I'm not sentencing your brothers or your sister because they didn't do anything wrong. *You* did."

Judge Rossetti commented on Anthony's second chance. "You got out of jail. I would have said, 'Thank God! I'm out of jail . . . I'm on my way. I'm going to get a job and start over again,' but, by God, you didn't do that. You have accomplished to destroy, tarnish, not only your well-respected name, your life to me has been . . . a charade of misrepresentation, self-centered, manipulative, disregard of the oaths and vows you've taken, disrespect for the law and, most important, disrespect for the value of human life."

Judge Rossetti commented that a piece of himself went with everyone he had to sentence, and that he felt sorry for Anthony's family.

"But I have to do what is just. I'm only a judge here on earth. The Judge you will finally face will give you whatever judgment that He will give you. That I can't do. We all face that Judge."

As Judge Rossetti began his sentence, Anthony seemed to shrink further. At this most crucial moment, a cell phone shrilled in the courtroom, annoying the judge. The cell phone owner fumbled frantically to turn it off.

Judge Rossetti sentenced Anthony to the top range available to him: fifteen years in prison, a sentence that was to run consecutively to the four years imposed by Judge Tills for the probation violation. Further, Rossetti said he would sign an order of protection for Debbie to begin eighteen years hence—in 2019—and continue for three years.

Judge Rossetti urged, perhaps in vain, that Debbie and Lena Pignataro try to find a way to put their differences aside. "I never had a grandmother or grandfather that I knew," he said a little wistfully. "But that's not my business. That's just an aside."

Anthony had 30 days to appeal his sentence, but for all intents and purposes, he appeared to have come to the end of the line. There would be no parole until he had served nine-tenths of his sentence. If he survives, he will be nearly 60 when he gets out of prison.

Anthony Pignataro no longer has a medical degree, a wife, a home of his own, a red Lamborghini, a Cadillac, or a mistress. His children can decide whether they want to visit him in prison, talk to him on the phone, or write to him.

The "modern-day Galileo" spends his days and nights in the Five Points Correctional Facility in Romulus, New York.

He has no contact with his children.

He did not honor his promise to tell authorities where he obtained the arsenic that he used to poison his wife.

Afterword

A year after Pignataro's sentencing, I had one of the most remarkable interviews of my career. Almost without exception, the victims I write about have been dead for years before I begin to research their stories, and, of course, I don't get to talk with them. I can only describe them through the memories of the people who knew them in life. But now I was sitting at a long dining room table in a warm and friendly home in West Seneca, New York. Almost all the people who were responsible for bringing justice to Debbie Pignataro were there, too, sharing antipasto and pizza, and remembering the myriad events of almost five years: Frank Sedita, Carol Giarizzo Bridge, Chuck Craven, Sharon Simon, Caroline Rago, Shelly Palombaro, Rose Gardner, Denis Scinta, and, most gratifying to me, Debbie Pignataro herself.

I had spoken to Debbie on the phone many times and early on learned to my chagrin at my own naivete that she wasn't the woman Anthony had introduced to me as his wife when he called me in 1998. I had no way of knowing then that it was Tami Maxell, Anthony's mistress, who greeted me graciously and assured me that she, "Debbie," had written the *Mass Destruction* manuscript. I had been only one of a long list of people Anthony tried to con into doing what he wanted.

If I had agreed to write a book defending him, then, I wonder: how would he have kept up his fake-wife gambit?

The real Debbie was someone I liked instantly. She was a little shy, and I'm sure she was apprehensive that this evening was going to bring back a lot of ghosts from her past. She bustled around the kitchen, waiting on her guests, and no one who didn't know about her long physical ordeal would have noticed the slight stiffness in her lower legs and feet. She had cleaned house for days and made a special effort to invite the prosecutorial team to her home so that I could meet them.

Ralph and Lauren and two of Shelly Palombaro's kids—D.J. and Aly,—and Gabby, the pup, romped around the house, which was clearly a house where children were important.

The room was filled with laughter, laughter that is still caught on the tape recorder they allowed me to place in the center of the table as everyone recalled the portions of Debbie's story that were most meaningful to them.

And yet, there were times when I looked at Debbie and saw a brief cloud of pain pass across her face. This was her life story, her tragedy, and we were in the house she had shared with Anthony for many years. Sharon Simon saw it, too. We exchanged a glance, but we didn't attempt to stop the conversation. None of us can fully share others' heartbreak—we'd go crazy if we did—but I saw Debbie's that night.

The walls were covered with photographs of Lauren and Ralph. In person, they were very nice kids, polite and respectful of adults but not in the least goody-goody. Lauren and Aly gave us a demonstration of gymnastics, and Ralph downloaded his father's book, *Mass Destruction,* from his computer for me.

Very few reminders of Anthony are left in his one-time

home. Only a snarling stuffed cheetah, which Ralph wants to keep, challenges visitors who walk up the stairway. There are still photographs of a younger Anthony in Debbie's wedding book.

Chuck Craven's daughter, Christine, came with him to what was basically a celebration of Debbie's life. She is a physical therapist, inspired by the therapists who helped her dad use his arm again after he was shot so many years ago in the drug raid in Arizona.

It was easy to forget why I was there in West Seneca. It was fun to hear Denis Scinta's stories of Debbie's father, "Uncle Junior," and to listen to the easy camaraderie among the district attorney's staff. It was chilling, however, when the conversation turned to Anthony and how close he came to succeeding in his carefully orchestrated plans to destroy his family and head off for a new life in a tropical climate.

We talked until long after midnight, but Sharon Simon's beeper went off, Frank Sedita had to get up early to fly to South Carolina to present a seminar to lawyers from around America, and, reluctantly, the group straggled off. It occurred to me how fortunate Debbie had been to have good old friends and good new friends. They had not only saved her life but helped her gain the dignity and confidence she has achieved.

Debbie drove me back to my motel, and I almost forgot that this was a woman whose feet hadn't been able to move a year earlier, much less press an accelerator or stomp on the brakes. I was exhausted, but happy to finally *know* someone who was supposed to be dead but who was triumphantly alive.

Finally, after hiding in her home, Debbie was able to rejoin life. She was no longer afraid to tell her story. She hopes that it might help other women by warning them and giving them the courage to walk away from abusive relationships. The only thing she asked of me was the opportunity to thank the people who had, quite literally, saved her life and locked away the man who wanted her dead.

That seemed a very reasonable request.

Debbie's Acknowledgments

With much love and thanks from Deborah Pignataro to:

My children. What can I say to the two most important people in my life? My son Ralph and my daughter Lauren. Without them, I wouldn't have had the courage to survive. Their constant love and courage made me fight even harder to make it through the most terrible of times . . . They have remained strong, bright, and well adjusted. I love them very much, and I will always be there for them no matter what.

My mother, Caroline Rago, who gave up her job, her home, and her social life to take care of me. Thank you from the bottom of my heart. I love you very much.

I thank God every day for my brother, sister-in-law, my nephew and niece. They welcomed my children into their home without a second thought and took care of them for a whole year. They came to court with me every day and gave me their strength.

My best friend, Shelly Palombaro, who appeared at my hospital bed and offered to help my mom nurse me back to now. She is my guardian angel. I would also like to thank her husband, Frank, who always dropped whatever he was doing to lend me a helping hand . . . and their kids, D.J. Striker, Aly, Chelsea, and Jacob Palombaro.

Denis A. Scinta, my attorney, and his law firm: Lipsitz, Green, Fahringer, Roll, Salisbury & Cambria . . . for the understanding and support they gave me. Not a day went by that I didn't have a phone conversation with Denis. He was my strength during the trial. He fought for my kids and me until the truth finally prevailed.

Many heartfelt thanks to my neighbor, Rose Gardner, and her family . . . and to my dear friend, Allan Steinberg, who have been there for us since Day One.

My sincere thanks to Dr. Michael C. Snyderman, Dr. Jahangir Koleini, and Dr. M. Raise Samie, all affiliated with South Buffalo Mercy Hospital. To my nurses—especially Teena Wise, Jackie Keller, Lima, Darrein, Marcia, Lucy, Donna, Debby, and Chris, who took such good care of me in my fight to live. To all the physical and occupational therapists, especially Ken and Joanne, who taught me to relearn the everyday things we all take for granted. And I will never forget Jerome, my bodyguard, who protected me! To the rest of the staff at Mercy Hospital. I will never forget you.

And thank you to Frank Clark, District Attorney of Erie County; Frank Sedita, Deputy District Attorney; Carol Bridge, Assistant District Attorney; Sharon Simon, Assistant Coordinator of the Victim/Witness Program of the Erie County D.A.'s Office; and Charles Craven and Patrick Finnerty, Confidential Criminal Investigators, Erie County D.A.'s Office. They all worked so hard on my behalf, and I will always be grateful to them.

And to all my family and friends who loved and supported my kids and me. Thank you from the bottom of my heart!"

It hasn't been long since I researched this book, and all the players are still in the same jobs they were in January.

Debbie hopes to regain her health enough so that one day she can find a job.

Ralph was the top student in his school at year's end, 2002, and Lauren is doing very well in school and in gymnastic competitions. Most weekends, Debbie drives her to either a meet or a practice.

Despite Judge Rossetti's hopes, Lena Pignataro has not reconciled with her son's family.

Dan Smith grieved for Sarah for a long time, and then he met someone he knew she would approve of. He has remarried, and he and his second wife, Kari, are raising Dan's children and theirs, although all four are *their* children, now. Dan's regret is that he asked for mercy for Anthony Pignataro before his first sentencing in Sarah's death. "I didn't want to see another young family ripped apart when their children were young, so I asked that he not be given a long sentence," he says, somewhat ruefully. "I thought Debbie and their children would be better off if they had their father come home to them. I was wrong, and in a way I blame myself that Debbie got poisoned. I never thought he would hurt his own family."

Barb Grafton, Sarah's mother, is the "Grandma" of all of Dan's children, and she visits often and spends holidays with them. "She's a special part of our family," Dan says.

Sharon Simon remains a close friend to Debbie, and she still works with victims and their families. In the spring of 2002, she was as busy as ever with some of the highest-profile cases ever to be adjudicated in Erie County. Sharon always seems to do more than her job description calls for.

Sharon had one young male client who barely survived being shot. His brain damage left him just at the edge of death, but he was determined to survive and learn to walk again. Although his mother suffered from emphysema and had to be on an oxygen tank, she took two buses and a subway every day to visit her son.

"But she's got a three-hour oxygen tank," Sharon said, "and it took her an hour and a half each way. So I started giving her rides on weekends and Christmas. This woman is lovely. She's five years older than I am, but she calls me 'Miss Simon.'"

That made Sharon feel embarrassed, and when the woman told her, "I'm gonna pray for you," Sharon's reaction was to "go mutter, mutter to myself, but then I took it back.

"I said, 'Miss Naomi, if your prayers got your son this far, I'll be grateful for them.'"

There are days in victim/witness advocacy when only prayer will get people through.

There are days in any police department and every district attorney's office when the same holds true. The lay public has no idea of how hard those people work to bring justice to crime victims.

But in Buffalo, New York, as Christmas arrives in 2002, there are scores of people who understand that sometimes good does overcome evil, and there can be happy endings.

And Debbie Pignataro changes the station whenever "Last Dance" comes on the radio.

There are sadistic sociopaths whose entire focus is on the destruction of other human beings—even though they appear to be ordinary citizens. Some of them are rich and famous, and some are everyday working people, but in all of them, the masks they wear are completely perfect, and therein lies the danger.

Every murderer in the stories that follow is a repeat offender, so entrenched in destroying the lives of others that it is easy to believe they would never stop of their own accord.

Some of them were blocked by detectives and the justice system.

Some simply grew too old to be dangerous.

And some died.

The Accountant

This story begins a very long time ago—more than fifty years have passed since it began—and it continued for decades. One of the smartest detectives in the Seattle Police Department was a young man when he first met the killer, and he was long past retirement as the story kept unfolding, layer after layer, as if it would never end. Austin Seth is well over 80 now, but he has an impeccable memory, particularly when he is asked about the case that began on July 10, 1948. Of the scores of homicides he solved, this case is the one he remembers the best.

In Seattle, it is often rainy in July. That hasn't changed in 54 years. Rhododendrons, impatiens, and hydrangeas thrive, but tomatoes and strawberries sometimes rot on the vine as the Emerald City grudgingly lets go of spring and plunges into summer. August is usually the only month you can count on to have more than three consecutive days of sunshine.

On that long-ago Saturday morning in July, it was warm and sultry, the air humid from a recent rain. A young man who lived in the northeast section of Seattle was taking a shortcut across vacant lots to the bus stop at E. 65th and N.E. 35th in the Ravenna district. There were a lot of vacant lots in Seattle in 1948, although today they are few and far between. Wild blackberry vines, bindweed, and straggly clover grew in tangles wherever builders weren't constructing new houses to meet the post–World War II demand. The bus commuter trotted across the clear spots between the verdant weed patches.

The sandy clay soil dipped in spots, leaving hollows, ditches, and rutted trails that were now filled with leftover rainwater from a Friday night storm. He leaped over a water hazard, and, as he did so, glanced down to be sure he'd cleared a ditch. His heart constricted and his breath caught in his throat as he wondered if his mind was playing tricks on him. Late as he was, he had to turn back and look more carefully.

When he did, he was sorry he had. There *was* a woman lying there motionless, facedown, in the ditch. It looked as if she was naked beneath the sweater-jacket that had been tossed carelessly over her pale white flesh.

All thoughts of catching the next bus vanished as the man ran to the nearest house and pounded on the door. He asked if he could use the phone. There was no 911 in 1948; indeed, one man per shift—Harmon Ensley on this First Watch from four until noon—handled all the emergency calls that came into the Seattle Police Department, as well as the ADT bank alarms. It seems impossible now, but it worked just fine then. Ensley could direct patrol cars into a crime scene as deftly as any air traffic controller and keep up a constant patter as he did so.

In those days, there was a captain overseeing the Homicide and Robbery Unit, and all the homicide detectives were designated lieutenants. "We didn't get any extra pay," Austin Seth recalls, "but we had the rank. It gave us a little more persuasive power if we needed it."

On the morning of July 10, patrol officers from the north end's Wallingford precinct were the first to reach the scene. The spot where the woman lay was only a half block off a well-traveled boulevard, Sand Point Way, but it still seemed isolated. Officers Henry Redick and J.B. Small were followed by the commander of the precinct, Captain Art Chaffee.

The witness who led them to the ditch hadn't known if the woman was alive or dead when he called, but the Wallingford officers could see that she was dead; her face was under a few inches of muddy water. She would have drowned if she'd been unconscious when she was thrown or fell there. Maybe someone had held her head down, or perhaps she was already dead.

They didn't disturb the body, waiting for homicide detectives to arrive from headquarters in downtown Seattle. It wasn't long before the weed-filled field was alive with police cars and plainclothes vehicles. Sergeant I.A. O'Mera and Lieutenants Austin Seth and his partner, Don Sprinkle, made the 10-mile trip in no time. King County Coroner John Brill came along, too. He would be the one to officially declare the victim dead, but he wouldn't remove the body until a search for possible evidence had been finished.

In the 1940s, detectives still wore fedoras, suits, white shirts, and ties. The group of men who gathered around the body resembled an outtake from a *film noir* movie.

Sprinkle and Seth were close friends as well as partners, and Seth would never in his life have a better partner. Austin Seth was 33 years old, six feet three, with thick dark hair; Don Sprinkle was a year younger, several inches shorter than Seth, with reddish-blond hair. He was a snappy dresser; his hat was woven of straw with an extra-wide brim and a cloth band in a tropical print. Seth was far more conservative. The two homicide detectives worked together so well that often they didn't even have to speak to know what the other was thinking.

Now, they tossed their suit jackets in their car and rolled up their sleeves. They dug a ditch in the dirt road next to the ditch so that the water would drain from the depression where the body lay.

They didn't know yet how she had died, but it wasn't likely that she had been hit by a car on the narrow dirt road—not when she now lay naked, except for the sweater with its ornate gold buttons. There were traces of blood on the sweater. Her long thick auburn hair floated in the muddy water, obscuring most of her face. But when they turned the body, already stiffening with rigor mortis, they had no doubt at all that the young woman had been murdered. *More* than murdered—if such a thing were possible. She had been beaten savagely. Her right eye was swollen and as purple as a ripe plum, her nose was broken, and her head and face were covered with multiple bruises and abrasions. A black strap of some kind protruded from her mouth.

Although Brill could not tell the actual manner of death, he said it was likely that she had been manually strangled. Deep black bruising on the front of her neck made that a strong possibility.

Worst of all, her killer had slashed at her breasts and pubic area with a razor-sharp instrument, mutilating her body in a way that suggested she had encountered an acutely disturbed sexual psychopath.

"I think these will prove to be wounds that were administered after death," Brill said. "But we'll have to see what Doc Wilson says after he does the autopsy."

The victim's body was removed and taken to the King County morgue, located in the basement of the County City Building. Hopefully, a postmortem examination would give the investigators an accurate picture of her time of death.

Precious little physical evidence was found at the body site. They found one sturdy woman's oxford shoe, the kind that nurses wear—although this one was brown— and a pair of panties. The chances were good that the actual murder had occurred someplace else and the killer had brought the body here to dispose of it.

The soil was very sandy, and Seth noticed fresh tire tracks not far from the ditch. The imprints were sharp; clearly, no other vehicle had driven over them. Max Allison, head of the crime lab, headed out to take a plaster of paris impression, known as a moulage cast, of the tread pattern. If they found tires to compare with the pattern, they might just have a positive piece of evidence.

The neighborhood was mostly residential, with neat little homes just across the street from the open field where the victim had been left. Their lawns sloped down to the street and were all carefully landscaped. A few blocks farther along, the houses became virtual mansions, with gated entries. Another major presence in the area was the Sand Point Naval Air Station, where hundreds of pilots and officers were assigned. The killer could have come from the naval base, from the neighborhood, or from someplace far away.

Austin Seth and Don Sprinkle followed the coroner's ambulance as it headed downtown; as the principal detectives assigned to this case, they would observe the autopsy. However, they had gone only a few blocks when the police radio announced that a stolen car, a brand-new gray Lincoln sedan, had been located at 36th Avenue West and West Bertona in the Magnolia district. The officer responding to the early morning report had found that the front seat and one of the doors were stained heavily with blood.

Seth and Sprinkle headed to Magnolia Bluff, a trip of several miles. Seattle is a city with large bodies of water on either side. The body had been found close to Lake Washington, on the east side of the city, and Magnolia Bluff was on the west side, overlooking Elliot Bay. The latter had several characteristics that were similar to the Sand Point region. The address where the car was found was only a few blocks from the Fort Lawton Army base. During World War II (and later the Korean War), thousands of troops passed through Fort Lawton headed for the Far East.

Seth and Sprinkle would probably have to sift through thousands of soldiers, sailors, and marines to find their killer. They hoped that wouldn't happen. For now, they were very curious about the car found on Magnolia Bluff, its keys still in the ignition.

"That Lincoln turned out to belong to a doctor," Seth recalls. "He'd parked it in the Olympic Hotel garage, and when he went to get it at seven the night before, it was gone. He reported it immediately to our department."

Seth and Sprinkle walked around the luxury car. It didn't have any exterior damage, and its white sidewall tires were perfectly clean. The interior was another story. The upholstery on the driver's side of the front seat was stained with dried blood; one spot had come from pooling blood, and the other looked like transferred blood. There were also flecks of castoff blood on the dashboard. They would have come from a weapon being raised again and again. On the upswing, the velocity of the movement would have flung droplets onto the dashboard, their "tails" showing the direction of the killer's swing.

The clutch, brake, and accelerator pedals were covered with sandy residue, and the floorboards had a good amount of sand and tiny pebbles, similar to the dirt found at the body site.

The physician himself, of course, became a suspect. He had reported the car stolen around 7 P.M. the night before. They didn't know yet when the murdered woman had died, but the autopsy was about to start, and they would have a better idea soon.

Max Allison arrived to process the car, dusting for fingerprints and taking dirt samples and tire impressions. There was enough blood to check for type—although it would be decades before DNA would assist police probes.

* * *

The postmortem was just beginning when Seth and Sprinkle arrived at the morgue. The young woman was five feet, five inches tall and weighed 120 pounds. She appeared to be in her late teens or early twenties. Her red hair was luxuriant, and she had a redhead's complexion with a profusion of freckles. It was impossible to tell whether she had been pretty, but she had a perfect figure, although it was marred now by the ugly perversion of her killer. There were more than two dozen thin cuts on her right breast, and both breasts had been laid open with deep horizontal slashes. The same weapon had been used to make a deep cut in her pubic area and then trailed up around her belly button and back down.

"What was the weapon?" Austin Seth asked.

"This beer bottle," Dr. Gale Wilson said as he showed the two detectives the broken bottle that had been removed from beneath the body. The bottom had been smashed as bar-fighters do. "He held it by the neck and used the sharp edges to cut her."

"I think he strangled her with her own bra," Wilson said. The bra had been cruelly jammed deeply into the victim's throat, leaving only a thin black satin shoulder strap visible in the corner of her mouth.

"At least this all happened after she was dead," Wilson said. "She was strangled first, and she was raped. I can't say if that happened before or after she died."

Forty years later, the semen left behind by the killer would be a vital clue. But, again, DNA testing was as unlikely in 1948 as a spaceship landing in downtown Seattle.

"Time of death?" Don Sprinkle asked, knowing that it wouldn't be as specific as fictional pathologists' opinions.

"Probably between 2 and 3 A.M., give or take an hour either way," Dr. Wilson said.

That let the physician with the new Lincoln off the

hook. He hadn't seen his car since the evening before the victim died. It wasn't very likely he would report his car missing and then go out and commit a murder. Besides, he had an impeccable reputation.

Dr. Gale Wilson was something of a legend in King County. He kept a small black notebook in his suit pocket and noted every autopsy he performed. When he testified in court, he always began by giving the latest tally. By the time he retired, he had done more than 40,000 autopsies.

However, this autopsy was far more troubling than most. This was the work of a sadistic sociopath. Although about 3 percent of all males and 1 percent of females are deemed to be sociopaths, only a tiny, tiny percentage of those people are diagnosed as sadistic. Sadists *enjoy* hurting people.

The person who had done this terrible damage to the victim before them had to be caught as soon as possible. Because of the rape, they were looking for a male. Whoever he was, if he had done it once, he would do it again, and Don Sprinkle and Austin Seth vowed that they were not going to allow that to happen.

Patrol officers and detectives who had spread out to search the entire neighborhood near Sand Point Way discovered women's clothing that had been tossed onto the median strip of the boulevard for two or three miles. They gathered the items up carefully and put them into evidence bags. There were slacks, a white blouse, panties, and stockings. All appeared to match the size of the dead woman.

The sweater that had been thrown over the woman in the ditch was drying on a rack in the homicide unit. When the detectives examined it more closely, they saw a name tag sewn inside the collar. It read "Velda Woodcock."

Sergeant O'Mera asked detectives H. W. Vosper and Stan Bowerman to check the Seattle phone book for the name Woodcock. They found sixteen Woodcock listings and began to dial them one by one. The tenth call went to a Mrs. Leona Woodcock, who lived on 43rd Avenue N.E. That address was fairly close to where the victim's body had been found.

A woman with a young voice answered, and when Vosper asked for Velda Woodcock, she surprised him.

"*I'm* Velda Woodcock," she said.

Vosper identified himself, and Velda immediately asked, "Is it about my sister? My sister, Donna, didn't come home last night. Was she in an accident? My mother and I have been so worried."

Vosper didn't want to give her the terrible news over the phone. He said that his sergeant was on the way to her house to talk with her. But noting the address, Sergeant O'Mera immediately called Captain Chaffee, who could get there a lot quicker.

At the Woodcock home, Chaffee met Velda, who was only eighteen, and her mother. Both of them were shaking with apprehension.

"We're not certain that the woman we're inquiring about is your sister," Chaffee said. "Could you describe her to me—maybe tell me a little bit about her?"

"Has something happened to her?" Velda asked nervously.

"We don't know—" Chaffee said. In this situation it was difficult to know what to say. The woman and the girl in front of him really didn't want to know the truth, but Velda's words came rushing out.

"My sister is 22," she said, "and she's really pretty. She has long red hair and blue eyes, and she's about five feet, five. She's a really nice person, and she would never want us to worry about her—"

"Where does she work?"

"She works hard because she has a lot of ambition," Velda said. "She's studying law, so she has to work nights. She works at the Triple XXX Barrel drive-in on Bothell Way. She used to be a receptionist in a doctor's office, but she didn't make enough to pay for school, so she took the carhop job. She gets big tips. That's why she works the night shift. The tips are bigger at night."

"What time does she usually get home?"

"Her shift is over at 3 A.M.," Velda said, her words tumbling one on top of the other. "She always comes straight home. She doesn't have a car, but she usually gets a ride with one of the other employees, or maybe with some guy she knows if one of them comes by at closing time. But she didn't come home last night at all, and she didn't even call. She always calls."

Velda Woodcock was fighting back tears now. "Please tell us. Was she in an accident? Is she in the hospital?"

There was no way to tell the victim's mother and sister and not have it hurt. Chaffee took a deep breath and told them that Donna Woodcock was dead. "The woman we found was wearing your sweater—we think that someone killed her," he said, carefully avoiding the horrific details of the homicide.

"I loaned her my sweater last night. It gets so cool in the middle of the night," Velda sobbed. "But are you sure it's Donna?"

"The description matches. The victim has long red hair and blue eyes, and she was wearing your sweater. I'm sorry."

When Leona and Velda Woodcock had finally steadied themselves from the shock, they said they thought they could answer Chaffee's questions.

"Was Donna afraid of anyone?" he asked quietly. "Was there anything in her life that might have led to this? Anyone hanging around her work who scared her?"

They shook their heads. Donna wasn't afraid of any-one. She was strong and independent. "My husband died last year," Leona Woodcock said. "Since then, Donna's been the only one working. She supported all of us. I have a law degree, but I never practiced because I got married right after law school."

Neither of them could imagine that Donna would have gone with someone she didn't know. "She was too intelligent for that," her mother said. "I kept telling her you couldn't trust people until you know something about them—"

"Wait," Velda Woodcock said. "Someone might have been waiting for her to rob her. She took $250 out of her postal savings account yesterday. She needed it to pay for summer quarter tuition. She had it in her purse when she went to work last night. Maybe somebody saw it there when she opened her purse."

They hadn't found a purse. But they had found the scattered clothing along Sand Point Way. Those clothes were taken to the Woodcock home, and Velda identified the slacks as the ones Donna had worn when she left for work the night before.

Donna's mother thumbed through a photo album and gave detectives a picture of her daughter. Donna had been a truly beautiful young woman, her red hair swept up into a pompadour in front and hanging in shining waves to her shoulders. Her features were lovely.

Austin Seth and Don Sprinkle went to the Triple XXX Barrel drive-in on Bothell way, a few miles north of the field where Donna Woodcock was found. The owner was there, but he said he hadn't been the night before. He gave them the name and address of another carhop who worked the same shift as Donna did.

The two detectives located the young woman, Sandy

Graham*, who had just awakened after working the late, late shift. She was making coffee, but she hadn't turned the radio on yet. She hadn't heard anything about the murder victim found near the Sand Point Naval Air Station.

Sandy Graham was stunned when they told her about Donna's murder. Tears filled her eyes.

"Did you see her leave last night—ahhh—this *morning?*" Austin Seth asked.

"Let me think . . . it's hard to think," the shocked girl said. "Donna said she had a ride home with a guy named Bruce. We knew him. He used to come into the Triple XXX. He drove up around nine, I remember. He was in a jeep. But when Donna went off duty at a quarter to three, I saw her get into another car."

"What kind of a car?" Don Sprinkle asked.

"It was a big gray car. It looked like a very expensive car. It was parked near the restaurant."

Sandy didn't know Bruce's last name. She said that Donna had never talked much about him. "But Donna had very good judgment, and she must have thought he was O.K."

Sandy couldn't give them a detailed description of Bruce, and she didn't know if he had been the driver of the Lincoln or not; she wasn't close enough to see the driver—and, of course, it was dark.

Seattle newspapers carried the story of Donna Woodcock's murder on the front page, along with a request for any information the public might have about the driver of the stolen gray Lincoln.

The phone rang in Homicide the next morning. It was the officer of the day at the Sand Point Naval Air Station.

"One of the marines stationed here just picked up the newspaper," the naval officer said. "He recognizes the murdered girl and the Lincoln. He thinks he may know the man the girl left with. I have him here in my office now."

"Keep him there," Don Sprinkle said. "We're on our way."

Sprinkle and Austin Seth were at the Naval Air Station within 15 minutes. A young marine was there, waiting for them. His name was Fred Haws.

"Seattle is my home town," he told Seth and Sprinkle. "And I graduated from Lincoln High School. I knew this guy in high school—and I saw him in the Triple XXX on the night the waitress was killed. I think he took her home that night."

"Tell us about it," Seth said.

"I got there sometime before two in the morning," Haws said, "and this pretty, red-haired girl waited on me. I was kind of kidding—kind of serious—about asking her to go out with me. She said no, but she didn't say why. She was a nice girl, and I didn't really expect she would go, anyway.

"Anyway," he continued, "this new gray Lincoln sedan pulled in. I was surprised to see that Jack Gasser was driving it. I left my car and walked over and talked to him. I hadn't seen him for two years. He left high school to join the Navy before he graduated. He told me he was sent to China, and after his Navy service, he finished high school at Broadway High. I didn't see how he could afford the fancy car, and then he told me the Lincoln belonged to his uncle."

Fred Haws said he'd gone back to his own car to eat his sandwich, and he saw the girl he now knew was Donna Woodcock come out of the Triple XXX and go over to the Lincoln.

"They were talking, and I think Jack was asking her out, or maybe he knew her from before, and he already had a date with her. Anyway, they were still talking when I left."

"We think she did go out with him that night," Don

ANN RULE

Sprinkle said. "Another waitress saw her leave in a gray Lincoln. Do you know where this Jack Gasser lives?"

"I couldn't tell you the address—but I could lead you there," Haws said.

Seth and Sprinkle followed the young Marine to a house in the north end, but when they rang the doorbell, the man who answered said that the Gassers had moved two years earlier. He told them that the head of the household was named William Gasser.

The phone book showed a William Gasser on 35th Avenue West. Seth and Sprinkle felt a thrill of excitement. The address was only two blocks from where the stolen Lincoln had been abandoned a few hours after the murder.

"We drove there," Austin Seth remembers. "It was a really hot night—I remember that well."

Moths fluttered around the porch light, and a faint breeze made the heavy shrubbery around the steps brush against the railing. When they knocked on the screen door, a good-looking young man who looked to be about nineteen or twenty answered.

"We walked right in," Seth says, "and I said, 'Is Jack Gasser here?' The boy who answered the door said, 'That's me.' He didn't seem nervous at all."

In the light of the foyer, the two detectives studied Jack Gasser. He was six feet tall and very trim and muscular. His thick dark hair was heavily pomaded and combed straight back, except for one errant lock that he had deliberately curled so that it fell over his forehead in a style popularized by movie star Robert Mitchum. Jack Gasser had clear light eyes, but Seth recalls that there was a "dead" quality about them.

Of more interest to Seth and Sprinkle was the cluster of scratches on the left side of Jack Gasser's face. They were deep and had barely begun to heal.

"Can we talk to you for a minute?" Seth asked.

"We're just eating supper," Gasser said, but he led them into the dining room, where his family sat around the table. His parents and his older brother stared at the detectives in open-mouthed surprise.

While Jack Gasser seemed to grow tense, his father was angry at the interruption and demanded to know why the two detectives were there. The elder Gasser, who owned an insurance agency in the University District, explained that he had just been elected commander of his district's American Legion veterans' group and that his installation was that evening. He didn't appreciate being interrupted at such an important time.

"We told him that nevertheless we needed to talk to Jack, and we took him out to our car," Seth recalls.

The Gassers were puzzled, but they didn't object to Jack's being questioned. Don Sprinkle and Jack Gasser slid into the back seat of the detectives' unmarked car.

"It's about a Lincoln sedan that was stolen last night," Sprinkle said.

And, with that, Jack noticeably relaxed.

"It was found just a short distance from here," Sprinkle said.

"Oh, that," Gasser finally admitted. "I did steal that car. I didn't hurt it, though. I just took it for a joyride. I know that was wrong. I'm sorry."

Seth left his partner talking with Jack Gasser and went back inside the family home. Isabel Gasser was close to tears and her husband was apoplectic when he told them that they would be taking Jack downtown to police headquarters.

"This could ruin us socially," Isabel said faintly. "Just when his father was going to get such a big honor tonight."

"Well, I'm sorry," Seth said, a little puzzled by her priorities, "but we're going to have to talk to him some more. You can come down later, if you like."

As Seth pulled away from the curb, Don Sprinkle asked Gasser what he had been wearing the night before.

"Just slacks and a shirt, " he answered.

"Where are those clothes now?"

"At the cleaners—the one right up in the next block."

Seth's eyes met Sprinkle's in the rearview mirror, and they both looked instinctively at their watches. It was almost 7 P.M., time for the cleaners to close. Seth hit the accelerator and wrenched the wheel, pulling to a skidding stop in front of the cleaners.

"I left Gasser sitting with Don and raced in to get those clothes before they were dry-cleaned. If any of Donna Woodcock's blood was on them, we'd lose that evidence if they were cleaned. We made it just in time. All there was was a pair of slacks, but you could see they were heavily stained with dried blood. Later, Max was able to type it and match it to Donna Woodcock's blood type."

Austin Seth recalls, "At first, Gasser seemed relieved that we were only taking him to the station because of a car theft. He told us he'd been in the Navy, and he got a dishonorable discharge for punching out an officer. He was going to college and was in his sophomore year at Seattle University. But he didn't want to talk any more about the car or anything else we might have in mind."

It was hard for them to look at this kid with the clear eyes and realize that he was probably the monster who had mutilated the body of his victim after he raped and strangled her. He was polite and soft-spoken.

At headquarters, Sprinkle and Seth escorted Jack Gasser to an interview room. Seth began rolling a tape from a recorder, a machine considerably larger than today's tiny tape recorders. The big spools revolved slowly, committing their conversation to posterity.

"Since you've admitted that you stole the car, you might as well tell us why you killed Donna Woodcock."

"I didn't kill anyone," Jack Gasser said, his voice suddenly apprehensive.

"Her blood is all over that car you just told us you stole. We already have a witness who saw Donna get into your car Friday night."

"Somebody's wrong," Gasser muttered, refusing to meet their eyes.

"And then," Austin Seth said, "it was like he couldn't hold it in. Within five minutes, he began to confess to killing her."

Jack Gasser said he had had a couple of beers, and then he'd driven to the Triple XXX Barrel drive-in. He insisted he'd never seen Donna Woodcock before the moment she walked up to his car to take his order. He had kidded around with her.

"I offered to give her a ride home at closing time," he said, "and she accepted."

Gasser told a story that warred with the facts. He said he'd driven Donna home, and she'd gone inside and fed some scraps from the drive-in to her dog. "She came back to the car, and we went and parked in the field and drank a couple of beers apiece."

Seth and Sprinkle knew that Donna Woodcock's blood alcohol level was zero. She hadn't drunk any beer—and if she *had* gone into her house, her mother and sister, who always checked to be sure she was home safe, would have heard her.

Gasser said he was kidding Donna. "I was just sitting there," he said, surprise in his voice. "I hadn't laid a hand on her."

But he admitted he'd been teasing her, claiming that

all carhops were floozies and easy, saying that he had no respect for them. And then she flared up at him, very angry. "I evidently said something she didn't like at all. She slapped me," he said.

"I grabbed her and started to choke her and everything seemed to go black."

Austin Seth had heard the words, "Everything went black" too many times. He pressed Gasser to give them a few more details. Gasser admitted that he remembered having Donna down on the seat on her back, and that he'd punched her in the nose and in the right eye. But he wouldn't discuss cutting her or stuffing her bra down her throat. And he certainly would not admit to sexually assaulting her. He did remember wanting to see her naked.

"I started to take her clothes off, and then I pushed her out of the car. She fell partway into the mud hole. I pushed her into it until she lay there facedown. Then I threw the sweater on top of her. I knew she was dead. I felt for her pulse, and there wasn't any."

Still, Gasser hadn't mentioned the sexual assault or the way Donna's body was mutilated. If she had any scratches, he insisted that that must have happened when he was dragging her toward the ditch. Maybe she'd been cut by one of the beer bottles they'd thrown out the window.

"He did admit to me," Seth says, "that he didn't get any kick out of raping a woman—it was the act of overcoming her that he found exciting. He liked to have complete control."

After he left the body site, Gasser said he'd noticed Donna's clothes in the back seat of the car, and he'd thrown them out of the car window while driving down Sand Point Way. He had driven to Magnolia Bluff and left the stolen Lincoln a block and a half from his home.

William Gasser and his wife, Isabel, had waited anxiously while their son was being questioned. After Jack was placed under arrest on suspicion of first-degree murder, they were allowed to see him. They asked to see him alone, but Austin Seth told them that wasn't possible.

"He put on a really good act for them," Seth remembers. "He told them that Donna Woodcock came on to him and wouldn't take no for an answer. He made it sound as if he were just an innocent young boy, and this older woman with no morals had practically attacked him. His mother hugged him and sobbed."

They promised they would get him a good lawyer and that it would all be straightened out.

The next morning, Jack Gasser led Don Sprinkle, Austin Seth, and Edmund Quigley, the Senior Deputy Prosecuting Attorney of King County, to the empty lot where he had left Donna Woodcock's body, reenacting the crime for them. He held out his arms, showing Quigley how he had pulled Donna from the car and dragged her to the ditch.

There was no question any longer that he had killed Donna: he went unerringly to the exact spot where her body had been found. He showed the first emotion he'd exhibited since they arrested him, complaining that it really depressed him to have to come back to this place. "You really know how to make a guy feel bad," he whined.

Velda Woodcock insisted that Donna must have known Gasser before the night she was killed. "She wouldn't have gone with a stranger—I'll bet he'd been into the Triple XXX Barrel before. She probably thought she knew him. But I know she would have fought him. She was really strong for a woman, and she would have struggled hard to save her life."

As indeed she had—from the look of the many deep scratches on Gasser's face. Donna's purse, containing her tuition money, was never found, despite intense searches at the body site and near where the stolen Lincoln was left.

Jack Gasser had people who spoke up for him, too. His parents, of course, were his biggest support. One of his professors at Seattle University, a Jesuit school where only the brightest students were admitted, described him as a "nice boy who had everything going for him.

"He was industrious and he did above-average work. He was a nice boy—very pleasant, and seemed to get along with everyone."

John Russell Gasser went on trial in Superior Court Judge Howard M. Findley's courtroom on November 29, 1948. Despite the fact that extensive psychological testing indicated he was quite sane and understood the difference between right and wrong at the time he killed Donna Woodcock, Gasser pleaded not guilty by reason of mental irresponsibility.

Deputy Prosecuting Attorney John Vogel, 38, represented the state as he told a jury of eight men and four women about the death of Donna Woodcock.

Dr. Gale Wilson, the pathologist who had performed the autopsy on the victim, explained her wounds to the jurors. Besides being strangled with her own bra, her nose was fractured, two of her teeth were broken off when her bra was stuffed down her throat, and she had suffered a terrible beating. The jurors' faces paled as they looked at the morgue photographs that showed the repetitive slicing of her body with the broken beer bottle. It looked as if the killer had been studying Krafft-Ebing and the Marquis de Sade, carrying murder far beyond the death of his victim.

"I ask you for the death penalty," Vogel said. "I doubt

that you ever have heard—or ever will hear—of a more cold-blooded crime."

Jack Gasser sat at the defense table, his youthful face a study of innocence and regret. He was only 20; to recommend that he be executed would require that the jurors believed that he could never be rehabilitated. Attractive defendants traditionally have much less chance of being sentenced to death than those who look dangerous. And Gasser looked like a choirboy.

On December 2, the jurors retired to deliberate. They were back in three hours with their verdict. Jack Gasser had been found guilty of murder in the first degree, but two of the women on the jury had balked at voting for the death penalty. They all believed that he would be locked up forever.

Five days later, Judge Findley sentenced Gasser to a mandatory life sentence without possibility of parole in the Washington State Penitentiary in Walla Walla. The community breathed a sigh of relief.

The physician whose brand-new Lincoln had been stolen got it back. "It still looked new and didn't have a scratch on it," Austin Seth remembered, "but his wife would never ride in it again. He had to turn it in on another sedan."

Laws can change. Voters swing back and forth from one extreme to another when it comes to punishment of criminals. And in the late forties, *rehabilitation* was the key word. The death penalty was considered cruel and unusual.

By 1951, the State of Washington had a new policy regarding "life" sentences. The new law set a 20-year minimum for those sentenced to life in prison, and reduced that by one third with time off for good behavior. As a result, most life terms really meant 13 years and 4 months. If a killer had used a deadly weapon—such as a gun or a knife—in his crime, a mandatory 5 years could be added, to run either consecutively or concurrently.

For Jack Gasser, it was a "Get out of jail free" card. He had been a model prisoner, a friend to other prisoners and guards alike. He took a two-year correspondence course in basic accounting, and he even earned four postgraduate credits in accounting. He passed a shorthand course, worked as a clerk in the inmates' store at Walla Walla, and then was put in charge of the curio store, where he handled money for both guards and prisoners. He was charming and cooperative and seemed to get along well with almost everyone he met in prison.

From 1956 on, there were notations in his file that he should be considered eligible for parole; he seemed an ideal candidate for rehabilitation. In 1962, two members of the Washington State Parole Board went over Gasser's files carefully. They certainly had dealt with hard-core antisocial personalities before. Helen Shank had been superintendent for the state's Maple Lane School for delinquent girls. H. J. "Jimmy" Lawrence had been the chief of the Seattle Police Department. They read all the reports from psychiatrists and psychologists about Jack Gasser. They read a study that said sixty-five murderers had been paroled in Washington State since the new law came in, and not one of them had killed anyone.

"I recall many, many cases that were murders of passion and were a one-time thing," Helen Shank remarked a long time later.

But Jack Gasser's crime hadn't been a traditional "murder of passion." It wasn't a case of a one partner in a love relationship catching the other in *flagrante delicto* with another person. Jack Gasser had killed a complete stranger because he wanted to control her and torture her.

Nevertheless, on Shank's and Lawrence's recommendation to the parole board, Gasser was paroled on August 7, 1962. He was still a young man—only thirty-three—when he walked out of prison.

The murder of Donna Woodcock had been one of the most shocking ever to hit Seattle. Citizens remembered it, even though the general public never heard all the grotesque details. When newspapers reported that the killer who'd been sent up for the rest of his natural life was walking free among them, there were letters to the editors, editorials, and outraged disbelief.

It didn't change things at all. Jack Gasser was free.

Austin Seth and Don Sprinkle weren't partners any longer, although they were still close friends. Sprinkle had been elected the sheriff of King County. He also coached the semipro football team, the Seattle Ramblers. Seth stayed on in the Seattle Police Department.

"And then we started getting reports," Austin Seth remembers. "It seems that Jack Gasser was back trying to lure women into his car. He had a drinking problem—a big problem—and when he drank, he got mean. There were just too many complaints from women who'd been frightened by some guy in his thirties. One got his license plate number, and I checked it out. It was the Gasser family car.

"Don and I got together and reported him to the parole board. They started the process of revoking his parole."

But Don Sprinkle didn't live to see Gasser's parole revoked. Tragically, Sprinkle suffered a massive heart attack in August 1963, as he rode in a car in the Chinatown Parade as part of the Seattle Seafair Festival. He was dead at the age of 47. It was a loss that Austin Seth would carry with him forever. He had other partners over the years, but none was ever as close as Don Sprinkle had been.

In January 1964, Jack Gasser was arrested for public intoxication after another incident when a woman was frightened by his behavior. His parole was instantly revoked, and he went back to Walla Walla. He served a little over five more years. He was paroled again in September 1969. By this time, Austin Seth had retired from the Seattle Police Department, but he was far from retired. He became the chief of security at the Olympic Hotel, Seattle's poshest hotel, where visiting presidents stayed when they were in town. So did national celebrities, some of whose antics shocked even the long-time homicide detective.

Austin Seth also took the photo-finish pictures at the Longacres Race Track. An accomplished photographer, he had taken thousands of crime scene photos over the years.

Although Seth never forgot Jack Gasser, he was no longer in a position to keep track of his movements.

Actually, Jack Gasser, now forty, appeared to be the poster boy for rehabilitation of felons. He moved to Bellingham, Washington, where he attended Western Washington University and earned his accounting degree in 1971.

The Bellingham Police Department has no record of any contact at all with Jack Gasser. However, Bellingham is in Whatcom County, and the Whatcom County Sheriff's Department has an unsolved murder dating back to 1970. There are startling similarities to the case of Donna Woodcock more than two decades earlier.

Nancy Winslow was a pretty 22-year-old waitress. She was five feet four and weighed 123 pounds. July 26, 1970, was actually her first full day on the job at the Beaver Tavern after three days of training. She was supposed to work only from two until five, and a teenaged relative was looking after Nancy's two toddlers. Nancy didn't have a car, and she didn't have a ride either—but she planned to walk home when she finished her shift at the tavern on the outskirts of Bellingham. It would still be light out at five.

The afternoon went well, but the woman who was supposed to work the late shift called in to say she was ill. Nancy volunteered to stay until ten, even though it meant canceling her plans to go to a picnic that night. Always a thoughtful and responsible mother, she called home to arrange for an older girl to baby-sit until 10:30. The afternoon sitter was too young to stay out so late. Nancy also bought hamburgers from the restaurant and sent them in a cab to her house to feed her children and the sitters. She wanted to keep her new job, but she was worried about her children.

Nancy Winslow made several calls during the evening to try to find a ride home. She finally located her husband, but he said he wouldn't be able to pick her up. He had to work late, too.

"That's O.K.," the cook heard her say. "I'll find a ride."

Nancy finished her shift and did her side work, filling catsup and mustard containers, sugar bowls, and salt and pepper shakers. She even did some dishes; she wanted to make a good impression. The owners of the Beaver Tavern offered to drive her home, but she said she didn't want to bother them. She had found a ride.

After she washed the last glasses, she put on her white mohair sweater with orange trim, picked up her straw purse, and started watching out the window.

"There he is now," she called to the owners, and she waved as she headed out to the parking lot. They saw her get into what looked like a 1952 gray or light tan Plymouth. They couldn't see who was driving, but they were positive that there was only one person in the car.

Nancy Winslow never made it home that night. Her worried husband went to the Bellingham Police Department to file a missing persons report the next afternoon. He was insistent that she would never have left her children willingly. He'd come home from work late the night before to find a worried baby-sitter, who hadn't heard from Nancy since she had sent hamburgers home for them to eat. She had promised she would be there by 10:45 at the latest.

Although the Bellingham police checked with hospitals and surrounding law enforcement departments, they found out nothing about Nancy Winslow. She had simply walked out of the Beaver Tavern into the darkness and driven off with someone. They didn't even know whether the driver was a man or a woman.

It was two weeks to the day on August 9 when a couple, enjoying an outing in the forested tranquility of the Bridge Camp Ground some 40 miles east of Bellingham, noticed that their dog was behaving strangely. He kept dashing to the edge of the Nooksack River, barking and growling. The camping area near the foot of Mount Baker is a virtual wilderness, and they assumed that their dog had caught the scent of a bear or a cougar. But he seemed to be barking at something that lay on a rocky bar that jutted out of the river below. They walked over to see what it was.

As they moved closer they saw the naked body of a woman sprawled on the rocks. They corralled their dog and hurried to the closest ranger station. An urgent call went into the Whatcom County Sheriff's Office, and Sergeant Ward Crutcher and Detective F. Scott Notar were dispatched to the body site on the Nooksack River.

The detectives and the ranger waded through the swift current to the gravel and rock bar. The body of the woman was badly decomposed by the ravages of summer heat. Most of the head and neck were nearly skeletonized. It would be impossible to identify her visually.

She was completely naked except for a nylon stocking that had been used as a garotte around her neck. They would learn it was a type sold by J. C. Penney, called "Clingalon," with lacy elastic at the top.

"She was probably thrown into the river upstream," Crutcher surmised. "With the heat of the last two weeks, the river's gone down a lot, and it exposed this bar. Otherwise, the body would have ended up much farther downstream."

The body in the river was taken to Whatcom County Coroner Dr. Robert Rood's office for a postmortem examination.

The corpse appeared to be that of a young woman, well under thirty. With the high temperatures and the body's long immersion in the river, it was no longer possible to tell the extent of the injuries the victim might have suffered, or whether she had been raped. Nor could Dr. Rood give a time or even a day of death. The murder weapon was the stocking; she had died of strangulation by ligature.

Nancy Winslow, the 22-year-old waitress, was the only woman missing in Whatcom County who fit the general description of the body in the Nooksack. A comparison of her dental records and those of the river victim verified that she had been found.

She had disappeared from the city of Bellingham, but her body was found in Whatcom County, so it became essentially a county case, although the sheriff's detectives would work closely with the city investigators.

An outdoor crime scene is very difficult to work; wind, water, changing weather, and wild animals all combine to move or destroy any evidence that might have been left behind by the killer. Detectives Pete Kuehnel from the county and Telmer Kvevin from the city drove the 40 miles to the lonely river campsite. They knew that they had little chance of finding Nancy's clothing; it had probably all washed away in the river—but they hoped they might find *something*.

With the help of forest rangers, Kuehnel and Kvevin searched the campgrounds. They dug through garbage piles and even probed portable "Honey Buckets" placed there for campers to use. It was an onerous task. They were looking for the bright orange and white daisy-printed shift Nancy had worn, her black patent-leather pumps, the white sweater she'd borrowed, and her big straw basket of a purse. But, after frustrating hours under a burning sun, they found nothing they could connect to the murdered woman.

Nor did they discover anything they could link to her killer.

"Let's try upstream," Pete Kuehnel said, and they made their way a quarter of a mile to the Dead Horse Creek Road bridge. Inching along the railing, they found a clump of black hair caught in the wood rail, and they sealed it in a plastic bag.

They were already convinced that the killer had thrown Nancy Winslow into the river from one of the bridges upstream. The hair, however, would prove to be animal hair.

They got a break the next day. A mountain rescue volunteer, Doug Hamilton, who operated a power plant further upriver, called Pete Kuehnel to say that he had found a sweater on the Wells Creek Road that might have some connection to the murder.

"At first, I thought it was a deer hide that some poachers had thrown there," Hamilton said, "but then I got closer and it was a sweater."

He led Kuehnel to where it lay—150 feet from the Mount Baker Highway and 20 feet down a mossy bank. It was the white mohair sweater with orange trim that Nancy Winslow had borrowed the night she vanished.

Optimistic after this find, detectives and Explorer Search

and Rescue Scouts spent the next two days searching the area for more clothing or her purse. They found nothing at all.

Although both the Whatcom County Sheriff's men and the Bellingham police worked on this baffling murder case for months—for *years*—questioning scores of witnesses and a dozen suspects, they never solved it. Nancy Winslow might as well have walked into another dimension when she left the Beaver Tavern at 10:30 on the night of July 26, 1970. But she was gone, lost to her children and her husband. Today she would be 54 years old.

Nancy *had* arranged for a ride home, but the cook, who answered the phone, said that all of the calls coming in for her were from women or girls, and all the calls she made—except for the one to her husband—were to women. The only other way she could have found a ride was with someone who was a customer at the restaurant.

Nancy Winslow was a faithful wife, and while she might laugh and joke with a customer, she would never consider dating another man. The owners of the Beaver Tavern were able to remember most of the customers who had come in on that Sunday afternoon and evening 32 years ago.

One of them was a man who sat in the bar section of the restaurant. "He spent a lot of time teasing Nancy," the owner's wife said. "He kept calling her over to him, and he was kind of hustling her. I think he got to her with his jokes, because he made her nervous enough to confuse her orders."

"What did he look like?" Pete Kuehnel asked.

It was hard for the witness to judge age, but she guessed he was in his thirties, somewhere around six feet. He had dark brown hair, combed over his forehead in waves and then slicked back on the sides. "He had on a dark ski jacket and dark pants."

"Moustache?" Kuehnel asked. "Beard?"

"No, he was clean-shaven."

"When did he come in?"

"About eight or nine. He finished his meal and left about an hour before Nancy finished her shift."

More than three decades have passed since Nancy Winslow drove away with her killer. However, although her murder remains unsolved, there are too many connections to Jack Gasser not to wonder:

- Like Donna Woodcock, Nancy was a 22-year-old waitress.
- She accepted a ride home with a stranger after working a late shift.
- Her killer threw her clothes away after he killed her.
- Her body was left in water.
- She was killed in July.
- She was strangled with an article of her own clothing.
- She was probably beaten in the face and on the head (injured portions of the body decompose first).
- Her purse was never found.
- She was found nude.

Jack Gasser lived in Bellingham, attending college, at the time Nancy Winslow died.

Although another waitress knew Jack Gasser as a regular for breakfast at the Beaver Tavern, she never connected him to Nancy's murder. He lived in a rooming house nearby, and he seemed like a good guy to her. In 1970, she certainly didn't know Jack's background. He was just another young guy going to college. It would be many years before she finally read something in the paper that made her wonder.

At any rate, Jack Gasser was never a suspect in Nancy Winslow's murder. His name never even came up in 1970. He was on active parole and had to report to his parole officer regularly until December 1975. As far as the parole officer could tell, Gasser was making a remarkably successful return to society.

In the fall of 1970, a few months after Nancy Winslow was murdered, Jack Gasser got married. His wife, Trudy*, was divorced and the mother of four children. Jack told her about his past, or at least some of it. "He said that he had killed this girl, but he twisted it around so that it didn't sound so bad," Trudy recalled later.

When he graduated from Western Washington University in 1972, Jack and his new family moved to Olympia, Washington, the state capital. He had a job there as an accountant for the state Department of Ecology. He got a better job with the State of Washington in 1974 as an auditor with the Department of Social and Health Services (DSHS). His work required that he travel around the state frequently.

Jack and Trudy became the parents of two sons in the early years of their marriage. He seemed to be completely rehabilitated, although Trudy worried sometimes. He still had a problem with alcohol. His personality changed radically when he drank. When he was sober, you couldn't ask for a nicer guy. When he was drunk, his wife was afraid of him. She hoped she wasn't being paranoid, but there always seemed to be news of a woman being murdered in the cities where Jack went to go over the books of the different DSHS offices.

On January 31, 1981, Trudy and Jack separated at her instigation. She filed for divorce and asked for a restraining order against him.

On July 4, however, he came to her home, drunk, and attacked her physically. On December 8, Trudy Gasser asked for a second restraining order that would bar Gasser from being "inebriated or consuming alcoholic beverages" in front of her six children.

In her divorce petition, she said that he had piled up $8,000 worth of debt without her knowledge, and that she had reluctantly agreed to refinance their house so they could get $15,000 in cash. It was either that or file for bankruptcy.

Through it all, Gasser kept his job with the State of Washington. He made $1,370 a month, which wasn't a munificent salary, but he had good benefits, and he could do free-lance accounting on the side. Ironically, the State of Washington was now paying him approximately the amount it had cost each year to keep him in the penitentiary.

The Gassers' divorce became final on July 6, 1982. Trudy Gasser was awarded custody of the children, but Jack was given visitation rights.

It had been 34 years, almost to the day, since a young Jack Gasser had killed Donna Woodcock, and 12 years since Nancy Winslow's murder. Gasser scarcely resembled the handsome young man he'd once been. He was almost 54 now, and he carried a lot of weight. His features seemed larger, too; his nose was hawklike, and his brow was deeply furrowed. In repose, his face could look like a study of rage. But Jack had kept his full head of dark hair, and many single, middle-aged women were attracted to him.

He was still a ladies' man, and he continued to drink— more heavily all the time. However, his neighbors in the apartment complex on Martin Way in Olympia found him a great guy, even when he was drinking. There were several single women in nearby apartments. One, a 49-year-old waitress, said, "Every woman up here was treated as a lady by him. He was a gentleman, nice in the halls. Even if he came in drinking, he did not cuss and raise Cain. He was a very quiet man."

Perhaps.

He had been officially single for only eleven days when John Russell Gasser made headlines again. It was July once more, which might have been mere coincidence, or perhaps it was a month that brought Gasser's buried anger to the surface. He was bitter about women, he told friends. His wife had left him, and he couldn't see his children when he wanted to.

At 11:30 on the morning of July 17, 1982, two boys were walking near a ditch on Johnson Point Road about five miles north of Olympia. The Nisqually River empties into the Henderson Inlet there, where Henderson Bay nudges the lowlands off Interstate 5. The boys looked down into the ditch and saw what they first thought was a store mannequin.

But it wasn't. It was the naked body of 49-year-old Gerri Barker. Gerri was a lonely woman, worried about her health, nearing middle age. Someone had thrown her away in this ditch, her battered body mute evidence of a terrible beating.

Geraldine Ann "Gerri" Barker had once been an Air Force wife, and she had lived in many exotic spots around the world, although her life began in Craig, Minnesota, a town so small that it no longer exists. She'd been married and divorced twice, and she'd come to Olympia from Utah 13 years earlier. She had worked in the office of the Parks and Recreation Department for the city of Lacey, a small suburb north of Olympia, but now she lived in a small apartment, subsisting on welfare. She had borne two sons and a daughter, all grown.

Gerri loved to read, and she always had a couple of novels going. She also read everything she could find about foods that were good for health. Sadly, she defeated any beneficial effects of healthy eating by drinking too much alcohol. That hot July of 1982, Gerri was very worried about her health; she had recently had surgery for a growth in her esophagus (the tube leading from the throat to the stomach), and she was very frail. At 49, she sometimes felt that all her good times were behind her.

When Gerri Barker's body was removed from the ditch and taken to the Thurston County Medical Examiner's Office for a postmortem examination, the deputy medical examiners carrying the litter barely felt her weight; she was so thin.

Gerri had been sexually assaulted and strangled. She also had a broken nose, a broken jaw, and a broken rib. She couldn't have put up much of a fight. Rather, it looked as though she had been beaten by someone in a towering rage. The pathologist performing the autopsy estimated that she had been dead for less than 12 hours.

Thurston County Sheriff Dan Montgomery's detectives went to the apartment house where Gerri Barker was said to live. The manager said that she often frequented the bar at the VFW Hall in East Olympia in the late afternoons and evenings. The bartender there nodded when they asked about her.

"She was in yesterday afternoon about 4:30," he said. "We had to cut her off at about 8 P.M. She had had too much to drink."

But Gerri had stayed at the club, nursing a soft drink and visiting with other patrons. Jack Gasser, who was also a member of the VFW club, showed up about 11 P.M. He had stayed for only half an hour, but when he left, he was with Gerri Barker.

"They know each other before?" a detective asked.

"I think so. They're both regulars."

The Thurston County detectives obtained Gasser's driver's license photo and started a check to see if he had any prior record.

Back at Gerri Barker's apartment house, her neighbors recognized the photograph of Jack Gasser. Frank Braun, the manager, told detectives that he had seen him there at least a half dozen times. In early June, he'd seen Gasser knocking loudly on Gerri Barker's apartment door. "I knew she was home," Braun said, "but she didn't come to the door."

They must have cleared up their differences. Gerri had left the VFW Hall with Jack Gasser on the night she was killed, and witnesses said they were getting along fine. She hadn't had a drink for three hours, but she was probably still slightly affected by the drinks she had had earlier.

Detectives found witnesses in Gasser's apartment building, which was only a half mile from the club, who recalled seeing the pair together in the hallway near his apartment the night before. "It was about midnight," one woman said.

When the investigators finally located Jack Gasser on Tuesday, July 20, he wasn't at his apartment in Olympia; he was in Everett, Washington, 90 miles north, doing an audit for the Department of Social and Health Services. Although at first he denied any part in Gerri Barker's murder, he didn't put up a fight when his car was seized with a search warrant. He returned to Olympia the next day and turned himself in to the Olympia Police Department, where he was arrested. He was surprised by that and refused to give any statement. He had long since become con-wise and didn't care for cops.

Search warrants were obtained for his apartment. The detectives found human blood inside the apartment, in the doorway, in the stairwell, and in Gasser's 1978 Mazda. It was not of his blood type, but it did match Gerri Barker's.

On Thursday, July 22, 1982, Jack Gasser faced Thurston County Superior Court Judge Carol Fuller, charged for the second time with first-degree murder. Fuller ordered that he be held without bail.

On December 28, 1982, Jack Gasser was convicted of first-degree murder for the second time. With the sentencing matrix, his first possible parole date was set for June 7, 2012, when he would be 84 years old.

Gasser began his third trip to prison in the penitentiary at Walla Walla, but alcohol and perhaps genetics caught up with him. He was no longer the good-looking young kid; he was an old man in poor health. Whereas he had once been charming, Gasser was surly and full of complaints, more so with every year that passed.

Just before Christmas 1996, Jack Gasser was transferred to the Ahtanum View Assisted Living Facility. Located near Yakima, Washington, it is a kind of nursing home for convicts. He was angry about being there and refused to cooperate with intake workers who tried to fill out their forms and evaluations.

"He is a 71-year-old inmate," his report read in 1999. "With extensive medical problems, given his sentence structure, he will likely not survive until release."

Jack Gasser knew the prison system well, and his subsequent evaluations reflected his discontent at his present quarters. He would have much preferred to be at the new and modern prison facility, Airway Heights Corrections Center, due to open soon, where he felt the accommodations and amenities were more pleasing. Airway Heights also had a section for minimum security prisoners, although even now Gasser was still considered a medium risk.

Doctors suspected he had either had a stroke or was suffering from Parkinson's disease. He said he could not walk with a walker or push himself in his wheelchair. He commandeered other prisoners to help him, insisting that he was unable to care for himself.

Jack Gasser bombarded his corrections counselor with demands. He still wanted a transfer to Airway Heights in April 2000. He claimed he wasn't strong enough to stay at Ahtanum, but the impression he gave was of a manipulator and malingerer.

He still wasn't eligible for the new prison, but he was happier when another prisoner was assigned to serve as his wheelchair pusher and to stand by his side when he used his walker.

The public tends to think of convicts as young, strong, and tough, but those with life sentences grow old in the system. Jack Gasser had never lost his air of barely repressed hostility—even when he needed help getting in and out of bed and went everywhere in a wheelchair.

"He is 74 years old," his last report read. "His percentage to re-offend is 31.1. This is his second time for the same crime . . . He has not done a lot to improve himself. If released, he would still be very dangerous . . ."

Had she lived, Donna Woodcock would be 76 now, but she has been gone for 54 years. When retired King County Assistant Prosecuting Attorney John Vogel heard about the murder of Gerri Barker, he summed up what any number of detectives and grieving relatives thought: "He should have been hanged in 1948."

Retired Homicide Lieutenant Austin Seth, 87, agrees. "No one will ever really know how many women Jack Gasser killed. He spent a lot of time in prison—but he was free and traveling around Washington State for 25 years. I know that I, for one, will never stop wondering what the whole story is."

The Killer Who Begged to Die

Like Jack Gasser, there was another man who served his time in prison in the Northwest and who was paroled when he should have stayed locked up. He himself knew he shouldn't be walking free. In the end, he felt he should not be allowed to live. And yet, he had to fight his way through crowds of people who wanted to save him. His is a backward or "inside-out" kind of story. When I wrote about him the first time, I never expected to write about him again.

But I did.

The only thing at all flamboyant about the neat little motel on Seattle's Aurora Avenue North was its name: the Eldorado. When Bertha Maude Lush bought it, it had seen better days. That was why she could afford it. She cleaned it up and kept it spotless, and she made sure that it was always freshly painted.

Before Interstate 5 was built, Aurora Avenue was the main route from Seattle to Canada and points north. Back in the thirties and forties, the Eldorado was considered modern. Now it catered to those who couldn't—or wouldn't—pay the asking price for a night in one of the huge glass-and-stone motels that had sprouted along the new freeway.

Many of Bertha's guests were return customers, visitors from Vancouver, British Columbia, who made it a habit to stop there on trips to shop in Seattle.

Ironically, it was the reasonable cost of a room at the Eldorado that drew a killer there.

Bertha Maude Lush, sole owner and proprietor of the Eldorado since her partner's death 18 years earlier, had worked all her life to gain a modicum of security. Originally hired to take a man's job during World War II, Bertha was in the wave of women personified as "Rosie the Riveter." She rode the bus to work at the Boeing Airplane Company every day until she'd put in enough years as a mechanic to retire.

In May 1974, Bertha was in her 60s, and she had never married. She was a loner, devoting all her energies to keeping her motel going; the travelers she dealt with were enough company for her. She had a car, an old white Studebaker, but she never drove it any more. She even banked by mail. Maybe it was because she had begun to be afraid—although she hated to admit it.

But she was a woman alone, dealing with strangers every day of her life, in an era when the small-business person had abundant reason to be afraid. Mom-and-pop grocery stores and small motels were robbed frequently.

Bertha Lush's neighbors kept an eye on her, noticing when the "No Vacancy" went on at night and the office lights dimmed, but they tried not to let her know that they were watching over her. She was fiercely independent, and she wouldn't have liked it.

Only Bertha's closest relative knew that she kept a gun hidden in a clothes hamper behind the office. She had never had to use it. When the time came that she needed it, she didn't even get the chance to reach for the gun.

The weekend of May 18–19 was a national holiday in Canada, and Bertha Lush had welcomed many familiar guests on Saturday. These preferred customers, along with some new clients, filled all the units by 3 P.M. and allowed Bertha to turn the "No Vacancy" sign on early.

It was much later—a quarter after ten that night— when one of the guests pounded on the door of the manager's office. He had returned to the motel to find his unit double-locked, and he needed Bertha's master key to get in. But no one responded to his knock. Exasperated, he peered through the glass. He didn't see Bertha, but the lights were on, and his eyes were drawn to a scarlet smear along the pale aqua wall inside.

It was such a large stain that he ran to a nearby pay phone and called the police.

Patrol officers responding to the motel found the door to the office firmly locked, but they could see evidence of a violent struggle inside. They asked the police radio dispatcher to call the motel's phone. They could hear it ringing, but no one answered. The officers broke out a pane of glass in the door to gain entry.

There was no one in the office, no one behind the counter. The officers opened a door leading to the rear area and stopped. They could see now why the phone had rung unanswered. A woman lay motionless just inside the door, the back of her head virtually destroyed. The three patrolmen shut the door and put in a call to homicide detectives.

Detective Sergeant Ward Dutcher and Detectives P. R. Forsell, George Cuthill, and Jess Cook responded. They worked their way into the crime scene gradually, careful to stick to a narrow path so they wouldn't contaminate any evidence that might be there. First, they looked at the outer office. Ironically, a cross hung on one wall bearing the inscription "Peace to All Who Enter Here."

Next to it hung a scroll with a prayer often known as the Serenity Prayer, used by Alcoholics Anonymous, but also cherished by many people seeking tranquility:

God Grant Us the Serenity
to accept the things we cannot change,
Courage
to change the things we can,
and the
Wisdom
to know the difference

Both sentiments were now spattered and streaked with what must surely be blood. If the woman who lay face-down in the living quarters was Bertha Lush, she would never again be able to change anything. When the guest who had called police described the motel owner-manager, there was no doubt that the dead woman inside *was* Bertha Lush; she still wore the green house dress, blue sweater, and white shoes she had worn when the man checked in. The witness said Bertha had given him his change from her black leather wallet, which had quite a bit of money in it at that time.

The black wallet now lay beside the dead woman, and it was empty. The motive for her murder was obvious. So was the weapon: a blood-encrusted ball peen hammer rested against the victim's right leg.

This was going to be one of those investigations rife with clues, but the detectives didn't know at the outset how very little those clues would help. It might have been better that they had no expectations—because it wasn't going to be easy.

The detective crew at the scene was soon joined by Homicide Detective Lieutenant Pat Murphy and George Ishii, director of the Western Washington Crime Lab, with his assistant, Bob Sullivan. Ishii pointed out that the attack had begun behind the counter in the outer office. There were marks on the plywood walls where the hammer had glanced off, and a formidable amount of blood had gushed from the victim's head wounds and stained the floor and walls there.

The killer had then dragged the woman into the living quarters in the rear so that she could not be seen through the glass in the office door.

Bertha Lush's living quarters were filled with the accumulation of many years of living: papers, family portraits, letters, books, and other memorabilia, and none of them had been ransacked. Her killer, it seemed, wanted only cash. He had probably been in a hurry and had been too apprehensive to search for money Bertha might have hidden in her apartment.

Bertha Lush had been very cautious. Every door in both the office and living quarters had three separate locks—the usual doorknob lock and two deadbolt locks. The outer door of the office could be locked by merely pulling it shut from the outside, and it looked as though that was what her killer had done as he left, probably hoping to delay discovery of her body.

And he *had* left in a rush. There was a suitcase in the office, possibly left there by the killer in his flight. It contained clothing that would fit an average-size male, from five feet eight to ten inches, 150 to 160 pounds. There were also some men's toilet items and a tooled leather belt made in New Mexico among the effects.

But there was always the chance that the suitcase had been left there by someone else—someone who had nothing to do with the murder and might even come forward later.

King County Medical Examiner Dr. Donald Reay arrived at the scene at 1:30 A.M. and made a preliminary examination of the body. He estimated that death had occurred some two to four hours earlier, although he leaned toward the earlier figure. There was no rigor mortis as yet, and the body was still warm to the touch. Lividity had begun on the front of the body, as was to be expected because the victim had lain on her stomach. The dark purple striations of livor mortis always appear in the lowermost parts of the body, as the heart no longer circulates the blood.

Bertha Lush had suffered many, many bludgeon blows to the skull and had almost certainly sustained fatal brain injuries. There did not appear to be any evidence of sexual assault; her pantyhose were still in place, and although her clothing was in disarray, that had probably occurred while she was dragged from the office into the back room.

The body was removed shortly after 1:30 on Sunday morning, and Detectives Cook and Cuthill secured the crime scene at 3 A.M., leaving a patrol officer stationed outside the motel office to guard it until detectives returned to view it in daylight. Homicide detectives, accompanied by criminalist Ishii and departmental illustrator Ben Smith, were back early in the morning. The entire office and the victim's apartment were dusted for latent prints.

It looked as though the killer had washed up in Bertha Lush's bathroom, and Ishii removed a water sample from the P-trap beneath; with any luck there might be enough blood suspended there to isolate its type.

There were also red smudges on a fresh roll of toilet paper in the bathroom. It was a long shot, but there could be a usable print that would emerge after Ninhydrin processing, a technique that can lift prints from paper decades after they are left there.

A paper sack near the suitcase in the office seemed to be empty—and it was, except for a sales slip. The slip was from a hardware item sold at Ernst's Hardware, a well-known Seattle chain store. The item was a ball peen hammer. The death weapon was so new that it still bore a price tag. This sales slip matched that price tag. And the sale had taken place on May 18. How cruel, cold-blooded, and premeditated a killer would have to be to deliberately purchase a hammer with which to bludgeon an old woman! Had the killer already met Bertha Lush, or was the hammer a weapon he carried in case he needed it?

Detective Benny DePalmo, working the Sunday shift in the Homicide Unit back at the office, read a teletype out of Salem, Oregon. It was an all-points bulletin on a convict named Carl Cletus Bowles, who had escaped from a conjugal visit to a local motel. The woman he'd gone to spend four hours with had been introduced to prison officials as his fiancée; in actuality, she proved to be his niece. Authorities believed that Bowles, who had killed a cop, might head for the Canadian border and slip across into British Columbia.

The Eldorado Motel was right along such a route. Bowles was known as a vicious "over-killer," and the person who had slain Bertha Lush had struck her approximately 28 times in the head with a hammer.

DePalmo and Detective Ted Fonis called prison officials in Salem and asked for any information and mug shots available on Bowles and his niece. They learned that the couple had escaped through a rear door of the Motel 6 in Salem while a guard waited in front. The niece's car was a white Thunderbird.

It looked good for a while, especially when a patrolman in Seattle's north end precinct reported that he'd followed a suspicious-looking couple in a 1962 white T-bird on the fatal Saturday.

But a lot of suspects looked good. Detective DePalmo, along with Ted Fonis and Detective Wayne Dorman—the partners who would be assigned the follow-up work on the case—would have to sift through any number of suspects before they found their killer.

Another patrolman reported that he'd shaken down and F.I.R'd (Field Investigation Reported) a white male, 32, outside the motel on the night before the murder. The man had given his name as Albert Selleck* and he said he was staying in Unit 2. He explained that he'd had a fight with his wife and moved out of their house in the north end of Seattle. The man had been highly nervous and had driven away in his clunker of a car when the officer turned away for a moment.

But the cop got the license number. He ran it through auto records in Olympia, and it came back listed to Albert Selleck. At least, he hadn't lied about his name. Maybe he hadn't lied about anything.

After several tries, the detectives found Selleck at his north Seattle address. He had left the motel even though he still had another day paid for. He said he'd made up with his wife, and he had a solid alibi for May 18. Sheepishly, he admitted he'd panicked when the officer stopped him. He felt stupid for driving away.

Other guests at the motel told detectives that they had come home to find their units double-locked on Saturday afternoon. Bertha told them she'd had trouble with a man who hadn't paid his bill, and she'd locked the units to be sure he couldn't sneak back in if he'd had a key copy made. To the best of the witnesses' recollection, she hadn't mentioned his name or anything else about him.

The mystery man couldn't have been Albert Selleck; his rent was paid well in advance. And reports on sightings of Carl Bowles placed him 300 miles south of Seattle, near Eugene, Oregon.

Detectives Fonis and DePalmo began a search for the store that had sold the death hammer, carrying a picture of the hammer to show the employees in the many outlets of Ernst Hardware stores. The sales slip showed the hammer cost $3.46. The purchaser had given the clerk a five-dollar bill and a penny and received $1.55 in change. Beyond that was the notation "256 18, May, 74."

The manager of the Ernst store in the Northgate area explained that 256 was not the number of the store selling the hammer, but rather the number of the sale in a particular store on May 18. It would be more difficult to find the store where the hammer had been purchased, but he said he would try.

Unfortunately, many of the motel guests had checked out and gone on their way before the body discovery. The investigators sent letters to everyone listed on the log for May 17–18, asking that the recipients call the Seattle Homicide Unit collect. Within a day all of them had responded, but none of them had any new information to offer.

Sergeant Ivan Beeson, Fonis, and DePalmo returned once again to the Eldorado, where they carried out a very thorough search. They found a black purse in a closet in Bertha Lush's apartment. It was empty except for her birth certificate, which showed she'd been born in Harlan County, Nebraska, on September 7, 1909, and two sets of keys for her Studebaker, parked out in back. They searched the car but found nothing connected to the murder.

A nearby business owner walked over to tell them that he and Bertha were friends, and that he'd tried to watch out for her. "She hasn't driven that car for a long time," he said.

"I noticed two guys outside her place Saturday night," he said. "They were jittery-acting."

"What did they look like?" Benny DePalmo asked.

"I'd say they were both in their 50s—and one was short and the other one was really tall."

Two more suspects in an already crowded investigation.

As the news of Bertha Lush's murder flooded the media, the detectives began to get phone calls from other people who knew Bertha. One reported that he knew her well from her days at Boeing and that he'd often ridden the bus with her.

"I visited with Bertha on Saturday, the 18th, from 1 P.M. until 3:30. I went over to her place to buy a tool that I needed at work. Bertha had one she didn't need anymore," he said. "Well, the funny thing is—she showed me this blue-green suitcase and a shaving kit or something. She said she was holding them for some guy who couldn't pay rent. She said she was kind of afraid of him. Some girl had dropped him off at her place to stay, and then he couldn't pay her. She said he tried to borrow money from friends but he couldn't get any."

So Bertha *had* been afraid on the afternoon before she died, and specifically fearful of the man who owned the blue suitcase. Unfortunately, she hadn't mentioned the name to her friend, or anything else that might help to identify the stranger.

Bertha's sister in Denver called to say that she'd talked with her between 9:00 and 9:30 (Seattle time) on Saturday night and that they'd had a perfectly ordinary conversation. "Bertha didn't say a thing about being scared."

They were shaving minutes off the vital time period. Bertha Lush was alive at 9:30 and dead at 10:15, yet no one had heard a scream or the sounds of a struggle.

When they'd opened the suitcase, they knew they were looking for an "invisible man" who was medium-sized and who wore Brut men's cologne. He'd fled without the possessions in his suitcase. He hadn't had enough money, apparently, to pay the seven dollars to rent a room at the Eldorado—but he'd had five dollars to buy a hammer.

Wayne Dorman and Denny DePalmo began a frustrating canvass of Ernst Hardware stores, looking for someone who could recall selling a 42-ounce Stanley brand ball peen hammer on the afternoon of May 18. The sales tally didn't match the Northgate store, but it did seem close to the number of sales made at the 6th and Pike store in downtown Seattle. Made at Register #1, it was the 256th of 277 sales that day.

Since the store closed at 6:30 P.M., store officials estimated that the hammer had been purchased at about 4:00 in the afternoon.

Dorman and DePalmo interviewed the clerk at Register #1, but they were disappointed again to find that she had no recollection of selling the hammer. Nor did any other Ernst clerks. It was only one sale among 277. Evidently the killer-to-be had looked and acted average enough to maintain a low profile.

Criminalists reported that they had been unable to lift any legible prints from the hammer. Nor had they found usable prints on the toilet paper roll. "What if you cut through the roll to the cardboard in the center?" Benny DePalmo asked Criminalist Ann Beaman. "Could the killer have grasped the roll with his fingers inside the core and left a print there?"

After Beaman made the cut, they found that he had done just that. One perfect print surfaced with the Ninhydrin process. It was the first break in an ultimately frustrating case. But this investigation occurred years before the computerized AFIS (Automated Fingerprint Analysis System) technique was established. The print would do them no good unless there was a suspect print to compare with it. The FBI kept single prints only for the ten most wanted fugitives in America.

Although Bertha Lush had lived a moderate life, neither smoking nor drinking, obeying the law and minding her own business, some of her male relatives had had runins with the police. Now the Seattle detectives attempted to locate those men. The family knew that Bertha was financially secure and that she always had cash in the motel office to make change. That might have been tempting to a few of them who always seemed to need money.

An active warrant was out for Bertha's grand-nephew on assault charges. The detectives soon found out where he was. They left their cards, and he walked into the Homicide Unit voluntarily to talk to them. He said he hadn't seen his great-aunt in seven months. He'd been in Everett—26 miles north of Seattle—with his sister on the evening of May 18. He produced a bus ticket that showed he'd left Everett for Idaho at 10:30 on May 19. Witnesses verified his story, and he passed a polygraph test cleanly.

Another nephew was located in Payette, Idaho. He said he hadn't been in the State of Washington for months; in fact, he couldn't travel because he was recovering from a back injury.

Bertha Lush had saved *everything,* and the detectives sorted through piles and piles of papers, receipts, and other records in the motel office. They found a receipt from a drug-abuse center in the north end of Seattle, which showed that Bertha had made a donation of some chairs for a garage sale. Was it possible that the men who picked up the donated items had thought Bertha would make an easy target for robbery?

It was possible, but it hadn't happened. The men who'd come for the items were the responsible directors of the center. They remembered going to the motel on May 15. Bertha Lush had given them bottles, vases, and chairs.

"She was a real nice lady—a little eccentric, maybe—but really nice," one man commented.

By the end of June, Detectives Fonis, Dorman, and DePalmo had come to a dead end on a case where so many promising leads fizzled out. They had a suitcase, a shaving kit, the print from the toilet paper core—and that was about it. Half a dozen suspects had had their prints compared with the killer's. None of them had matched. The mysterious woman who had dropped off the man Bertha was afraid of had never surfaced. Maybe she hadn't seen all the TV coverage on the case, or maybe she was part of the crime. It was possible that she was simply someone who had given a stranger a ride.

On July 17, Detective Sergeant Jim Lehner of the Albuquerque, New Mexico, Police Department called the Seattle Police's Homicide Unit. He inquired if Seattle had an open case involving the murder of a woman in a motel.

It was the kind of break that detectives dream about and devoutly hope for—but that happens infrequently. Benny DePalmo called Lehner back the minute he arrived for the early morning shift. Lehner said that two detectives from his department had staked out a downtown corner after they got a tip that a man wanted for murder in Seattle would be there soon.

"Our informant tipped us to this guy," Lehner said. *"Your* guy's name is James Homer Elledge. He had a lot to tell us. I'll fill you in—and I'll send you his mug shots and fingerprints."

Lehner said that he'd gone through Elledge's wallet and found the name and phone number of a Seattle woman. "Her name's Kim Lane*."

After two months of dead ends, the solution to Bertha Lush's death seemed close. DePalmo called Kim Lane and talked to a very startled young woman. She said she was unaware of the murder because she never followed crime news.

"But I know Jim Elledge," Kim said. "I met him on a bus from Texas to Seattle on May 10. He seemed like a good guy. We had coffee together at all the rest stops along the way. He told me that he was regional manager for a big restaurant chain. He said he'd worked so much overtime for so long that he just made up his mind to take a leave of absence. He was traveling around the country to see old friends.

"He got off the bus in Wichita Falls, Texas—"

DePalmo's heart sank. If Elledge had gotten off the

bus in Texas and he was in New Mexico now, how could he be Bertha Lush's killer?

"He asked for my phone number," Kim continued. "He said he was planning to come to the Northwest soon. I really never expected to see him again."

"*Did* you see him again?" DePalmo asked.

"Yes. I got home to Seattle on May 12, and I got a phone call two days later about 7:30 in the evening. It was Jim. He told me he was in Portland, Oregon, and was just about to get on a plane for Seattle. He asked if I could pick him up at the airport."

A plane ride from Portland only took half an hour or forty-five minutes, and Kim met Jim Elledge at the Seattle-Tacoma Airport a little over an hour later. "We had a drink in the airport lounge—and then Jim said he had to make some phone calls to a friend in Phoenix. He said his friend would wire him some money."

But Elledge had returned to their table looking grim. "He said his friend wouldn't be able to wire the money until the next day—this was on a Sunday."

Kim admitted to DePalmo that she was beginning to wonder if Jim's story about his high-paying job as an executive in the restaurant business was true. He didn't seem to have any money at all. She ended up paying for their drinks.

"I offered to loan him $20," she said, "and I said I could take him to a motel. I wasn't about to take him home with me."

Elledge had accepted the offer, and Kim headed for the I-5 freeway. She exited at the first off-ramp, and he went into a newer motel there. "He came back out, and he looked pretty disturbed because they wanted $20 a night. He said he wouldn't pay that much, so I headed for "Old 99" and Aurora Avenue. I took him to an older motel there. Well, *that* was too expensive for his taste, too. Finally, I drove him to the Eldorado."

Kim Lane said she'd begun to be really nervous about Elledge. She just wanted to be rid of him and get home. "But I waited. I saw him talking to an older woman in the motel office, and then they walked out and went to the first room at the end of the driveway. Jim came out to my car and asked me to come in and see his room. I only went as far as the open door and peeked in.

"Then the woman—the manager, I guess—came in with a coffee pot and coffee for him, and I just made my excuses and left."

"Did you see him again?" DePalmo asked.

"He called me the next day and asked me to go to dinner with him at the Space Needle. I said 'No,' and I don't know why—just *something*. I never saw him again."

Kim Lane said that Elledge was about 30 and good-looking and wore his blond hair in a crew cut.

"How tall is he?" DePalmo asked.

"Maybe five nine or ten—and he was average weight."

They probably knew now who the man was who matched the suitcase left in Bertha Lush's office. Jim Elledge had checked into the Eldorado on Tuesday, May 14. He'd had $20 then—just about enough for three nights at the Eldorado prices.

Bertha had talked about a man who couldn't pay his rent. Maybe Elledge hadn't paid for three nights; maybe he'd held out five dollars to buy a hammer. At any rate, by Saturday night, May 18, he would have been at least three days behind. Bertha was kind, but she wasn't a pushover; she would have asked him to leave.

Sergeant Jim Lehner in Albuquerque filled in more chinks in the case's structure. Lehner said he had been tipped to Elledge's alleged crime by one of the suspect's own friends. Elledge had never been a restaurant executive, but he'd been a cook.

The man who called Lehner was an air traffic controller. He said that he'd had a phone call from Elledge around the middle of May. He'd been calling from a motel in Seattle and asked that the informant wire him some money.

"The woman who owned the motel came on the line," Lehner said, "but our guy here said he didn't promise to send Elledge money. Instead, he told her that if Jim didn't pay her, she could bill him and he'd send it to her. He wasn't about to wire money to Jim."

Calls kept coming into Elledge's friend for the next two months, and Jim was always in a different spot on the map.

"Elledge got back to Albuquerque on July 16," Lehner said. "He told his friend here that he'd been so desperate that he started to rob the woman in the motel in Seattle. When she fought him, he said he had to hit her with a hammer. And he claims that he killed her. I guess he blamed himself for panicking. He said, 'It was stupid—because I left the hammer there.' "

"Yeah, he sure did," DePalmo said. "We found it."

Elledge's claim to be a murderer had been too much for the air traffic controller, and he called the police.

"I told him I'd meet him on a certain corner of First Street," the informant said. "He thinks I'm bringing him money. He says he's driving a Buick with Louisiana plates."

Lehner and his crew had been on the prearranged corner on the evening of July 16. They spotted a 1967 Buick with Louisiana plates and asked Radio to run the plates through the National Crime Information Center (NCIC) computers. It came back as stolen from West Monroe, Louisiana, six days earlier.

As they watched, the suspect left the car and walked south on First. He leaned against a light pole, his eyes searching the street for someone. The Albuquerque detectives moved in and arrested him on suspicion of auto theft. Elledge had a loaded .38 Smith and Wesson snub-nosed revolver tucked into the waistband of his pants. The cylinder had two spent, and three live rounds.

"When we inventoried his car later," Lehner said, "we found a bowie knife under the driver's seat.

Something lay heavily on Jim Elledge's conscience. The Seattle detectives hadn't even packed their bags to go to Albuquerque when Jim Elledge felt the need to unburden himself again. He talked to Sergeant Jim Lehner.

Lehner called DePalmo to relate his confession. Elledge had confirmed that he'd stayed at the Eldorado, and that he'd run out of money after three days. He hadn't been able to get money from his friend in New Mexico, so Bertha Lush had taken the phone and received a promise that she would get her money if she billed the friend.

"But that wasn't good enough for her," Lehner said. "She told Elledge he had to leave. He spent a couple of nights sleeping in a field across the street from the motel. Is there a field there?"

"Yeah," DePalmo said. "There is."

"So he goes back on Saturday and offers to do some chores to pay for a room, but she said no. Then he told her he had jewelry and personal items worth $200 and she could hold them if she'd give him a night or two in the motel. But she didn't want him there."

Lehner read from the confession Jim Elledge had signed:

". . . She got angry and called me a bum and an 'S.O.B.' I think I was leaning on the counter and she was coming at me. I don't remember who grabbed who first. I remember having the hammer in my hand. She grabbed my wrist, and I remember hitting her in the face with the blunt side of the hammer.

"We struggled, and I came to standing over her. I had blood all over my hands, face, and white shirt. I got a pink shirt out of the suitcase and washed at the basin. I do remember that I was scared as hell. After I washed my hands, I remember grabbing money from the office—$80 or $85— took a taxi to the airport, and took a plane to Portland."

In a fictional mystery, a confession would be enough. But in reality, direct physical evidence is better. The best evidence of all is a fingerprint in blood. The Seattle detectives had that. When Jim Elledge's fingerprints arrived from New Mexico, Criminalist Jean Battista was able to match his left middle finger to the bloody print inside the toilet paper roll and his left thumbprint to a partial latent print left on the Brut spray bottle.

Elledge was turned over to the New Mexico Parole Board for a hearing in Santa Fe. He still had ten years hanging over him for an earlier sentence for assault and robbery. He hadn't proved to be the ideal candidate for parole.

Detectives DePalmo and John Boren flew to New Mexico to bring Elledge back to Seattle to face charges of first-degree murder. Jim Elledge said he was afraid to fly, and under New Mexico law he had the right to refuse to fly, so DePalmo and Boren had to take the tediously long train trip with their prisoner handcuffed to them. Once arraigned in Seattle, he was held without bail.

James Elledge went on trial in Judge Horton Smith's courtroom in March 1975. His defense was "diminished responsibility" because of his long history of alcoholism.

The jurors didn't believe it, particularly when they heard how he had bought the hammer hours before Bertha Lush was killed. They returned with a verdict of premeditated first-degree murder with the use of a deadly weapon.

Under existing Washington statute, Elledge's earliest release would be in 13 years, four months *plus* a mandatory five years for the deadly weapon. This was to run consecutively to the 10-year New Mexico sentence. The jurors who convicted Jim Elledge believed that he would not be released until he was almost 60.

For Elledge, prison was safer than being on the outside. He rapidly became institutionalized. He admitted that he "didn't feel comfortable at all" outside prison, and almost all of his crimes had been exacerbated by imbibing alcohol. In prison, he had limits, and he knew he would have a bed and three meals a day.

Although it didn't excuse his crimes, anyone who knew James Elledge's background might understand that—as well as wonder that he survived to grow up. He had begun life in a rural area in Louisiana, living in grinding poverty.

Elledge was one of six children in a family that could barely afford to raise one child. He was closer to a sister than he was to his parents, who had no time for him. But she died when he was 6. In his family, the answer to despair was alcohol. "I started so durned young in drinking," he once said. "Hell, I'm talking about a little kid—7, 8 years old. I think that's what destroyed me."

Elledge's father was committed to a mental institution when Jim was 10, and a few months later Jim was arrested for breaking and entering. His long rap sheet began.

After his father went insane, his mother began to drink, too. She couldn't cope with supporting five children emotionally or financially.

Jim's father died when he was 13, and two of his half-siblings committed suicide, allegedly because they were grief-stricken over the loss of their father. His mother would always blame Jim's trouble with the law on the loss of his father.

Jim went to reform school in his early teens. He was badly burned while working in the kitchen there, and spent months in the hospital. Even so, he preferred reform school to his home. He once asked his parole officer to put him back in prison because he was literally "starving" at home. He was told that they couldn't do that; his sentence was up.

He left home when he was 15, seeking some life that might be better than what he had known. He was 21 when he was arrested for his first serious crime: he kidnapped a Western Union Clerk during an armed robbery in New Mexico in 1964.

In 1966, while Elledge was serving time for that robbery, he managed to slither through an air vent and escape from the New Mexico Penitentiary. Recaptured, he made yet another attempt at freedom: He jumped from a second-story window at the city jail, but he was free for only 11 hours.

His records showed that he had tested as "very intelligent," but psychological tests indicated that he suffered from antisocial personality disorder, meaning, essentially, that he had no conscience.

When Kim Lane met Jim Elledge on the bus, she saw a rather attractive man—a man who told lies with a great deal of conviction. But she sensed the danger there.

Jim wasn't a complete sociopath. He was a survivor, but he seemed to have episodes of feeling empathy for others. Had his childhood not been so cruel, he might have grown up to be an entirely different man.

Three years after he went to the Washington State Penitentiary, he tipped prison officials to an escape plot planned by several high-profile offenders. They were well on their way to tunneling out of the prison.

"Snitches" don't last long in prison, and his life was threatened.

He was moved to a prison in Atlanta for protection. Ten years later, during the Cuban prison riots in the Georgia prison, he risked his life again—this time to save a prison guard. The Cubans were about to take a prison lieutenant hostage and gain control of his ring of security keys—keys that would open a series of doors that led to the outside. Jim barred a door between the rioters and the guard and said he "would fight for as long as he could hold out."

He earned his GED high school equivalency diploma in prison, and he went to classes in anger management and support groups for substance abusers. His sentence was reduced from premeditated first-degree murder to second-degree murder.

Still, every time Jim was paroled, he managed to do something that violated the trust placed in him, usually after he had been drinking. He was released on parole after 14 years, but in 1989 he got drunk and tried to rob a tavern in Louisiana. And back he went to prison. It may well have been that he actually craved the security of being inside, away from the world. He never seemed upset about going back.

On one occasion when he broke the rules of his parole, a corrections officer wrote in 1990: "No use. Might as well go get him and attempt to save another life."

Jim was now back in Washington State. "It is obvious that Mr. Elledge cannot adjust to life outside of prison," a community corrections supervisor wrote in 1994, warning a parole review board. "Be extremely careful in deciding if you ever want to let him out of prison. I believe he is at *high risk* to kill again." The supervisor said he had little hope for Jim Elledge's "redemption."

But Jim was placed in a work-release program that

year, the first step in allowing him to go entirely free. He soon got drunk and walked away from work-release. He went back to prison.

Elledge became a Christian in prison after a delegate from the Free Methodist Church came into the penitentiary to minister to him. And he was finally paroled from the Monroe Reformatory in 1995. He moved to Tacoma, Washington.

Jim Elledge was no longer the muscular tanned man with the crew cut who had murdered Bertha Lush. He had aged in double-time while he was locked up. He was thin and balding, and his short gray beard and moustache and horn-rimmed glasses made him resemble an Amish elder more than an ex-con.

He looked harmless. But *he* knew there was another side to him, a violent side that he had to struggle to control. Rage often bloomed in him.

Duane Grooters, who had come into the Monroe Reformatory to share the Bible with him, believed that Jim could learn to be good. The Free Methodist Church had a portion of their belief system that said they must help prisoners, using compassion, to seek the right path. "Jim seemed like someone who really had a desire to change. He had a desire to get out and do something and help others and make it on his own."

Although the Lynnwood Lighthouse Free Methodist Church that had helped him while he was in prison was fifty miles north of his apartment in Tacoma, Jim took a bus to attend services there. He eventually moved to Lynnwood after one of the church members, Bill Hubbard, who was a local city councilman, said he could sleep on his couch.

"Jim was like a cheerleader to me," the good Samaritan said. "He greeted me with coffee after late nights at work or council meetings. This guy would cook and clean. He was a real trouper."

Jim walked three miles to the red brick church for Bible study, and never missed Sunday service. The Lighthouse Free Methodist Church hired him as a janitor. He was popular with the members, a very friendly and likable man. Many knew he had been in prison; fewer knew what his crimes had been.

Jim found a girlfriend who loved him and agreed to marry him. She described herself as "slow," but Jim made her feel smart and beautiful. He and his fiancée, Ann, were married in late 1997. He started a little side janitorial business. He seemed to have made it through, despite the warnings of corrections and parole officers.

Sometimes he drove by the cemetery where his 1974 victim was buried. "Bertha," he recalled. "Bertha Maude. Every time I'd drive by the graveyard out there where's she's buried at—well . . . I just felt so damn guilty."

Jim Elledge might as well have had "love" and "hate" tattooed on either hand; the compassionate, helpful side of him did exist, but so did the vengeful, angry part of him. He harbored intense hatred for a woman named Eloise Fitzner, who was 47 and single. She lived in the Sherwood Springs Apartments in Lynnwood in a unit upstairs from the apartment Jim shared with Bill Hubbard, his benefactor. Jim got to know her there in the midnineties. But it wasn't Eloise he was attracted to—it was her friend, Rita Bentson*, 39, who fascinated him.

"He loved her," Lynnwood Detective Mike McBride said later. "He had the hots for her. It was not a mutual feeling at all."

Rita, fifteen years younger than Jim Elledge, wasn't the least bit attracted to him. Besides that, he was newly married to Ann; he was practically on his honeymoon.

Eloise just didn't like him. That was unusual because Eloise Fitzner liked almost everyone. Eloise was an attractive woman who wore her dark blond hair in bangs. Her photographs usually showed her smiling, even though she had suffered for years with fibromyalgia that left her with severe muscle pain much of the time.

"Eloise was always on the side of the lost and the wayward, always pulling for the underdog," her brother, Mike Helland, commented. "She often bonded with people who needed help."

Nothing had worked out in Eloise's life, but she still had an optimistic attitude. Born in Spokane into a happy family, she had gone to secretarial school and worked in Hawaii, Houston, and New Orleans. Neither of her two marriages succeeded, and one was marred by domestic violence. Frightened by her husband's threats and stalking, she moved far away to escape him. Eventually, she came back to Washington State.

Eloise Fitzner was dedicated to God, Bible study, and her church—which was a different church than the Free Methodist church, where Jim worked. She was a compulsive rescuer of animals and people who needed her, even though her chronic disease often confined her to bed.

Maybe Eloise didn't like Jim Elledge because she was sensitized to men who could be cruel to women. Perhaps she had encounters with him that frightened her. At any rate, she warned both Rita Bentson and Jim's wife, Ann, to put him out of their lives. Without thinking of the consequences, Eloise had written letters to Ann, trying to get her to think twice about marrying Jim, warning her about "that horrible man." She continued to warn Ann even after she and Jim were wed.

Ann didn't listen. From the time she met him where he

worked as a part-time janitor at a Boeing assembly plant, she had liked Jim, and she didn't believe Eloise Fitzner was right. She thought Eloise was lying when she said Jim was cheating on her—or trying to cheat on her with Rita.

But Ann told Jim that Eloise was badmouthing him, and he was furious. "There's something wrong with my nature," he explained later. "I had been able to control a lot of it by the power of prayer [but] the hate and the anger that was inside me just came up, and I made up my mind that I was going to get my evens with this woman."

It was April 18, 1998. It was spring again in the Northwest, almost exactly 24 years from the time that Bertha Maude Lush had died violently a few miles south of Lynnwood, Washington.

Jim Elledge had decided to kill Eloise Fitzner.

She was a naive, gullible woman who didn't realize the demons she had unleashed in Elledge with her constant meddling. Her friend Rita recalled that Eloise was actually excited when he knocked on her apartment door that Saturday in April. She was willing to forgive him. Jim had on pressed black slacks and his good shoes. He explained that his wife, Ann, was away at a church retreat.

"He told us he had presents for us at his church," Rita said. "He said, 'I have a lot of nice gifts for you girls, and you're really going to like these gifts.' He told Eloise that she should bring her car because we'd need it to get all our gifts home. He even said he would treat us to dinner out afterward."

Eloise had asked, "Oh! Can we go to the Olive Garden?"

"Sure," Jim said easily, "I'll take you to the Olive Garden."

Neither woman got many chances to go out to dinner in a restaurant, and they couldn't afford to go themselves. Now, they suddenly had plans for a Saturday night out. They got dressed up. Eloise put on a red linen skirt and a pale blue satin blouse. The two women even took photographs of each other so they could remember how good they looked all dressed up.

They left Eloise's apartment in her light blue 14-year-old Buick Skylark. They were going to meet Jim at his church. What could be safer than meeting a man they thought they knew at a church?

Neither Eloise nor Rita knew that Jim Elledge had once murdered a woman, or even that he had spent almost 20 years in prison.

It was nearly 8:30 in the evening when Jim Elledge, Eloise Fitzner, and Rita Bentson walked into the church. Jim seemed surprised to see that one of the assistant pastors was there, writing his sermon for the next morning. The pastor was a little surprised, too. He smelled the women's perfume before he saw them, and he noticed that Jim hadn't turned on the foyer lights as he'd led the women inside.

Jim introduced his friends to the pastor and said he was going to give them a tour of the church. The minister nodded and went back to his sermon. When he was finished, he left the church, aware, but unconcerned, that Jim and his friends were probably still inside.

Sometime on Sunday, Lynnwood police got an almost hysterical call from Rita Bentson. She had a terrible story to tell them.

Rita told detectives about Jim Elledge's invitation the night before. But there had been no gifts and no dinner out. Instead, she said he had taken them to an inner room of the empty church and barricaded the door.

Suddenly, he'd had a knife in his hand and some lengths of rope that he must have already cut to the size he wanted. Rita said Jim had tied them up, binding them at their wrists and ankles with the rope.

"Then he covered my eyes with a sweatshirt," she sobbed, "so I couldn't see what he was doing."

But she could hear. She knew that he was strangling Eloise, and it sounded as if he was stabbing her, too. She heard Eloise beg, "No! Stop . . . I can't breathe!" After that, there was only silence.

Rita waited, still helpless in her bonds, while Elledge went someplace with Eloise. And then, she said, Jim had taken her to the mobile home in Everett where he lived with Ann. But Ann wasn't there, and Jim had sexually assaulted Rita several times before he finally released her.

Rita didn't have any idea where he was at the moment, but she was afraid he might come back for her.

Lynnwood Detectives Jim Nelson and Steve Bredeson were assigned to the case. That Sunday night, they went to the Lighthouse Free Methodist Church, looking for Eloise. Humans alone couldn't have found her, but they had a search dog with them. The dog led them to a crawl space in the lower part of the church.

Eloise was there, her hands clasped together as if she were praying. But she was dead. She was still tied with carefully measured lengths of nylon rope. The discoloration in her face, the broken blood vessels, and the ligature marks around her neck showed that she had been strangled. She has also been stabbed in the throat in a sadistic overkill.

The Lynnwood detectives soon learned that Jim Elledge had a long criminal record that included murder. They put out a Wanted computer memo on him, sending it to the 13 Western states, and then all over America. Elledge had always been a traveler—at least, when he wasn't locked up.

He was probably driving Eloise Fitzner's car, which was missing. Rita told detectives that he had told them to bring the car because they would need it to carry home all the presents he was going to give them.

The blue Buick was found at 2:30 in the morning on Tuesday on South Commerce Street in Tacoma, sixty miles from Elledge's Everett trailer.

Jim Elledge might have been tired of running, or he might have finally faced the reality of the other side of his nature, the dark side. At 9:30 on Tuesday morning, he called Tacoma police and told them that he wanted to surrender. He told the dispatcher that he was staying at the Morgan Motel in the south end of Tacoma. He was as good as his word. As police pulled into the motel parking lot, Elledge walked out with his hands in the air. He had been staying there, he said, since Sunday.

Lynnwood detective Steve Bredeson felt that Elledge had come to the end of his resources. His image was all over newspapers and television, and he was running out of money. He didn't dare drive his victim's car, and he wouldn't get far on foot. Maybe he was only sick of fighting the violent impulses that whispered in his ear.

The man that Lynnwood detectives transferred back to their jurisdiction didn't look like a murderous monster. He looked like what he was: a wimpy, aging church janitor. He told them that he'd tried to kill himself—twice—but found he didn't have the nerve.

He admitted to police that he had killed Eloise, but he denied raping Rita Bentsen. "I hope I get the justice that Eloise got," he said bleakly. "And that's death. I want it so bad you can't believe it."

The congregation that had held out a hand of friendship and encouragement to a long-term prisoner was stunned, more so because Jim Elledge had chosen their sacred building for the scene of brutal murder. "Things like that aren't supposed to happen in a church," a departing member said. "Did I experience anger? Yes, I did."

Members and clergy of the Lighthouse Free Methodist Church held a massive cleansing service to rid their building of the real or imagined miasma of horror, pain, and bloody death. They gathered to pray on the grounds, asking God to give them back peace and love and to remove the sad mind pictures of an innocent woman trapped and dying in a dark crawl space.

One church elder visited Jim Elledge in jail. He was looking for answers as he asked Jim, "Was there anything we could have done to prevent this?"

Jim shook his head. It wasn't the church's fault. He was sure he hadn't given anyone any warning about the compulsion he carried within him.

He had hurt the church that reached out to him. Even though he had had no access to the nursery school, the state closed it down. Members drifted away, unable to shake the memories. Rita Bentsen would eventually bring suit against the church.

Duane Grooters, who had come into the Monroe Reformatory so many times to help Elledge find God, was shaken. He wasn't sure if he could ever be involved in prison ministry again. If Jim had fooled him so completely, how could he ever know what any convict was *really* thinking?

Eloise Fitzner was laid to rest, and her brother adopted the last two cats she had rescued—Bruce and Sheba—and took home a half-finished ceramic piece that she had been painting as a surprise for him when she died. Michael Helland said he had no interest in what happened to Jim Elledge as long as he couldn't hurt anyone else. Whether her confessed killer lived or died, it wouldn't bring Eloise back.

On May 27, 1998, Jim Elledge pleaded guilty to aggravated first-degree murder. Snohomish County Prosecutor Jim Krider said he would seek the death penalty. Elledge instructed his attorney not to send arguments against his execution to the prosecutors. Not only did he not want to fight to live, he seemed anxious to embrace death.

He would have no trial per se; when he faced a jury, they would decide only his punishment. Would he get a life without parole sentence? Or would he face death by hanging or lethal injection? In Washington State, he could choose the method of execution.

Bill Jacquette, Elledge's public defender, had promised him that he would argue—not for his client's life— but for the death penalty, as Elledge wanted. But, as trial neared in mid-October, there were those who stepped up to try to save him. A Seattle attorney made a motion to Superior Court Judge Joseph Thibodeau, asking to raise potential defense issues that would block the death penalty. She said she was speaking for a lawyers' group.

Judge Thibodeau denied her motion. "I'm satisfied it's not for the Court to override the constitutional rights of a fully informed and competent person in how he directs his particular defense."

If Jim Elledge wanted to die, he might just get his wish, although representatives of churches of many denominations wanted to rescue him. It was a most unusual situation: most accused killers fight to live; Jim Elledge was fighting to die.

The actual trial began on October 20, 1998. It was an abbreviated affair, although too long for Elledge.

Prosecutor Krider presented three witnesses the first day. Lynnwood detective James Nelson gave the jurors an overview of the case. He told them how Jim Elledge had hated Eloise and how he had carried out his plan. Nelson read a letter of warning that the victim had sent to the woman who was now the defendant's wife: "Please don't stay with that awful man anymore," Eloise had pleaded with Ann Elledge. "He told me he is just using you for sex and because he needs the income from your job."

That letter had made Jim Elledge angry.

The jurors learned of the grisly results of that anger from the forensic pathologist who performed the post-mortem exam of Eloise Fitzner's body. They blanched as autopsy photos were passed to them. The courtroom lights were dimmed, and they watched the Lynnwood investigators' video footage of the crime scene.

Next, they listened to Jim Elledge's confession to murder. In a way, even he didn't understand why he had done what he did, but there was no question that he had killed Eloise after planning and plotting how to accomplish it.

"There's something wrong with my nature," his voice, amplified in the courtroom, began. "An evil I can't control. I had to make my mind up that I was going to get even with this woman who tried to wreck my marriage earlier in the year. I had been carrying that anger inside of me for over a year . . . and it just spewed out."

Later in his confession, he seemed baffled. "I had no real reason to go after this woman. I mean, I have had a reason to be angry with her, but I didn't have a reason to kill her . . . and I threw away a fairly good life, you know . . . I couldn't control myself."

Elledge had written a letter to his wife before he lured Eloise and Rita into the church—a communiqué that added to the premeditation theory.

"My Darling Wife,

"I'm really sorry I screwed up our marriage . . . Do one thing for me. O.K.? Turn to God, honey. I know things will be bad for you for a while, but give God your heart and soul. I will always love you . . .

"Jim."

Although they had been forced to look at terrible pictures and listen to a killer describe his crimes, the jurors held up well until Eloise's brother testified in the late afternoon. At that point, several of them had tears in their eyes.

Mike Helland told jurors of his sister's strong faith. "She was a compassionate person who, to the extent that anyone can, lived by Christ's example. Her faith sustained her."

He recalled an idyllic childhood when he and Eloise were small. That made her seem more real than anything the jury had heard yet.

The next morning, Jim Elledge himself took the witness stand. He was 55, but he looked 15 years older. He was testifying for the defense, but in his case, he declared there *was* no defense. He looked impassively at the jury and tried to explain to them that he had no way of knowing when the "dark times" would creep up on him, although they usually happened just when things were going well for him. He spoke of rage that boiled up inside of him like a volcano erupting, explosive anger that burned like the fires of hell, even though someone watching him wouldn't be able to sense it.

And things *had* been going well for him. He was happily married, and shortly before the murder of Eloise Fitzner, he'd paid off a $3,000 debt. "I even bought a car. I don't think anyone who knew they were going to be in trouble would go out and make all those payments and buy a new car."

The jurors looked mystified. Was Elledge suddenly denying that he was guilty? He sat in the witness chair, his expression calm, if dour.

"There's no doubt in my mind," he said softly, but with profound conviction, "that there is a very wicked part of me. And this wicked part of me *needs* to die."

Final arguments began, and both Bill Jaquette and Deputy Prosecutor Mark Roe spoke of the need for Jim Elledge to be executed. It was an almost unheard-of situation, and it was difficult to tell which of the two brought up the most damning information from Elledge's past.

Jaquette was personally against the death penalty, but he was obeying his client's instructions to fight to get him the death penalty.

"If you are worried that you might be assisting my client in suicide, don't be. You won't be taking the law into your own hands. You will be *obeying* the law."

It was the first and only time in Jaquette's career that he had implored a jury *not* to show leniency for his client.

Roe spoke of Eloise's pain and fear as she lay on her back, bound and gagged, helpless to fight as Elledge cut off her airway.

Deputy Prosecutor John Adcock, the co-prosecutor, urged the jurors to remember Eloise and the brutal way she had perished at the defendant's hands.

When both the prosecutors and the defense attorney were finished, Jim Elledge thanked them all and hugged Bill Jaquette.

"I feel Mr. Jaquette has done an excellent job," he said. "I think the prosecutor's office has done an excellent job, too."

It took only 90 minutes for the jurors to return with a verdict. The nine men and three women gave Jim Elledge what he wanted. Death.

But it would not be soon. In death penalty cases, it is mandatory that the Washington State Supreme Court review the case. On July 5, 2001, the high court agreed that Jim Elledge had waived his right to appeal "knowingly, voluntarily, and intelligently."

Within a few weeks, the American Civil Liberties Union and the Catholic Archdiocese filed a clemency petition with the state Clemency and Pardons Board. They insisted that the jury might have voted differently if they had been told about Jim Elledge's miserable childhood or if they had known that he had once helped foil a prison escape and saved a guard.

On August 6, the Clemency Board voted three to two to recommend that Governor Gary Locke allow the execution to proceed. On August 17, Locke acted on their recommendation.

James Elledge's execution date was set for August 28, 2001.

There would be no delays. Bill Hubbard, the former Lynnwood City Council member who had once shared his apartment with Jim Elledge for a few months, lived in Kansas City in 2001. He left his telephone number at the prison in Walla Walla, just in case Jim wanted to call him collect. A week before August 28, Jim did call him. He declared his continuing faith and said he knew his death alone would not make up for killing Eloise.

He had something more to confess, too, so that he would go to his death with a clear conscience. "He said the $400 I thought I lost years ago wasn't lost; he had taken it," Hubbard said. "He was sorry."

On Monday night, August 27, 100 anti–death penalty demonstrators began to gather outside the prison in Walla Walla, holding signs that said, "Execute Justice— Not People!" They held hands and chanted as they held a candlelight vigil for a man who wanted none of their help.

James Elledge spent the night before his execution in a holding cell that had a mattress, a pillow, two sheets, two towels, and three blankets. He declined to make a request for a last supper. His last meal, then, was the breakfast he'd eaten that morning: apple juice, oatmeal, hash-browns, toast, a boiled egg, and coffee.

Shortly after midnight, Elledge was moved from his

cell to a gurney in the death chamber. He had chosen death by lethal injection.

Witnesses sat tensely in the room with a large window, where they could see the execution. Bill Jaquette was there, as was Deputy Prosecutor John Adcock, along with the two detectives who had worked on the Fitzner murder case. Jim Nelson said he felt little sympathy for Elledge. "I feel a lot worse about her than I do about him. He knows what's coming. He's had a chance to make his peace with whatever he feels he needs to do. And he did this to himself. He committed his second murder, and he's been given chance after chance."

At 12:30 A.M., a white curtain that hid the execution chamber from the witnesses suddenly rose. The witnesses could see Elledge lying on his back. A dark blue sheet was pulled up to his neck, and his eyes were closed. He seemed to be dead already, but then they saw the faint movement of his chest as he breathed in and out.

Prison Superintendent John Lambert announced, "Inmate Elledge has no last words."

At 12:39, the petcock was turned on the first of the drugs and it began to flow through the saline solution into Elledge's veins. All the witnesses saw was the two lines. Just as those who throw the switch on an electric chair never know which switch is a dummy, these executioners would not know which of them let loose the fatal drugs.

First, there was thiopental sodium to relax the muscles, then pancuronium bromide to paralyze the lungs, and finally potassium chloride to stop the heart.

Scott North, a reporter for the *Everett Herald,* sat watching, his notepad in his hand, almost forgetting to write.

Jim Elledge moved so slightly that it was almost undetectable. He seemed to take one deep breath. After several minutes, his mouth fell open slightly.

And then the curtain fell.

Almost immediately, Department of Corrections spokesman Veltry Johnson announced that Elledge was dead. It was 12:52. The entire process had taken 13 minutes. The oldest prisoner ever to be executed in the state of Washington was dead at the age of 58.

Eloise Fitzner's brother, Mike, didn't go to the prison to observe the execution. Instead, he stayed with their elderly mother, who was in a nursing home. They had both hoped that Elledge might ask for forgiveness for murdering Eloise—but, of course, he had not said a word.

"In my mind," Helland said, "Elledge is just kind of a nonentity. [My sister]—through no fault of her own—ran into a bad guy, a person who was broken. I'd just not like to think about him anymore."

There was no one left to talk to who could speak for Bertha Lush—not after 27 years.

No one can say for sure what event, if any, in Jim Elledge's early life had filled him with so much rage. It was probably a series of losses, disappointments, abandonments, griefs. It might have been nature or nurture, or a genetic predisposition to violence enflamed by his desperate childhood. But one thing was certain: he would surely have gone on hurting and killing people as long as he had the strength to do it.

He stopped that, fully aware of the black thing inside of him, even though he didn't understand it.

He took himself out of the game before he could do it again.

The Beach

Grays Harbor County, Washington, is a great sprawling county that edges the coast along the Pacific Ocean near the southwestern corner of the state. It isn't a heavily populated area, perhaps because it rains so much there—a relentless gray curtain of water that can leave even the most ebullient personality discouraged. The economy has driven some residents away; the timber industry has fallen on hard times.

The Beach

Aberdeen, the biggest town in Grays Harbor County, has under 20,000 residents, and the whole county has somewhere between 60,000 and 70,000 people. But that number doubles, often triples, during a clam tide. Commercial and sports fishing are a big draw; there are scores of shake mills, endless miles of beach, plush resorts, and modest cabin camps. It is a county with place names that sound strange to a visitor: towns named Humptulips and Satsop ring oddly to the ear. The hamlet of McCleary has the biggest summer festival, and the cuisine is bear stew.

In spots, the timberland of Grays Harbor County gives way to acres of bog, which is almost like quicksand. One oceanfront section was called—quite realistically—Washaway Beach. It did indeed give up more and more shoreline as the hungry ocean gnawed at it year after year.

The Quinault Indian Reservation is the northwest corner of the county and has its own tribal police force.

Grays Harbor has had both its stunning failures and its roaring successes. For those who truly love the wildness of the ocean as it has been for eons, Grays Harbor is a much desired destination, and that will never change. The Satsop Project, designed to convert atomic energy to civilian use, collapsed into a financial fiasco that left nothing but looming silos. A singular success was Kurt Cobain; perhaps the most brilliant—if troubled—musician ever to come out of the Northwest was born and raised in Grays Harbor County.

But Kurt Cobain was only a tow-headed, blue-eyed little boy on Monday, April 14, 1975. On that day, Grays Harbor County Sheriff Harold Sumpter and a friend who was a Superior Court judge were driving to a weekly lunch meeting. It had become something of a ritual for them over their years of association. They had just left the county seat of Montesano and were nearing Satsop on old Highway 12 when they noticed two young girls with backpacks walking along the side of the blacktop.

They shook their heads at the danger inherent in the situation, but they had no reason to stop the girls. Hitchhiking wasn't against the law at the time. The judge commented that it was "too bad" that their usual lunch companion, who was a juvenile court worker, wasn't with them. "He probably knows them."

If he *had* been with them that day, they might have found a reason to give the girls a ride home.

In mid-1975, young women in Washington and Oregon were still afraid of running into the mysterious "Ted," the faceless wraith who was wanted for the murders and disappearances of almost a dozen girls, some of whom had been last seen hitchhiking. These two young women had tucked their thumbs in when they saw the sheriff's car, but Sumpter knew they were hoping to catch a ride.

Law enforcement officers file away information almost unconsciously, and Sumpter remembered later that one girl was of medium height and the other much shorter and very petite; both carried orangy-red backpacks. Still, he was never absolutely sure that the young women he saw near Satsop were the same girls he would see later in horrifying circumstances.

Most homicides in Grays Harbor County erupted out

of family beefs and domestic violence situations. But there was no way to predict how many predators—not animal but human—prowled the highways and beaches looking for the vulnerable and the trusting. No, hitchhiking wasn't against the law, although the "Ted" case had spurred activists and police alike to circulate petitions to send to the Washington State Legislature to ask for a law that *would* ban it. No one knew yet that the real Ted—Ted Bundy—had moved on to Utah.

Harold Sumpter was a man born to the badge: his grandfather was a judge, and his father was the sheriff and then a marshal in Mason County, Missouri. The lawmen in his family warned him that if he ever expected to have any money, he'd better avoid police work. He knew they were right, but the urge was too strong. He signed on at Grays Harbor County in 1963 as a special deputy, rose through the ranks to resident deputy in the eastern sector of the county, and then became Chief Criminal Deputy. When he was off duty, Sumpter painted houses to add to his income.

Sumpter knew his citizens and the back roads of his county as well as most men know the block they live on. He had 27 working deputies (he included himself in this count), but he recalled only too well a time when he was the only officer on night patrol in the entire county. The idea of having a backup unit if he ran into a potentially dangerous situation was unheard of "unless you could wake up somebody at home, and then it was usually too late," Sumpter said with a grin.

He had just settled into his new post as Sheriff when he and his department were faced with one of the most brutal crimes in county history.

April 14 was a little early for the true tourist season to begin in Grays Harbor County; the weather was too mercurial, changing from sunshine and blue skies to bitterly cold, windswept storms in minutes. But Tina Jacobsen and Gaelisa (Gael) Burton loved the ocean beaches, and they were prepared to deal with the vicissitudes of Mother Nature. Sadly, they knew a lot more about camping than they did about human aberration, and they headed for the ocean without fear.

They had graduated together from Vashon Island High School in 1974. Vashon Island is a small community between Seattle and Tacoma, set in the middle of Puget Sound. The only way to get there is by ferry. Most of its graduates find jobs off the island in Seattle.

Gael had worked a while as an X-ray librarian at Virginia Mason Hospital; Tina still worked there as a dietary aide. At 19, Gael had given up hospital work and the big city. She lived alone on an old 20-acre homestead on Vashon. She was an apprentice in a moccasin and leather shirt business on the island, and she was so talented and hardworking that she had just been asked to become a full partner. It was a very small business, but orders were increasing all the time.

Gael had some unfinished moccasins in her backpack and intended to sew on them while they were camped out on the beach.

Gael Burton was only five feet, one inch tall and weighed about 95 pounds. She was a vegetarian, a young woman who deplored violence in either thought or deed. She had long straight dark hair and wore "granny" glasses.

Tina Jacobsen was five feet, five inches tall and weighed 125 pounds. Her face was as open as a flower, with a smooth high forehead and dark eyes, framed by masses of curly light brown hair that cascaded below her shoulder blades.

Tina often visited on Gael's farm, and she knew the Grays Harbor area well, too. She had visited the ocean beach towns several times before and had suggested to Gael that it was the perfect place for an early spring campout. There wouldn't be a lot of tourists yet, and the weather was warming up.

The two girls were well prepared for their trip to the coast as they rode the Vashon Island ferry to Tacoma on that Monday in April. From there, they hitched rides. They wore warm clothes and sturdy hiking boots, and they carried backpacks filled with carefully chosen food and equipment. Both of them had maroon sleeping bags, but they had more than enough money for emergencies and a few meals inside, out of the weather, if they needed to.

As always, their friends and Gael's mother had cautioned them about strangers, but they felt safe because there were two of them. They promised that they wouldn't have anything to do with strangers on the beach—they knew better than that. They just wanted to hike and camp.

They were due home on Thursday, April 17, but they didn't get back then. Nobody was really worried about them that night, thinking that they had just decided to camp one more day.

It was close to 5 P.M. on Friday, April 18, when a couple from Seattle walked slowly along the shoreline just inside the border of the Quinault Indian Reservation. They were only a few hundred yards from the small town of Moclips, Washington. They separated as each scanned the sands for interesting driftwood to take home.

The wife's attention was drawn to a shelter that looked as though kids had built it by stacking driftwood logs around a center pole. The whole thing was about five by six feet and barely five feet high. At high tide, it would be no more than fifty feet from the pounding surf. But the woman who looked at it didn't think anyone would actually use it for shelter. The spaces between the driftwood walls wouldn't afford much protection from wind and waves. It would make an ideal "fort" for kids with active imaginations, though.

Moving closer, she peered inside—and stepped back hastily in embarrassment. Through a crack in the gnarled logs, she'd seen what could only be someone's bare buttocks. She thought she'd stumbled across lovers who had taken advantage of the shelter. Somewhat red-faced, she walked back to where her husband stood.

They discussed what she had seen, and the more they talked, the more unlikely it seemed that anyone would be making love in the nude in such chilly weather. They walked closer to the shelter, called out, received no reply, and finally peered inside again.

What they saw was so shocking they couldn't believe it at first. There was no love-making—nor any life at all—inside. Pale light filtered in and cast shadows over two bodies. As their eyes adjusted to the dim light, they saw that there was blood everywhere.

With their feet sinking in the beach sand, they ran clumsily toward their truck and drove to a phone.

Sheriff Sumpter and Undersheriff Gene Niece led a crew of officers to the beach in Moclips. It was almost 40 miles from Montesano. The caravan of sheriff's units driven by Sergeant Larry Deason, Detective Nick Johnson, and Deputy George Sepansky tailed Sumpter's speeding vehicle. Even so, daylight disappeared as the sun dipped into the ocean.

The body site was only a few hundred yards from the houses and mobile homes that huddled near the sea in the tiny town. It wasn't easy to get to the driftwood hut. The investigators drove to the end of a narrow dirt road, and then they had to walk along a trail leading past a dump site for sawdust and shakes to the beach. Only the rising moon and their flashlights guided them. The Moclips River cut through to the sea near them, and the huge, jagged rocks marking Point Grenville were silhouettes against the last muted colors of sunset as they rose from the ocean to the north.

Sumpter knew that the Moclips River was within feet of the boundary that divided his county from the Quinault Indian Reservation. There was a very good chance that the shelter and the bodies inside were actually on federal property. He would probably have to coordinate his probe with Indian tribal police and with FBI agents. He had worked with them before, and it made a difficult case easier.

Even as the officers' flashlights sent cones of light through the beach grass and brush that separated the overgrown path from the beach, a storm gathered in the ocean. High winds and torrential rain bore down on the investigators, and the surf crept closer to the driftwood shelter. The waves were black now, capped by snowy foam, and the warmth of the day's sunshine was only a memory.

Grays Harbor County's prosecuting attorney, Curtis Janhunen and his deputy, David Edwards, were only 15 minutes behind the sheriff's party, and they joined the men on the beach. So did John Siemers, a criminal investigator for the Bureau of Indian Affairs.

The weather and the dark night cast the whole crime scene into grim flickering shadows as they peered inside the pile of gray wood. It wasn't a couple inside; they saw two young women who were obviously dead. They lay atop sleeping bags, the bags so saturated with blood that their life fluid had soaked through into the sand beneath.

The taller girl was facedown, her hands apparently tied in front of her, her feet effectively hobbled by her jeans and panties, which had been pulled down around her ankles. She wore a plaid shirt, and it and her bra had been pulled up to her shoulders. Even a cursory exam showed them that she had been stabbed several times.

The second girl lay on her side, her hands tied behind her with bloodstained twine. She was a tiny girl, with dark hair pulled into a ponytail. As with her companion, her clothing had been yanked both down and up until she was almost nude, her T-shirt and red-and-green plaid work shirt high above her breasts, her ankles pinioned by her jeans.

Both of the victims had been gagged with strips of the plaid material sliced by a very sharp knife from their own shirts.

As they listened to the roar of the surf and shouted to make themselves heard, the investigators commented that the gagging couldn't have been necessary. Any cries for help would never have carried back to town, even though the lights of houses seemed close enough to reach out and touch.

The smaller girl had been stabbed, too, again and again around the throat and chest.

Oddly, no sign of a prolonged struggle was evident inside the cramped shelter. The girls' hiking boots had been neatly placed upside down to keep them dry, and some wet clothing was spread out to dry. Their orangy-red backpacks had barely been opened, and their cooking utensils and food supplies were not disturbed. It looked as if they had arrived at the beach late at night and had been too tired and wet to do anything but change into dry clothing, crawl into their sleeping bags, and go to sleep.

If their killer came upon them while they were swaddled in the cocoon-like sleeping bags, he could have immobilized them and bound them before they ever had a chance to fight back.

It was obvious that the girls' hands had been bound before their upper garments were pulled up; that would account for the fact that they still wore clothes. The twine knots would have made it impossible to slip their shirts off past their hands.

Rape was the most probable motive, but it would take lab tests to determine whether the victims had actually been sexually attacked. Robbery was ruled out when Sumpter's men found a good deal of cash in their backpacks. They also found drivers' licenses and various kinds of identification.

According to their identification, the victims were Tina Jacobsen and Gaelisa Burton, both 19 years old, with addresses on Vashon Island, Washington. Now, they knew who the young women were, but they had no idea who had killed them, and it would take a medical examiner to estimate the time of death.

Harold Sumpter had a terrible feeling he had seen them before: two young women walking happily down the road a few days earlier, their orange-hued backpacks on their shoulders.

Undersheriff Niece set about measuring and diagramming the area while the other detectives looked for evidence at the scene. It was one of the most difficult crime scenes they had ever worked. The winds keened and howled, flapping the plastic tarp they had tied atop the shelter, while the rain only increased in intensity. They didn't even try to keep dry, but they wanted to preserve any evidence that might be there.

Sheriff Sumpter and his men and the investigators from the Bureau of Indian Affairs were battered by the storm for four hours before the bodies were removed. They would come back to search again in the daylight; now they had to find as much as they could before the heedless wind blew precious clues away.

It was 11 P.M. when Deputy Sepansky and Indian agent Charlie McBride were posted to secure the scene until morning. Sumpter would not be going home for three days and nights; he set up headquarters at the Tradewinds Lodge in Moclips.

Sumpter contacted the FBI, and Special Agents Pete Shepp and Bob Wick headed toward the tiny oceanfront town of Moclips. Bureau of Indian Affairs Officer Siemers confirmed that the girls' bodies had been found 200 feet inside the Quinault Indian Reservation, but said the case would be totally under tribal jurisdiction only if the killer or killers proved to be of Indian heritage. At this point, there was no way to determine that,

Sumpter had a hunch. He'd felt it the first time he'd seen the twine knots that were cut carefully off the victims' wrists. He'd mentioned it to Niece, but he knew he had to have a lot more to go on. There were advantages to being a lawman who had worked an entire county for so many years. Sumpter had a memory like a computer, and he'd worked on a troubling case in February eight years earlier, a case that came back to him now.

Several young boys had been abducted while they were playing in a nearby town. A dark-haired man about 20 years old had threatened them with a knife to make them go with him. The frightened youngsters were then tied to trees or hung by their wrists while their tormentor threatened to emasculate them with his knife.

Although none of them was actually cut, their terror had seemed to be enough to sexually satisfy the sadist who taunted them.

Sumpter had been assigned to that case, and he remembered the distinctive configuration of the knots, which had been saved by one father who rescued his boy from a tree in the woods. There were five twists, looping under and over: a variation on a square knot—like something a Boy Scout might have learned.

The knots on the dead girls looked to be identical.

The man arrested for tormenting the schoolboys was 20-year-old William Calvin Batten, a sometime shake-mill worker. On February 10, 1967, Batten had been found guilty of indecent liberties, and he had been sent to Western Washington State Hospital's sexual Psychopath program.

He was released shortly thereafter.

Sheriff Sumpter determined to find out just what William Batten had been up to in the intervening eight years. He'd heard that Batten had moved back to the west county area after living near Bremerton, Washington, for a while. Apparently he had kept out of trouble in Grays Harbor territory.

When the full crew of county, federal, and tribal investigators assembled on the beach at dawn, only the bloodstained sand remained to show that Tina and Gael had died there in the driftwood shed. The storm had passed, and the sun shone.

The victims' bodies were awaiting autopsy; their sleeping bags and backpacks were drying out back at sheriff's headquarters in Montesano. Hopefully, the postmortem exams would add information that would help find their killer.

Lieutenant Larry Clevenger, one of Sumpter's sharpest investigators, was at the scene now. Ironically, on one of his rare days off, Clevenger had been fishing in the ocean the day before, not far off the very beach he now surveyed.

The detectives were looking for some specific items as well as other evidence that might have been left behind by a killer. Gael's glasses were missing; relatives said she was very nearsighted and would never have gone on a trip of several days without them. When Tina was found, she wore only one earring, long before it was fashionable to wear a single earring. And the murder knife might be buried somewhere in the sand.

The searchers found neither the glasses nor the earring, but they did find a ball of twine, which appeared to be the same as the bloodstained bonds on the victims' wrists. And they found something considerably more damaging to a suspect: buried about four inches beneath the sand at the corner of the shelter was a bill from the public utilities department.

It was addressed to William Batten. There was also an envelope from a place called Futures Clear, addressed to his wife. The address listed was in Moclips, and it was that of an apartment that faced the ocean only a few blocks south of the driftwood shelter. The possibility that the items could have blown onto the beach and been buried there from the dump farther inland was most unlikely; the prevailing wind blew off the ocean, not toward it.

While Harold Sumpter traced William Batten's movements and any recent police contacts or arrests, his men, aided by every officer available from the Hoquiam Police Department, fanned out in a door-to-door inquiry in Moclips and along the route the dead girls had probably taken to reach the lonely beach where they had met their killer.

Disappointingly, although the teenagers would have had to walk right through Moclips to reach their camp, no one in town recalled seeing them. They hadn't shopped at the one local grocery store, or gone to the Tradewinds Lodge for coffee or a meal. This only seemed to further indicate that they had been killed shortly after coming to town. That probably would have been Monday in the hours after dark. Monday was the day they had left home for their trip. No one expected them back for a few days, so no alarm would have been raised.

The autopsy reports from Dr. Arthur Campbell indicated that the victims had succumbed to multiple knife wounds. The most immediately fatal were two deep penetrating wounds on each body to the right carotid artery in the neck. Hemorrhaging would have been profound. Gael had superficial wounds on the neck and chest. Tina had a stab wound to her right flank and a deep wound in her back, a wound that had penetrated a piece of plastic found on top her body.

Surprisingly, neither of the victims had been raped or sodomized. No semen was present, nor any evidence of trauma to the victims' vaginas or rectums. However, this did not eliminate a sexual motivation in the double murders, as suggested by the seminude condition of the girls' bodies when they were found. The killer might have panicked as he prepared to rape the helpless girls, or he might have been a sadist whose gratification came through his victims' terror rather than through an overt sex act.

He might even have had a premature sexual climax in the excitement of stripping his victims naked, and then been unable to achieve another erection. Then, too, he could have been impotent—a man who raped symbolically, with a knife.

Dr. Campbell estimated that the missing death weapon was a long knife, sharpened on one side only, with a blade two and a half to three inches in width: a butcher knife.

The time of the victims' death was much harder to determine. When the girls were found, rigor was present only in their upper arms and jaws. This area is the first to stiffen after death, and it is also the last to be affected as rigor mortis leaves. The bodies had been preserved almost perfectly by the refrigerated air of the chilled beach. Campbell's final assessment was only that they had been dead more than 48 hours.

Sumpter and his judge friend had seen two girls hitchhiking on Monday; other witnesses had seen a similar pair on the following Wednesday. Were they the same girls? Despite requests for information, the girls allegedly seen on Wednesday were never located.

One possibility to set the time of death was identifying the stomach contents of the victims. Gael had eaten salad for her last meal, and Tina a hamburger. Tracing back along the probable path the victims had taken to Moclips, detectives contacted employees at the popular Colonial West Restaurant and Burgess Motel on Perry Avenue running north out of Hoquiam. The day staff recalled that two teenage girls with backpacks had eaten lunch there on Monday.

One of the young women had cashed a large-denomination bill to pay for their lunch of a salad and a hamburger.

"They were sitting on that big log across the road," a resident at the Broken Arrow Trailer Park just down the road recalled. "They looked like they were resting. Then they were picked up by a man in a green 1964 Ford or Chevy."

William Batten drove such a car, but there were lots of green Fords and Chevrolets. The witness didn't have a license number or a detailed description of the driver. He had had no reason to be suspicious of him.

Sumpter learned that Batten had gotten himself into some familiar trouble in Kitsap County two years earlier. In October, he'd been found guilty on three counts of second-degree assault involving three young children. Free on bail after the conviction, he'd been released to undergo treatment at a mental health clinic in Grays Harbor County. His wife was still with him, but her children had been removed from the Battens' custody.

It is not the expected progression for a man who victimizes children to turn to attacking adults—but in the world of the sadist, nothing is truly predictable.

By Sunday night, Sumpter and his crew had gathered voluminous circumstantial evidence that pointed strongly to William Batten. They had learned that Batten was employed at the Saginaw Shake Mill, but that he had not worked during the week of April 14 until Friday, April 18, the day the bodies were found.

District Court Judge L. Thomas Parker issued a search warrant for the trailer where William Batten lived with his wife and for the adjoining apartment complex where relatives lived. The probable cause request also listed certain vehicles Batten had access to.

At 7:00 A.M., Lieutenant Clevenger, Sergeant Bob Baldarson, Detectives Nick Johnson and Veryl Hutchinson, Deputies Tom Hranac and Dan Crisp, Sergeant Larry Deason, and FBI agents Shepp and Wick arrived at the apartment complex where the Battens' 35-foot trailer was parked. They were armed with the search warrant.

Clevenger searched the trailer; the other investigators searched the relatives' apartment, grounds, and garbage cans. During his search Clevenger found a pair of stained men's jockey shorts (which the FBI lab later determined to have probable human blood and semen stains, although the garment had been washed and it was impossible to say positively what blood type the stains were). He found a jackknife atop a television set and, in the second right-hand kitchen drawer, a 10-inch blade, which had been ground down to a sharp edge on one side. A chunk of steel had been knocked off the blade. The suspect's wife said the knife had not been used in six months—but Clevenger noted that there was paper towel residue clinging to the blade, which appeared to have been left there very recently, as though the knife had been wiped free of some substance. He did not find the missing earring or Gaelisa's glasses.

The knife matched exactly the type of weapon used in the double murders. Just as important in evidentiary value were some items of men's clothing found soaking in a washer full of cold water in the apartment house next door.

Clevenger retrieved a pair of brown men's slacks and a green shirt. Dried, and sent to the FBI lab, they proved to be heavily stained with human blood. Again, the washing process made determination of blood type impossible.

William Batten was at work at the shake mill while the search was carried out; his wife was very cooperative with the investigators. Thinking back to the Monday night when the crime had probably occurred, Batten's wife recalled that he had been extremely upset and nervous, but she thought that was because he'd just quit smoking.

She said that she had asked him to come next door to the apartment house with her to watch television, but he said he was too nervous. He told her he thought he would take a walk instead. When she returned to their trailer about two and a half hours later, he was there.

Later on in the week—on Wednesday night—Batten left the trailer after she was asleep. She thought he'd gone to a local tavern. This didn't strike her as unusual at all. Her husband often went for walks at night after she was asleep.

A relative of the shake-mill worker said that Batten had commented to him that the newspaper pictures of the victims looked familiar—that he thought they were some girls he'd picked up hitchhiking.

The missing pieces of the case were rapidly falling into place. Gael and Tina had hitchhiked from the Vashon Island ferry to Olympia, Washington State's capital city, and then along the old highway west, where they had passed through Satsop and McCleary. They had eaten lunch and then been picked up by a man in a green Ford or Chevy heading north toward the ocean beaches.

At that rate, they should have arrived on the beach where they set up camp long before sunset, which occurred at 6:26 P.M. on April 14. Harold Sumpter mulled over a possible scenario.

Suppose Batten had given them a ride, left them at the beach, and bided his time until night cloaked the area with blackness? There would have been no hurry; his quarry was waiting, unaware, in the driftwood lean-to. He could return whenever he chose.

As they discussed whether they had enough probable cause to ask for an arrest warrant, Harold Sumpter kept full-time stakeouts on the mill worker. Rumors were rife around the close-knit community, and Sumpter particularly feared two things: that William Batten might leave the area before an arrest could be effected, or that angry citizens might decide to carry out their own punishment for the horrendous crime if the suspect was not soon put behind bars.

Batten continued to report to work at the shake mill and to return home to his trailer each night, but he went for no more walks on the beach.

Memorial services were held for Tina Jacobsen at the Island Funeral Services Chapel on Vashon Island on Tuesday, April 22. Gaelisa Burton's services were held the following day at the Vashon Island Episcopal Church. It was a poignant last goodbye for two young women on the brink of life who had expected to find three days of tranquility and meditation on a quiet beach. Instead, their bodies had lain undetected in the windswept shelter as the ocean changed from green to blue to angry black in its ageless ebb and flow while the gentle folk of Moclips went about their regular routines unaware.

At least, all but one of them were unaware.

As the week progressed and constant surveillance was kept on Batten, the case investigators continued to question townspeople and county residents about the movements of the dead girls and Batten on that fatal Monday. They finally located a truck driver who corroborated the story told by the witness who had seen the girls get into a green Ford near the Burgess Motel. But their trail ended there. No one who could recall seeing Gaelisa and Tina after that.

On Friday, April 25, William Batten was arrested at his home, and the green Ford was impounded. Two deputies drove him to Olympia, where Washington State Patrol Major John Kendersei, one of the Northwest's foremost polygraphists, awaited. Kendersei had been apprised of the evidence and facts of the case.

Batten, 28, was a big man with wildly tousled dark hair, a muscular six feet tall. He seemed a little antsy as he was ushered into Kendersei's office. He was informed of his rights and asked to take a lie-detector test, but he changed his mind, intimidated by the wires and needles that can winnow truth from lie.

He muttered, "I'd never pass it." Instead, the suspect said he would write out a statement in his own hand. He scribbled over six legal-size pages and then did it over. Although he was not satisfied with the first statement, both accounts were similar in detail.

Even though witnesses had seen Batten pick up two girls matching Gael's and Tina's descriptions only 2 miles north of Hoquiam (and about 28 miles from where their bodies were found), he insisted that he had picked them up much closer to the beach—at the Copalis Crossing. He said that he had given them a ride because he knew what it was like to hitchhike himself, and that he'd thought they were about 15 or 16. They had told him they were headed for Moclips or Taholah. He had asked them if they minded if he drove to Moclips via Pacific Beach— and that, he said, was fine with them.

He wrote that he had pointed out some campsites to them, but they weren't interested, and he'd assumed that they were planning to meet someone in the area. If that part of his statement was true, Tina and Gaelisa may have only pretended that they were going to meet someone as a protective, discouraging ploy with Batten.

According to Batten, he dropped the two young women off in Moclips, and they walked away. Then he went to the mobile home that he shared with his wife.

He wrote that he was nervous because he'd been laid up after an accident at work and because his mental health counselor had moved away, and he couldn't relate well to his new one.

That Monday night, he said, he told his wife he was going for a walk and invited her to come along. "She asked me to wait and she'd come with me—but I was too nervous. So I left."

He said he'd left, telling her he'd be gone an hour and a half to two hours.

Because it was chilly, he'd put on a pair of coveralls over his shirt and pants; he wrote that he headed first for a tavern and then changed his mind and walked out toward Moclips River. When he got out to the end of the tracks, he said he'd seen a campfire burning near the driftwood huts. He expected to find some of the "beach kids," or at least someone to talk to.

The investigators had never found any indication that the victims had built a fire on the beach.

Batten wrote that he had walked close enough to the fire to recognize the same girls he'd given a ride to. He joined them, and they talked.

As always, in a homicide situation, only the suspect's statement can be given. The victim has no voice at all, and Batten's version of what occurred demanded scrutiny.

He recalled that he had told the girls he was married

and told them his wife's name. He insisted that they had invited him inside the hut because the spray was up and it was cold. He then wrote that the girls had attempted to seduce him (a common fantasy in confessional statements) and that they had taken off their clothes.

Since Tina and Gaelisa had been bound before an attempt was made to remove their clothing, this statement had to be a blatant lie.

Batten's fantasy confession continued: he wrote that he started to leave, and the girls threatened to tell his wife that he had been intimate with them even though he had not. He said he had then been forced to tie them up with some twine he found in his jumpsuit pocket.

He said that he had tried to leave again, but the girls had laughed at him and said they could holler for help and say that he tried to rape them and that their bound hands would be proof. So then he'd been forced to cut gags from a shirt.

He admitted that he had gagged Tina and then Gael, when he heard a scream. As he turned around, the knife still in his hand had "just happened" to stick into Tina.

And then he had panicked because he thought he had killed her, so he had to do the same to Gael, or she would tell on him. He stabbed each of the victims several times and had turned to leave when Tina made a sound. It was then that he'd turned around and stabbed her in the back.

He said he had become nauseated then and had thrown up in the river. Then he had headed home to get advice from his wife about what he should do, but she hadn't been there. So he had washed his hands, wiped off the knife, and put it back in the drawer. By the time his wife returned, he'd been too "shook up" to talk.

For almost four days, the victims had lain undiscovered. He denied that he had returned to the beach after he left on Monday night.

Batten was taken back to the Grays Harbor County Jail and charged with two counts of first-degree murder. Judge Parker set his bail at $2,000,000 and appointed a local law firm to defend him, as he had no funds for an attorney.

Sheriff Sumpter was concerned that the suspect might attempt suicide, and even thought a lynching attempt might be mobilized against him. He kept an around-the-clock watch on Batten in his high-security cell, both with a special guard and with closed-circuit TV.

On April 29, William Batten pleaded not guilty to the murders before Superior Court Judge John Schumacher. At that time, he was denied bail.

On June 3, Batten appeared before Superior Court Judge Jay Hamilton in Kitsap County and was sentenced for his three earlier convictions on the second-degree assault charges involving the three children. He was sentenced to three concurrent 10-year terms on those charges, and returned to the Grays Harbor County Jail.

William Batten's initial defense was that he was not guilty by reason of insanity. It proved useless when he underwent psychiatric examination and the results did not establish mental illness that would meet the requirements under the M'Naughton Rule. Under M'Naughton, the killer has to have been unaware of the difference between right and wrong at the time of the crime, and to have made no attempt to escape or to cover up his crime. Batten *knew* that what he had done was wrong, and he told an elaborate story to take the blame off himself.

During the second week in September 1975, William Batten appeared before a jury of seven women and five men. Prosecutor Janhunen told the jury that the crimes were vicious and premeditated, and he scoffed at Batten's version of the fatal encounter wherein he asserted that the women had made sexual advances to him. Instead, Janhunen painted a picture of two young women stalked and taken by complete surprise.

He surmised that Tina and Gaelisa were trapped in their mummy-type sleeping bags when Batten's husky body loomed over them in their shelter.

"I suggest to you that a decision was made by two 19-year-old girls not to fight."

Pinned in their sleeping bags, Tina and Gael could have been quickly subdued if the heavy defendant had merely lain across those bags.

Prosecutor Janhunen pointed out that the girls' desperate ploy of nonresistance meant "submitting to being tied up and gagged and going along with everything until the stabbing began."

Major Kendersei's testimony regarding Batten's oral and then written confession was one of the most damaging in the trial. That, combined with the profusion of physical and lab evidence gathered by Sheriff Sumpter and his men, convinced a jury. It took them only two and a half hours to find Batten guilty on two counts of first-degree murder. Batten showed no emotion as the verdict was read.

On October 10, Batten was sentenced to two consecutive life terms in prison, plus the compulsory deadly weapon charge—meaning that he could not hope to be out of prison for more than 30 years.

The investigation carried out by Sheriff Sumpter was a classic melding of old-time seat-of-the-pants lawman's savvy and the utilization of modern forensic science. His detectives talked to hundreds of people, racking up more overtime hours than a small county's budget could ever hope to reimburse. They knew that, but it didn't matter to them. They found a killer, and they found him before he could harm anyone else. Prosecutor Janhunen's court-room expertise did the rest.

Gaelisa Burton's mother, Grace, had raised her as a single parent, and much of Gael's gentleness and philoso-phies about life came from her mother. After she buried her daughter, Grace Burton became active in Washington State's first group to support the rights of victims: Fami-lies and Friends of Victims of Violent Crimes and Miss-ing Persons, volunteering to help other parents who had suffered similar losses. She worked at her full-time job as a caretaker for the ill and the elderly in their homes, and then gave many hours a week to Families and Friends.

Harold Sumpter was named National Police Officer of the Month for his work on the Burton-Jacobsen case as well as for other successful investigations and service to the public in Grays Harbor County. He died of a heart at-tack in 1999.

William Batten is still incarcerated in the Washington State Penitentiary in Walla Walla, and his first possible release date is in 2043.

The Desperate Hours

There have probably been dozens of movies about killers on the run who burst into the homes of strangers and hold them hostage. It is a terrifying thought, particularly with the current rise of so-called home invasion robberies in cities. What would you do if you opened your door to find a man with a gun? Even worse, what would you do if you were a woman home alone with your three small children?

That ultimate nightmare happened to Patricia Jacque five days before Christmas. December 20 is the beginning of the winter solstice, the shortest day of the year. On that day it doesn't get light until after eight and the sun disappears well before four in the Northwest.

The Jacques' house in Maple Valley, Washington, was set far back from Wax Road in a forest of tall fir trees. Usually Pat didn't feel isolated; their property was ideal for raising children. Now her three—Steve, 7; David, 5; and Diane, 3—were wired with excitement over having a Christmas tree with packages underneath. Patricia had managed to corral them and sit them in front of the television to watch cartoons.

Hoping she had a free fifteen minutes or so, she headed for the kitchen to fix supper. When she glanced out the window it was so dark that it might as well have been midnight. The rain lashing at the windows made it seem as if their house was in a black cocoon. In the daytime, it was easier to see neighbors' homes, although they were a good distance down Wax Road. When it got dark, she sometimes felt as if they were all alone. Still, Pat was never afraid. The very fact that they *were* so far from heavily populated areas helped to keep street crimes and burglars away.

ANN RULE

Pat was reaching into the refrigerator when she was startled to hear a loud knock on the front door. Her first thought was that something had happened to her father-in-law. He lived several hundred yards down—and across—the road, and he had recently had a stroke. They all worried about him, and she hurried to answer the door, thinking maybe he was in trouble.

"A man was standing there," she said. "He said there had been an accident and he needed to use the phone. I didn't open the door right away, but he just pushed his way inside. That was when I saw that he was carrying a rifle."

Pat Jacque screamed in alarm. The stranger wasn't very big—but his gun was. She cut her scream short, aware of three little pairs of eyes looking at her from the living room. She didn't want them to be frightened. The man with the gun seemed agitated, and she fought to stay calm so he wouldn't lose control.

The stranger asked where her husband was, and she lied, telling him that her husband was right next door at his father's house—and that he was due home any minute.

"You'd better leave before my husband gets home," she warned, trying to frighten him into leaving.

"I'll wait," the man said. "I need to be someplace, and he's gonna drive me."

Pat's children were afraid, and they began to sob. She asked if she could take them to their bedrooms, and the intruder agreed. But he insisted on following them down the narrow hall to be sure she wasn't headed to a back door.

She whispered to the children, telling them to be very quiet and not to open the bedroom door. "Everything will be all right," she promised, although she had no way of knowing whether it would.

Once her children were a wall away from the gun,

Pat's mind raced frantically to find a way for them all to survive. She would do whatever she had to do to keep them safe. At this point, she still hoped that she could persuade the man to leave. Maybe he would take money or whatever he wanted and just go away.

She studied the man who held the rifle. He certainly didn't look menacing. He looked a little like an Irish leprechaun, with fine features and big ears that stuck out. He had black hair, combed in careful waves, and he wore glasses. He was short and thin, and she wondered if she might be strong enough to actually overpower him. But she knew men were stronger than women, and she dismissed that idea quickly.

He wore a plaid shirt and work pants, and he paced around her house, asking questions. Even though it was a cold night, he was perspiring heavily.

The stranger asked Pat if she had a radio, and she took him to the kitchen and pointed to the small radio there. He carried it back to the living room and plugged it in next to the television set.

He both watched and listened to the evening news broadcasts, but apparently there was nothing on that interested him. He kept turning the radio dial and switching television channels. "Something's wrong," he said, shaking his head in disbelief. "There should have been something by now."

Then he looked up at Pat Jacque and said, "You screamed when I came in. You know about me, don't you? You've heard about me?"

"I don't know what you're talking about," she said firmly. "I have no idea who you are or what you're doing here."

"You know, all right."

"No," she said truthfully. "I *don't* know. I've been here

with my children all day, and I haven't had the radio on and all that's been on the TV is cartoons. I don't even know your name."

"You can call me Denny," he said.

She looked around the room covertly, looking for possibilities of escape. If she had to, she could take the children out through the bedroom window. But "Denny" never left her side; he stayed within a foot or so from her, constantly.

It made her more nervous the way he kept emptying and reloading the rifle. He asked her if she knew anything about guns, and she told him she didn't.

"See that wall behind your head? This will make a mighty big hole in that wall. Don't make any noise, because it's cocked and ready."

Now she was more afraid. Her children weren't really safe in their room. And she was scared to death that one of them would come out to see where she was. She prayed silently that they would obey her, this most important time of all.

"What does your husband look like?"

"He's big—tall and pretty muscular. He works in construction."

"What kind of a car does he drive? What's he gonna do when he comes in and finds me here in his house?"

She lied to him about the make of car, too. Pat knew that her husband, Roy, would probably try to jump on the stranger and take the gun away from him. She was afraid of a struggle in which Roy might get shot. If he had any warning at all that Denny was inside, Roy could take him easily—but if he just walked in unaware . . .

The minutes crawled by.

Pat continued to speak gently to the gunman. It quieted him down quite a bit, and she tried to use whatever worked. He seemed very unhappy, and he told her that he had a lot of problems in his romantic life.

"People are interfering with my life," he said bitterly. "You can't trust anybody."

He was alternately sorry for himself and threatening, and he kept glancing at the television set as if he expected some major news bulletin to flash across the screen at any moment.

Pat's overwhelming purpose was to get him out of her house. She didn't want him there when Roy came in, and she could hear her children beginning to whimper. That was making him more jittery.

Finally, Pat suggested that Denny take *her* car so that he wouldn't have to wait for her husband to drive him.

"I won't call anyone," she said.

He gave her a look, and sarcastically said, "I'll bet you won't."

It rained harder, and Pat Jacque froze every time she heard the sound of a car out on the street. She longed to have her husband there to protect them, but she was so afraid he would be shot and wounded—or killed.

And so they waited. She tried not to suggest too many alternatives for Denny because that seemed to make him antsy, too. But she took her car keys from her purse and put them where he could see them.

Pat's captor was telling the truth when he said that other people were interfering with his life. He had taken care of that earlier in the day and only now was beginning to panic about what he had done.

Almost three years earlier, he had met the woman who was to become both his obsession and his frustration. Her name was Cherie Mullins*, and she was a buxom blonde in her thirties, who worked as a nurse's aide. Denny Lee

Tuohmy* and Cherie Mullins were immediately attracted to each other, and early on their relationship seemed wonderful.

Cherie and Denny began living together in April, 32 months before he crashed into Pat Jacque's home. They took a long trip to California, and it was like a honeymoon, with no responsibilities and no worries about jobs or money. It didn't even matter that Denny was still married to another woman and their trip couldn't be a real honeymoon. The trouble began when they returned to regular, everyday life.

They moved into a small cabin in a trailer park, and Cherie became the breadwinner in the household. Denny's resistance to getting a job was one of the biggest sore points for Cherie.

"I wanted him to get a job and be a decent, upright human being," Cherie said later. "I wanted him to see about getting his divorce through. I told him if he ever hit me, I was finished. Then he hit me in November, and I had two broken ribs. I left that night, but then I went back for my things and he begged me to stay and I felt sorry for him, so I stayed; but only for about a week. He was using my car to date other women."

It was the all-too-familiar pattern of domestic violence: Denny was so pathetic when Cherie left him that she truly believed he was going to change. But a few weeks after she came back to him, he returned to his old behavior.

What started in April as bliss ended in early December. The couple separated, and Denny moved to Seattle but continued to call Cherie every day.

For a few weeks, Cherie moved in with her mother, Gladys Bodine, in Kent, 20 miles southeast of Seattle and not far from Maple Valley.

But Cherie couldn't bring herself to separate completely from Denny. Part of it was that she really did care for him, and part of it was that she felt sorry for him. But she was also afraid of him. Like many women who are hounded and stalked by men who won't let go, Cherie made the mistake of leaving the door slightly open.

"We were partners in a mixed-doubles bowling league, and I told Denny I would continue to bowl with him on Friday nights," Cherie recalled. "He kept calling me at work, wanting to see me, to ask how I was; sometimes he just wanted to borrow my car.

It was Friday the 13th when Cherie had what was to be her last date with Denny. "He came out to Kent, and we went bowling," she said. "Afterwards, he asked me to drive him into Seattle. We sat and talked in the parking lot for a long time. He wanted me to go back with him."

Cherie wanted to be back together, too, but she wanted things to be different. She laid down some rules. "I told him again if he'd get a job and support me, I would go back to him."

After she told Denny what she needed to make a relationship work, she drove him back to Seattle. Apparently, he had intended that they would return to intimacy that very night, and he was angry that he had to prove himself to her. When they were halfway to Seattle, somewhere in Tukwila, he asked Cherie to pull over and park. She agreed. "But he kept arguing, and I told him I had to get home to my mother's house because she went to bed early and she didn't like to have me come in late."

The truth was that Cherie no longer lived with her mother, but she didn't want Denny to know the address of her new apartment. If he thought she was with her mother, he'd be lulled into believing that he could always locate her when wanted to.

"I just didn't want him to know where I was living."

Denny's mood changed rapidly, and he turned to her and said a strange thing in a flat, monotone voice: "You won't have to worry about your mother. You won't have to worry about tomorrow. Neither will I. We'll both be dead."

That frightened Cherie. Denny could be a lot of fun, but when he was in his depressed or angry moods, she didn't know for sure what he might do. "I *was* scared then," she remembered. "I told him I loved him and asked him how could he hurt someone who loved him, and the *only* one who loved him? He looked up at a hill nearby where a cross was lighted up on a church, and then he shouted, 'Damn you God! Damn you!' "

Then he seemed to calm down, and Cherie started the car and drove him into Seattle.

Pat Jacque didn't know any of Denny's background. As far as she was concerned, she was dealing with a man who had no past at all.

Denny was getting more nervous, pacing like a lion and pulling the curtains back more frequently to see if anyone was coming. He kept shaking his head when she begged him to take her car and leave. He didn't trust her at all.

And then he turned to her and said, "You will have to drive me."

It was a terrible decision that would have taken the wisdom of Solomon to determine. If she went with him, her children would be safe from him, at least. But then again, they were so young. She never left them alone, even to run across the street. There were so many dangerous things little kids could get into. Worse, if they wandered out to the road looking for her, they might be hit by a car coming along Wax Road. What if the house caught fire? What if they fell—or got into poisonous cleaning supplies? Mothers always worry about things like that. Most are nervous even with baby-sitters.

But she had to get the man with the gun out of her house, and Pat prayed that Roy would be home soon. At age 7, Steve *might* be able to tell his father what had happened. She hoped that somehow Roy would find her.

Wondering if she would ever see her family again, Pat Jacque stepped from the warmth of her home into the icy drizzle of December rain. Denny motioned for her to get in the driver's seat. "You drive," he ordered. "I'll be right behind you."

The lights of her house faded quickly from her rearview mirror as Pat drove. Denny sat right behind her with the .303 aimed at the back of her head.

Denny Tuohmy directed her precisely. "Turn here. Now here." He knew where he wanted to go, but Pat didn't know if they were headed for a deserted gravel pit where he was going to shoot her and kill her or were about to take off on a 150-mile drive to Canada. She kept hoping that her husband would come home and the kids would be safe. Somehow, she knew Roy *would* find her—if she could just stay alive.

Cherie Mullins had heard from Denny several times on December 19 and 20. On Thursday evening, he had called her at a beauty parlor where she worked part time. It was 6:20 P.M., and she was having her hair done. It made her nervous that he always seemed to be able to track her down. He wanted to borrow her car to drive to Tacoma.

"I told him I was busy and I needed my car. And I couldn't drive him down, either. I almost begged him to leave me alone."

He did not call again that night, but at 8:30 the next morning, Friday, December 20, just as Cherie walked into the nursing home where she worked, the phone was ringing. It was Denny again. He still wanted a ride to Tacoma. He asked her again to borrow her car or to have her drive him.

Cherie was exasperated. "I told him I was working, and not to call me at work again or I would lose my job."

"Is everything all right?" Denny's voice softened as he asked her that.

"Yes—but I'm *working,* Denny," she said in a kinder tone.

"Do you still love me?" he asked.

". . . Yes."

"Will you go to Tacoma with me after work?"

"I can't, Denny—"

"I'll be there anyway," he said. She didn't know what he meant. Would he be in Tacoma? Or was he coming to the nursing home?

Cherie went about her Friday morning duties at work, but she got another personal call. It was her mother's next-door neighbor.

The woman said that all the lights in Gladys Bodine's house were on—even the outside Christmas lights. They'd been on all night, she thought. Gladys's car was in the driveway, and her dog was barking in the house. But no one would answer the door.

Cherie made arrangements to leave work immediately and drove hurriedly to her mother's home. With the help of neighbors, she tried every door. They were all locked. A neighbor finally crawled through a side window and opened the front door for Cherie.

She walked through the quiet rooms, filled with a dread she couldn't really explain. She tried to tell herself that her mother could take care of herself. She was only 58, and she was almost six feet tall and weighed about 180 pounds. It wasn't likely some burglar could hurt her mother.

"I checked the front bedroom, but my mother wasn't there," Cherie said. And then she saw her mother's bedroom slipper lying in the back hallway.

Slowly, Cherie walked toward the rear of the house. Then she saw two feet sticking out through the back bedroom door. Her mother was lying on her back next to the bed, and two jackets had been tucked around her head.

"I pulled the jackets away from her face, but then I saw she was dead," Cherie Mullins recalled with a sob.

She was too shocked to try to figure out how her mother had died, and she ran to call the police.

Cherie was afraid she knew who had killed her mother, but it was too terrible to think about. King County sheriff's detectives worked the crime scene in Gladys Bodine's home on that Friday, but they made sure that the local news media wouldn't know about the case right away. For the moment, the investigators had a few hours' head start before a suspect might be spooked by being on the news.

Cherie Mullins didn't hear from Denny again that Friday, but she kept remembering how he had told her that she didn't have to worry about anything any more. She would be dead and he would be dead—but he hadn't mentioned anything about her mother. Of course, Denny resented her mother sometimes. Gladys Bodine hadn't found him a perfect mate for her daughter, and sometimes she warned Cherie that she was getting in too deep with him, and she could do better.

But she'd always felt so sorry for him because he hadn't had much happiness in his life. He and his two older brothers had been deserted by their mother and had gone from foster home to foster home. They were eventually placed in a Roman Catholic home for boys near Portland, Oregon. Denny stayed there several years before he was released to his father. That didn't work out either, and in his mid-teens he'd been placed in the Luther Burbank school for boys on Mercer Island, Washington. It wasn't a reform school, but it *was* for teenagers who had deep problems.

Denny ran away from Luther Burbank, and when they caught up with him, he was given a choice of going to a state reform school or joining the Army. Denny chose the Army.

He didn't do well in the service. He had a violent temper, and Cherie knew he'd been in trouble and had a dishonorable discharge, but she didn't know all the details. In fact, for the Army at least, his decision was not a happy choice. Once, while he was in the stockade for being intoxicated, Tuohmy took a gun away from a guard and beat him over the head with it. When a superior officer was called, the defendant attacked him, too. Taken to a prison hospital, Tuohmy had insisted that he had no memory of the events.

Cherie had seen his temper, but she just couldn't believe he would hurt her mother. She didn't want to believe that.

Pat Jacque didn't know about Gladys Bodine, or anything about Denny's past. Perhaps it was better that she didn't. After circling through the woods for a long time, they parked in back of a house—which was actually within a few miles of her own.

Three boys came out of the house and said, "Hi, Uncle Denny. What is it? Why do you have that gun?"

"I'm serious," Denny told the youngsters. "I mean business."

Surprised, the boys looked at Pat, and she nodded and said softly, "He really means it."

Denny Tuohmy's brother lived in this house, and once more Denny was set on getting to Tacoma, which was less than 20 miles away. He said he wanted his brother to drive him there. But his elder brother wasn't home.

For a moment, Pat Jacque felt relief. If he wanted to have his brother drive him, maybe that meant she would be allowed to go home. It was a bizarre experience. She sat there with his nephews and Denny in a silent tableau and waited. Denny balanced the high-powered rifle across his knees, ready for use.

Pat Jacque asked if she could use the bathroom, and Denny allowed her to go, but he followed her, and kept talking to her constantly through the door to be sure that she didn't try to escape out the window. Of course, she *had* thought of that, but she didn't think she could make it out and away before he came around the house and caught her.

Even though it was December, the room where they waited seemed to grow warmer with Denny's anger and frustration. His brother finally came home, but he was furious when he saw the gun. He ordered Denny out of the house and told him to take the gun with him. Denny refused. He insisted that his brother should drive him where he wanted to go.

The scene was getting more hysterical all the time. Denny's sister-in-law was pregnant and was due within a few days, and she became so upset that she started having labor pains. At this point, Pat realized she was more worried for the other woman than she was for herself. She was afraid that Denny was going to hurt his sister-in-law, because he was getting so infuriated with her, but he quieted down.

Denny's family apparently assumed that Pat was with Denny by choice, and that she was his girlfriend. Should she tell them that he'd kidnapped her? No. That might set him off. All she could do was sit there and watch this absolutely unreal spectacle take place.

Their conversation turned to family problems, and then the sister-in-law said suddenly, "Gladys is dead. They found her this morning, and they think she was strangled."

Instantly she got a frightened look on her face, as if she knew she'd said the wrong thing. She backed up, saying, "No, no, that's not right. They think she died of a heart attack."

Pat had no idea who Gladys was, but she saw Denny's face change when her name came up. She could tell that he didn't believe the second version of the news about Gladys.

Pat felt as if she had come in during the middle of some horror film. She didn't know what any of them were talking about, and she tried to concentrate on how she could get away from Denny while there were still people around.

Now Pat Jacque was finally able to put the pieces together. This was why Denny had been so curious about the news. This was why he had said, "You know about me, don't you?"

At the time, she truthfully had had no idea what he was talking about. But now Pat thought about what she had heard on the radio during the noon news. There had been a brief mention of a woman who had been found murdered in Kent, but it meant nothing to Pat. Not then. Now it did. She had a terrible feeling that Denny had murdered Gladys. Pat didn't know whether Gladys was his girlfriend or his wife or *who*. She had been scared before, but now she realized that she was being held captive by a man who was probably a killer. She tried to concentrate on the conversation to get some clue about Gladys.

Denny kept telling his sister-in-law that he didn't know anything about what happened to Gladys.

Denny Tuohmy's brother didn't catch on that Pat Jacque was an unwilling hostage. He refused once more to drive his brother anywhere, saying, "You've got a car and a woman; drive yourself."

By this time, Pat's gas gauge was on empty, and she didn't have any money with her. If they left in her car, it was going to stall on some back-country road. She mentioned that, hoping Denny's brother would change his mind. Instead, he wrote out a check for $5.00 and told them the location of a gas station where they could cash it.

Numbly, Pat watched Denny tuck the check in his pocket and stand up. He signaled to her to lead the way to the door. She followed him, sure that she had lost all hope of rescue.

Once again, Pat Jacque was alone with him, hurtling over rural roads in the pitch-black night, the .303 rifle aimed at her head. Following his directions, she eventually turned onto the Kent-Kangley Road.

Feeling even more desperate, she happened to glance up at her rearview mirror and saw the headlights of a car moving up right behind them. She waited for it to pass, thinking she might be able to flash her lights or give some signal, but it stayed with them.

Then Denny saw the lights in the mirror, and he turned around to watch the car. As he did, it dropped back. He told Pat to drive very, very carefully. But if she noticed a car with a blue light, or heard a siren, she was to "step on it."

A few moments later, she *did* hear the wail of a siren and saw a flashing blue light in the rearview mirror.

"Turn right and speed up," Denny ordered in a tight voice.

She did as he said, but suddenly there were cars with flashing lights all around them. Denny poked the gun at her back and told her to floor the accelerator.

She was going so much faster that she was afraid to look at the dashboard and check her speed. She felt as if she would lose control of her car at any time, and they would all be killed.

"I just can't go any further," Pat cried.

She was completely terrified, and her arms and feet felt leaden, but he screamed at her to keep driving. She expected Denny to start shooting at the patrol cars, and she knew that she was in the way. He would probably blow her head off when he fired at the cars ahead of and beside them.

Expertly, the sheriff's officers slowed their speed, forcing Pat to slow hers. She had no place to go but to the shoulder of the road, and there was a deep ditch just beside it.

Her car was forced off the road, and she stomped on the brake frantically, coming to a stop just inches from a ditch.

Pat would remember this moment for the rest of her life. "An officer waved at me to get out, but I was afraid to move," she said. "Then other officers came around on the right and opened the door and pulled Denny out. Someone opened my door and I got out."

She could barely stand, but she was grateful to simply be alive. She began to believe that she *would* see her family again—that there would be a Christmas.

"Are my children all right?" she begged one of the county patrolmen.

He smiled and said, "They're fine. Your husband is with them."

Roy Jacque had come home shortly before eight. "I came in the back door, and there were three little kids all lined up, with great big eyes and trying hard not to cry. They said, 'Mommy went away with a man with a gun.' I knew Pat would never have left the children alone if she had a choice, or left without a note. I called the King County sheriff."

Jacque had spent truly desperate hours waiting for some word of his wife, imagining what might be happening to her and trying not to let his thoughts go that way.

Alerted first by Roy Jacque and next by Tuohmy's

brother—who *had* realized that something was wrong—the sheriff's patrol units had converged in the Kent area, blocking every road leading from town. They were looking for the Jacques' Ford station wagon, and their radios were alive with chatter as they kept in touch.

Reserve officers Kent and French first observed the vehicle on Sweeney Road near Wilderness Corner, and they immediately put that information on the air. Detective Sergeant Dave Urban had been taking a report from the defendant's brother when the call crackled over his radio. He immediately drove to the area where the car had been sighted and spotted it on the road ahead of him. Urban followed the Ford station wagon for three miles, coming up close and then dropping back for fear he would be spotted by Denny Tuohmy. It was when the two vehicles eased onto the Benson Road and Kent-Kangley intersection that he knew he had to move. The fugitive was forcing his captive into a more heavily populated area.

"I turned on my siren, but there was no response," Urban recalled. "Then I pulled alongside it with my bubble lights going and the siren blowing—but Mrs. Jacque just speeded up. I then proceeded to force the car off to the shoulder of the road. My car was parked diagonally in front of the Jacque vehicle and I left by the driver's door, crouching low with my revolver out, and moved around the back of my car. I motioned to Mrs. Jacque to get out. Then Kent and French pulled in behind the station wagon and came up on the passenger side, where they pulled Tuohmy out."

The powerful rifle was lying on the seat between Pat Jacque and Denny Tuohmy. It was turned over to Sheriff's Sergeant John McGowan and Detective George Helland. Helland found that it was loaded with five shells in the magazine and one in the firing chamber.

Pat Jacque went home to comfort her children and

count her blessings. Denny Tuohmy was taken at once to King County Sheriff's headquarters in the downtown Seattle courthouse building. There, Lieutenant Leonard Givens advised him of his rights under Miranda.

He was the prime suspect in the murder of Gladys Bodine, but no one yet knew everything Denny Tuohmy had done during the previous 30 hours. There were big gaps in time between Thursday evening and his capture late Friday night.

The investigators noted that he did not smell of alcohol and didn't appear to be under the influence of drugs.

Denny Tuohmy's state of mind as he sat in the interview room would become very important. Lieutenant Givens recalled that he had found Tuohmy "calm and lucid."

He said he was hungry, and he sipped coffee and ate sandwiches provided by the jail kitchen as he talked to Givens and Detective Ted Forrester.

Tuohmy had expressly asked that Ted Forrester be present as he was interrogated. Forrester had spoken to Tuohmy several months earlier when he was investigating reports of some minor family fights. Now, Tuohmy looked upon him as a friend; the presence of the easygoing, kind detective put him at ease. And Forrester was a man who really cared about people—although, admittedly, killers were not on the top of his list.

Despite the Miranda warnings, Tuohmy seemed anxious to talk to the two detectives. Maybe he needed to ease his conscience. Maybe he relished the attention. Or, as he would claim much later, maybe he *was* mentally ill and didn't understand the consequences of what he had done.

As he spoke, Givens and Forrester thought it was a miracle, indeed, that Pat Jacque had survived her ordeal without being injured or killed.

Later, Tuohmy signed his confession. He prefaced his

unburdening by telling them how he had tried to get back with Cherie. He felt that other people were deliberately trying to break up their relationship, and he had gone to talk with her and with her mother, Gladys, on the morning of December 19. He believed that Cherie was living there, but realized she had lied to him. She had moved away to be free of him.

Cherie had already left to get her hair done when Denny got to her mother's house in Kent very early in the morning, long before it was light out.

"On December 19," Denny Tuohmy's statement began, "I walked and ran down to Gladys Bodine's. I went to see Cherie Mullins. Gladys came to the door in a robe and said, 'Hi, Denny,' and I said, 'Hi, Gladys.' I asked her if she had some coffee, and she went to the kitchen to warm some up. She told me Cherie didn't live there any more. I told her I wanted all three of us to get together and talk. I kept talking to Gladys, but I wasn't getting the right answers—not the answers Cherie had given me. I put my arm under her chin. She said, 'Denny, please let me go and I'll give you the right answers.' I moved toward the back bedroom and laid her down. One hand moved. Then I got scared and I left by the back door."

It seemed impossible that Tuohmy had been able to overpower Gladys Bodine so easily. The detectives knew that she was almost six feet tall and had outweighed him by about 40 pounds. And yet, they had seen her body, and she had been brutally strangled.

"I went downtown and had a few beers with [my friend] Fritz Donohue," Tuohmy continued. "I rested in his car for a while alone, and then he came out and we went to his place to sleep. I stayed up and I tried to call Cherie at 8:15, then 8:30. I went down to my sister-in-law's car and got my rifle and my bowling ball. Then I went home and packed my clothes to go to Cherie's house in Kent and see if she would go to California with me. I called Fritz to take me to Cherie's nursing home on the West Valley Highway near the Smith Brothers' Dairy. He said he would if he didn't have to work overtime; he'd be by at 3:15."

Apparently, Fritz had kept his promise to Denny, and he had come home to pick him up around three in the afternoon. The next part of the confession was a complete surprise to the detectives.

"We went out to Kent and missed turns and came to a bridge where we couldn't go any further. We started to back up, and then decided to get out of the car and relieve ourselves. I said, 'Hey, Fritz, I want to show you something.' He looked at the rifle and said, 'Yeah, your gun.'

"I carried the rifle in my right hand. I remember my foot slipping. The rifle went off and I saw a shadow moving. I got scared and tried to start the car. It wouldn't start, so I ran through the woods and the branches slapped me in the face."

Denny seemed to be telling them in an oblique way that he had shot Fritz. But there hadn't been any reports of a dead man found near Kent. Was he only saying that he had left his friend in the woods with a broken-down car?

Givens looked at Denny to see if he was making a bad joke or if he was tricking them. But he seemed rational enough, so Givens immediately detailed a patrol car to search the area for Fritz Donohue.

"Our prisoner says that he's lying out there somewhere, wounded."

At this point, Fritz Donohue's fate was in limbo. Radio had received a complaint from a couple who lived in the south end of the county. They reported that an older model car was parked at the end of the road past their home with its lights on. Hours passed, and still the car sat there with its lights burning. Near midnight, when no one had approached the car, the couple called the sheriff's office. The deputies sent there walked toward the abandoned car.

Fritz Donohue had been found. He lay on the frozen ground, his left leg outstretched and his right leg under it, crossed at the knee. His sightless eyes gazed up at nothing, and the ground beneath his head was soaked with blood.

Working in the icy early morning rain, detectives brought in floodlights and took triangulation measurements so that later they could tell exactly where the victim's body had lain and where evidence was found. They marked the scene off into grids, looking for the spent bullet casing from a .303 Britisher bullet, like the bullets in Tuohmy's gun. They finally found it 43 feet from the car. Carefully, they checked to see if the victim's car would start, and it wouldn't turn over. So far, Tuohmy's information was accurate.

Fritz Donohue, a small man like the suspect, was finally removed from the crime scene and taken to the morgue to await autopsy.

The postmortem exam of Gladys Bodine's body began first. Dr. Gale Wilson described the procedure in his report, as he would in trial testimony one day.

"The deceased was a woman of 58, 5'10" tall and weighing 174 pounds. Her face was livid, her lips blue," the pathologist dictated. "A large number of petechiae—small reddish spots resembling paprika and resulting from rupture of capillaries—were evident on her forehead, cheeks, lips, within the small vessels of her brain, the left strap muscle of her throat, her larynx, and her heart."

Since most laymen have never heard of petechiae, Wilson explained further. "These result from the damming of capillaries which burst from prolonged pressure. The whole picture is one of manual strangulation. There are two rounded depressions on the right forehead and concurrent hemorrhaging in the brain itself, but no skull fracture. The hemorrhages in the neck area are of the type caused by *fingers*.

"To make marks on the neck like this, it requires a great deal of pressure. The victim would have lost consciousness in 15 or 20 seconds. I would say she was clinically dead in a couple of minutes. In my opinion the person strangling Mrs. Bodine would have had to apply steady pressure for at least two minutes. She died at approximately 7 P.M. on December 19, 1963."

Gladys had been dead since Thursday evening, but her daughter had had no inkling of the horror in her mother's house when Denny Tuohmy called her as she arrived at work Friday morning. Now she understood why he had asked her if anything was wrong, and wanted to be sure that she still loved him. In all likelihood, he had strangled her mother the night before. He must have been checking to see if she knew about her mother's murder yet.

Dr. Wilson performed the autopsy on Fritz Donohue's body next. It was still early on Saturday morning, December 21.

"Donohue was a man of 39, 5'7" tall, weighing 135 pounds. His body showed a large caliber gunshot entry wound just in front of the left ear canal. The bullet passed horizontally through the base of the skull and emerged through the right ear. The skull in these cases is so fragmented that the head feels like popcorn in a bag, the whole head has a putty-like feeling. There were no other injuries."

Dr. Wilson felt that the location of the single bullet wound was consistent with a bullet fired by a person holding his gun to his shoulder and aiming carefully. "Assuming the victim was standing up, the bullet traveled horizontally, approximately five feet above the ground."

The only other alternative would be more damning for Denny Tuohmy. He would have had to aim straight down at a victim lying on the ground. That was not, however, consistent with Tuohmy's height. He was too short to have held the gun far above Fritz's head, and the entry wound didn't have the characteristic powder burns and gun barrel debris of a near-contact wound.

Denny Tuohmy was arrested and charged with murder in the deaths of Gladys Bodine and Fritz Donohue.

Cherie Mullins visited him in jail on Christmas Eve, not because she felt affection for him but because she was completely stunned and shocked, and full of questions.

She found that Tuohmy was quite clearheaded. "But he seemed sad and tired. I looked at him and I said, 'Why Denny, why?' and he said, 'I don't know, Mama,' and I said, 'Do you know what's going to happen to you?' "

Tuohmy's response was with a hand gesture. "He drew his finger across his throat like this."

He would spend the six months following his arrest in the King County Jail. He wrote letters—rational, lucid letters—to relatives and to Cherie Mullins.

The most significant question was this: *Was Denny Tuohmy sane or insane at the time of his crimes?* Under the M'Naughton Rule, the killer must have the ability to perceive reality at the time of the crime and must be able to differentiate between right and wrong in order to go to trial. Defense attorneys worked feverishly to prove that

Tuohmy had been certifiably psychotic when he killed Gladys Bodine and Fritz Donohue *and* when he kidnapped Pat Jacque.

Until his discharge from the Army seven years before these felonies, Denny Lee Tuohmy had spent periodic sojourns in service hospitals. But opinions regarding the cause of his problems differed from one Army psychiatrist to another. One diagnosed his actions as schizophrenic and found him mentally ill.

Yet, there were other excerpts from Army records with different viewpoints on Tuohmy's personality problems. One mental evaluation declared him to be "extremely immature, impulsive, with no insight into his own problems."

Two years after that conclusion, a report read: "No delusions or hallucinations. Inability to postpone gratification. This man cannot profit from punishment or experience. Hopeless to treat. Probably will be life-long."

That psychiatrist may have been right on the mark.

Dishonorably discharged from the service, Denny Lee Tuohmy had spent his next seven years working sporadically and getting into minor skirmishes with the law that landed him behind bars from time to time.

The winter rains were long gone on May 28 when Tuohmy talked with Dr. Richard B. Jarvis, a Seattle psychiatrist who testified frequently in criminal cases. Jarvis made a startlingly accurate prediction in his summary of that interview.

"It is quite possible that during the course of the trial, Mr. Tuohmy may become angry and lose his temper. This is not evidence of mental disease but of his inability to hold his temper."

Days later, Denny Tuohmy appeared in King County Superior Court Judge Eugene Wright's courtroom for a preliminary hearing. Although he had an attorney to represent him, Tuohmy rose and asked to address the court. He insisted upon a change of venue, demanded that witnesses be kept in the hallway before testimony, and refused the judge's request that he sit down and remain quiet.

All witnesses were routinely required to stay outside the courtroom until they had testified, and there hadn't been enough publicity to warrant a change of venue. Tuohmy seemed to enjoy hearing himself talk.

When admonished by the judge again, he shouted that he would not sit still for what he considered a "travesty of justice" and announced that he was going back to jail. And then, the slight, wiry Tuohmy launched an attack that has not been forgotten by either those present in that courtroom or by King County sheriff's deputies. Screaming like an animal, Denny Tuohmy picked up the heavy tables in front of the bar and threw them across the room at the judge as if they were toothpicks.

Deputies—many weighing over 200 pounds—rushed to subdue him. In the words of a witness, "He bounced them off the wall. Blood was drawn, but it wasn't Tuohmy's."

While women spectators screamed and raced for the comparative safety of the hallway, more and more deputies ran into the courtroom. They threw shoulder blocks on Tuohmy, trying to stop him without hurting him, but he continued his rampage. The court reporter, hunched over his machine in an attempt to avoid the flying debris, recorded the incredible melee.

Eventually, it took eleven deputies to pin down Denny Lee Tuohmy.

As a result of his display in Judge Wright's court, Tuohmy was found incompetent to stand trial and was committed to the Eastern Washington State Hospital.

Throughout his stay at the facility, located in Medical Lake, Tuohmy continued to perplex psychiatric personnel. Some found him to be a psychopathic personality, sane but without the normal restraints of conscience of the average person. Some speculated that he was indeed schizophrenic. Twice, he walked away from the grounds but returned without incident. Whatever his state of mind, patients and attendants alike feared him.

On two occasions, Tuohmy repeated his familiar pattern of violence and held off a score of hospital attendants with weapons fashioned from a floor mop and his own dismantled steel bed. He attempted to strangle fellow patients and threatened them with homosexual attacks.

Eventually, the day came when psychiatrists in the state mental hospital declared that Denny Tuohmy was no longer insane—if he ever had been insane—and was competent to stand trial. Almost eight years had gone by, and it wasn't at all difficult to pick a jury. Nobody in Seattle remembered him—except, perhaps, for Cherie Mullins, Fritz Donohue's relatives and friends, and, of course, Pat Jacque, who would never forget him.

King County deputies who had worked courtroom security remembered him, too. They double-staffed the trial in Superior Court Judge George Stuntz's courtroom.

Denny Tuohmy seemed calm enough. The short, almost frail-looking defendant smiled benignly at the jury.

On that sunny, crisp morning of January 11, court habitués who had heard this might be an interesting trial filed in. Some of the old-timers who lived in drab hotels around the courthouse had attended so many trials that prosecutors and defense attorneys alike valued their perspective and occasionally asked, "How do you think it's going?" in one trial or another. The "expert" legal advisers in the gallery had learned to bring cushions, since the wooden benches became hard as rock by the afternoon sessions.

* * *

Judge George Stuntz had a reputation for being peppery and taking no nonsense, so his trials always drew extra court-watchers. They would not be disappointed. Stuntz ran a tight ship. Still, tempers flared and old hatreds among witnesses revived as special prosecutors Paul M. Acheson and Darrell E. Lee and defense attorney Anthony Savage, Jr., elicited testimony.

The opposing attorneys had the most astute minds in criminal law in the county. Paul Acheson, who had resigned his position as assistant chief criminal deputy on January 1 to form a law partnership with two other winning ex-prosecutors, William Kinzel and C. N. (Nick) Marshall, had prosecuted over 200 felony cases during his tenure in the prosecutor's office. He and Darrell Lee, another former assistant prosecutor, had been rehired to prosecute this case, which they had spent so many years preparing.

Tony Savage, arguably the top criminal defense attorney in Seattle, had been appointed to defend Denny Tuohmy, who was now 36, by the office of the public defender. Savage was a most worthy opponent. He too had once been assistant chief criminal deputy in the prosecuting attorney's office.

Tony Savage was totally against the death penalty. He always would be. Some thirty years later, an older—and grayer—Savage would be appointed to defend Gary Ridgway, the man accused of being the infamous Green River Killer. Savage would be just as adamantly against the death penalty as he was when he was a young attorney.

In his opening statement, special prosecutor Acheson recalled the grim events of December 19 and 20, for the jury. He said the defendant had confessed to King County detectives that he had strangled Mrs. Gladys Bodine, 58, in her Kent home because he believed she had broken up his romance with her daughter.

The next day, Tuohmy had driven to a desolate road outside Kent and "accidentally" shot his best friend in the head. Fred Garfield "Fritz" Donohue, a hospital orderly, had been found with his skull literally "blasted to small fragments." Tuohmy's initial confessions had been enhanced, however, Acheson said, when he told a detective he had committed both murders "on purpose."

After shooting Donohue, Tuohmy had admitted that he ran through the densely wooded Kent area with his rifle and forced his way into the home of Mrs. Patricia Jacque. He had threatened her with the powerful gun and forced her to drive him from her house, leaving her three young children behind.

With the rifle aimed at her head, Mrs. Jacque had been forced to drive a meandering route through the back roads of South King County until she was rescued uninjured by several sheriff's deputies, who forced her automobile off the road and disarmed Tuohmy.

Defense attorney Tony Savage, who had entered a plea for his client of innocent by reason of insanity at the time of his crimes, told the jurors that his client was mentally ill and that there would be no evidence from the state to show premeditation—an essential factor in proving first-degree murder.

"From the day Denny Tuohmy was born, he lived anything but a happy life," Savage told the jury, and the eloquent attorney promised that he would produce lengthy records supporting his contention that Denny Tuohmy was, and had been, a schizophrenic for many years. With voluminous medical and Army records, and with testimony from the defendant's family, he would attempt to show that Tuohmy had acted as a man medically and legally insane. The diminutive defendant viewed the proceedings with equanimity as Tony Savage rose to present the case for the defense.

The most difficult questions facing the jury were whether Denny Lee Tuohmy had been legally insane in December seven years before. Was he unable to distinguish right from wrong at the time he killed Gladys Bodine and Fritz Donohue?

There is no machine, no recording device, no computer that can accurately evaluate the condition of the human mind at a specific time in the past. The jurors who would decide Tuohmy's fate would have to rely on testimony from friends and relatives who knew the defendant before and after his crimes, testimony from strangers who dealt with him during that period, and testimony of expert witnesses in the field of psychiatry.

Three questions had to be answered by the statements of witnesses: (1) Was Denny Lee Tuohmy legally insane at the time of the murders, insane during his stay at Eastern State Hospital, and still insane at the time of his trial, or had he recovered to a point where he could move freely within society? (2) Was Denny Lee Tuohmy legally sane at the time of the crimes, and had he only succumbed to mental illness in the aftermath? (3) Was Denny Lee Tuohmy legally sane at the time of his crimes, and had he, as some experts speculated, faked a schizophrenic reaction to avoid being tried?

Special prosecutor Darrell Lee called Cherie Mullins, the dead woman's daughter, to the stand. Answering his questions, she related the ups and downs of her affair with Tuohmy.

"Did you hear from him on December 19?" Lee asked.

"At about six that evening—he called me, and wanted to borrow my car. I told him to leave me alone."

"Did you ever see your mother alive or talk to your mother after that phone call?"

"No."

Cherie described the phone call she had received from the defendant the next morning at the nursing home where she worked.

"Did you see Denny Tuohmy after your mother's death?"

She explained her visit to him in jail on Christmas Eve, when she hoped to get some answers.

"When you found her, did you see marks on your mother's body?"

"No, not then," she answered softly. "Later, at the morgue, I saw that she had black and blue marks on the backs of her hands and on her throat, and her throat was all swollen."

Cherie identified the contents of a suitcase that Denny Tuohmy had taken with him the day after her mother's death. Virtually all of his clothes and possessions had been packed as if he planned an extended trip. She then identified more than a score of letters he had written to her after his arrest. They were not the ravings of a maniac.

The gallery buzzed when Patricia Jacque was called to the stand to tell the jury the chilling story of the hours she had spent with Denny Tuohmy.

Dark-eyed and delicately pretty, Pat had such a soft voice that it needed to be amplified by a microphone. Yet, despite her seeming fragility, Pat Jacque had displayed a backbone of steel when confronted by the gun-wielding stranger. Her children were in danger, and her instincts to protect them were stronger than her own terror.

"When did you first see the defendant, Denny Tuohmy?" Paul Acheson asked.

"I answered the knock at the door," she said, and then related the terrifying hours that began for her, her children, and her husband.

"At any time that the defendant was with you," Acheson queried, "did you notice any odor of intoxicants or drugs?"

"None . . . Never."

"Was his conversation rational? Was he purposeful in his actions?"

"Yes. He had a reason for everything he told me to do."

Pat darted a look at the defendant, where he sat beside his attorney. He smiled at her as if she were an old friend.

It was clear to everyone in the courtroom that Pat Jacque had believed that she wasn't going to survive. She still seemed thankful that she was alive.

Tony Savage bore down heavily on Detective Lieutenant Givens as he asked about Tuohmy's state of mind during his first contact with the detectives, shortly after he was arrested. Givens recalled that they had talked casually at first about the weather and sports events and that Tuohmy had appeared perfectly competent.

"And when you questioned him about Fritz Donohue?" asked the defense attorney.

Givens answered that Tuohmy made complete sense and that he had given excellent instructions about the route they should take to find Fritz, even though he didn't come right out and admit that he had shot Donohue.

The final days of the lengthy trial might be called the "war of the psychiatrists."

Dr. Nicholas Godfroy, called by Savage for the defense, stated unequivocally that Denny Tuohmy had been legally insane at the time of his crimes and was a "schizophrenic, undifferentiated type." Godfroy, who had not interviewed Tuohmy until five months after the murders, insisted nevertheless that he could be positive that Tuohmy had been insane the previous December.

Throughout four hours of cross-examination by prosecutor Acheson, Godfroy remained steadfast in his original diagnosis.

The second defense psychiatrist, S. Harvard Kaufman, had interviewed Tuohmy six years after his crimes. Kaufman, too, said he found the defendant to be a chronic schizophrenic. In cross-examination, prosecutor Darrell Lee asked him, "If you saw a patient five months after a crime, could you state what his condition was at the time of the incident?"

Kaufman replied, "No, there would be no way of knowing."

The first psychiatric witness for the prosecution, Dr. Jack Klein, was questioned by prosecutor Lee. Klein, who had talked to Tuohmy on December 26, six days after the two murders and the kidnapping, found no overt evidence of abnormal mechanisms in the mind.

"I would not have recommended that he be committed."

During rebuttal, Dr. Jarvis, the final witness for the prosecution, said that he had also talked to Denny Tuohmy on December 26. In subsequent years, he had talked to him five more times. Jarvis's basic assumption was that the defendant was a psychopath—or, in current terminology, an antisocial personality.

"If Tuohmy was as disturbed as he claims to have been, close associates would have noticed it. Even strangers would have noticed," Jarvis said flatly. "Nobody saw it."

The day after Christmas, Tuohmy had admitted his crimes to Jarvis, saying he wanted to talk about them. In discussing his capture by sheriff's deputies, he had remarked, "If I'd really wanted to hurt somebody, I could have kicked out the back window and shot the patrol car. I'm not insane, but I will be if things keep going like they have."

One aspect in the marathon courtroom debate on mental illness was brought out by the prosecution. All the psychiatrists agreed that the mere fact that an individual suffered from schizophrenia did not mean that he was unable to differentiate between right and wrong.

Asked if they had ever been "fooled" by a patient mimicking mental illness, each doctor in turn admitted that he was sure he had been.

The time had come for final arguments. Darrell Lee walked to the bar to speak for the prosecution.

"In making your decision on this case, you must operate on a premise of reasonable doubt. A reasonable doubt can be written down: The defendant had a girlfriend; her mother was trying to drive them apart. He went to the woman's house to get the right answers. He knocked her down. He fought her. He choked her. And then he heard her gurgling. He went to her and placed his full weight with his knees on her chest, and as Dr. Wilson says, he choked her for two minutes. He knew Cherie Mullins was not living with her mother, because he called her the minute she arrived at work the next morning. He packed all his clothes. He bought shells for his gun. He called Cherie's place of employment and found she'd already left. He called Fritz Donohue and wanted to go to Kent. He led him up a lonely road— Denny Lee Tuohmy wasn't lost; he knew all those roads, but he wanted a car. He couldn't steal a car. Stolen cars are reported, but not if you kill your best friend and take his car.

"Then the car wouldn't start, so he took his gun and his shells and he ran. Why was the rifle loaded? He picked up that rifle and lifted it to his shoulder. He says that gun fired when he slipped, but the bolt action of that rifle takes many steps. Fritz was 5'7" and that gun was held five feet above the ground. Tuohmy shot him right through the head at a range of four or five feet.

"The defendant once told Cherie Mullins that he had faked insanity in the Army because the hospital was more comfortable than the stockade. Why not then fake insanity again and wait in the hospital in comfort for seven years for witnesses against him to die and disperse?

"You, as jurors, represent King County; you are six women and six men, a cross-section of our community. Capital punishment is an individual question for an individual case. When you think of Denny Lee Tuohmy, consider the safety of state employees, of fellow prisoners, of you and me. Consider what will happen when he escapes . . . because he has a history of escape. Think what it will mean to our fellow citizens if he should make another rampage throughout the county."

Tony Savage was a large, sardonic man with a wry sense of humor, and he lumbered like a bear when he walked. Now, he rose to address the jury for the final time on behalf of his client.

Once again, he recounted the defendant's history of mental aberration.

"It borders on the ridiculous to say these killings were premeditated acts. He strangles the mother so he can resume the relationship with the daughter. That is supposed to be the act of a sane, rational, man? He wants to 'escape' to Tacoma so he can get a divorce from his wife and come back and marry his girlfriend."

Although the defense had contended that Tuohmy had now regained his sanity, Savage conceded, "I'm not suggesting any more than anyone else that you should give him a verdict that will let him walk out the door. But to say you're going to hang a mentally ill person to act as a deterrent for other mentally ill persons just doesn't make sense.

"Do you think this man could fool doctors for nineteen years?"

It was well into Friday evening and other courthouse business had ceased when special prosecutor Paul Acheson began his rebuttal statement. It had been a long, long day for participants and spectators alike, but no one made a move to leave the courtroom.

"The test is whether Tuohmy knew right from wrong, not whether he has suffered from schizophrenia. Dr. Jarvis has told us that Denny Lee Tuohmy knows right from wrong; it simply doesn't make that much difference to him. Mr. Savage says he cannot imagine how the defendant could fool doctors for nineteen years. He didn't fool them. Over and over in the Army records, he is referred to as a sociopath, an antisocial personality. The record is replete with indications that this person is hostile, a bully, obnoxious, *not* that he does not know right from wrong.

"This man has a record of violence. He has been in Monroe Reformatory and Walla Walla Penitentiary. Gladys Bodine was trying to take away someone he loved, so he killed her. There is no evidence to support Fritz Donohue's death as an accident. Fritz never even saw it coming. Then the defendant walked right by the body of the person he'd just shot to try to start the car.

"Of course, he has to arrange things so that Cherie won't know. So he'll say, 'Just go with me to Tacoma,' but he's *really* thinking California. Just get her with him part of the way, and he'll take care of the rest.

"Why did he buy shells for the gun, and how did those shells get from the box into the chamber?

"He wasn't lost when he told Fritz that he was. He told Mrs. Jacque: 'Turn left, turn right, turn left,' right to his brother's house. He needed a car, so he killed his best friend in cold blood. Fritz wouldn't report him because Fritz would be dead.

"When we consider the death penalty, we have to consider the protection society needs and the question of rehabilitation, but what do the records say? 'This man will never change.'

"He walked away from Eastern State Hospital twice. He needs the maximum security of death row in Walla Walla. Maybe he will never hang. Mr. Savage tells us he'll appeal, and appeal, and appeal. But you can be sure of one thing. A man in the maximum security on death row will never 'walk away' to prowl the countryside again."

The jury retired on Saturday evening to deliberate. Those spectators who had stayed until the end walked along the now empty marble hallways of the courthouse, their voices echoing.

It was a long night for everyone concerned. Not until after four on Sunday afternoon did the jury send word that they had reached a verdict.

Denny Lee Tuohmy was found guilty of first-degree murder in the death of Fritz Donohue and condemned to hang, guilty of second-degree murder in the death of Mrs. Gladys Bodine, and guilty of armed first-degree kidnapping of Mrs. Patricia Jacque, but he was not given the death penalty in that crime.

A heavy guard of four deputy sheriffs was prepared for trouble, but Tuohmy only smiled cheerfully upon hearing the verdicts and shook hands with his attorney. Still smiling, he was led off to jail.

The witnesses, who had been summoned from throughout the western half of the United States, returned home. Of all the principals, only Patricia Jacque still lived in the same house.

If, as the saying goes, something good comes from everything, it may be that her experience resulted in the one positive aspect of the convoluted case: Immediately after his wife's kidnapping, Roy Jacque adopted a dependable watchdog to protect his family. Subsequently, the Jacque menagerie would include two Dobermans and four German shepherds, all trained search and rescue dogs. Jacque and his dogs, along with thirty other King County members of the Search and Rescue Dog Club, were available day and night to help law-enforcement officials in everything from finding a lost child to locating a body in a homicide case.

Although Denny Tuohmy was sentenced to die, he never came close to the execution chamber in the Washington State Prison in Walla Walla. His sentence was commuted. By the 1990s, Tuohmy's crimes were ancient history. No one noticed when he was released from prison, and he successfully completed his parole supervision. He was finally discharged by the parole board at 4:39 P.M. on December 17, 1991, at the age of 57.

Today, Denny Tuohmy is 67. His commutation to a life sentence didn't really mean life at all. He is free.

But Gladys Bodine and Fritz Donohue are still dead.

Visit the
Simon & Schuster Web site:
www.SimonSays.com

and sign up for our
mystery e-mail updates!

Keep up on the latest
new releases, author appearances,
news, chats, special offers, and more!
We'll deliver the information
right to your inbox — if it's new,
you'll know about it.

SIMON & SCHUSTER
A VIACOM COMPANY
www.SimonSays.com

POCKET BOOKS

POCKET STAR BOOKS

2350-01